REGULAT...

The Police and Criminal Evidence Act 1984 (PACE) was an innovative and controversial attempt to regulate the investigation of crime. Two decades on, it now operates in a very different context than in the mid-1980s. Whilst legal advice has become established as a basic right of those arrested and detained by the police, the police service has become increasingly professionalised but also increasingly driven by government objectives and targets. The Crown Prosecution Service, originally established to separate prosecution from investigation, is now becoming involved in the investigative process with the power to make charge decisions.

Although the basic structure of PACE has survived, almost continual revision and amendment has resulted in a markedly different creature than that which was originally enacted. Further changes are imminent as the government has embarked on a further review of PACE, promising to 're-focus the investigation and evidence gathering processes [to deliver] 21st century policing powers to meet the demands of 21st century crime'.

This collection brings together some of the leading academic experts, police officers and defence lawyers who have a wealth of experience of researching and working with the PACE provisions. They examine the critical questions and issues surrounding PACE, providing unique and exciting insights into the demands and challenges of the regulation of policing.

# Regulating Policing

## The Police and Criminal Evidence Act 1984 Past, Present and Future

Edited by

### Ed Cape

and

### Richard Young

·HART·
PUBLISHING

OXFORD AND PORTLAND, OREGON
2008

Published in North America (US and Canada) by
Hart Publishing
c/o International Specialized Book Services
920 NE 58th Avenue, Suite 300
Portland, OR 97213–3786
USA
Tel: +1 503 287 3093 or toll-free: (1) 800 944 6190
Fax: +1 503 280 8832
E-mail: orders@isbs.com
Website: http://www.isbs.com

Hart Publishing Ltd, 16C Worcester Place, Oxford, OX1 2JW
Telephone: +44 (0)1865 517530 Fax: +44 (0)1865 510710
E-mail: mail@hartpub.co.uk
Website: http://www.hartpub.co.uk

British Library Cataloguing in Publication Data
Data Available

ISBN: 978-1-84113-861-9

Typeset by Columns Design Ltd, Reading
Printed and bound in Great Britain by
TJ International Ltd, Padstow, Cornwall

# Contents

# Notes on Contributors

**Ed Cape** is Professor of Criminal Law and Practice, University of the West of England.

**John Coppen** is a member of the Joint Central Committee of the Police Federation of England and Wales, and is lead spokesperson in matters relating to police custody issues. He served in the role of custody officer both pre and post PACE.

**David Dixon** is Professor of Law, University of New South Wales, Sydney, Australia.

**Anthony Edwards** is Solicitor and Partner, TV Edwards, London.

**John Jackson** is Professor of Public Law, Queen's University, Belfast.

**John Long** is Assistant Chief Constable, Avon and Somerset Constabulary.

**Andrew Sanders** is Professor of Criminal Law and Criminology, University of Manchester.

**Barbara Wilding** CBE QPM CCMI is Chief Constable, South Wales Police.

**Richard Young** is Professor of Law and Policy Research, University of Bristol.

# 1

# Introduction

ED CAPE AND RICHARD YOUNG

2007 marked the twenty-first anniversary of the implementation of the Police and Criminal Evidence Act 1984 (PACE). This statute was an innovative and controversial attempt to regulate the investigation of crime and, in particular, the detention and questioning of suspects. Based upon the recommendations of the Royal Commission on Criminal Procedure (RCCP), which envisaged that it would represent a balance between 'the interests of the community in bringing offenders to justice and ... the rights and liberties of persons suspected or accused of crime', it was founded upon the principles of 'fairness', 'openness' and 'workability'.[1]

Whilst the basic structure has survived, it is now a markedly different creature than that which was originally enacted. PACE itself has been amended on numerous occasions, generally giving the police greater investigative powers, and lowering the threshold and extending the circumstances in which they can be exercised. The result is a complex piece of legislation which, for those who are unfamiliar with its intricacies, is hard to understand. The PACE Codes of Practice, which were intended to set out straightforward, detailed rules about various aspects of crime investigation, have grown in number from four to eight, and from 92 pages to 270 pages. Sometimes these changes have been consulted on and other times not, but none of the changes have been based on the kind of careful, principled and evidence-based approach adopted by the RCCP.[2]

PACE now operates in a very different context than that in the mid-1980s. On the one hand, crime rates have declined and the Human Rights Act 1998 has resulted in a greater awareness of the human rights implications of policing powers. On the other, attitudes have changed with regard to the collection and retention of personal information, and the demands on those suspected of crime to cooperate with the police has increased. Relations between the police and suspects (and their defence advisers) have been further complicated by the

---

[1]  RCCP, *Report*, Cmnd, 8092, London, HMSO, 1981, para 2.18.
[2]  For a critique of the various twenty-first century 'New Labour' modernisation exercises in relation to PACE see E Cape, 'Modernising Police Powers—Again?' [2007] *Crim LR* 934.

growing recognition of victims' interests at the pre-charge stage, and by the fact that responses to terrorism have resulted in a parallel system of regulation which is, nevertheless, closely interrelated with PACE.

There have also been substantial changes within the organisations and groups that operate within the PACE framework. The police service, for example, has become increasingly professionalised, but also increasingly driven by government inspired incentives, objectives, targets, inspection and audit. The Crown Prosecution Service (CPS) has gained the power to charge suspects and impose punishments upon them. And there are now far fewer firms of defence solicitors, subject to far greater governmental regulation, than was the case in the mid-1980s.[3]

Our use of the term regulation within this introduction requires clarification. In line with other writers in this field, we see 'regulation' as having three main elements: the goal (the rule or standard against which behaviour is to be assessed); monitoring (to evaluate what happens in reality); and realignment (through mechanisms for enforcing rules or promoting adherence to standards where monitoring shows significant deviation from them).[4] It follows that it is critical to good regulation that sound evaluative research be undertaken. Only through such research is it likely that the need for, and preconditions of, effective realignment can be identified.

In the first decade after the implementation of PACE, its effectiveness and limits were indeed subject to searching enquiry through both independently funded research and studies sponsored or conducted by the Home Office.[5] This body of research resulted in many important changes to PACE and its Codes of Practice. A second wave of research also proved invaluable in uncovering the effects of major amendments to the regulatory framework[6]—such as the changes

---

[3]  It would neither be desirable nor feasible in this introduction to enumerate, still less analyse, all aspects of the shifting terrain of criminal justice in general or policing in particular. For a good assessment of the latter see A Henry and D Smith (eds), *Transformations of Policing* (Aldershot, Ashgate, 2007).

[4]  See Ch 3 by Sanders in this collection, which draws on A Crawford, 'Networked governance and the post-regulatory state? Steering, rowing and anchoring the provision of policing and security' (2006) 10 *Theoretical Criminology* 449.

[5]  See, in particular, D Brown, *Detention at the Police Station under the Police and Criminal Evidence Act 1984* (Home Office Research Study no 104) (London, HMSO, 1989), M Maguire, 'Effects of the PACE provisions on Detention and Questioning' (1988) 28 *British Journal of Criminology* 19; A Sanders, L Bridges, A Mulvaney and G Crozier, *Advice and Assistance at Police Stations and the 24 Hour Duty Solicitor Scheme* (London, Lord Chancellor's Department, 1989); D Dixon, A Bottomley, C Coleman, M Gill and D Wall, 'Reality and Rules in the Construction and Regulation of Police Suspicion' (1989) 17 *International Journal of the Sociology of Law* 185; D Dixon, A Bottomley, C Coleman, M Gill and D Wall, 'Safeguarding the Rights of Suspects in Police Custody' (1990) 1 *Policing and Society* 115; D Dixon, C Coleman and A Bottomley, 'Consent and the Legal Regulation of Policing' (1990) 17 *Journal of Law and Society* 345, and M McConville, A Sanders, and R Leng, *The Case for the Prosecution* (London, Routledge, 1991).

[6]  See, eg, D Brown, T Ellis and K Larcombe, *Changing the Code: Police Detention under the Revised PACE Codes of Practice* (Home Office Research Study no 129) (London, HMSO, 1992), T Bucke and D Brown, *In Police Custody: Police Powers and Suspects' Rights Under the Revised Pace Codes of Practice* (Home Office Research Study no 174) (London, Home Office, 1997).

to the right to silence ushered in by the Criminal Justice and Public Order Act 1994.[7] For a time it was possible to say that the regulation of policing was informed (although rarely led) by solid evidence.

In retrospect it is possible to identify the Home Office overview of this research—'PACE ten years on', published in 1997, as the high-water mark of this reflective approach.[8] The author, David Brown, afforded chapter-length treatment to the following subjects: stop and search, entry search and seizure, arrest and detention, treatment of suspects, legal advice, interviews with suspects, the right of silence, juveniles, the mentally disordered, and supervision and accountability. On the plus side, PACE was depicted as introducing greater clarity for the police and more effective protections for suspects in a number of areas. On the negative side, police compliance with the requirements of PACE was adjudged often mechanistic and in some areas largely lacking. Brown concluded by assessing whether PACE (as amended) did represent a reasonable balance between the public interest in bringing offenders to trial while safeguarding the rights and liberties of suspects. He opined that:

> It would be difficult to argue that PACE has produced a system that is in a state of balance . . . it might be argued, on the evidence presented in this review, that suspects are at a disadvantage relative to police powers in several key areas. Among these may be included stop and search, search and seizure, and the treatment of at risk groups.[9]

This implied a need for further changes to the regulation of policing accompanied by further research to assess their impact. Moreover, in his final words Brown argued that the assessment of PACE would necessarily have to be an ongoing process:

> achieving balance between the suspect's rights and the public interest in convicting the guilty is a continually shifting process of adjusting to circumstances as they change or as weaknesses in the existing provisions become apparent. . . . While, for the present, the conclusion might be drawn that the balance intended by PACE has not been achieved, the state of play must be regularly reviewed in order to take account of the effect of new initiatives affecting the pre-trial process.[10]

Unfortunately the arrival of a 'New Labour' government in 1997 signalled the virtual end of what had been a sustained commitment to keep PACE under review. Instead the research agenda was switched to assessing 'what works' in reducing crime.[11] Indeed, the government appears to have lost virtually all

---

[7]  T Bucke, R Street and D Brown, *The right of silence: the impact of the Criminal Justice and Public Order Act 1994* (Home Office Research Study no 199) (London, Home Office, 2000).

[8]  D Brown, *PACE ten years on: a review of the research* (Home Office Research Study no 155) (London, Home Office, 1997).

[9]  *Ibid*, 254.

[10]  *Ibid*, 256.

[11]  This shift in the agenda is all the more regrettable given the flawed nature of the policy and research programme that ensued. See further M Maguire, 'The Crime Reduction Programme in England and Wales' (2004) 4 *Criminal Justice* 213.

interest in in-depth research into the operation of police powers, including the many new ones it has created in relation to 'anti-social behaviour'.[12] Similarly, it has shown little interest in the fairness and effectiveness of safeguards for suspects. The exception is stop and search powers, where the legacy of the Macpherson Inquiry into the death of Stephen Lawrence can be seen in a plethora of research studies and reforming efforts.[13] The intense focus on stop and search has, ironically, brought into stark relief the dearth of research taking place into other aspects of police investigatory powers and rights for suspects.[14]

We are thus unlikely to see a repeat of the kind of overview of PACE that David Brown carried out on PACE a decade ago. We both author textbooks in the field of criminal justice[15] and know only too well that the solid research evidence that would be needed for a comprehensive up-to-date assessment of the operation of the criminal process is simply not available. For this reason, in 2006 we decided to organise a one-day conference to bring together academics, researchers, defence lawyers, police officers and policy-makers to examine the critical questions and issues surrounding PACE. Our aim was to highlight that the debates about the regulation of policing remain as important as ever and to stimulate discussion and research in the area. We were also succumbing to that human temptation to invest a particular number of years (in this case 21) with a particular significance.[16] We did not want this milestone in the life of the operation of PACE to pass by without comment. To ensure that the conference was more than just an analytical flash in the pan, we also organised a follow-up colloquium for the speakers so that their papers could be further debated with a view to their refinement and publication in the form of an edited collection.

Choosing who to invite proved relatively easy. There was very little research into policing in England and Wales prior to PACE and the work of the RCCP (and its associated research programme) was able to address only some of the most glaring gaps. Ideally, therefore, we wanted speakers who could give a long-term perspective on PACE, including some with experience of the pre-PACE regime. We were thus delighted when a Chief Constable (Barbara Wilding), a (then) Chief Superintendent (John Long), and a long-serving custody officer

---

[12] As noted by the Comptroller and Auditor-General, *Home Office: Tackling Anti-Social Behaviour* HC99 Session 2006–2007 (London, The Stationery Office, 2006) 5.

[13] See, for example, Home Office Police Research Papers nos 127–132 (various authors) available at http://www.homeoffice.gov.uk/rds/policerspubs1.html (accessed 12 June 2008); P Waddington, K Stenson and D Don, 'In proportion: Race, and Police Stop and Search' (2004) 44 *British Journal of Criminology* 889, and the official web-site dedicated to the issue at http://www.stopandsearch.com/ (accessed 31 December 2007).

[14] See T Newburn, M Shiner and S Hayman, 'Race, crime and injustice? Strip-search and the treatment of suspects in custody' (2004) 44 *British Journal of Criminology* 677.

[15] E Cape, *Defending Suspects at Police Stations*, 5th edn (London, Legal Action Group, 2006) and A Sanders and R Young, *Criminal Justice* 3rd edn (Oxford, Oxford University Press, 2007).

[16] In May 2008 the Centre for Criminal Justice Studies at the University of Leeds held a conference entitled 'The Crime and Disorder Act 1998: Ten Years On' while in 2007 a colloquium was held at the University of Bristol to mark the tenth anniversary of the Criminal Cases Review Commission.

(John Coppen) accepted our invitations to contribute papers to this collection and further agreed to include some personal reminiscences of life before and after PACE. From the defence perspective, Ed Cape and Anthony Edwards are able to draw on their work as practising solicitors both pre- and post-PACE. From an academic researcher's perspective, both David Dixon and Andrew Sanders were leading figures in the first wave of in-depth research studies into PACE, while John Jackson and Richard Young have similarly long-standing research interests in this field.

The conference itself took place on 29 March 2007 at the University of the West of England. Over 150 lawyers, police officers, academics and policy-makers attended, which we took as a heartening sign that interest in PACE is far from dead. The conference also proved very timely—two weeks earlier the Home Office had published a consultation document, *Modernising Police Powers: Review of the Police and Criminal Evidence Act*, which raised fundamental questions about the future of PACE. We thought it important to make room at the conference for the civil servant overseeing the consultation exercise, Alan Brown, to present a Home Office viewpoint. Other Home Office officials participated in the colloquium the following day.

Refined versions of the papers that were given at the conference (with the exception of Alan Brown's) are presented in this collection. They speak for themselves and there is little to be gained by discussing them in detail here. Brief summaries coupled with some contextual analysis may help, however, to give a flavour of the conference and the contents of this book. A few key passages from their chapters are reproduced here, chosen on the basis that they help convey the gist of an argument.

Drawing on his research into policing in Australia and England, David Dixon provides a cross-cultural analysis of the conditions that gave rise to PACE. He argues that, contrary to the views expressed by some contemporary critics, and his own initial suppositions prior to carrying out research, PACE did not involve a huge increase in police power. Rather it had the effect of providing statutory authority for what the police were already doing 'by consent', while simultaneously subjecting policing to a complex web of regulation (including limits on detention, custody officers, duty solicitor schemes and so forth). As he puts it: 'Rather than revelling in their new powers, operational officers moaned about having their practices restricted and being held to account by supervisors and via bureaucratic regulation.'

The 'authorise and regulate' strategy inherent in PACE is analysed as a creature of its time which may not survive the shift in ideologies and priorities of twenty-first century governments. In particular, the shift towards managing risky populations for the benefit of the 'law-abiding majority' has led to impatience with the limitations on police powers implied by rights for suspects, and enthusiasm for allowing the police to control and sanction citizens without any meaningful oversight. Counter-trends are also evident, however, in the rise of human rights and the increasing recognition of the importance of police legitimacy.

One lesson that might be drawn from Dixon's analysis is that it is reasonable to expect a certain amount of incoherence and inconsistency in the regulatory framework for the foreseeable future, as these various trends and counter-trends work themselves out in practice. Another is that there is still room for creative debate on the future of PACE.

In such a debate the contribution of Andrew Sanders may prove to be important. He situates the PACE model within the burgeoning literature on regulation—a literature which rarely engages with 'the police' as that term is conventionally understood. He notes how the literature on the 'post-regulatory state' and 'smart regulation' advocates regulatory pluralism, in which there are intersecting regulatory networks aimed at achieving an effective mixture of self- and external-regulation (the ultimate guarantor of which is coercive law).

The problem with the PACE framework is that it relies very heavily on the police regulating themselves, a reliance that has become more pronounced over time. Typically, officers monitor their subordinates' activities on the basis of information provided by the latter, thus rendering effective control nigh impossible. Regulatory pluralism is thus needed in this arena and might be achieved by empowering those with an interest in seeing suspects treated fairly (their family and friends, lay visitors and so forth) to have much greater access to the police station. Moreover, defence lawyers should be funded to be present in police stations on a permanent basis so that key decisions (such as whether to seek medical assistance) would no longer be taken by the police, and so that suspects would no longer be deterred from seeking legal advice by the thought of the delay involved in bringing a solicitor to the station.

Sanders argues that this kind of dispersal of regulatory power holds out the promise of a range of important benefits, including fewer deaths in custody. That is something that virtually all police officers would welcome, which might suggest there is room for some coalition building around this set of proposals. As John Coppen notes, the ultimate concern for a custody officer is whether a death in custody will happen on their watch.

Coppen provides a fascinating account of front-line policing prior to PACE, which chimes well with Dixon's analysis of the importance of 'consent' in achieving policing goals. He highlights the relative absence of legal limits and opportunities for review or challenge of police actions. He recalls, for example, how he commonly acted as custody officer for a detainee, interviewed witnesses in relation to the same matter, and prosecuted the case in the local magistrates' court the next day.

He also notes how the introduction of PACE initially made little difference to patrol officers as few forces made any serious investment in training prior to implementation. Over time, however, the police came to accept PACE as providing a fundamental guide to how an investigation should be conducted. As an aside we might observe that this implies that the early wave of research studies conducted into the impact of PACE are not a reliable guide to the longer-term difference PACE is likely to have made to policing. This increases our sense of frustration at the lack of in-depth research into PACE since the mid-1990s. As Dixon argues in this collection, the opportunity to assess the police's shifting response to PACE against the baseline created by the early research studies has largely been squandered.

In any such follow-up research the role of the custody officer would clearly be of prime importance. Coppen argues that PACE gave custody officers a vested interest in the welfare and proper treatment of detainees and enabled them to take decisions that did not necessarily favour either the interviewer or the suspect 'but were fair and unbiased'. While Coppen may be right in saying that a major strength of PACE is the clarity it brought to the custody officer's responsibilities, the police service's commitment to reinforcing a custody officer's sense of independence from the investigation seems less clear-cut. Thus Coppen reveals that he received no formal training in the 12 years he served as a custody officer from 1990. His account highlights that training across all aspects of policing remains somewhat haphazard and that matters have not been made easier by the flood of new criminal laws and procedures introduced over the last decade. Thus the 'training' offered by several forces in respect of the sweeping changes to the law of arrest introduced by 2005 legislation came in the form of an e-mail on the day before implementation.

Coppen concludes his analysis by examining specific issues that concern custody officers, including the bureaucracy and delays created by the new CPS-controlled statutory charging scheme, the difficulties caused by designating police stations as 'places of safety' for the mentally disordered, and the moves towards civilianising the custody officer function. On the latter point he argues that: 'A trained, experienced police sergeant has the power and authority to safeguard the independence and integrity of the process, and does not have the obligations owed by an employee to an employer.' As against this one might argue that civilians would not be so prone to sharing in a policing outlook in which occupational solidarity may take precedence over protecting suspects' rights. Much depends on who the civilians are, of course, as well as how they are trained and supported. Coppen's observation that Thames Valley Police intends to recruit ex-custody officers as their 'civilians' suggests that we might end up with the worst of all worlds. An in-depth comparative study of different custody officer arrangements is clearly what is needed, but it seems unlikely that the resources and access needed to allow this to happen will be forthcoming.

John Long begins his contribution by reflecting on his early days in the Metropolitan Police prior to the implementation of PACE. He points out that to some extent PACE simply replaced and rationalised existing police powers 'provided by a melee of longstanding legislation'. Under the old legislation, however, safeguards for suspects were far from systematic. Thus Long recalls how only 'resented' stop and searches were recorded, rendering the pre-PACE statistics unreliable. Drawing on Brown's review of research into PACE (discussed above) Long highlights how the new framework made a marked difference in some areas (such as interviewing techniques and provision of legal advice) while proving less successful in others (such as scrutiny by custody officers of the grounds for arrest). Echoing Coppen's recollections, Long indicates that the initial training on PACE in the Metropolitan Police was inadequate: 'The Act's objectives, and why the criminal process was being changed to achieve a certain balance, were hardly touched upon at all and this must inevitably have had an impact on how it was interpreted by practitioners.'

The central question tackled by Long, however, is whether wider developments in policing have rendered PACE no longer fit for purpose. The first of such developments examined is the new statutory charging scheme. In line with Coppen, Long notes how the CPS are not resourced to provide the 24–7 service that police officers have to deliver. Obtaining CPS advice and decisions on charging has thus become a major source of delay in custody. The solution posited is to amend PACE so that the detention clock could be paused, an idea supported by Coppen in relation to delays caused by waiting for appropriate adults, defence solicitors and medical practitioners to arrive in custody. The second post-PACE development in policing that Long examines is the emphasis on diversity issues that arose in the wake of the Macpherson Inquiry into the murder of Stephen Lawrence. As well as ushering in the use of Independent Advisory Groups to help raise awareness of the needs of diverse communities, the Inquiry's recommendations led to a new requirement to record stops that did not result in a search. Long notes how this has added to the complexity of the law and the bureaucratic requirements that surround it, while nonetheless welcoming the raising of professional standards brought about by Macpherson.

The third development discussed centres on the duties now placed on police officers to provide higher standards of service to victims. The danger depicted here is that police officers may come to see themselves as representing the interests of victims, which in turn might make them less willing to adhere to the spirit and wording of PACE insofar as that legislation protects suspects' rights. Fourthly, Long examines the impact of new terrorist legislation and how this has increased the complexity of the law facing the police practitioner, thus making it harder to meet operational needs (as specialist knowledge is now required in order to process terrorist suspects). Finally, the managerial shift towards 'policing by targets' is put under the microscope. Long emphasises how league tables and performance reviews by senior officers have resulted in quantitative activity (for example, numbers of stop and searches for minor offences) taking precedence over quality policing (careful investigation of serious crime aimed at ensuring the exoneration of the innocent and the conviction of the guilty). Echoing Coppen, he also notes how the drive to increase levels of police 'detections' may come into conflict with the drive to reduce the levels of unsuccessful CPS prosecutions. Thus the police may be pushing cases into the system that should not be there at the same time as the CPS may be unduly cautious in charging cases.

Long notes how Brown's review of the PACE research (discussed above) identified four preconditions for successful regulation of police powers within the pre-trial criminal process: 1) new rules should be clearly expressed; 2) implementation should be accompanied by adequate training; 3) rules should be backed up by effective sanctions and supervision; and 4) the public need to be aware of rights and police powers. The problem is that post-PACE developments have introduced exactly the kind of patchwork complexity that PACE was designed to supersede. Moreover, the provision of training to cope with the torrent of new law has, not surprisingly, proved problematic (although, as Long notes, the effectiveness of police training has not attracted much research interest).

Supervision arrangements have proliferated in the post-PACE era and arguably gained more teeth (for example, the advent of statutory charging, surveillance commissioners, the Independent Police Complaints Commission, and greater managerial oversight of front-line policing following Macpherson). While concerns about rendering policing truly visible to the regulators are seen by Long as valid, the greater use of technology (for example to record stop and search encounters) is suggested as one way forward. The post-PACE efforts to educate the public about their rights is noted, but Long accepts that the complexity of the law will have detracted from levels of understanding.

If we reflect on Long's analysis, we can see that three (points 1, 2 and 4) of Brown's pre-conditions for the successful regulation of police powers are not met under current conditions. Moreover, the proliferation of state-led supervision arrangements does little to meet Sanders' argument that regulatory-pluralism requires the empowering of those who currently occupy structurally weak positions such as the friends and family of suspects. Indeed, the suggestion that the detention clock be stopped during periods when lawyers or appropriate adults are travelling to the police station to attend suspects may end up enhancing the relative power of the police still further. We know that the length of detention is a source of great anxiety for suspects.[17] If they are made aware that requesting legal advice could result not just in a delay while the advisor is summonsed, but also in the extension of the normal overall limits for detention, the chilling effect on seeking help from 'outside regulators' may be considerable.

Wilding presents the final police perspective offered in this collection. Having joined the police in 1967 her insights into the pre-PACE era are particularly rich. She writes: 'The police force I joined was testosterone driven and fuelled with frustration at a criminal justice system perceived as being loaded in favour of the suspect. …. Pressures from senior officers to get results as a means of proving fitness for promotion also played a part in the culture of the day.' As a result, corruption of various kinds flourished and rules designed to protect suspects

---

[17]   See, eg, Ch 9 by Edwards in this collection, where he comments: 'The client's first concerns are always about ancillary matters, primarily about the period for which they will be detained and letting others know where they are.'

were commonly flouted with the connivance of supervisors. PACE was thus an understandable attempt to give police officers the powers they claimed they needed to tackle rising crime levels while at the same time introducing clear rights for suspects and mechanisms designed to ensure respect for those rights.

Wilding's account of the initial reception of PACE chimes with those of Coppen and Long. Training was superficial and did little to challenge the existing police culture, in which investigations were oriented towards finding the evidence that would secure a conviction. Over time, however, PACE is depicted as having achieved greater success. It clarified police powers and suspects' rights and set much higher ethical standards for the police. Moreover, the chief mechanism introduced to secure those standards is said to have proved effective, with Wilding having personally witnessed 'many fierce debates' between old-school detectives and custody officers who 'refused to compromise their role'. It might be responded that researchers conducting observational research have not uncovered similar evidence.[18] That may be in part because detectives know better than to seek custody officer approval (whether tacit or explicit) for subversion of suspects' rights when a researcher is watching[19] and, in part, because custody officers are unwilling to have stand-up rows with colleagues in front of outsiders.[20] The notion that researchers do not affect the very things they seek to study is hopelessly naive in many instances and this is one reason why the personal recollections of police officers are valuable.

On the negative side, Wilding identifies a number of problems with PACE. Chief amongst these is the bureaucracy and delays associated with compliance which results in police officers spending more time in the station than on the streets. With regard to some police powers, such as stop and search, the safeguards are said to have increased post-PACE to the point where the attendant bureaucracy discourages the police from using their powers.

Wilding argues that, since PACE was introduced, the police have become a professional and highly accountable public body. She questions whether the checks and balances that were thought necessary in the mid-1980s are still in the public interest today. Support is therefore expressed for streamlining criminal justice through such measures as penalty notices, street bail and on-street DNA and fingerprinting. Interestingly, she simultaneously expresses her opposition to

---

[18] Indeed, some researchers have gone so far as to say that custody officers actively seek to undermine suspects' rights through a variety of 'ploys', such as reading out those rights at a speed designed to ensure incomprehension: A Sanders, L Bridges, A Mulvaney and G Crozier, *Advice and Assistance at Police Stations and the 24 Hour Duty Solicitor Scheme* (London, Lord Chancellor's Department, 1989).

[19] For an insight into how a custody officer and an investigating officer behaved when they believed no one was watching, see M McConville, 'Videotaping Interrogations: Police behaviour on and off camera' (1992) *Crim LR* 532.

[20] Though this would not explain the failure of custody officers to protect suspects' rights when there are no outsiders present, but that are caught on videotape. For examples, see *ibid*, and IPCC, *Report, dated 27th February 2006, of the Review into the events leading up to and following the death of Christopher Alder on 1st April 1998*, HC 971-I (London, The Stationery Office, 2006).

the government's emphasis on 'bringing more offenders to justice' through increasing 'sanction detections', since this is resulting in the criminalisation of young people for minor offences. In other words, Wilding is advocating that minor deviance should be 'defined down'[21] as should the attendant safeguards. Another line of critique concerns the over-emphasis within PACE on police powers and suspects' rights, and the lack of provisions on the role of the defence solicitor at the police station, or concerning the fair treatment of witnesses and victims in the courtroom.

She concludes by expressing concerns about co-locating prosecutors and police officers in police stations and the growing tendency for prosecutors to direct investigations as part of the new statutory charging scheme. As she rightly notes, this begins to blur the distinct roles of investigator and prosecutor that was achieved by creating the CPS. Impartial prosecutorial review of a case built independently by the police was intended to be a bulwark against miscarriages of justice. Whether such review is possible when the CPS has itself contributed to the building of a case remains to be seen.

Looking to the future, Wilding's plea is for the police to be given more trust as impartial investigators into the truth, and for the spirit of adversarialism to be removed from police stations. While supporting a major codifying effort along the lines of PACE she argues that it should not make the mistake inherent in that legislation of focusing on the police alone but rather encompass the entire criminal justice system and all who have to interact with it.

Richard Young's chapter focuses on one of the main trends discernible in post-PACE developments—the drift to police-led summary justice. This has been facilitated through: increasing police investigative powers (especially stop and search and arrest); widening the ambit of the criminal law (notably through measures that target such nebulous concepts as 'disorderly conduct' and 'anti-social behaviour'); and adding to police dispositive powers (such as penalty notices for disorder). Of equal importance has been the shift in political culture. Whereas PACE had been based on the notion that fairness to suspects was crucial to securing police legitimacy and, thus, public cooperation with policing, subsequent developments have posited a misleading dichotomy between the interests of the 'law-abiding majority' and a dangerous minority who would seek to 'undermine our way of life'.[22] Safeguards for suspects have accordingly been pared away at the same time as the police have been encouraged to increase the net of social control so as better to manage 'risky groups' and to meet the government target of bringing more offenders to justice.

---

[21] In line with a strategy that was popular pre-New Labour. See D Garland, 'The Limits of the Sovereign State: Strategies of Crime Control in Contemporary Society' (1996) 36 *British Journal of Criminology* 445.

[22] This demonising language is to be found in *Rebalancing the criminal justice system in favour of the law-abiding majority: Cutting crime, reducing reoffending and protecting the public* (London, Home Office, July 2006) 4.

Young offers a radically different perspective to Wilding on the extent to which the police can be trusted, arguing, for example, that the police regularly flout the law when using their stop and search powers. His main focus, however, is on the rise of penalty notices for disorder. He notes how PACE cemented the place of the police station as an evidence-gathering site and the effective start of the adversarial process. It has thus become difficult to resist calls for many of the safeguards associated with court processes to be made available in the police station. In the government's eyes this has resulted in unacceptable inefficiency, delays and diversion of policing resources from the street. The response has been to give the police the power to issue fixed penalty notices for a wide range of offences, including theft, criminal damage and the controversial Section 5 Public Order Act 1986 offence. The police have used these powers enthusiastically, and massive net-widening has resulted—fully in line with the government's intentions to 'define deviance up'. Whereas previously the police would have exercised discretion and told disorderly youths to 'go home or get arrested', now the more likely option is the imposition of an £80 on the spot fine.

The rapid development of the penalty notices scheme has been police- rather than research-led, with no attempt made to ascertain the views of the recipients of these notices or to scrutinise the scheme from other perspectives, such as racial equality. Young argues that even the government's limited research into the scheme demonstrates a variety of forms of abuse and that independent research would no doubt show an even more worrying picture. Young concludes by arguing that more general policing research and the lessons of history indicate that the government's strategy is misconceived: 'If any part of our "way of life" is being undermined, it is the notion that the police should be subjected to the rule of law as articulated through the kind of sophisticated regulatory structure embodied in PACE.' The drift to summary justice is undermining police legitimacy and the willingness of large sections of the public to cooperate with the police when it comes to tackling more serious crimes, thus putting 'the freedom and safety of us all at risk'.

In his chapter, Ed Cape shifts the focus of analysis from summary justice on the streets to the process of building cases in the police station. The powers covered include arrest, detention for custodial interrogation, the taking of bodily samples, and bail. He presents a careful analysis of the changes made to the PACE framework, with a particular focus on the radical 're-balancing' (away from suspects' rights) that has taken place under New Labour. Cape critiques the government's claim that the twenty-first century fight against crime is being hindered by a (now outmoded) nineteenth century approach introduced to protect the accused against the 'savage standards' of the day. This is a peculiar image for ministers to have invoked given that PACE was fashioned in Thatcherite (not Victorian) times. Moreover, PACE was based on the recommendations of the RCCP which itself sought a reasonable balance between suspects' rights and the interest of the community in bringing offenders to justice. The RCCP thought that the use of coercive investigative powers could be justified so long as there was (at least) reasonable suspicion of a specific crime, a necessity for using the powers in question (with safeguards in place to test whether the necessity condition was met), and proportionality in their use (meaning, in broad terms, that more intrusive powers should apply only to the more serious offences).

Cape shows how these principles were only imperfectly realised in PACE as originally enacted. He then goes on to explore how necessity and proportionality as prerequisites for the exercise of most investigative powers have subsequently either been removed or rendered nugatory. Thus whereas PACE divided offences into 'arrestable' and 'non-arrestable' (with arrest for the latter possible only if a necessity test was met), the law now allows arrest for any offence, however trivial, subject only to a reformulated necessity test devoid of any truly restrictive content. The chapter also reviews the way in which the courts have interpreted the PACE framework (usually with the effect of weakening safeguards for suspects) and the research demonstrating the lack of interest shown by the police in honouring the spirit of those safeguards in practice. One key consequence of all this is that: 'Once a person is arrested, if the officer chooses to take them to the police station for investigation, nothing will prevent their detention irrespective of whether detention, judged objectively, is really necessary.'

Once in detention, PACE as enacted was designed to ensure that suspects were treated in a proportionate way. Thus, for example, questioning had to cease (and a charge decision made) as soon as the investigating officer believed there was sufficient evidence to prosecute successfully. Changes to the PACE framework now enable questioning to continue after this point has been reached. In other words there is no effective limit (other than the time limits for detention) to how long the police can use custodial interrogation to build a case against a suspect. Cape argues that this amounts to a fundamental shift in the relationship between the state and the citizen effected by incremental change without any debate of the issues involved. In one sense the lack of debate is unsurprising—the constitutional devil can barely be discerned amongst the blizzard of legislative detail.

A similar observation might be made about many of the other changes Cape reviews, such as the successive 'reforms' that broke the link PACE created between 'serious arrestable offences' and the power of the police to detain for more than 24 hours. That power is now linked to whether an offence is indictable or not. While proportionality still plays some part in the revised statutory scheme, the reality is that far more offences are now eligible for extended detention than hitherto. No less complex are the changes to the rules on taking bodily samples from suspects and police bail. The overall result of all the detailed changes is that the bodies and minds of citizens may now come under the coercive control of the police for extended periods of time without any effective mechanism by which this can be challenged. Cape concludes by warning that this drift towards police control will continue unless future legislative action is guided by a more principled approach in which change is based and evaluated on thorough and objective evidence.

Anthony Edwards examines PACE through the lens of the practising defence solicitor. As he notes, neither the RCCP nor PACE provided a clear definition of the role the solicitor should play in the police station. This both reflected and reinforced the lack of an adversarial mindset within the profession at the time PACE was enacted. It took time for solicitors to treat events in the police station as if they were the first day of a trial, and to provide competent advice and assistance accordingly.

Thus research conducted in the decade after PACE found poor standards of defence advocacy. Solicitors, for example, often: gave advice by telephone rather than in person; sent junior, unqualified, staff to the station; failed to attend any or some of the police–suspect interviews; failed to intervene appropriately during interviews to protect the interests of their client; and provided bad legal advice.[23]

Edwards charts how this situation was addressed by the Law Society and the Legal Aid Board (the predecessor of the Legal Services Commission). The key reform was the introduction of an accreditation process, itself backed up by a series of publications advocating and explaining 'active defence', and by a 1995 revision to Code C which stressed that: 'The solicitor's only role in the police station is to protect and advance the legal rights of their client.' While there is no doubt that these developments drove up standards, Edwards reminds us that starting the adversarial process within the police station puts solicitors and their clients at a significant disadvantage from the outset:

> critical advice now had to be given immediately, in circumstances that were often wholly unsatisfactory. A solicitor has to give advice on the basis that much information is withheld by both the police and the client, often at unsocial hours, and in relation to a client who may be in no fit state clearly to understand and act upon it, either as a result of voluntary intoxication or because of their vulnerability.

Edwards analyses a number of legal issues arising from the post-PACE clarification of the defence solicitor role, namely legal privilege and client confidentiality, conflict of interests, and perverting the course of justice. He then goes on to look at how significant post-PACE amendments to criminal law, evidence and procedure have affected the content of the advice that defence solicitors should give. Thus, for example, the increases in police powers to take bodily samples from suspects (as charted by Cape) mean that the scope for 'active defence' has been greatly narrowed:

> great skill is needed to persuade the client that the solicitor is 'on their side'. Police officers routinely use solicitors to persuade a 'difficult' client to co-operate with the process and the law is such that solicitors have to advise clients to co-operate in order to avoid additional allegations of assault on or obstruction of a police officer in the execution of their duty.

---

[23] See Ch 10 by Jackson in this collection and the studies cited therein (nn 22–3).

Similarly, the virtual abolition of the right to silence makes it problematic for the solicitor to advise a policy of non-cooperation during interrogation. However, as Edwards shows, relevant case law accepts that it *may* be reasonable for a solicitor to advise silence (and for a client to rely on that advice without suffering adverse inferences at trial) depending on the interplay of a large number of relevant factors. What Edwards' detailed analysis of a wide range of issues (including character evidence, bail, diversion from prosecution, and post-charge advice) makes clear is that the legal complexity that now perplexes police officers is just as much of an issue for defence solicitors.

This growth in complexity would not matter so much if the government was prepared to pay for it through increased funding for defence services. But it is not so prepared, as the market-driven Carter reforms to the legal aid system demonstrate. Edwards highlights a number of dangers inherent in these reforms. For example, the drive to reduce the number of defence firms still further may result in individual lawyers spending their working day solely in a particular police station. As he notes: 'There is a danger that too close a working relationship between individual lawyers and police officers can dull sensibilities and weaken the adversarial approach.' Also troubling is the proposal to introduce a fixed fee to cover an entire investigation rather than the fee reflecting the time actually spent on an individual case. The obvious danger is that solicitors will not attend key stages of an investigation (such as identification procedures) in order to maximise profits (or minimise losses). Edwards' suggestion that this risk might be reduced by requiring the permanent attendance in the police station of a defence representative answerable to the professional head of the Public Defender Service rubs up uneasily against his early warning against allowing defence lawyers and police officers to spend too much time in each other's company. As with developments in the custody officer role, research is needed to illuminate whether the advantages of permanent defence representation in the police station (as advocated by Sanders and Edwards) would outweigh any disadvantages. Initial and continuing assessment of the impact of the fixed fee regime will also be needed, given that the operation and effects of the regime will be crucially affected by what seems likely to be ongoing legislative hyper-activity in the field of criminal justice. Just as important will be research into the proposed shift away from direct Legal Services Commission supervision of defence work towards peer review backed up by oversight from the Law Society.

In the final chapter in the book, John Jackson argues that the context within which PACE operates has been transformed since the mid 1990s with implications more radical than those which flowed from the initial implementation of that legislation. Echoing Dixon's analysis, Jackson argues that the main effects of PACE were to legitimise custodial interrogation aimed at building cases against suspects, and to make the custodial regime operate in a much more transparent and accountable fashion. Post-PACE developments have, however, gone far beyond this initial 'authorise and regulate' strategy. The police station is no longer merely the site of investigation, but also of accusation and disposition.

One key change was the curtailment of the right to silence effected in England by the Criminal Justice and Public Order Act 1994. Now the police could call on the suspect to give an account in interview, accompanied by a warning that a failure to do so could damage their case in court. The courts have responded by recognising that the police interview and the trial are part of a continuous process in which the suspect is engaged 'from the beginning'. Jackson's own research in Northern Ireland shows how the police have adapted to the new regime by portraying the interview as the 'one big opportunity' to provide an explanation. Defence solicitors too have adapted by ensuring that explanations are put on record where appropriate. What is lacking, argues Jackson, are the safeguards typically associated with an accusatory phase of criminal procedure, notably full disclosure of the prosecution case and oversight from a judicial figure.

Jackson next looks at the effect of the transformation that has been taking place (through the statutory charging scheme) in the role of the CPS prosecutor from the passive 'case reviewer' of the police file after investigation, towards a more active 'case builder' working with the police in the police station. The aims behind the partial transfer of the power to charge from the custody officer to the CPS include ensuring that robust cases are built against the guilty and that the right charges are proceeded with from the outset. Discontinuances and charge-bargaining will thus be frowned upon. As Jackson notes (echoing the concerns expressed by Wilding): 'The danger is that the new management systems being built to forge closer relations between the police and prosecutors will lead to a new 'canteen culture' driven by performance targets to stick to the first charge even when the evidence points to weaknesses down the line when the case gets to court.' He suggests that the danger would be reduced if the prosecutor who built the case also had to present it in court, an idea that finds support from research into the operation of civil justice.[24]

Jackson also analyses the growing responsibility of the CPS (through the expanding system of conditional cautions) for disposing of cases altogether before they reach court. The significance here lies in the power of prosecutors to attach punitive conditions to these cautions, including up to 20 hours of unpaid work or a fine not exceeding £250. The intention is to divert from the courts large numbers of summary offences. As with penalty notices for disorder, the upshot is that punishments are being imposed outside of the courtroom and its attendant safeguards. Jackson analyses the compatibility of this scheme with Article 6 of the European Convention on Human Rights and finds it wanting. With the pre-court system now taking on many of the functions of trial and punishment, a raft of beefed up safeguards are required. Thus, prior to any police interview, defendants should be more actively encouraged to seek legal advice and legal representatives

---

[24]  J Baldwin, N Wikeley and R Young, *Judging Social Security* (Oxford, Oxford University Press, 1994).

should be given full disclosure of the case against the suspect, and full access to police and prosecutors to make representations about disposal afterwards. And far more steps need to be taken to ensure that the suspect gives fully informed consent to a conditional caution, 'including, as in the case of defendants considering a plea in court, a full opportunity through a legal adviser in attendance to make representations to prosecutors on the conditions for accepting a caution'. All of this will cost a great deal of money and it seems likely that the government will continue to want to have its cake (greater disposal of cases at the pre-court stage) and eat it (no enhancements to defence rights) unless the European Court of Human Rights demands otherwise.

The conference itself concluded with a presentation by Alan Brown, the Head of Police Power and Procedures at the Home Office, who explained the thinking behind *Modernising Police Powers: Review of the Police and Criminal Evidence Act (PACE) 1984*[25] (the 2007 review). As one might have expected, the presentation did not stray far from the indications provided in that document. The purpose of the consultation is set out in the foreword by the Minister of State, Tony McNulty, and in the introduction by the Director of the Home Office Policing Policy and Operations Directorate. Referring to the 'bureaucratic and over-complicated procedures' governing the safeguards and protections for suspects, the Minister states that the aim is to 're-focus the investigation and evidence gathering processes on serving the needs of victims and witnesses and helping raise the efficiency and effectiveness of the police service'.[26] The Director refers to the need to ensure that PACE and its codes 'serve the demands of the modern police service' and that PACE powers and procedures 'fully reflect what is needed in a fast changing world' whilst ensuring that 'every opportunity is taken to simplify and rationalise wherever possible'.[27] One of us has presented a critical analysis of this consultation paper elsewhere, noting that: 'At best the 2007 review appears to assume that the existing safeguards for suspects are adequate; at worst, it appears to place them below managerialist concerns, and conditional on the 'needs of the criminal justice system', a particularly opaque phrase.'[28] The presentation by Alan Brown did little to make matters more transparent, and many delegates, including both police officers and defence lawyers, were far from reassured that the consultation would lead to improvements to PACE.

The debates sparked during the conference from which this book stems suggests that plenty of practitioners still care deeply about the future of PACE. Young's paper provoked particularly heartfelt and telling reactions when delivered at the conference. From the audience a senior police officer commented

---

[25] London, Home Office, March 2007, available at http://police.homeoffice.gov.uk/news-and-publications/publication/operational-policing/PACE-review?view=Binary (accessed 31 December 2007).

[26] *Ibid*, 2.

[27] *Ibid*, 3.

[28] See Cape, n 2 above, 937.

defensively that the police felt they had no choice but to use the penalty notices scheme expansively given the pressure they were under to meet government targets. Most, if not all, of the police officers present loudly applauded this intervention. The underlying message that 'it's not our fault' was coupled with a sense of dismay (echoed in Wilding's chapter) at the 'loss of discretion' implied by the push to bring more minor offenders into the net of social control. Defence solicitors also expressed concern. One asked the Home Office official Alan Brown how he could possibly defend the penalty notices scheme given the evidence just presented of how it was being used. The solicitor personalised the question by revealing that he had teenage children of his own and was concerned at how easily they could be criminalised and have their life chances ruined. Brown responded coolly by asking the solicitor whether his children were committing criminal offences when on the street. Gasps of disbelief could be heard around the lecture theatre at this rigid reply. The black and white, zero tolerance view of crime implicit in Brown's reply is, however, characteristic of Home Office thinking since Labour came to power in 1997. As noted in Young's chapter, there are (a few) signs that the shift in leadership from Tony Blair to Gordon Brown may be prompting something of a reassessment.

Consistent with those signs, there is some indication that the 2007 review of PACE will be more thorough and considered than the others that have occurred since the turn of the century, and that there may be further opportunity to comment on concrete proposals that emerge from the initial consultation. The consultation paper itself is rather vague about the precise process: having examined responses to the consultation 'with departmental colleagues and police representatives',[29] a PACE Review Board is to be established, composed of representatives from a range of interests and organisations, including the judiciary, lawyers, the police, the voluntary sector and academics. The scope and nature of the Board's work is yet to be made clear, as is the process of review thereafter, and it is similarly unclear whether the Board will continue after the current consultation process has been completed.[30] Potentially, however, such a Board

[29] 2007 review, n 2, para 2.12. This aspect of the review process was criticised by Michael Zander in his response to the consultation paper: 'What is striking about this list is that it consists entirely of governmental or police bodies. The Home Office might find that consultation with others (the Criminal Bar Association, the Law Society, Justice, Liberty, academic PACE experts, etc), would also be of value'. His response is available at http://www.lse.ac.uk/collections/law/staff/michael-zander.htm (accessed 31 December 2007). The Home Office subsequently published a summary of responses to the consultation paper, available at http://police.homeoffice.gov.uk/news-and-publications/publication/operational-policing/PACEReviewsummary310707.pdf?view=Binary (accessed 31 December 2007), which indicated that there would be series of regional seminars in the autumn, culminating in a national conference in December 2007, with a final phase of consultation following publication of the government's response in spring 2008. It made no mention of the proposed PACE Review Board, but see next note.

[30] On 4 December 2007 the Home Office announced that the proposed regional seminars had been 'postponed' on the basis that they would not have represented value for money due to the level of responses received (no mention was made of the planned national conference). The intention was to publish a final PACE review consultation paper by the end of March 2008, although this later

could start to build something of a principled consensus about the future regulation of the criminal investigative process along the lines that Long argues for in his chapter. This would involve promoting the notion that all parties are stewards of fair procedures and outcomes within the system, and a mutual understanding and respect for each other's proper roles within the adversarial system. Such a Board could also agitate for, or itself commission, a body of research that would enable future reforms to be based and evaluated on sound evidence. However, if the Board is to play a constructive role in advising on the future regulation of the investigative process there must be a commitment by government to fund it sufficiently and to treat its recommendations with respect. The fact that at its first meeting the Board was presented with a draft of the government's final response to the consultation does not provide grounds for confidence. It will also be crucial that the Board does not get bogged down by the ever-changing detail of criminal procedure, and instead focuses on the fundamental trends and issues as identified by the various contributors to this book.

slipped to the end of May 2008. The December announcement also noted the first meeting of the PACE Review Board on 3 December, and provided a list of its members (who include Professor Michael Zander). It met twice more (on 7 January and 14 February 2008). Terms of reference and minutes were supposed to have been published by the end of December, but were not available at the time of finalising this chapter in early June 2008 (and neither was the consultation paper promised for the end of May). See http://police.homeoffice.gov.uk/operational-policing/powers-pace-codes/PACE-Review/ (accessed 12 June 2008).

# 2

## Authorise and Regulate: A Comparative Perspective on the Rise and Fall of a Regulatory Strategy

DAVID DIXON

## I  Introduction

This chapter looks back at the enactment of the Police and Criminal Evidence Act 1984 (PACE) and seeks to reinterpret its story by placing it in a broader historical and comparative perspective. I review the historical context of its emergence and relate it to developments in other common law jurisdictions, notably Australia, drawing on my experience of empirical research on policing in both England and Australia. In the second half of the paper, I argue that the distinctive regulatory strategy expressed in PACE was a product of a socio-political conjuncture. Times have changed, and there are new priorities and strategies in the contemporary social and political climate.

## II  The politics of PACE

When PACE was enacted, it was generally understood by academic commentators as primarily providing a great increase in police powers. Most initial assessments ranged from critical to hostile. Emerging when Thatcherism was in its pomp, PACE was closely identified with the government's political agenda: it 'consolidated and embodied the Thatcherite programme within the law'.[1] Controversies over industrial disputes, public disorder, racial discrimination and miscarriages of justice dominated debates about policing. The dominant academic interpretation of the period was that the government was building a strong

---

[1] P Scraton, 'Editor's preface', in *Law, Order and the Authoritarian State* (Milton Keynes, Open University Press, 1987) viii.

state to partner and protect a free economy and that its policies were fuelled by an ideology of authoritarian populism which fed off law and order panics. Expanding police powers and restricting suspects' rights were seen as integral techniques of power.[2] More specifically, PACE was understood by many to be the Conservative government's generous response to years of public and private pressure from vocal senior police officers for more powers.

This is how I saw PACE at the time: in my files from the early 1980s, I have notes from lectures to students and talks to civil liberties groups about the Thatcher government's reckless expansion of police powers. However, my conventional academic perspective was challenged when I started doing observational fieldwork and interviews for one of the research projects in the (then) Social Science Research Council's programme of assessing the impact of PACE and the Prosecution of Offences Act.[3] Rather than revelling in their new powers, operational officers moaned about having their practices restricted and being held to account by supervisors and via bureaucratic regulation.

The relationship between pre-1986 policing practice and what was authorised under PACE is contentious. The dearth of empirical research on pre-PACE investigative activity encouraged some commentators to commit the legalistic fallacy of assuming that practice and law were consistent. This allowed PACE to be seen as providing a major increase in police power. Antagonism to the political status quo encouraged looking back to 'how things used to be' through rosy glasses. For example, Ewing and Gearty claimed that there was 'a benign vagueness to the law on detention before the 1984 Act … (P)olice practice drifted benevolently in the uncertainty'. This uncertainty was in the nature of the common law, 'the traditional guardian of the people', while the Thatcher government was 'relentlessly pushing back' its 'frontiers'.[4] Necessary corollaries of this view were that judges and magistrates (the operators of the common law) were active in protecting civil liberties and that judicial decisions significantly affected policing practice. For example, Ewing and Gearty claim that the courts developed rules concerning pre-charge detention of suspects which by 1984 'had crystallized into a firm control on the police power to detain without charge'.[5] This unjustifiably assumed that what a few judges said in appeal cases[6] determined general police practice: there is no evidence to establish this interpretation.[7]

---

[2]  See, eg L Bridges and T Bunyan, 'Britain's new urban policing strategy—The Police & Criminal Evidence Bill in context' (1983) 10 *Journal of Law and Society* 85.

[3]  For the project report, see A Bottomley, C Coleman, D Dixon, M Gill and D Wall, *The Impact of PACE: Policing in a Northern Force* (Hull, Centre for Criminology and Criminal Justice, 1991).

[4]  K Ewing and C Gearty, *Freedom under Thatcher: Civil Liberties in Modern Britain* (Oxford, Clarendon Press, 1990) 29 and v.

[5]  *Ibid*, 30.

[6]  Such as *Holmes* [1981] 2 AER 612.

[7]  See D Dixon *Law in Policing: Legal Regulation and Police Practices* (Oxford, Clarendon Press, 1997) 129–42 for an alternative history of this period (hereafter Dixon). Recollections of the pre-PACE era can be found in chs 4, 5 and 6 by John Coppen, John Long and Barbara Wilding (all serving police officers) in this collection.

Fieldwork provided access to a rather different reality. A major finding of our research was that officers could evade PACE's restrictions on stop and search, search of premises, and (to a lesser extent) pre-charge detention for questioning by relying on the suspect's 'consent'.[8] If the suspect agreed to being searched on the street or to letting officers into their home, or to going voluntarily to the station, then statutory power was not used—and the accompanying suspects' rights and bureaucratic controls did not apply.[9] The realities of relations between police and suspects meant that such 'consent' was very rarely the informed, empowered agreement of legal mythology. Much more often, it was an acquiescence stemming from a realistic appreciation of the lack of alternatives. Otherwise, 'consent' would be called upon as ex post facto justification in the rare circumstance of complaint or a supervisor's inquiry. These findings informed early revisions of the PACE Codes of Practice on search of premises and stop and search.

Initially, we considered the use of 'consent' as primarily an adaptive response to the requirements of PACE. However, my fieldwork in Australian policing in the early 1990s made me appreciate that the issue was much wider. In making inter-jurisdictional comparisons, there is of course a danger of simplification: the longer I work in Australia, the more I realise that a shared language can be deceptive. Nonetheless, there are fundamental similarities between law and policing in Australia and in England and Wales. Researching policing in New South Wales was, in legal terms, to step back a decade.[10] This was a jurisdiction which largely relied on the common law: significant reform and consolidation of powers was to await legislation (strongly influenced by PACE) on pre-charge detention in 1997 and a more general consolidation in 2002. What I found in New South Wales was a system of policing by 'consent' which was not just an adaptive response, but rather the normality, a longstanding, traditional way of doing police work. People were stopped and searched, had their houses searched, and were taken to police stations for questioning in processes in which legal formality was largely notable by its absence. This should be no surprise: a key lesson of the observational studies which founded modern policing research was that policing has other resources and purposes than those set by law.[11]

This Australian experience suggested the need for a reinterpretation of practices in England and Wales. 'Helping the police with their inquiries' was a conventional cliché. It is an indicator of a more general practice by which the police achieved their objectives without relying on formal powers. It is to this that

---

[8]   *Ibid*, ch 8; D Dixon, C Coleman and A Bottomley, 'Consent and the legal regulation of policing' (1990) 17 *Journal of Law and Society* 345.

[9]   Experience in Scotland of voluntary attendance being used to avoid the controls of the Criminal Justice (Scotland) Act 1980 led to PACE s 51 and Code C ss 3.15–16 largely removing the advantage of consent in this context (see Dixon, n 7 above, 113–14).

[10]   *Ibid*, ch 5.

[11]   See, eg M Banton, *The Policeman in the Community* (London, Tavistock, 1964).

David McNee (as Metropolitan Police Commissioner) was referring when he argued for increased police powers to deal with a society which was becoming less willing to accept the fiction of consent:

> many police officers, early in their career, learned to use methods bordering on trickery or stealth in their investigations ... (I)t is now increasingly clear that the days when investigating officers could expect to bluff their way into obtaining consent to take body samples, or enter premises, were numbered.[12]

The police could also use other ways of securing suspects for investigative purposes: the holding charge and 'three day lie-down' were useful devices.[13]

It should be noted that this is not to suggest that either Australian or pre-PACE English policing was a mass of malevolent malpractice. The absence of law does not necessarily mean a vacuum: other institutional, cultural and social norms may be significant. While the New South Wales Police had a dubious reputation, by the time my fieldwork began, it had undergone the first of a series of reforms. Systemic corruption and misconduct continued, but they were being challenged in a series of reform programmes which would run through the decade.[14]

In considerable contrast to the 'benign benevolence' account of pre-PACE law in policing, some commentators claimed that police lobbying sought to legitimise police malpractice and that therefore it should be resisted. A convenient resource for this approach was the writings and public statements of Metropolitan Police Commissioners Sir Robert Mark and Sir David McNee. Central to their case for expanding police powers was the argument that inadequate powers led the police to operate outside the law, and potentially into corruption.

> The right to silence has always afforded the strongest motive for police malpractice. Conversely, its abolition will eliminate the strongest temptation for police misbehaviour ... Detectives are under occasional temptation to bend the rules to convict those whom they believe to be guilty, if only because convention has always inhibited them from saying how badly they think those rules work ... A detective who finds general acceptance of a system which protects the wrongdoer can come to think that if crime seems to pay for everyone else, why not for him?[15]

It was easy to caricature this as inviting rewards for bad behaviour and as part of a constant pressure from the police to go beyond the law and then demand that the law should catch up. While it may be more academically fashionable to

---

[12] D McNee, *McNee's Law* (London, Collins, 1983) 18 and 181.

[13] See Dixon, n 7 above, 136–7.

[14] J Wood, *Final Report of the Royal Commission into the New South Wales Police Service* (Sydney, Royal Commission, 1997); D Dixon, 'Reform, Regression and the Royal Commission into the NSW Police Service', in D Dixon (ed), *A Culture of Corruption: Changing an Australian Police Service*, (Sydney, Hawkins Press, 1999) 138.

[15] R Mark, *Policing a Perplexed Society* (London, George Allen & Unwin, 1977) 40 and 67. See also R Mark, *In the Office of Constable* (London, William Collins, 1978) and D McNee, *McNee's Law* (London, Collins, 1983).

criticise Mark's approach, his claims had a significant kernel of truth. This is particularly so as regards pre-charge detention.

The common law required that people arrested by the police should be taken to a magistrate without delay. This reflected a division of labour between police and magistrates which was long gone, having significantly changed in the mid-nineteenth century when magistrates retreated to an essentially judicial role, while the police became crime investigators. English common law eventually recognised police power to detain before charge for investigative purposes[16] but the Australian High Court restated the common law's prohibition on pre-charge detention.[17] It did so not out of naivety, but in order to send a clear message to the authorities that statutory reform was needed. In both countries, the lack of clear legal authority to carry out what had become a basic, expected police function was reprehensible. This meant that police practices developed and authority expanded without appropriate regulation and without protection for suspects' rights.

So when the police argued that the lack of powers was making them act unlawfully and risk other temptations, they deserved a hearing. They made their case forcefully and overstated their argument in ways which had not previously been accepted practice for the police in Britain. But it is surely this earlier historical record of political reticence which is more remarkable than the fact that a group lobbied for its interests. Indeed, the activities of English police seem remarkably restrained when set against those in Australia, where police departments and police unions continue to enjoy considerable political power in some states.[18]

Given the strength of police pressure and the politics of the government of the day, it is surprising not that PACE extended police powers, but rather that this extension was accompanied by measures of bureaucratic regulation and the provision of substantial rights to suspects. The academic literature focuses on failings and inadequacies.[19] Like the glass which is half full or half empty, it depends on how you look at it—and from where. For example, when I was in England, some of my work examined the shortcomings of legal advice for people detained in police stations.[20] Looking from Australia—where lawyers in police interview rooms are as common as English sporting successes[21]—what was notable (indeed, extraordinary, given the timing of its establishment) about the PACE system is the existence of substantial provision for free legal advice. Similarly, English critics point to the problematic aspects of the custody officer's

---

[16] See Dixon, n 7 above, 127–8.
[17] *Ibid*, 180–83.
[18] M Finnane, *When Police Unionise: the Politics of Law and Order in Australia* (Sydney, Institute of Criminology, 2002).
[19] A Sanders and R Young, *Criminal Justice* 3rd edn (Oxford, Oxford University Press, 2007).
[20] See Dixon, above n 7, ch 6.
[21] D Dixon, *Interrogating Images: Audio-visually Recorded Police Questioning of Suspects* (Sydney, Institute of Criminology, 2007).

role, notably the extreme rarity of a custody officer refusing to accept a suspect into custody. My experience in Australia was to see suspects taken into police stations by arresting officers who did not even bother to inform a supervisor of the detention. From this perspective, the positive aspects of the PACE custody officer seem more significant than the negative.

English critics of PACE faced problems in reconciling its restrictions on police powers and its provisions for suspects' rights: why would a Thatcherite government hell-bent on expanding police powers do this? The usual response was to emphasise the maximum power available, to point to exceptions in requirements to provide rights, and to suggest that restrictions and controls were ineffective. Notably, the notional availability of four days of pre-charge detention attracted more attention than the procedures requiring review and authorisation of continued detention (the result of which is that most suspects are charged or released within six hours and very few are held for longer than 24). Ewing and Gearty emphasised the deliberate complexity of PACE's bureaucratic regulation:

> The greatly increased power [to detain before charge] is enshrouded in a mist of complicated statutory provisions. It is protected from public scrutiny by the technicality of its jargon. Words rarely mean what they seem to say. Grandiose guarantees of freedom are liable to be contradicted in a couple of discreet subparagraphs, loitering at the end of a page. Safeguards offered to detainees turn out to be more apparent than real ... It is a bureaucracy of incarceration beyond the dreams of the bleakest writers.[22]

This hyperbole exemplifies how political antagonism led to misinterpretation of the regulatory structure of PACE.

A conventional account of elements of PACE which are inconsistent with a linear increase of police powers would focus on the ways in which 'balance' between police powers and suspects' rights was built into the Philips Commission's Report[23] and in which balancing measures appeared in PACE as part of the parliamentary process. Use of the balance metaphor in criminal justice has been the target of sustained criticism.[24] Nonetheless, in providing an account of the legislative process, its use can be justified. Take, for example, the role of the House of Lords in revising what eventually became section 78 of PACE.[25] However I would argue that understanding this aspect of PACE requires us to put the legislation in a broader context, moving beyond description of the political process.

---

[22] K Ewing and C Gearty, *Freedom under Thatcher: Civil Liberties in Modern Britain* (Oxford: Clarendon Press, 1990) 30–31.

[23] Report of the Royal Commission on Criminal Procedure, Cmnd 8092 (London, HMSO, 1981).

[24] See, eg, A Ashworth, *The Criminal Process* (Oxford, Oxford University Press, 1994).

[25] L Leigh, 'Some observations on the parliamentary history of the PACE Act 1984', in C Harlow (ed) *Public Law and Politics* (London, Sweet & Maxwell, 1986) 91.

# III  The authorise and regulate strategy

The relationship between law and policing before PACE is primarily to be explained as the product of a distinctive set of beliefs about policing in England, which were carried over to Australia.[26] Originating in the particular conditions under which reform of policing in early and mid-nineteenth century England had been possible, the ideas of the police officer as a 'citizen in uniform' and as the holder of the ancient office of constable were crucial.[27] Taken together, these distanced the the police from the rest of the state and emphasised their connection with the community and (at a largely rhetorical level) with the law. In 1929, the Royal Commission on Police Powers and Procedure (in England and Wales) reported that:

> The Police ... have never been recognised, either in law or in tradition, as a force distinct from the general body of citizens ... (T)he principle remains that a Policeman ... is only 'a person paid to perform, as a matter of duty, acts which if he were so minded he might have done voluntarily'. Indeed, a policeman possesses few powers not enjoyed by the ordinary citizen, and public opinion, as expressed in Parliament and elsewhere, has shown great jealousy of any attempt to give increased authority to the Police.[28]

In 1962, another English Royal Commission endorsed 'the principle that police powers are mostly grounded in the common law and differ little from those of ordinary citizens'.[29]

The potent myth about the English tradition overlaid a reality in which, to do their job, the police had to do more than the law allowed. As suggested above, the police had either to exploit legal loopholes or to evade the law by relying on the suspect's notional consent. Another alternative was simply to rely on the courts' persistent unwillingness to exclude unlawfully obtained evidence.

Indeed, policing was practicable largely because the courts abstained from active supervision of police practices. This was particularly significant in Australia, where the courts were, notionally, the primary means of controlling police practices. Despite conventional grumbling from the police about lack of support from the courts, empirical studies demonstrate just how limited judicial intervention was.[30] External factors played their part too: so long as there was no great

---

[26] For an outstanding account, see K Alderson, *Powers and Responsibilities: Reforming NSW Criminal Investigation Law,* PhD thesis (University of New South Wales, 2002).

[27] I Loader and A Mulcahy, *Policing and the Condition of England* (Oxford, Oxford University Press, 2003); R Reiner, *The Politics of the Police,* (Oxford, Oxford University Press, 2000).

[28] *Report of the Royal Commission on Police Powers and Procedure,* Cmd 3297 (London, HMSO, 1929) 6.

[29] *Report of the Royal Commission on the Police* (London, HMSO, 1962) 11.

[30] B Presser, 'Public Policy, Police Interest: A Re-evaluation of the Judicial Discretion to Exclude Improperly or Illegally Obtained Evidence' (2001) 25 *Melbourne University Law Review* 757.

public concern about crime, the popular press took a civil libertarian line, opposing the extension of formal police powers.[31] As Alderson concludes, in the years between 1945 and 1968:

> Dominant ways of thinking ... emphasised faith in police, belief in an ideal of police/community cooperation, and a playing down of the importance, and desirability, of formal legal powers. [They] also emphasised faith in the courts as the best forum for redressing injustice, controlling police misconduct and upholding citizens' rights.[32]

Until the final third of the twentieth century, the marginality of law was a notable feature of everyday police practice in Australia and England. Police forces were disciplined organisations, but such discipline came principally from internal police management rather than external law. Formal police powers were very limited. In carrying out their key tasks of controlling crime and maintaining order, officers could draw upon broad offences (particularly, in Australia, public order offences related to drunkenness). Notionally, the criminal process was dominated by magistrates and judges. The judges instructed the police on how to carry out their duties by issuing various versions of the Judges' Rules. These were written in a way that demonstrated the authors' very limited understanding of police practices.[33] In Australia, these were reproduced and adapted as part of (increasingly voluminous) Commissioner's Instructions which (like most such rules) had very limited impact on policing practice.

In summary, the defining characteristic of this period in law–policing relations was legalistic rhetoric which masked an essentially permissive policing environment. According to an authoritative Australian survey in the mid-1960s:

> Little interest has been shown in this country ... in reassessing the adequacy of police powers ... Understandably the police themselves are rather reluctant to press claims for additional power for fear that their intentions might be misconstrued or that their representations might focus attention on existing practices of questionable legality. Only on rare occasions is the legality of police actions challenged in the courts, but there must be many occasions on which police officers ... feel it necessary in the interests of law enforcement to adopt measures which technically are not within the scope of their authority.[34]

In this respect, the position in England and Wales and in Australia was very similar.

The final third of the twentieth century saw the development of a new and distinctive approach to police powers in common law countries. This discussion focuses on England and Australia, but similar trends were evident in New

---

[31]  K Alderson, *Powers and Responsibilities: Reforming NSW Criminal Investigation Law,* PhD thesis (University of New South Wales, 2002) 61.

[32]  *Ibid,* 83.

[33]  See Dixon, above n 7, ch 4.

[34]  E Campbell and H Whitmore, *Freedom in Australia,* (Sydney, Sydney University Press, 1966) 32.

Zealand[35] and Canada.[36] By the turn of the century, the law of criminal investigation was an increasingly complex structure of laws, subsidiary rules and codes of practice. They provided clear authorisation to the police to intrude on individual liberty in various ways—including stop and search, search of premises, and detention for investigative purposes. As explained above, the police had routinely done these things before the new laws, exploiting the gaps and uncertainties in the common law and local legislation, and relying on their targets' ignorance of, or inability to enforce, their rights. What was new was that the police now had clear authorisation for such practices.

However, the new laws did not merely legalise what the police had always done or provide new powers. In defining police powers, the law both clarified them and set their limits. For example, if the police were authorised to detain suspects between arrest and charge, such detention was made subject to specific time limits. In addition, new powers were complemented by rights for suspects which were to be shifted from the airy rhetoric of judicial neglect to specific rules on, for example, access to legal advice. Indeed, while legal police powers were substantially extended during this period, '(p)rovision for provision, most of the criminal investigation legislation enacted has been about regulating the conduct of law enforcement officers and restricting the availability and use of powers'.[37] The manner in which powers and rights are exercised was made subject to extensive administrative control with requirements of record-making, managerial supervision, and external review. Often seen at the time as merely an extension of police powers, the strategy should be understood as being to 'authorize and regulate'.[38] To characterise this as abandoning the rigour of law for the permissiveness of self-regulation is to misunderstand the realities of policing both before and after PACE.[39]

Why did such regulatory developments occur? Their origin is to be found in a series of related social and political developments in Anglophone societies from the mid-1960s. Increasing levels of recorded crime and public concern about crime pushed policing into the political arena, provoking demands for increased police powers. A symbiotic relationship developed: proposals and demands from one side provoked contrary responses from the other. A significant factor here

[35] New Zealand Law Commission, *Criminal Evidence: Police Questioning*, Preliminary Paper No 21 (Wellington, Law Commission, 1992).

[36] Law Reform Commission of Canada, *Arrest* (Ottawa, LRCC, 1985); *Our Criminal Procedure* (Ottawa, LRCC, 1988); *Recodifying Criminal Procedure*, vol 1 (Ottawa, LRCC, 1991).

[37] K Alderson, *Powers and Responsibilities: Reforming NSW Criminal Investigation Law*, PhD thesis (University of New South Wales, 2002) 8.

[38] *Ibid.*

[39] In his paper in this collection, Andrew Sanders argues that PACE places too much reliance on 'self-regulation'. A central point of my own recent work is that New South Wales police have been left to regulate themselves in recording interrogations and that more effective legal and other regulation is required—ie an explicit argument against relying solely on self-regulation: D Dixon, 'A window into the interviewing process?' (2006) 16 *Policing & Society* 323. The real issue (as in any regulatory enterprise) is how to combine external and internal regulation: each depends on the other.

was the professionalisation of policing: for an occupation with aspirations to professional status, relying on legal loopholes and the public's ignorance was unsatisfactory and demeaning. At the same time, the growth of social liberalism led to pressure for protection of civil liberties and suspects' rights. The influence of the US civil rights movement and the Warren Supreme Court is evident in Australia and elsewhere.[40]

At another level, the 'authorise and regulate' strategy was a product of a general shift towards formalisation and extension of regulation in and by states. When a need to deal with problems in policing was recognised, it was simply consistent with other contemporary trends in state activity for processes of bureaucratic regulation to be introduced. Statutory specification, codes of practice, record-making, and supervision were all the standard tools of late twentieth century states in countries such as Britain and Australia.

Equally, there were changes in the status of the objects of police attention: social democratisation in the mid-twentieth century meant that 'informality' in dealing with suspects became less appropriate. In legal and political rhetoric (even if not in police practice), suspects were no longer merely 'police property'[41] but citizens whose alleged delicts did not set them outside the political community. They were therefore to be treated according to liberal democratic principles. These were best expounded by the Royal Commission on Criminal Procedure (in England and Wales) which provided a 'framework of first principles'—fairness, openness, accountability and efficiency.[42] This is a distinctively liberal democratic form of governance: while the need for state action is accepted, interventions into the life of any citizen required legal authority and justification which had to respect the citizen's liberties. Criminal justice in the twentieth century was constructed around a group of concepts, values and purposes which originate in liberal democratic politics. These include: the primacy of the individual and the individual's rights; the need for guilt to be proved by the prosecution beyond reasonable doubt; due process; a need for certainty; reactive response as the key role of policing agencies; punishment based on desert; and processes providing fairness and justice.

While Australia was ahead of Britain in conducting an inquiry committed to authorisation and regulation—the Australian Law Reform Commission's (ALRC) influential report on criminal investigation[43] appeared in 1975—it took longer than England and Wales to legislate. The Royal Commission on Criminal Procedure was followed by legislation in England and Wales, principally PACE. But it was not until 1991 that the Australian Commonwealth finally reformed

---

[40] Notably, see ALRC, *Criminal Investigation: Interim Report*, Report No 2. (Canberra, Australian Government Publishing Service, 1975).

[41] R Reiner, *The Politics of the Police*, (Oxford, Oxford University Press, 2000).

[42] *Report of the Royal Commission on Criminal Procedure*, Cmnd 8092 (London, HMSO, 1981) 126.

[43] ALRC, *Criminal Investigation: Interim Report*, Report No 2. (Canberra, Australian Government Publishing Service, 1975).

federal investigative law, while New South Wales took even longer: its Crimes Amendment (Detention after Arrest) Act 1997 was eventually followed by a consolidating measure, the Law Enforcement (Powers and Responsibilities) Act in 2002. What accounts for this lag between the jurisdictions and the relative weakness of the Australian legislation's protection for suspects?

An important factor is that the liberal lawyers who called for change in Australia were outside the formal political process. For example, while Lord Scarman could directly influence the PACE Bill in the House of Lords, Justice Michael Kirby (ALRC chairman) was able only to complain in extra-judicial speeches that criminal procedure had become a 'graveyard of reports'.[44] A second factor was that Australian jurisdictions have regarded audio-visual recording of police interrogation as a panacea which made other reform of criminal investigation at best less pressing, at worst unnecessary.[45]

A third factor was the relative weakness in Australia of the permanent civil or public service in the area of criminal justice. In part this was a consequence of the fact that policing and criminal justice have been primarily the responsibilities of the various states rather than of the federal government. (A major development in recent years—and particularly since 9/11—has been the growth of central policing and security agencies.) By contrast, the Home Office had a powerful and established bureaucracy with significant commitments to liberalism. As Ian Loader argues, these 'platonic guardians' had a major influence on criminal justice policy. The 'organizing motifs' of this ideology were 'a concern with the primacy of individual freedom and the threat the state poses to it, coupled simultaneously with the belief that a strong, effective, rule-bound state is vital to the preservation of order and hence liberty'.[46] PACE is best understood as a product of this, as well as, of course, of a Royal Commission which embodied the 'liberal elitism' described by Loader. By contrast, the picture painted by some of PACE's critics of the Home Office and senior police in a conspiratorial, illiberal partnership to extend police powers is unconvincing. These civil servants collaborated with politicians (notably William Whitelaw and Douglas Hurd) whose involvement in the Thatcher governments was tempered by an old-Tory liberalism.[47] This political strain has always been weaker in Australia. By the time legislation on police powers was seriously considered in New South Wales, it was entirely absent. The political process had come to be dominated by a simplistic

---

[44]  M Kirby, 'Control over investigation of offences and pre-trial treatment of suspects' (1979) 53 *Australian Law Journal* 626.

[45]  D Dixon, 'A window into the interviewing process?' (2006) 16 *Policing & Society* 323.

[46]  I Loader, 'Fall of the "platonic guardians": liberalism, criminology and political responses to crime in England and Wales' (2006) 46 *British Journal of Criminology* 561. See also D Faulkner, *Crime, State and Citizen* (Winchester, Waterside Press, 2006).

[47]  *Ibid*, 576. Like Loader, my comment on this liberalism is made 'without any prior commitment either to defending it, or to viewing it in some wistful mode' (*ibid*, 562, n 1) and certainly should not be read as an expression of political sympathy. Taking a seat in Margaret Thatcher's cabinet involved the compromising of principle. On the other hand, it is hardly more blameworthy than the shallow, authoritarian paternalism of some of their successors.

politics of law and order. In this context, the social and political forces underlying the 'authorise and regulate' strategy had lost their momentum.

This is not the place for a review of the evidence on the impact of PACE.[48] However, it is perhaps worth noting my general conclusion that success of the authorise and regulate strategy depended on the rules' relationship with other police norms and priorities and upon the potential for supervision and bureaucratic regulation to get to grips with policing practice.

Stop and search demonstrates the limitations of the authorise and regulate strategy. As noted above, police officers could simply evade its restrictions by purporting to stop and search not by using legal authority, but by relying on the suspect's 'consent'. By its very nature, the interaction between officer and suspect on the street is difficult to supervise. Unless every exchange between police and people is to be electronically recorded, what was said will be open to dispute. The English authorities' response to abuse of 'consent' was to direct officers that they should only stop and search using statutory powers. This suggests excessive faith in authorisation and regulation.

The strategy conceives of stop and search as a preliminary stage of a linear criminal investigation and justice process punctuated by decisions about individuals (as in the flow charts of the criminal justice system found in introductory student texts). A police officer decides whether he or she has the appropriate level of suspicion about an individual's possession of certain items. However, this is a misleadingly narrow view of stop and search both in terms of its general functions and the way it is used in specific encounters. Officers stop people not just to search them for specified articles, but also to obtain information, to impose authority on individuals, groups and areas, and to disrupt activities such as drug markets. In dealing with an individual, an officer's suspicion may be prompted by the kind of specific indicator contemplated by legislators (for example slipping a packet into a bag), but it is more likely to be a complex mixture of preconceptions about what is normal in a particular place at a particular time, stereotypes, and assumptions about particular types of people. Specific encounters are to be understood not as characterised by discrete legalistic decision-making, but rather as a process of interaction between officer and citizen in which suspicion is constructed or dispelled.[49]

By contrast, PACE has had more impact on the way in which suspects are detained and questioned. As noted above, the custody officer system may not be ideal, but it looks more attractive when one has experienced a system without any semblance of independent overview of the detention process. Similarly, I prefer to look at the achievements rather than the failings of post-PACE police questioning of suspects. It is certainly true that the review of investigative interviewing by

---

[48] See A Sanders and R Young, *Criminal Justice* 3rd edn (Oxford, Oxford University Press, 2007); Dixon, n 7 above.

[49] D Dixon, A Bottomley, C Coleman, M Gill and D Wall, 'Reality and rules in the construction and regulation of police suspicion' (1989) 17 *International Journal of the Sociology of Law* 185.

Clarke and Milne found that many officers were not using the specific techniques known by the acronym PEACE: indeed, there was little difference between the performance of officers who were trained and those who were not.[50] However, as they suggest, it would be more appropriate to compare the interviews in their sample as a whole with those conducted before 1991 (when the PEACE programme was launched). From this perspective, 'there was clear evidence ... that since the introduction of PEACE an improvement in the ethos and ethical approach to interviewing has taken place' and 'PEACE training has developed the skills used by police officers to interview suspects of crime'.[51] While 'ten per cent of the sample was rated as possibly breaching PACE',[52] the picture presented is very different from the pervasive misconduct and incompetence found in earlier research by Williamson, Moston and Baldwin.[53] Investigative interviewing is more important for its impact in undermining previously accepted strategies than for the specific techniques of information gathering and checking which it incorporates. From another comparative perspective, this is a considerable achievement: compared to the academically discredited and error-producing interrogation techniques which dominate US police training, investigative interviewing looks more like success than failure. It should not be forgotten that two decades ago some English police forces were training their officers in US methods. They were stopped from going down that dangerous path by judicial decisions on PACE (notably in *Heron* and *Paris et al*) which pushed the police into developing a better way of questioning suspects.[54] So soon after the sad death of Tom Williamson, a key architect of investigative interviewing, it is appropriate to focus on its achievements—and to wonder how many miscarriages of justice would have occurred if the American model had been adopted generally.

# IV From authorise/regulate to the politics of risk

In retrospect, the 'authorise and regulate' strategy has to be seen as a governing style suited to a particular moment in the trajectory of social–liberal democracy,

---

[50] C Clarke and R Milne, *National Evaluation of the PEACE Investigative Interviewing Course* (2001) Police Research Award Scheme Report No 149. (PEACE stands for 'Preparation and Planning, Engage and Explain, Account, Closure, and Evaluate').

[51] *Ibid*, 100 and 113.

[52] *Ibid*, 100.

[53] T Williamson, 'Strategic changes in police interrogation', PhD thesis (University of Kent, 1990); S Moston and G Stephenson, 'The changing face of police interrogation' (1993) 3 *Journal of Community & Applied Psychology* 101; J Baldwin, 'Police interview techniques' (1993) 33 *British Journal of Criminology* 325.

[54] D Dixon, 'Regulating police interrogation', in T Williamson (ed), *Investigative Interviewing: Developments in Rights, Research and Regulation* (Cullompton, Willan, 2006).

one in which the metaphor of balance was well-suited. As noted above, there was real commitment to the objective of providing both for the police to have the powers that they need to do their job and for suspects to have substantial rights. Its zenith came with the establishment of the Royal Commission on Criminal Justice in 1991: the belated acknowledgement that the criminal justice process had convicted the wrong people in a long series of cases was expected by many to lead to significant reform which would give greater substance to measures protecting rights. However, by the time the Royal Commission reported in 1993,[55] times were decisively changing. Far from a reconstitution of criminal justice around liberal principle, this Commission paid homage to the new gods of efficiency and effectiveness.

The central concepts of liberal democratic criminal justice are devalued in the new criminal justice. The key concern is now the minimisation of risk and the security of the group. The target is 'the offender not the offence': what someone has done is less significant than what he or she may do in the future.[56] Policing intervenes proactively, preventing and pre-empting problems rather than retrospectively solving them. The buzzword is 'preemption'.[57] There is less emphasis on the individual's rights and the need to prove the individual's guilt beyond reasonable doubt through a system of due process. Legality is bled out of criminal justice by incentives and pressures to plead guilty, the expansion of summary jurisdiction, and the collapse of adjudication into enforcement through the proliferation of fixed penalty notices.[58] Flexibility replaces certainty as a virtue. Compliance, efficiency and outcomes are more important than individual punishment or due process: cautioning schemes, preventive detention for potential sex-offenders and others, anti-social behaviour orders, behaviour management contracts, non-association and space restriction orders, and the use of bail conditions as a proactive crime control measure are just the more prominent examples. There is less interest in understanding crime's causation than in accepting crime as normal, a choice to be controlled and insured against, in which 'attempts to cure or punish appear less logical than do moves to manage crime and minimize its costs'.[59] This has two contrasting facets. On one hand, crime is ubiquitous and to be controlled by measures noted above. On the other, 'criminals' are specific, targeted, enumerated groups of repeat, prolific and serious offenders. The state's responsibility for crime control is 'contracted out to private providers wielding state franchises, delegated to individuals and communities, or completely over taken by the growing private security industry'.[60]

---

[55]  *Report of the Royal Commission on Criminal Justice*, Cmd 2263 (London, HMSO, 1993).
[56]  HM Government, *Building on progress: security, crime and justice* (London, Cabinet Office, 2007) 4.
[57]  A Dershowitz, *Preemption* (New York, WW Norton, 2006).
[58]  See further ch 7 by Richard Young in this collection.
[59]  L Zedner, *Criminal Justice* (Oxford, Oxford University Press, 2005) 284.
[60]  *Ibid.*

Simply to say that all this goes against basic principle is rather like complaining that a game of chess is not being played according to the rules of draughts. The game has changed, allowing those in government to dismiss the standard civil libertarian response to new police powers as anachronistic and irrelevant. While these developments have been underway for some time, they accelerated quickly after 9/11. Parliaments are now in a constant cycle of extending criminal and anti-terrorism legislation in ways that routinely deviate from liberal democratic principles in the name of security.

As a consequence of these general developments, key elements of the 'authorise and regulate' strategy have weakened. First, the distinctive liberal caution about extending police powers has evaporated. When the individual's rights are set against the community's interest in self-protection against public disorder (let alone terrorist attacks), insistence on the primacy of the former is dismissed as anachronistic. This position has been forcefully stated by Tony Blair, who, when Prime Minister, presented the decline of individualism as a desirable consequence of a rediscovered social democratic communitarianism. Speaking of proposals to extend powers to deal with anti-social behaviour, Blair claimed:

> These powers have a strong philosophical justification, from within the Labour tradition. One of the basic insights of the Left, one of its distinguishing features, is to caution against too excessive an individualism. People must live together and one of the basic tasks of government is to facilitate this living together, to ensure the many can live without fear of the few.[61]

Blair rightly identified the need to respond to social change and to encourage a new politics of community in which mutual respect replaces deference. However, he tried to satisfy this need by drawing on a Labour tradition of moralistic authoritarianism and expecting too much of policing and criminal justice.[62]

In Blair's approach, the meaning of basic concepts is renegotiated:

> This is not a debate between those who value liberty and those who do not. It is an argument about the types of liberties that need to be protected given the changing nature of the crimes that violate them. And it is an attempt to protect that most fundamental liberty of all—freedom from harm by others.[63]

In his foreword to key policy statements, Tony Blair made explicit the view that construction of a new criminal justice is underway. We are told that 'the system we inherited had been designed for a previous era'.[64] It was archaic, a response to 'the need in Victorian times to counter the gross unfairness of the past by safeguarding the rights of the accused, with no real concern for the victim'. We are

---

[61] T Blair, 'Our citizens should not live in fear' *The Observer* 11 December 2005.

[62] I Loader 'Rebalancing the criminal justice system?' paper for PM's *Our Nation's Future* series, http://www.pm.gov.uk/output/Page9701.asp (accessed 15 May 2007).

[63] T Blair, 'Our citizens should not live in fear' *The Observer* 11 December 2005.

[64] T Blair, Foreword, HM Government *Building on progress: security, crime and justice* (London, Cabinet Office, 2007) 3.

now, apparently, 'in a modern world stripped of the bonds of the past'.[65] The then Home Secretary, John Reid, repeated this message, telling us that the criminal justice system's 'unfairness and savagery in Victorian times . . . led to a priority being placed on extra safeguards for the accused'.[66] This is a bizarrely ahistorical account: the miscarriages of justice which defiled British criminal justice in the 1970s and 1980s indicate that 'gross unfairness' was not confined to Victorian times and that care should be taken before stepping into the 'modern world'. The 'need to modernise' is played as if it trumps all concerns. However, if the player understands neither the past nor the present of criminal justice, it may be better to reserve 'modernisation' for talk about what to do to the kitchen or bathroom.

Balancing the rights of the individual against those of 'the community' is particularly problematic in the contemporary context of concern about terrorism. When the balance is 'between the security interests of the majority and the civil liberties of that tiny minority of persons who find themselves subject to state investigation', giving priority to the former is almost automatic.[67] In this self-interested utilitarianism, the 'only balance in question is the balance between the majority's security and *other* people's rights'.[68] When those others are racial, ethnic or religious minorities, the outcome can be deeply problematic. Police powers are no longer to be evaluated in terms of what 'we' would regard as acceptable for our political community, us or our children: they are powers to be applied to other people. Blair was unrepentant about this:

> It's no use saying that in theory there should be no conflict between the traditional protections for the suspect and the rights of the law-abiding majority because, as a result of the changing nature of crime and society, there is, in practice, such a conflict.[69]

When the stakes are high, there can be only one winner in such a conflict:

> This is not an argument about whether we respect civil liberties or not; but whose take priority. It is not about choosing hard line policies over an individual's human rights. It's about which human rights prevail. In making that decision, there is a balance to be struck. I am saying it is time to rebalance the decision in favour of the decent, law-abiding majority ...[70]

The re-balancing process is 'personalised' by constant references to another rhetorical trump—the victim. Set against the suspect/defendant/criminal is not (just) a general social interest, but the very specific interest of the victim. Indeed,

---

[65]   T Blair, Foreword, *Rebalancing the Criminal Justice System in Favour of the Law-abiding Majority* (London, Home Office, 2006) 2.

[66]   *Ibid*, Introduction, 3.

[67]   L Zedner, 'Securing Liberty in the Face of Terror', (2005) 32 *Journal of Law and Society* 507 at 513.

[68]   R Dworkin, 'Terror and the Attack on Civil Liberties', *New York Review of Books*, 6 November 2003, 37.

[69]   'Our Nation's Future—Criminal Justice System' 23 June 2006, http://www.pm.gov.uk/output/Page9737.asp (accessed 15 May 2007).

[70]   *Ibid.*

Minister of State McNulty asserted in his foreword to a consultation paper on *Modernising Police Powers* that his 'aim is to re-focus the investigation and evidence gathering processes on serving the needs of victims and witnesses'.[71] As Michael Zander forcefully argues in a submission to the PACE review, such references to victims are really 'code for rebalancing criminal justice in favour of the prosecution'.[72] Victims and witnesses should, of course, be treated better (not least because doing so will improve the quantity and quality of evidence they provide) but 'criminal investigation and evidence gathering processes cannot sensibly be driven by looking at the needs of victims and witnesses'.[73]

The second element of authorisation and regulation's weakening is that the divisions of function between elements of the justice process collapse. As chapters seven and ten in this collection by Young and Jackson show, the new criminal justice elides boundaries between investigation, accusation and disposition. Restriction of the right to silence and the location of prosecutors in police stations mean that the interview room provides the venue for disputes previously conducted in court.

The third element is shortening of the law-making process, making possible swift legislative responses to threat. A civil servant interviewed by Loader refers to 'almost hyperactive legislative behaviour' on crime and criminal justice in England and Wales.[74] Politicians who genuflect to the fashion for evidence-based policy are apparently happy to legislate without, or contrary to, the findings of any research base. Australia, and New South Wales in particular, suffers from a virulent form of this infection. Spurred on and harassed by media commentators whose influence is bizarrely disproportionate to their knowledge, governments legislate at the drop of a cliché. New powers are provided to the police whether they need them or not (and no time is spent investigating whether they will be useful and how they relate to police practice). The rhetoric of war is de rigueur: insistence that wars are being fought against drugs and terrorism justifies the apparently endless expansion of police powers.

Such legislation has a crucial symbolic dimension: its specific provisions are less important than the message that the public's fears of crime and insecurity are taken seriously even though (in a classic example of amplification) such fears can be increased rather than allayed by the reaction. Politicians must be seen to be doing something, and passing a law is a particularly effective way of being seen to

---

[71] *Modernising Police Powers: Review of the Police & Criminal Evidence Act (PACE) 1984: consultation paper* (London, Home Office, March 2007) 2. See Tony Blair's argument that liberalism has become detached from concern with victims in 'Our Nation's Future—Criminal Justice System' 23 June 2006, http://www.pm.gov.uk/output/Page9737.asp (accessed 15 May 2007).

[72] M Zander 'Response to Home Office Consultation Paper *Modernising Police Powers*', (March 2007, unpublished).

[73] M Zander 'Change of PACE' *New Law Journal*, 13 April 2007, 157: 504 at 504. See also M Zander 'If it ain't broke, don't fix it', *Police Review*, 1 June 2007.

[74] I Loader, 'Fall of the "platonic guardians": liberalism, criminology and political responses to crime in England and Wales' (2006) 46 *British Journal of Criminology* 561 at 578.

act—even if appearance and reality do not correspond. Action must be swift: so when the New South Wales Parliament legislated in 1998 in response to incidents of assaults with knives, the Police Minister commented approvingly 'This is instant law, this is as quick as instant coffee'.[75] Moral panics used to involve lengthy processes of amplification through the media, professionals and 'experts' before the law was changed.[76] Now, the process is cut short: almost before the broken glass had been cleared from the streets of Cronulla and Maroubra after outbreaks of disorder in late 2005, the New South Wales Parliament had been recalled and, in a single day, the Law Enforcement Legislation Amendment (Public Safety) Act 2005 had been introduced, 'debated' and passed into law.[77] Maximum penalties were increased, access to bail was reduced, a new offence was created, and police powers to stop and search, close down areas, and control alcohol consumption were provided. The Premier told Parliament 'I have recalled Parliament for one simple reason: new powers to uphold public order. And we are here to make sure that the police get the powers they need. Louts and criminals have effectively declared war on our society and we are not going to let them undermine our way of life'.[78] As if trying to exemplify the process of 'normalisation' of exceptional powers described by academic critics,[79] the second target of the new law (which had been introduced in response to inter-racial crime against a background of metropolitan concerns about terrorism) was an Aboriginal housing estate in a country town, Dubbo.

During the period when the 'authorise and regulate' strategy was dominant, the police had to lobby for powers. Now, such lobbying is barely necessary: legislatures shower the police with gifts. A New South Wales Premier provided notable examples:

> If police can identify another power they need to protect order and public safety, they will get it … If the police commissioner ever comes to me and says 'I need additional powers to arrest drug dealers', it goes without saying he gets them.[80]

Such statements express a relationship between government and police which is quite different from that conventionally associated with a liberal democracy, in which some healthy tension exists between the powers that the police want and the powers that they have.

---

[75] Quoted in D Dixon, 'Reform, Regression and the Royal Commission into the NSW Police Service', in D Dixon (ed), *A Culture of Corruption: Changing an Australian Police Service* (Sydney, Hawkins Press, 1999) 138 at 164.

[76] S Cohen, *Folk Devils and Moral Panics* (London, Paladin, 1972).

[77] Similarly swift law-making in 2006 at Westminster saw major changes to PACE powers of arrest: see ch 8 by Ed Cape in this collection.

[78] NSW Hansard, Legislative Assembly, 15 December 2005.

[79] P Hillyard, 'The Normalization of Special Powers', in N Lacey (ed), *Criminal Justice* (Oxford, Oxford University Press, 1994) 63.

[80] Bob Carr quoted in D Dixon, 'Reform, Regression and the Royal Commission into the NSW Police Service', in D Dixon (ed), *A Culture of Corruption: Changing an Australian Police Service* (Sydney, Hawkins Press, 1999) 138 at 166.

The final element of authorisation and regulation's decline is the conversion of 'bureaucracy' into a term of abuse, as if it is mere red tape to be cut. The target is not just excessive or unnecessary bureaucracy, but bureaucracy per se—a strange position for organised government to adopt. This tendency found notable expression in the Blair government's breezy and worryingly ill-informed first review of PACE.[81] My experience of this was to be rung by an official who seemed more concerned to tell me about PACE's problems than to hear what I had to say. The clear impression was that the only purpose of the call was to tick a box marked 'Consultation with academics'. The consultation paper on PACE issued in March 2007[82] does not encourage optimism that the lessons of 2002 have been learnt. On the contrary, the consultation paper fails to explain its purpose beyond three simplistic slogans (focusing on victims is good; modernising is good; bureaucracy is bad) before diving into a number of very specific issues.

These exercises by the Home Office contrasted with my experience in the late 1980s of dealing with departmental officials who were keen to feed the results of academic research into the policy-making process. However, even then, their approach was becoming less influential, as criminal justice policy became increasingly politicised and dominated by a managerialist style of administration.[83] One regrettable consequence is that—with a few exceptions—official sponsorship of qualitative research on PACE and associated powers has dried up. The SSRC research programme mentioned above provided a series of benchmarks: the failure to use them in subsequent research was an unfortunately wasted opportunity. This is just one product of a more general change in official attitude towards academic research in criminal justice.[84]

# V  Counter-trends: legality, efficiency and rights

While the trends identified in the preceding section are clear, there is a real and obvious danger in overstating the generality, linearity and unity of such change. It is therefore appropriate to conclude by looking at two flows which runs against those noted in the previous section. One notable contemporary development is the appreciation that legitimacy is crucial to efficiency, in the sense that effective

---

[81]  Home Office/Cabinet Office, *PACE Review*, (London, Home Office, 2002). For critique, see M Zander, 'The joint review of PACE—a deplorable report' *New Law Journal* 14 February 2003, 204.

[82]  *Modernising Police Powers: Review of the Police & Criminal Evidence Act (PACE) 1984: consultation paper* (London, Home Office, March 2007). For critique, see M Zander 'Change of PACE' *New Law Journal*, 13 April 2007, 157: 504. See also M Zander 'If it ain't broke, don't fix it', *Police Review*, 1 June 2007.

[83]  I Loader, 'Fall of the "platonic guardians": liberalism, criminology and political responses to crime in England and Wales' (2006) 46 *British Journal of Criminology* 576–7.

[84]  *Ibid*, 580.

crime control can only be accomplished by police who use their powers in ways which secure the approval of the communities in which they operate. The second is the intrusion of rights into the British constitution.

In England and Australia, a crucial source for connecting legitimacy and efficiency is Lord Scarman's report on the Brixton Disorders,[85] which provided authoritative impetus to the rise of community policing and a classic restatement of the relationship between law and policing. In Scarman's approach, police could no longer simply invoke the law to justify their actions. If the enforcement of law would lead to disruption of public peace, then the appropriate use of discretion would put preserving the peace above enforcing law. All too often caricatured as justifying 'no-go' zones and improper toleration of illegal activities in minority communities, Scarman's approach provided overdue recognition of the significance, difficulty and complexity of the police role. He argued that the police could only get the balance between law enforcement and maintenance of public peace right if their discretionary decision-making was informed by contact and consultation with the communities they police. While this led to a series of community consultative activities characterised by disappointment and frustration on both sides, the fundamental message of Scarman's report remained valid: enforcing law is not a trumping argument.

The Scarman message became all the more relevant after another inquiry once again exposed deep problems in relations between the police and minority communities in Britain. The Macpherson Report identified stop and search as a major source of problems.[86] A subsequent programme of research by the Home Office concluded strongly that the legitimacy of stops and searches depended upon three elements: public trust and confidence, legality, and effectiveness. It suggested ways to combine them.

> These three principles, far from being in opposition, are largely consistent. The programme's recommendations do not involve trade-offs between them but reinforce one another. For example, interventions to improve the effectiveness of searches are likely ... to improve public confidence. Similarly, there is a close link between the legality of searches, and their effectiveness against crime and acceptability to the public.[87]

Far from legality and efficiency being counter-posed (as the balance metaphor implies), this research on stop and search showed that they are interdependent.

It is notable that in a parallel but apparently quite separate stream of theorising and policy analysis, similar conclusions were reached by a major review conducted for the National Research Council in the USA.[88] This confluence is not

---

[85]  L Scarman, *The Brixton Disorders*, Cmnd 8427 (London, HMSO, 1981).

[86]  W Macpherson, *The Stephen Lawrence Inquiry* (London, HMSO, 1999).

[87]  J Miller, P Quinton and N Bland, *Police Stops and Searches: Lessons from a Programme of Research* (London, Home Office, 2000) 1.

[88]  Committee to Review Research on Police Policy and Practices, *Fairness and Effectiveness in Policing* (National Academies Press, 2004) ch 8.

coincidental: the reports by Scarman, Macpherson and the National Research Council's Committee stem from some fundamentally similar problems in relations between the police and minority communities.

A conceptual foundation from which these British and American reports could be developed can be found in the increasingly influential work of Tom Tyler on procedural justice.[89] Tyler's empirical work demonstrates the crucial importance of the manner in which police officers exercise their powers. In an important corrective to the dominant tendency to insist on the instrumental effectiveness of crime control policing in building public support, Tyler shows that how the police are seen is as important as what they do. Public cooperation with and support for the police depends not just on a belief that they are effective in controlling crime, but also on perceptions of how they go about their work. Working within the law is vital: legality is a precondition for legitimacy. This is equally true for the general public, for those people who call for police assistance, and for those whom the police stop, search, and arrest.[90] Contrary to many assumptions, outcomes of encounters are less important for those involved than their experience of 'procedural justice—an evaluation of the fairness of the manner in which their problem or dispute was handled'.[91] Such perceptions are particularly significant in minority communities which are most likely to experience police crime control activity. As Tyler and Fagan argue, 'the public cooperates with the police when they view them as legitimate authorities who are entitled to be obeyed. Such legitimacy judgments, in turn, are shaped by public views about procedural justice—the fairness of the processes the police use when dealing with members of the public'.[92]

Once again, the old contrast between due process and crime control, between rights and powers proves to be misleading: efficiency and legitimacy are not on opposing scales of a balance, but are interdependent. (Miscarriages of justice mean not only that the innocent are punished, but also that the guilty remain free to offend again.) The danger is that this couplet can slip into being little more than rhetoric. For example, the introduction to a strategic policy document, *Directions in Australasian Policing,* notes that 'To be effective police must enjoy the confidence, trust, cooperation and active support of the community'.[93]

---

[89] T Tyler, *Why People Obey the Law* (New Haven, Yale University Press, 1990) and T Tyler and J Fagan, 'Legitimacy and Cooperation: Why do People help the Police fight Crime in their Communities?', *Columbia Law School Public Law & Legal Theory Working Paper* 06–99, 2005.

[90] Committee to Review Research on Police Policy and Practices, *Fairness and Effectiveness in Policing* (Washington DC, National Academies Press, 2004) 292–3.

[91] *Ibid,* 301.

[92] T Tyler and J Fagan, 'Legitimacy and Cooperation: Why do People help the Police fight Crime in their Communities?', *Columbia Law School Public Law & Legal Theory Working Paper* 06–99, 2005, 36–7.

[93] Australasian Police Ministers' Council, *Directions in Australasian Policing* (Adelaide, Australasian Centre for Policing Research, 2005) 1.

Unfortunately, however, the body of this document treats efficiency and legitimacy as separate matters: crime reduction is considered in 'Direction 1: Innovation in policing', while 'the proper exercise of authority and discretion' is considered separately under 'Direction 3: Professionalism and accountability'. This unhelpfully conforms to the conventional approach in which crime fighting is prioritised, while the manner in which power is exercised is considered as relevant only to control of misconduct. This misses the point that legitimacy is crucial, not just a desirable but secondary consideration. As Scarman argued, such trust, cooperation and active support must be generated from the way in which police officers interact with people and the way in which police departments are open to public consultation and accountability. The distance from community which was characteristic of the mid-twentieth century model of US police professionalism and of more recent crime control focused policing is precisely the opposite of what is likely to produce the best results.

The need to give priority to legitimacy is particularly significant in responses to terrorism. The Australian government's own review of anti-terrorism legislation gave a sharp warning about 'a considerable increase in fear, a growing sense of alienation and an increase in distrust of authority' among Muslim and Arab Australians and expressed 'serious concerns about the way in which the legislation is perceived' by these communities.[94] Similarly, the 2007 UK Policy Review on *Security, crime and justice* recognised 'rising sympathy with extremist sentiments' in British Muslim communities.[95] The London bombings of July 2005 illustrated starkly the costs of alienating minority communities and exposed the fallacy of treating efficiency and legitimacy as if they sit at opposite ends of a balance.

Another challenge to the conventional due process/crime control dichotomy comes from the change to Britain's law-making, judicial and policy processes following the incorporation of the European Convention on Human Rights (ECHR) into domestic law via the Human Rights Act 1998.[96] Despite the constitutional angst which this caused, both the minimalist nature of the ECHR and the constraints on its incorporation have limited its impact. Most rights are qualified and subject to the power of derogation: notably, these have allowed the

---

[94] Review Committee *Report of the Security Legislation Review Committee* (Canberra, Australian Government, 2006) 5.

[95] HM Government *Building on progress: security, crime and justice* (London, Cabinet Office, 2007) 89.

[96] In this respect, Australia lags well behind. It is now the only large jurisdiction in the common law world which lacks significant domestic human rights protection. While there is considerable activity at local level (with the Australian Capital Territory's Human Rights Act and Victoria's Charter of Human Rights and Responsibilities), the Commonwealth government's commitment to incorporating human rights remains vague. Nonetheless, it seems likely that, later rather than sooner, Australian law will change. The longer that change is delayed, the greater will be the cost of isolating Australian law from the mainstream development of the common law: see H Charlesworth, M Chiam, D Hovell, and G Williams, 'Deep Anxieties: Australia and the International Legal Order' (2003) 25 *Sydney Law Review* 423.

enactment of exceptional anti-terrorism powers. As parents of Britain's new rights, Tony Blair's Home Secretaries were hardly proud fathers.[97]

While the direct effects of incorporating rights may not be dramatic, it would be wrong to understate the indirect effects. As Sanders and Young suggest, the ECHR sets 'outer limits' on what government can do: 'The influence of the Convention should be seen as much in what the state has not done in the criminal justice arena as in particular developments of law and practice'.[98] Other informed commentators on Britain (and Canada) point to the entwined changes in process and culture which have flowed from incorporating rights. This inevitably will affect future legislative reform, judicial consideration, and police implementation of PACE. In terms of process, legal change has to include consideration of the human rights implications of legislative proposals. As regards judicial culture, Sanders and Young suggest that 'the interpretation of the ECHR by domestic courts since the 1998 Act came into force has been minimalist in many areas. The judges' assessments of when the community interest in law enforcement outweighs human rights usually express crime control values'.[99] However, other commentators consider that the requirement to consider rights has had a significant impact: 'From the bland view of democracy as requiring deference to legislators, courts have begun to see human rights as constitutive of democracy rather than ranged against it'.[100] Such change may flow down through other sectors of the criminal justice process. As Neyroud explains, the Human Rights Act 'brought both a new language to policing and a new decision-making calculus'. Discretionary decisions must refer to the principle of proportionality, balancing 'the means proposed against the outcome intended and to ensure that any action is proportionate to the legitimate aim pursued'.[101] In place of simplistic appeals to 'balance', a 'rights-based' approach necessitates fundamental reconsideration of the principles and purposes of criminal justice.

# VI Conclusion

My argument in this paper has been that a historical and comparative perspective throws new light on PACE. Rather than either a simple extension of police powers or a balance between due process and crime control, PACE is better understood as the distinctive product of a governing strategy—'authorise and

---

[97] A Ashworth and M Redmayne, *The Criminal Process* (Oxford, Oxford University Press, 2005) 57; A Sanders and R Young, *Criminal Justice* 3rd edn (Oxford, Oxford University Press, 2007) 29–34.

[98] *Ibid*, 33.

[99] *Ibid*.

[100] S Fredman, 'From Deference to Democracy: The Role of Equality under the Human Rights Act 1998', (2006) 122 *LQR* 53 at 53.

[101] P Neyroud, 'Policing and ethics', in T Newburn (ed), *Handbook of Policing* (Cullompton, Willan Publishing, 2003) 578 at 585.

regulate'—which fitted a particular conjuncture in twentieth century liberal democratic societies. That conjuncture has now passed, and new ideologies, priorities and rhetoric have come to dominate our world.[102]

---

[102] See D Garland, *The Culture of Control: Crime and Order in Contemporary Societies* (Oxford, Oxford University Press, 2001); I Loader and R Sparks, 'For an historical sociology of crime policy in England and Wales since 1968' (2004) 7 *Critical Review of International Social and Political Philosophy* 5; and I Loader, 'Fall of the "platonic guardians": liberalism, criminology and political responses to crime in England and Wales' (2006) 46 *British Journal of Criminology* 581–2 for eloquent, contrasting accounts of this change.

# 3

# Can Coercive Powers be Effectively Controlled or Regulated? The Case for Anchored Pluralism

ANDREW SANDERS*

## I. Introduction: why PACE?

When the Police and Criminal Evidence Act 1984 (PACE) was created it was unusual in having a large number of regulatory elements. These included requirements to seek authorisation to exercise many police powers, and obligations to record the fact that many of these powers had been exercised. These regulatory aspects of PACE are often dismissed by critics as 'bureaucratic', 'red tape', 'obstacles to policing' and so forth. There is an element of truth to this. Filling in forms and records (for example for stop and search and for custody), securing authorisation (for example to search, mount surveillance operations and extend detention), allowing or requiring people (for example legal representatives and 'responsible adults') to attend interviews as well as recording them—the list could go on and on. This is bureaucratic. And it does obstruct policing, even if only by using time and resources that could be used for more direct investigation.

Another reason for the 'bad press' that these elements of PACE get is that much of the 'PACE regime' is aimed at protecting suspects—and that often goes hand-in-hand with obstructing policing in the sense that police actions have to be extensively justified and/or authorised and/or monitored.[1] It is this issue that I want to deal with in this chapter.[2]

* I would like to thank Graham Smith and Richard Young for invaluable advice and help at various stages of preparing this chapter.

[1] By 'PACE regime' I refer not just to the regulatory elements, but also the extensive sets of police powers—eg to detain without charge—that PACE expanded and then set out to regulate. See later in this section and A Sanders and R Young, 'The PACE regime for suspects detained by the police' (1995) 66 *Political Quarterly* 126.

[2] I am not dismissing the problems that the PACE regime cause for the police, and thus for the security of all of us. But that aspect of PACE receives treatment elsewhere in this collection in chs 4, 5 and 6 written by John Coppen, John Long and Barbara Wilding, all serving police officers.

To begin with, we need to say a little about why PACE was introduced in the first place, in a form that still shapes criminal justice over 20 years later. In 1977 a government-appointed former judge, Sir Henry Fisher, delivered a damning report on the *Confait Affair*, in which three youths were convicted of murder, arson and related offences in the early 1970s. All three had been arrested, taken into custody, denied contact with family or legal representatives and questioned until they made confessions of some kind. At trial, they retracted their confessions, saying they had been coerced into making them, and denied having anything to do with the death of Confait. At that time they were not believed, and so were convicted, but evidence later emerged that the time of Confait's death had been fudged in order to neutralise the alibi of one of the defendants, Lattimore. The convictions were therefore quashed by the Court of Appeal.

Fisher's investigation showed that Lattimore's alibi was unshakeable and that he could not have been involved in the offences. Fisher concluded that the details in his 'confession' had to have been made known to him by someone at the scene of the crime—that is, the 'real' criminals or the police. Fisher was not prepared to believe that the police would have fed him such details and then made him 'confess', particularly as this would entail believing that several officers had engaged in coercion and then covered it up. So Fisher concluded that Lattimore's two friends (one of whom was 14, and the other 16) were probably responsible for the crimes and for supplying Lattimore with the relevant details.[3]

Lattimore was an 18 year-old with mild learning disabilities. Fisher argued that had he had legal advice and support from, or at least communication with, family members, Lattimore (and suspects like him) would not have been put under such pressure, and confessions would be more reliable. Had he known at that time what later emerged—that the real killer actually had nothing to do with any of the youths—doubtless he would have argued this even more strongly.

The Royal Commission on Criminal Procedure (Philips Commission) was established to see, among other things, whether the problems identified by Fisher were confined to the occasional case or were widespread. Philips reported in 1981. Regrettably, many questions, such as how widespread coercion of the *Confait Affair* kind actually was, were not answered. But the report and its research studies did show, for example, that legal advice and other advice/support was hardly ever provided for suspects, and that large numbers of suspects were held in the unregulated limbo of 'helping police with their enquiries', allowing them to be detained and questioned without clear limits.

The impetus behind the establishment of the Philips Commission was concern for the safety of suspects and any convictions that ensued. It was motivated, in other words, by 'due process' concerns. Groups such as JUSTICE, for example, were concerned that the Judges Rules (that loosely governed police powers and

---

[3] The events are summarised in J Baxter and L Koffman, 'The Confait Inheritance—Forgotten Lessons?' (1983) *Cambrian Law Review* 14.

suspects' rights) had become progressively more 'crime control' oriented.[4] But the government was heavily lobbied by the police and police-oriented lobby groups, arguing for more, not fewer, police powers (accentuating the 'crime control' direction of the law), even before the Philips Commission was established—as is evident from its terms of reference.[5] The lobbying continued while it deliberated. The eventual report attempted to satisfy both camps. It tried to square the circle by granting the police more powers in many respects—for example allowing involuntary detention without charge, extending stop and search, arrest and entry-search-seizure powers, and allowing intimate and 'non-intimate' samples to be taken from suspects involuntarily in many circumstances. Perhaps most important of all, it recommended that it be clear that the police had the right to question suspects regardless of whether those suspects wished to be questioned, and to be able to do so repeatedly in the 24 hours it recommended be available for detention without charge (extendable to 36 hours or more in serious cases such as the *Confait Affair*). But it sought to control or regulate those powers more effectively than had hitherto been done—by providing free legal advice to all suspects, recording all interviews, regulating what happened to suspects in police stations by creating 'custody officers' to look after their interests, and so forth.

It was clear from much of the research commissioned by Philips that it was recommending *coercive* powers for the police. For example, involuntary questioning when in involuntary police detention was recognised as coercive virtually by definition. The research showed that the idea of 'voluntary' responses to questioning in such conditions is illusory. Listen to this suspect:

> There I was, banged up in a cell and I hadn't done anything and I was being taken away from my place of work, I'd been separated from my family ... Here was a policeman telling me that I had nothing to fear from him and he couldn't see the stupidity of his statement.[6]

The controls and regulations referred to above were not designed to protect suspects from *all* the effects of this coercion—after all, there is no point pressuring suspects who wish to remain silent to speak if you then protect them to the extent that the pressure is ineffective. Instead, they were designed to protect suspects from the *worst* effects—such as making false confessions. But herein lies one of the main problems. Controls and regulations cannot be so finely tuned. A protection regime that is deliberately half-hearted will almost inevitably be problematic.

---

[4] The terms 'due process' and 'crime control' were first coined by Herbert Packer in his *Limits of the Criminal Sanction* (Stanford, Stanford University Press, 1968). They are generally accepted as referring to opposite ends of the civil liberties spectrum, although it is now equally generally accepted that this spectrum does not capture anywhere near all the important criminal justice considerations. See A Sanders and R Young, *Criminal Justice* (Oxford, Oxford University Press, 2007) ch 1 (hereafter Sanders and Young).

[5] For discussion, see chs 7 and 8 by Richard Young and Ed Cape in this collection.

[6] P Hillyard, *Suspect Community* (London, Pluto, 1993) 186–7.

PACE enacted the broad scheme recommended by Philips, although departures from the recommendations were in more of a 'crime control' than 'due process' direction (for example in extending arrest powers and in reducing the role of summons to vanishing point in non-Road Traffic Act cases). However, as Dixon observes in chapter two in this collection, and as should be evident from its regulatory regime, PACE did not (and still does not) embody the undiluted authoritarianism that some of its most frenzied critics claimed.

## II  Ways of approaching police powers and their control or regulation

So far, I have established that many of the police powers that we now take for granted are intrinsically coercive. This is not a value judgement, but a simple matter of fact. I have also showed that in the late 1970s and early 1980s there was no serious opposition to the idea that these powers should be controlled or, at least, regulated. It may be that times and circumstances have changed so much in the last 20 years that opposition to this proposition might now be serious. But I believe that what follows will show this is not so, or, at least, should not be so.

David Dixon has identified three ways of understanding how legal regulation and control works:[7]

1.  **Legalistic:** People who take this approach believe that simply stating what the rules and controls are, will ensure conformity. For example, custody officers should not allow police officers to visits suspects in their cells, and are obliged to record who visits them, when, and for what purpose. People who take the legalistic approach view that as a good enough control: custody officers will not allow unauthorised visits, and if there are such visits they will be recorded. This is so naive that it hardly needs discussion. After all, if a custody officer does allow an unauthorised visit, s/he is hardly likely to record it, or to record it as being unauthorised. It is worth noting two further points. First, that much police power is nowadays ostensibly controlled, but clearly ineffectively, in just this way (for example the police have to complete stop and search, as well as custody, records). Secondly, much police power is *genuinely* controlled—in other words, wholly or largely effectively—in just this way. At one time it was not unusual for officers to beat suspects up. This is now very unusual. But to acknowledge that much power is genuinely controlled, and that abuse is very rare, is not the same as saying that power is never abused. Indeed, when officers wish to abuse their power, and to allow

---

[7]  D Dixon, *Law in Policing* (Oxford, Oxford University Press, 1997). Also see the first part of ch 2 in this collection, where he contrasts legalistic ways of understanding police use of their powers with more realistic ways.

other officers to do so, what in the PACE regime is there to stop this and/or to ensure that abuse is made apparent? This will be one of the key issues in this chapter.

2. **Culturalist**: People who take this approach see legal rules as a resource for the police to use for their own policing ends. In other words, legal rules are seen as largely ineffective in constraining their police. The requirement that arresting officers convince custody officers that there are valid reasons under PACE for detaining suspects prior to charge is a good example: one of the main reasons is to 'obtain evidence by questioning'. Since questioning is not allowed if there is enough evidence to charge (and since, if there is enough evidence to charge, the police can detain anyway in order to charge—or, now, to hold the suspect pending the Crown Prosecution Service (CPS) agreeing to charge) it is impossible to imagine a situation where, following a valid arrest, it would be wrong to authorise detention. Even when arrest and involuntary detention is patently unnecessary because the suspect is cooperative, as in the *Al-Fayed* case, the courts have upheld the right of the police to arrest.[8]

3. **Structural**: People who take this approach stress the broader social structures which shape police behaviour, and argue that legal rules are in harmony with those structures. An example would be the control of street demonstrations and protest. The control of public order has been at the heart of the police mandate ever since the establishment of the first professional English police forces in the nineteenth century, and for some time before that. The legal rules have always allowed the police great latitude to control order, and they continue to evolve in this way. They allow the police to arrest in huge numbers and then de-arrest without any formalities, because arrest is simply a way of exerting control, with prosecution rarely being the objective, regardless of whether any criminal laws have been broken. At such times as the miners strike of the 1980s a wide range of laws and powers (such as bail laws and the use of great force) were displayed to these ends.[9]

So examples can be found of legal rules, and of their use by the police, to illustrate all three approaches. The question is which approach best explains police behaviour, for that will help us understand how, if at all, police behaviour can be controlled or regulated. Crucially, if the legalistic approach is largely inadequate, would it be better to put the onus more on the police themselves—to require self-regulation, as many writers in other fields of regulation argue.[10] Self-regulation, as compared to the other forms of regulation, will be the central issue in this paper.

---

[8] *Al-Fayed v MPC* [2004] EWCA Civ 1579.

[9] For discussion and references, see Sanders and Young, n 4 above, 129–31.

[10] For discussion of the issues in a non-police context, see eg R Baldwin, 'Is better regulation smarter regulation?' (2005) *Public Law* 485.

# III   Control or regulation?

This paper has thus far used the phrase 'controlled or regulated' as if the two terms are synonymous. It is time to distinguish them.

'Control' refers to a situation where powers can only be exercised on the basis of a command or permission; where any abuse of, or deviation from the scope of, the power would be apparent to some form of higher or supervisory authority; and where that abuse or deviation would be the subject of some form of reprimand or discipline.

'Regulation' has three elements: the goal (the rule or standard against which behaviour is to be compared and contrasted); monitoring (to monitor or evaluate what happens in pursuance of the goal); and realignment (a mechanism for enforcing rules where monitoring shows significant deviation from them).[11]

In the debate about the 'regulatory (or even post-regulatory) state', the idea that 'control' is, or can be, the main regulatory mechanism is rejected. This would involve the state 'rowing' all aspects of the societal boat itself. Given the complexity of the modern state, this is plainly unrealistic in most respects. It is probably undesirable too. Instead, the State seeks to 'regulate' as defined above, which entails 'steering' instead of rowing. In other words, behaviour is regulated by setting the course (rules), monitoring the direction of travel (monitoring) and altering the course when deviations occur (realignment). Implicit in this debate is the idea that monitoring and realignment mechanisms and strategies draw on the knowledge and resources of the organisation being regulated—in other words, that there be a major element of self-regulation. But supporters of 'smart regulation'[12] advocate 'regulatory pluralism'. This includes a mix of methods: not just self-regulation, but also the use of third parties. 'Appropriate adults' and legal advisors for suspects in custody, and the Independent Police Complaints Commission (IPCC) in relation to complaints against the police, would be examples. But, as we shall see, regulatory theory shows that these are, as currently constituted, flawed examples.

Shearing takes the idea further in his argument that we should see beyond the State by, 'using many different oarsmen'[13] to implement their policies (or, by implication, to regulate the use of power). Noting that, almost by definition, the strong have power over the weak, he argues that instead of (ineffectively) attempting to rid the world of power, we need to empower the weak: to enable those outside the 'power nodes' to hold the powerful to account. 'What is required is ... the construction of nodes ... that recognise and mobilise the

---

[11]   A Crawford, 'Networked governance and the post-regulatory state? Steering, rowing and anchoring the provision of policing and security' (2006) 10 *Theoretical Criminology* 449.

[12]   See eg R Baldwin, 'Is better regulation smarter regulation?' (2005) *Public Law* 485.

[13]   This phrase is actually from D Osborne and T Gaebler, *Reinventing Government* (New York, Plume, 1993), who first coined the 'rowing' and 'steering' analogies.

resources of the weak'.[14] He envisages networks of intersecting regulatory mechanisms. Shearing is concerned here with the world stage, but the idea was adopted by the Independent Commission on Policing in Northern Ireland (Patten Report) at the level of community influence on policing.[15] This is particularly important in a province with deep community divides and a police institution that historically is identified with one of these two communities. Rather than the police controlling itself better, or even having a supervisory body to attempt to control it, the Patten report recommended devolving police authority to local police commanders, and those commanders being accountable to local communities. Thus policing would be acknowledged as being 'everybody's business' rather than just the business of the police and government.

The idea can be applied to the everyday use of police powers.[16] Rather than expect the police themselves, or a police supervisory agency, to monitor or control the treatment of suspects in custody, for example, we could empower legal advisors, appropriate adults, watchdogs, lay visitors and so forth. Elements of this already exist, as we saw above, but whether they have *power* is the crucial matter to which we will return.

In the context of police coercive powers, the question becomes whether there are clear rules or standards, whether compliance is monitored effectively, and whether there are adequate realignment mechanisms. Thus a hard distinction between 'self-regulation' and other forms of regulation should become artificial and unnecessary. The important question should be the effectiveness of regulation, not who or what does it. In reality, one might expect a mix of self- and outside-regulation to create the most workable and effective regulatory mechanisms. But whether this is so, and—if so—what the precise mix should be must surely depend on the context.[17] As we shall see, going with the grain of the regulated is not always compatible with securing adherence to the rules in question if the rule is due process oriented, and the behaviour is crime control oriented. At the very least these circumstances require some form of 'anchored

---

[14] C Shearing, 'Reflections on the refusal to acknowledge private governments' in J Wood and B Dupont (eds), *Democracy, Society and the Governance of Security* (Cambridge, Cambridge University Press, 2006).

[15] Independent Commission on Policing in Northern Ireland, *A New Beginning: Policing in Northern Ireland* (2000). The 'fit' between Patten's recommendations and Shearing's ideas is no coincidence, as Shearing was a (presumably influential) member of the Commission. See C Shearing, '"A new beginning" for policing' (2000) 27 *Journal of Law and Society* 386.

[16] This is what I do in the rest of this section and in the rest of the paper. Remarkably, I could not find the insights of the 'post-regulatory State' debate applied to the use of police powers in either the 'policing' or the 'regulation' literatures. The only exception is P Gill, 'Policing and Regulation: What's the Difference?' (2002) 11 *Social and Legal Studies* 523, who notes that 'the literatures regarding regulation and policing are separate' (p 524). However, rather than looking at regulation of police he concentrates on how far 'regulation' and 'policing' are different, rightly concluding that they are essentially identical.

[17] See, especially, advocates of 'responsive regulation' eg J Braithwaite, *Restorative Justice and Responsive Regulation* (Oxford, Oxford University Press, 2002).

pluralism'. Crawford identifies in this term of Loader and Walker[18] one element of particular concern to me: that is, the use of coercive law as a backup of last resort. But equally important is the element in this concept, shared by Shearing, of a pluralism of regulatory mechanisms. As recommended by the Patten report, for example, these may be outside as well as within the state apparatus in question.

# IV   The PACE model: an example of the (self-) regulatory state

Let us look, necessarily rather schematically in the limited space available, at the main areas covered by PACE in the terms of the earlier discussion.

## A Stop and Search

Whether or not to stop and search an individual is a matter entirely for officers on the street. These discretionary decisions are supposed to be in accordance with PACE section 1 and PACE Code of Practice A, and no doubt many are. But many are not, as we shall see.[19] There is no control over these decisions. PACE's innovation (to counterbalance its huge expansion of stop and search powers) was to require that the officer(s) doing the stop and search complete a record, setting out the reasons for the stop. The records can be used as a basis for challenge by suspects and they should be scrutinised by senior officers. Thus police officer A provides the basis on which senior police officer B judges the appropriateness of the actions of police officer A; challenge to the actions of police officer A is based on evidence provided by that police officer.

This is not so much *classic* self-regulation as something very close to the *ultimate* self-regulation. It is only a little more than regulation of individuals by those self-same individuals, whereas 'self-regulation' would usually be the institution regulating itself, but with some individuals in that institution regulating others. And it is ineffective regulation (judged in terms of compliance with Code A). Little over 10 per cent of all stops are followed by arrest, suggesting that 'reasonable suspicion' (the section 1 requirement) is often absent, as is also evident from much research. As one study concluded, 'The guidance on reasonable suspicion in the PACE Code of Practice is not clearly understood, or

[18]   I Loader and N Walker, 'Necessary Virtues: The Legitimate Place of the State in the Production of Security', in J Wood and B Dupont (eds), *Democracy, Society and the Governance of Security* (Cambridge, Cambridge University Press, 2006).

[19]   In order not to over-complicate matters, the many additional stop and search powers that have been added since PACE came into operation—discussed in Sanders and Young, n 4 above, ch 2—will not be considered here. The same arguments apply to them as to s 1 powers, however.

remembered, or put into practice ... the 'culture' on divisions will have a stronger impact on probationary officers than classroom teaching'[20]. And the over-representation of members of ethnic minorities suggests that stop and search is discriminatory, whether deliberately or unconsciously as MacPherson argued.[21]

If this discrimination works by ethnic minorities being stopped and searched lawfully in circumstances where white people would not generally be stopped this would not show up in even the most scrupulously completed record—for there is no such thing as a 'record of no stop'. It is true that records are supposed to be analysed within police forces to see if they reveal patterns of discrimination. Post-Macpherson, this is finally happening to some extent,[22] and it might lead to more pressure on officers not to discriminate, and to consider more carefully how their use of discretion skews patterns of stop and search. But it does not deal with individual officers who discriminate in individual cases, nor does it help black people (such as the Bishop of Stepney)[23] who get stopped in circumstances where white people would not be stopped.

## B Authorising Detention and the Rights of Suspects

Arrest should normally be followed by detention (though suspects can be de-arrested first—again, a matter for the police). Detention can be only author-ised on certain grounds specified in section 37 of PACE and Code of Practice C. It is done (or not) by a custody officer—usually a police sergeant. Then there are periodic reviews of detention and authorisation of extended detention by ever-more senior officers. The usual ground for authorising detention is to secure evidence by questioning. When people exercise their rights of silence this objective is clearly being thwarted. So the ground for extending detention in most cases where it is sought is obvious: the suspect's resistance has not yet been broken, but another few hours of questioning, isolation, degradation in the threatening and fetid atmosphere of the cells will probably change that:

> Yea I understood me rights but do you get rights in here? The loo don't flush, it stinks. You get breakfast in a cardboard box and its freezing cold ... it's not the law, its just the fucking conditions ... no fags, nowhere to wash, you've no idea what time it is[24]

---

[20] Nacro, *Policing Local Communities: The Tottenham Experiment* (London, Nacro, 1997) 41. Also see eg M Fitzgerald, M Hough, I Joseph and T Qureshi, *Policing for London* (Cullompton, Willan, 2002).

[21] W Macpherson of Cluny, *The Stephen Lawrence Inquiry* (London, HMSO, 1999). Sanders and Young, n 4 above, ch 2. See generally, C Phillips and B Bowling, 'Ethnicities, racism, crime and criminal justice' in M Maguire, R Morgan and R Reiner, *Oxford Handbook of Criminology* 4th edn (Oxford, Oxford University Press, 2007).

[22] J Foster, T Newburn and A Souhami, *Assessing the Impact of the Stephen Lawrence Inquiry* (Home Office Research Study 294) (London, Home Office, 2005).

[23] A particularly striking example we give in Sanders and Young, n 4 above, ch 2.

[24] S Choongh, *Policing as Social Discipline* (Oxford, Oxford University Press, 1997) 178.

Why would anyone doubt that most reasonable people would change their mind and speak in these circumstances? And if they do not? Well, for serious crimes, this can go on for 96 hours. After 36 hours there is an element of control (by the courts). But not before that. Before 36 hours, it is the police who do the authorisation—more self-regulation. Yet over half of all detentions following arrest lead to no further action.[25] At best, this suggests that in many cases no realistic assessment was made of:

(a) whether detention should have been authorised in the first place. Research carried out in the 1980s and early 1990s shows that there had been hardly an example of a custody officer refusing detention.[26] Recent figures from one police area indicate that this might be changing a little—in one month, out of a total of more than 8,000, detention was refused in 45 cases.[27] Whilst this means that self-regulation is not entirely illusory, a refusal rate of less than 1 per cent suggests one or more of, in most cases: custody officers not taking the issue seriously, custody officers not having time to probe adequately, and arresting officers being able to hide the true basis of the arrest;

(b) whether further questioning would produce significant evidence. Again, there is hardly an example of a custody officer or senior officer refusing continued detention, to 24 hours at any rate. Many authorisations by senior officers are done over the phone—hardly providing the opportunity for genuine scrutiny—and custody officers' checks on suspects often consist of a bang on the door, a call of 'alright mate?' and disappearance before the answer can be heard.[28] The self-regulation here is, truly, illusory.

At worst, it suggests, as Choongh argues, that in large numbers of cases there never was any intention of securing sufficient evidence to prosecute, but that the purpose of arrest, detention and questioning was to impose summary punishment and intimidation.[29] Either way the regulation is, again, ineffective.

When we look at what else goes on during detention, the picture is similar. Suspects should have reasonable access to visitors, telephone calls, lawyers and so forth. Requests should be recorded on custody records so that unreasonable denials of these things are regulated. But again this self-regulation is inadequate: custody officers complete the records, and in one study requests for a telephone call were made in 10–12 per cent of cases, but recorded in just 7–8 per cent of

---

[25] P Hillyard and D Gordon, 'Arresting statistics the drift to informal justice in England and Wales' (1999) 26 *Journal of Law and Society* 502.

[26] See, eg, M McConville, A Sanders and R Leng, *The Case for the Prosecution* (London, Routledge, 1992) and other studies discussed in Sanders and Young, n 4 above, ch 4.

[27] Private communication from a custody officer trainer (2007).

[28] D Dixon, K Bottomley, C Coleman, M Gill and D Wall, 'Safeguarding the rights of suspects in police custody' (1990) 1 *Policing and Society* 115.

[29] S Choongh, *Policing as Social Discipline* (Oxford, Oxford University Press, 1997).

cases.[30] Custody officers are supposed to help suspects understand their rights but while study after study has found systematic failure in this regard, this is rarely evident from the custody records.[31] Then there is the taking of samples and strip-searches. Again, this is regulated by custody officers. The fact that the introduction of CCTV into custody areas reduces the number of strip-searches[32] suggests that, once again, self-regulation is ineffective. Custody records, completed by custody officers, are not so much regulatory mechanisms (much less control mechanisms), as:

(a) memory aids. Police officers cannot be expected to remember every detail of what happens. Evidence may have to be given in court (or in a disciplinary hearing) weeks or months later. Like the writing down of what suspects and witnesses say in police notebooks, to be referred to in the witness box much later, the custody record is an aide-memoir. Like the police officer's note book, though, it can be flawed.

(b legitimating mechanisms. As much as recording reality, they *construct* reality. No one else is making notes (suspects are not allowed to—but why not?). So the hazy and possibly faulty—let alone possibly mendacious—memory of the suspect alleging non-compliance with PACE and the Code of Practice is counter-posed against the apparently solid evidence of writing on a form, signed by a police officer. Thus custody records are *protections for* officers as much as they are *regulators of* officers. And they are of little value as protections for suspects.

## C Interviewing

There are two main issues here: 'informal interviewing', where the interview is not recorded and may not officially take place at all; and interviewing that is coercive despite conforming with the rules.

Some 'informal interviewing' is entirely lawful. The problem with regulating formal interviewing is that it inevitably leads to more informal interviewing. This is, by definition, unregulated. For some years now, Richard Young and I have argued, in successive editions of *Criminal Justice*, that the police have huge scope to interview informally when they want to do or say things that they would not want recorded in formal interviews.[33] Thus in *Kerawalla*, for example, the

---

[30] D Brown , T Ellis and K Larcombe, *Changing the Code: Police Detention under the Revised PACE Codes of Practice* (Home Office Research Study 129) (London, HMSO, 1992). See also S Choongh, *Policing as Social Discipline* (Oxford, Oxford University Press, 1997).

[31] For a fairly recent study see N Britton, 'Race and policing: A study of police custody' (2000) 40 *British Journal of Criminology* 639. For vulnerable suspects—the victims of the *Confait* Affair—the failures are even more systematic. For discussion of several sets of research findings see Sanders and Young, n 4 above, ch 4.

[32] T Newburn, M Shiner and S Hayman, 'Race, crime and injustice? Strip-search and the treatment of suspects in custody' (2004) 44 *British Journal of Criminology* 677.

[33] Sanders and Young, n 4 above. The 1st edition was published in 1994 by Butterworths.

defendant was arrested in a hotel room and interrogated there without being taken to the police station. This was held to be in accord with PACE section 30 (requiring that suspects be taken to the station following arrest as soon as reasonably practical) and the Code of Practice; the legal consequence was that the normal protections of sections 56 and 58 (for example to legal advice), and the tape recording of the questioning, were circumvented. It is not that the police *usually* browbeat or offer illegal inducements to confess when out of earshot and unobserved—it is that they have the opportunity to do so, and they take those opportunities when the chances of securing strong evidence by other means look thin.

Another reason why it is difficult to control this is because suspects themselves often seek informal chats, and are often unwilling to say things 'officially' that they are willing to say unofficially. If they seek a 'deal' that may involve informing on someone, for example (as the police say happens frequently)[34], they will usually want this not to be recorded. Dealing is central to police–suspect relations—to stop it would deprive policing of one of its most fundamental underpinnings. Yet to facilitate it is to facilitate uncontrolled interaction. And detention itself facilitates it, because suspects often wish to deal simply because the alternative is to remain in custody at the mercy of the police. The PACE regime that makes detention normal leads to abnormal behaviour by suspects. Thus Dunninghan and Norris found that 84 per cent of the informers in their sample were in custody or had proceedings against them when they were recruited. In 85 per cent of cases the police handlers initiated the process of becoming an informer.[35]

It might be said that there is nothing wrong with creating conditions conducive to cooperation. Even if this is conceded, the problem is that by giving the police this power without control the scope for abuse arises. The liberty or even safety of family members, for example, become bargaining chips.

I and colleagues such as Richard Young have been criticised by many, including David Dixon,[36] for arguing that the police were in this, and other similar respects, controlled ineffectively. Yet in his most recent research Dixon makes a similar point in relation to policing in New South Wales, Australia. Huge numbers of formal, recorded interviews were preceded by informal interviews. 63 per cent of police officers interviewed said they had done this in the case about which they were being interviewed. It is also evident from recorded questions on the lines of 'do you agree that you said that ... ?'[37] It is true that in New South Wales this is not necessarily unlawful or contrary to any Code of Practice. But it seems that

---

[34] See, eg C Norris and C Dunninghan, 'Subterranean blues: conflict as an unintended consequence of the police use of informers' (2000) 9 *Policing and Society* 385.

[35] C Dunninghan and C Norris, 'A risky business: the recruitment and running of informers by English police officers' (1996) 19 *Police Studies* 1.

[36] D Dixon, 'Legal regulation and policing practice' (1992) 1 *Social and Legal Studies* 515.

[37] D Dixon, 'A Window into the Interviewing Process? The Audio-visual Recording of Police Interrogation in New South Wales, Australia' (2006) 15 *Policing and Society* 323.

similar practices occur in England and Wales. Moston and Stephenson's analysis of taped interviews shows the 'inadequacy of tape recording inside the police station as a wholly adequate record of all relevant verbal exchanges between suspect and interviewer'.[38] In other words, when there are cameras around, behaviour that the police do not want observed is simply transferred off camera.[39] Interviews outside the station are supposed to be contemporaneously recorded, but Moston and Stephenson found that the police admitted failing to do this in two thirds of all such interviews that they admitted to, and suspects were rarely asked to check the records that were made (both are breaches of the Codes of Practice unless it was impractical to make a record and/or ask the suspect to check it). Since we know that legal rules and Codes of Practice count for little in the UK with regard to the regulation of informers,[40] why should the regulation of interviews be any different?

Coercive interviewing need not be overtly violent or threatening. It starts by the interview being on police territory, at a timescale dictated by the police, and where those who might help or support the suspect are largely controlled by the police (that is, visitors and phone calls are allowed at the discretion of the custody officer, and legal representatives usually attend only shortly before an interview). The police control when there are breaks for meals and what those meals consist of. Autonomy is stripped away—yet answering questions is supposedly voluntary. Statements like, 'I'll decide when the interview finishes' and 'Don't think we'll let it go just because in one interview you make no replies—we're just starting'[41] are all the more threatening when the suspect is in the hands of the police for the next 36 hours.

Dixon notes a formal interview where the suspect was asked no less than 96 'do you agree … ?' questions in 15 minutes, all of which were answered 'yes'.[42] In my research in the 1980s a suspect was dragged into an interviewing room protesting that she would not answer any questions. The response was that this was her right—but it was equally the right of the police to ask them nonetheless. We might ask what the point is of asking questions if the suspect refuses to answer them. Changes to the law on the right of silence means that one answer is that silence can be used as evidence. But it is also the case that many suspects who protest their intention to be silent do nonetheless talk—this is what the police are trained to elicit. So what does 'regulation' mean in this context? It means that we

---

[38] S Moston and G Stephenson, *The questioning and interviewing of suspects outside the police station* (Royal Commission on Criminal Justice Research Study No 22) (London, HMSO, 1993) 36.

[39] M McConville, 'Videotaping Interrogations: Police behaviour on and off camera' (1992) *Crim LR* 532; T Newburn and S Hayman, *Policing, Surveillance and Social Control* (Cullompton, Willan, 2001).

[40] Sanders and Young, n 4 above, ch 6.

[41] Some of many examples given in Sanders and Young n 4 above, ch 5.

[42] D Dixon, 'A Window into the Interviewing Process? The Audio-visual Recording of Police Interrogation in New South Wales, Australia' (2006) 15 *Policing and Society* 340.

can reduce—perhaps even eliminate—overt violence by the police. But is psychological aggression aimed at, and often successful in, breaking down the will of suspects necessarily less distasteful? The combination, in New South Wales, of these techniques with the use of material written down—or purportedly written down—from informal interviews to elicit (unreliable) confessions is well documented by Dixon, and similar British examples are given by Gudjonsson.[43]

It must be emphasised that the police do not usually browbeat or overtly coerce suspects, or use tactics against them to get them to talk. Many suspects are passive and/or cooperative, and many want to 'deal' from the outset. But where none of this is so, PACE allows the police to try to break down resistance. Thirty-six hours allows one tactic after another to be tried. If the first one fails, there is always time to try another. If threats and isolation do not work—try covert taping of the suspect's conversations with a co-suspect, solicitor or member of the family.[44] Or how about deceiving the suspect into thinking there is more evidence than there really is or that his story had been undermined by a co-suspect?[45] Or into thinking that family and friends will be arrested if he or she does not 'cough'? Empathy is another good tactic—many suspects are ready to be befriended by a police officer if they are isolated and scared.[46] It is true that 'ethical interviewing' has been promoted as an alternative, but despite great claims for it, its use and effects are uneven, and have made little difference to the availability of coercive tactics when other methods do not produce results.[47] Even then, some—actually very few—suspects still do not talk, and some talk but say nothing incriminating. So police tactics do not always work. But the damage done in the attempts should not be discounted.

## D Entry and Search of Premises and Seizure of Property

The powers under which the police may enter and search premises vary, and are largely set out in PACE and yet another Code of Practice (B). When using these powers the police can sometimes search the people on the premises, but this is a complex matter that we will not pursue here. All the powers described here may be carried out with the consent of the suspect—indeed, the Codes of Practice

---

[43] G Gudjonsson, *The Psychology of Interrogations and Confessions: A Handbook* (Chichester, Wiley, 2003).

[44] See, eg *Allan* Crim LR [2005] 716.

[45] See, eg *Higgins* [2003] EWCA Crim 2943.

[46] M Innes, *Investigating Murder: Detective Work and the Police Response to Criminal Homicide* (Oxford, Oxford University Press, 2003) 149, 151.

[47] For such a widely touted innovation there has been remarkably little research on it. The main study is C Clarke and R Milne, *National Evaluation of the PEACE Investigative Interviewing Scheme* (Police Research Award Scheme, Report no PRAS/149 (London, Home Office, 2001). This, and the approach as a whole, is evaluated in Sanders and Young, n 4 above, 263–7. Dixon's view, as expressed in ch 2 in this collection, that PEACE has led to a general improvement in interviewing techniques is not inconsistent with my argument. For Dixon does not tackle the question—can the police be stopped from adopting non-PEACE methods when all else fails?

recommend this. The same forms should be completed as with forcible searches, and the Codes recommend that the police only do this where they have the same reasonable suspicion needed to exercise the powers by force. Yet when the police 'ask' people to answer questions or allow a search, for example, this is very different to 'ordinary people' asking such things—people will agree more readily when they perceive the power of authority lying behind the request. This gives the police real power that is hardly regulated at all.[48]

Sometimes the police enter premises to make an arrest. Sometimes this is in pursuit of a suspect, in which case it would be self-authorised, (as it would be unreasonable to require prior authorisation). But frequently it will be to execute an arrest warrant or be because of 'information received'. In these cases there must be 'reasonable suspicion' that the suspect will be there,[49] but this may simply amount to a tip-off from an informer (a notoriously unreliable source).[50] No authorisation is needed from a senior officer, or even from a court in circumstances where a warrant is not needed. At other times the police enter premises following an arrest (to search for weapons, stolen goods, and so on). If they wish to do this after the suspect has been detained in the police station, authorisation in writing must be given by an officer of at least the rank of inspector. But even this regulatory element is absent when search is sought following arrest but before taking the suspect to the station. Like stop and search, the officers exercising the power simply give themselves permission if they consider their actions to be 'reasonable', though they have to account for it to a senior officer afterwards.[51]

In all these circumstances, the police may seize property that they reasonably believe to be a product of crime or evidence of crime. Not only is this a judgement of the officer conducting the search, but there is no need for the crime to be connected to the crime for which the search is being carried out. Thus if the police search a house in relation to theft, but find what they believe to be illegal drugs, they can seize them.[52] The barely regulated power that this gives individual officers hardly needs comment. The only exceptions to this are documents or articles of a highly confidential nature, usually relating to business, journalistic or legal matters—rarely the stuff of 'the usual suspects', and far too complex to be discussed here.[53]

---

[48] This is pursued, particularly with reference to the rule of law, in A Sanders and R Young, 'The rule of law, due process and pre-trial criminal justice' (1994) 47 *Current Legal Problems* 125, and also in A Sanders and R Young, 'Police powers' in T Newburn (ed), *Handbook of Policing* (Cullompon, Willan, 2003).

[49] PACE, s 17 as amended (indeed, expanded) by the Serious Organised Crime and Police Act 2005, Sch 7 para 43(4).

[50] Sanders and Young, n 4 above, ch 6.

[51] This is all covered by PACE s 18.

[52] PACE, s 19.

[53] A mind bogglingly complex account can be found in S Sharpe, *Search and Surveillance: the Movement from Evidence to Information* (Aldershot, Ashgate, 2000).

The only situation where there is apparently strong regulation or control is where the police apply for search warrants, as application has to be made to magistrates or judges. Apart from special cases, such as the confidential material mentioned above, search warrants are usually needed where the police have reasonable suspicion that evidence of a suspected crime might be located in a particular place but have not yet made an arrest. They are also sometimes needed following an arrest if substantial time has elapsed since that arrest.[54] Judicial control is more apparent than real, as few requests for warrants are challenged, let alone refused, by magistrates. However, this is as much due to the police having to show little justification for their request as anything else, making warrants virtually a matter of self-certification.[55]

Despite the weaknesses of the system, obtaining a warrant is more of a hurdle than authorisation by another officer. In view of this, the decline of use of warrants over the years is striking. Partly this is because PACE gave the police so much power to enter, search and seize on their own authority, as we have seen.[56] But this was a trend even before PACE—Lidstone in the early 1980s found that less than 10 per cent of all search warrants were issued to the police.[57] The overwhelming majority were issued to other enforcement bodies, such as HM Revenue and Customs. This is ironic: these bodies, which enforce the law (insofar as that is what they do) do so by 'regulation' (that is non-coercively), yet the exercise of their powers is relatively tightly controlled. By contrast, the exercise of police powers, which is done much more coercively, is subject to the lightest touch regulation.

## E Covert Policing

When PACE was created in 1984 no one considered the need for the control or regulation of covert policing—such things as the use of informers, surveillance, bugging, undercover work and so on. It was not that these forms of policing were rare or unknown. It was probably because PACE was primarily about extending and regulating coercive police powers (stop and search, entry and search, intimate search, arrest, detention, and so on), and also extending the rights of suspects in relation to those powers. Covert policing does not involve the use of coercive powers, and so was 'under the radar'.

Yet there are many reasons for seeking to control or regulate covert policing. They include preventing: unwarranted invasion of the privacy, protected by Article 8 of the European Convention on Human Rights (ECHR), of suspects or

---

[54]  PACE, s 15.

[55]  Again, the word of an anonymous informer will usually suffice: Sanders and Young, n 4 above, ch 6.

[56]  Thus warrants used to be deployed in about 17% of police searches pre-PACE, but less often now: D Clark, *Bevan and Lidstone's The Investigation of Crime* (London, Butterworths, 2004) 122.

[57]  K Lidstone, 'Magistrates, the police and search warrants' (1984) *Crim LR* 449.

their associates; unfair pressure being put on (potential) informers; undercover officers or informers encouraging crime by acting as *agents provocateurs*; and officers becoming corrupted by informers and turning into informers for criminals.[58] Only with increased numbers of challenges in the European Court of Human Rights and then the incorporation of the ECHR into UK law (via the Human Rights Act 1998) were calls for regulation eventually acted upon. This was done by passing the Regulation of Investigatory Powers Act 2000 (RIPA), and it uses the kind of techniques pioneered in PACE—in particular, authorisation of the use of most powers by senior officers, and a Code of Practice to give detailed guidance that is not directly enforceable in the courts.

The regulation of informers in RIPA has the objective of increasing the visibility of the police–informer relationship to police managers.[59] What is most definitely *not* intended is increased visibility to the courts, supervisory bodies or the general public. Most types of informer—characterised in RIPA as 'covert human intelligence sources' (CHIS)—have to be registered and authorised.[60] Self-authorisation is allowed exceptionally, and otherwise it is reserved for designated senior officers, who must give reasons in writing. Further, what the CHIS is authorised to do has to be specified in writing (though only in very general terms), and separate 'handlers' and 'controllers' are appointed. This is all intended to ensure that authorisation is taken seriously, but since the only sources of information for those senior officers are the officers seeking authorisation, this is closer to the ultimate self-regulation we saw in the stop and search and detention contexts than it is to classic self-regulation. Further, even the government-appointed Chief Surveillance Commissioner notes, year after year, that many people who ought to be registered as CHIS are not.[61] As little as 10 per cent of the informer network may be officially recognised as such,[62] which means that, in most cases, regulation does not even get past first base.

Similar problems arise with the interception of communications. Under RIPA section 5 a warrant is needed from the Secretary of State. The Interception of Communications Commissioner is more sanguine than the Chief Surveillance Commissioner, and believes that—apart from genuine errors, such as the transposing of telephone numbers by mistake—there are few, if any, causes for concern.[63] The latest report was written before the Metropolitan Police Commissioner admitted secretly taping numerous conversations with individuals and

---

[58] Without diminishing the importance of any of these issues, we should note that corruption is highlighted by senior police officers as a particularly serious problem. See the contributions of Clark and of Williamson and Bagshaw to R Billingsley, T Nemitz and P Bean (eds), *Informers: Policing, Policy, Practice* (Cullompton, Willan, 2001).

[59] M Innes, 'Professionalising the role of the police informant' (2000) 9 *Policing and Society* 357.

[60] RIPA 2000, s 26.

[61] Chief Surveillance Commissioner, *Report, 2005–6* (House of Commons HC 1298) (London, HMSO, 2006), para 2.3.

[62] Sanders and Young, n 4 above, 287–8.

[63] Interception of Communications Commissioner, *Report, 2005–6* (House of Commons HC 315) London, HMSO, 2007.

officials.[64] It will be interesting to see if, in the light of this, his air of complacency is maintained. Even leaving this incident aside, it is unreasonable to expect a busy cabinet minister to give sufficient time to deal with such matters properly. The work can only be done on the advice of officials, who are not objective, legally trained, or subject to public scrutiny.

Where the police seek to bug conversations or engage in surveillance, the degree and type of regulation depends on the degree of intrusion. The most intrusive forms require authorisation by a surveillance commissioner, but less intrusive forms require only police authorisation—in some cases, the Chief Constable, but in most cases a middle-ranking officer.[65] Exactly the same problems arise as with the regulation of informers and interception of communications. A police sergeant in charge of a local drugs squad commented that requests for surveillance were 'never' rejected: 'It's just a waste of time—bureaucracy!' He said his senior officers trusted him, and were right to do so, and that since resources were too limited the problem was not too many surveillance operations, but too few.[66] The Commissioners authorise and/or approve over 2,000 of the more intrusive types of surveillance each year, and police authorisations of less intrusive surveillance runs at over 23,000 each year.[67]

We do not know how often illegal bugging occurs, but occasionally we learn of some of the circumstances. In a recent case it emerged that the police secretly recorded conversations in the police station between suspects and their solicitor. This is one of the few types of situation where bugging would not be authorised, so they did it without permission.[68] Given that the police control who is in custody, in what room, and when, installation of secret bugging equipment is not difficult, and regulating it is impossible. We can only rely on the honesty of the police—which may be fine most of the time, but clearly is not fine all the time. The problem is knowing how large or small the underlying iceberg actually is.

In most cases the measure sought (whether the use of an informer, or of a surveillance method, to take two examples) has to be proportionate to the crime suspected, and necessary.[69] These requirements are designed to ensure that these measures do not fall foul of the ECHR. However, the only source of information on whether or not the crime in question is sufficiently serious, and the measure sought necessary, is the officer requesting authorisation, who will be well aware of these legal requirements. It is true that actual crime seriousness can be gauged following arrest and conviction where that occurs. But these are far from the usual consequences; even then, the fact that the actual crime may have turned out to be minor does not mean that there was no reasonable suspicion of something

---

[64] See http://news.bbc.co.uk/1/hi/uk/4801032.stm (accessed June 12 2008).

[65] For a detailed discussion see Sanders and Young, n 4 above, 289–97.

[66] Private communication, reported in Sanders and Young, n 4 above, 296–7.

[67] Chief Surveillance Commissioner, *Report, 2005–6* (House of Commons HC 1298) (London, HMSO, 2006) paras 6.1–6.7.

[68] *The Guardian*, 2 December 2003.

[69] See, eg in relation to informers, RIPA s 29 and its associated Code of Practice para 4.8.

more significant. As for the 'necessity' requirement: PACE is peppered with similar requirements (see, for example, the earlier discussion about authorising detention), and there is no reason to believe that it is any more meaningful in the RIPA context than in the PACE context. In other words, these requirements amount to little more than self-certification. The result is that fewer than 10 authorisations are quashed (always on the grounds of non-necessity) per year.[70]

Further, instead of the (albeit limited) judicial oversight provided on PACE matters by the courts—if someone is prosecuted, confession evidence, for example, will be judged in the context of their custodial experience—oversight of covert policing is by government-appointed Commissioners and the Investigatory Powers Tribunal. There are at least three fundamental problems with these arrangements. First, there is the appearance of injustice when matters such as this are determined by government appointees. Secondly, the reality is not encouraging: only in 2005 was the first—and, so far, only—complaint upheld by the Tribunal.[71] Thirdly, since covert policing is by definition ultra-low profile, most illegal activity of this kind will not be known about by those suffering the invasion of privacy, and therefore will not know they have something to complain about. The reliance of this system on complaint by those who have no knowledge, and authorisation by those whose knowledge comes only from those who seek authorisation, is doubly flawed. If disclosure were required in all cases where there was either no prosecution or where someone was acquitted, some genuine redress and (retrospective) regulation could be secured. But there is no such requirement in RIPA.

## F Overview and Recent Developments

When police forces were first established in their modern form in the early to mid-nineteenth century, and for many decades thereafter, the exercise of police powers was very strictly controlled, at least in theory. Stop and search did not exist, and arrest could usually only be done on the basis of a warrant. Warrants were issued by the judiciary (usually magistrates), and only if they were convinced by the police or victim that there were reasonable grounds to suspect that the person(s) in question had done the alleged crime. Arrest was simply a way of bringing those suspects before the court, for arrested persons had to be brought before magistrates as soon as possible, greatly circumscribing the possibility of interrogation. Search of premises, again, required a judicial warrant. The prosecution decision was a matter for magistrates: they either granted an arrest warrant, which in effect was a decision to prosecute, reviewable if and when the arrestee was brought before them; or they granted a summons, which was sent to,

---

[70] Chief Surveillance Commissioner, *Report, 2005–6* (House of Commons HC 1298) (London, HMSO, 2006) para 6.5.

[71] Interception of Communications Commissioner, *Report, 2005–6* (House of Commons HC 315) (London, HMSO, 2007).

or served on, the suspect who was supposed to surrender him/herself to the court at an appointed time, where again the prosecution decision would be reviewable.

Thus the police did not, in principle at any rate, regulate themselves—they were regulated or controlled by the judiciary, who took decisions (albeit based on what the police told them).[72] This picture is hardly recognisable today. Virtually all arrests are summary—that is, on the initiative of the police, usually the arresting officer, alone. Most prosecutions follow arrest; summons and its equivalents having largely withered away. Detention is a matter for the police, prior to judicial oversight. Prosecution decisions used also to be a matter for the police until recently, but they are now usually taken by the CPS. And search warrants are very rare, entry and search usually being a matter for the police, along with most surveillance decisions. At the general level, then, we can see how control of police powers has passed from the judiciary largely to the police themselves, in the form of a system of self-regulation.

In many of these matters racism raises its ugly head. The police have done a lot to attempt to eradicate it since many chief constables admitted that Macpherson was right to talk about 'institutionalised racism' in the police (and indeed in most British institutions). But the undercover BBC report on trainee officers in Manchester in 2003 showed that there was, four years after Macpherson reported, a long way to go.[73] There is little reason to believe much has changed a further four years on. Indeed, successive versions of Code of Practice A have amplified what does not amount to 'reasonable suspicion'—from the first version saying little; then to the statement that race is not relevant; and, in the 2006 version, 'A person's religion cannot be considered reasonable grounds for suspicion' (para 2.2). This can only be a response to the (alleged) targeting of Muslims (or people thought to be Muslims) in the wake of the terrorist atrocities on 9 September 2001 in New York and 7 July 2005 in London. If it was not believed in Home Office and police circles that officers on the ground needed to be told this, why spell it out in the Code of Practice? A major Home Office report on research assessing the impact of the Macpherson Report concluded that, while much progress had been made, racism still exists in the police, and more subtle forms of discrimination (often unintended) still structure much everyday policing.[74] An exemplar of all this was the apparently criminal beating of Toni Comer in 2006: one woman, held down by several police officers, one of whom was caught on CCTV hitting her several times. That she is black can hardly be a coincidence, at least according to several people interviewed in her locality by journalists.[75]

---

[72] The history is sketched by S Sharpe, *Search and Surveillance: the Movement from Evidence to Information* (Aldershot, Ashgate, 2000) ch 1.

[73] Discussed in Sanders and Young, n 4 above, ch 2.

[74] J Foster, T Newburn and A Souhami, *Assessing the Impact of the Stephen Lawrence Inquiry* (Home Office Research Study 294) (London, Home Office, 2005).

[75] *The Guardian*, 8 March 2007.

Yet police powers have been increased since PACE was passed. Stop and search, for example, is available for an ever-growing range of offences;[76] and increasingly without individualised reasonable suspicion.[77] Arrest powers have been extended, and street bail has been introduced.[78] Custody can now be for 36 hours for all indictable offences.[79] The list could go on for a long time.

And yet the regulation of these powers—the original ones and these additional ones—has been steadily loosened in the last few years, not tightened. Loosening at the general level (the erosion of judicial control) has already been noted, but there has also been more specific loosening. The Criminal Justice Act 2003, section 6, for example, legitimised reviews of detention over the phone as a matter of routine, rather than on an exceptional basis. And whereas PACE required that a new search warrant be sought after each search, and that it would in any event lapse after one month, now a warrant is valid for three months, and can be used time after time for the same premises, or for multiple premises owned or controlled by a particular person if a new 'all premises' warrant is granted.[80]

The most remarkable example relates to the Terrorism Act 2000, section 44. This empowers the police to search without reasonable suspicion for articles intended for terrorist purposes. This can, like the Criminal Justice and Public Order Act section 60 power, be only for a limited amount of time, and in a specified area—though it can be a whole police force area—and when authorised by a senior officer. The officer must be of at least assistant chief constable rank in the terrorism example, but this is, again, self-regulation. One might have thought this not so, as authorisation has to be confirmed by the Home Secretary. However, it was discovered that the Home Secretary had (secretly) made rolling authorisations ever since section 44 came into operation. This was challenged in court. The view of the Court of Appeal was that:

> It did no more than enable the commander in a particular area to have the powers available when this was operationally required without going back to the Secretary of State for confirmation of a particular use.[81]

So even when legislation specifies a form of control or extraneous regulation this is subverted by the Home Secretary and police in practice, and the subversion, creating complete self-regulation, is then endorsed by the courts. Although Dixon, in chapter two in this collection, takes a more positive view of the role of

---

[76] For example, Criminal Justice Act 2003, s 1: search for articles for use in criminal damage; Serious Organised Crime and Police Act 2005, s115: search for prohibited fireworks.

[77] For example, Criminal Justice and Public Order Act 1994, s 60.

[78] Serious Organised Crime and Police Act 2005 s 110 (amending s 24 PACE). See Code of Practice G.

[79] Criminal Justice Act 2003 (amending PACE s 41); Serious Organised Crime and Police Act 2005, Sched 7, s 43 (7).

[80] Serious Organised Crime and Police Act 2005, s 114.

[81] *Gillan* [2004] EWCA (Civ) 1067 at para 51. Confirmed by the House of Lords in [2006] UKHL 12.

the courts than I take, he and I do agree that, overall, the attempt in PACE to exercise some constraint over police use of their powers has been steadily eroded in the last decade or so.

# V  The homicidal PACE regime: deaths in police custody[82]

Some of the unfair, degrading and inhuman consequences of the PACE regime and the weak regulation of officers working within it have become apparent in the course of this discussion. Many of the problems discussed above combine to produce the worst consequence of all: a death rate of which Britain should be ashamed. Yet it attracts little attention and little official response. Between 1990 and 2003, over 600 people died in police custody—nearly one per week. Yet only 11 of these led to unlawful killing verdicts and/or prosecutions, and none of them led to criminal convictions.[83]

Many horror stories could be recounted. Space permits just three. The first is Christopher Alder. He was arrested, handcuffed, and dumped—dying—onto a police station floor in 1998. Gasping for breath, he was accused of 'faking it' by one of the several officers who watched him die. By the time they tried to save him, it was too late. We know this is all true as it was captured for a long 12 minutes on a police CCTV tape.[84]

Then there was Paul Croker, who was arrested at home in 2005 following a struggle in which he was heard to shout, 'You are killing me. You are killing me.' The police carried him out of the house to the station. He was not struggling. He died in the station two hours later.[85] Only one year before, a study for the Police Complaints Authority (PCA) (shortly before it was replaced by the IPCC) commented that a major warning sign was if a detainee had to be carried to the station,[86] yet the lessons had not been learnt.

Finally, let us spend a little longer considering the case of Marlon Downes, who was found hanging in his cell in 1997.[87] We don't know how or why Downes died as there was no tape. The police said he committed suicide. For this to be true:

- he would have had to have stood on two rolled-up mattresses. Yet police photos showed only one;

---

[82]  This section is a summary of Sanders and Young, n 4 above, 191–4. For a police perspective, see ch 4 by John Coppen in this collection.

[83]  G Vogt and J Wadham, *Deaths in Police Custody: Redress and Remedies* (London, Civil Liberties Trust, 2003).

[84]  *The Guardian*, 25 August 2000.

[85]  *The Guardian*, 18 August 2005.

[86]  D Best and A Kefas, *The Role of Alcohol in Police-Related Deaths* (London, PCA, 2004).

[87]  T Newburn and S Hayman, *Policing, Surveillance and Social Control* (Cullompton, Willan, 2001) ch 2.

- the shoelace with which he allegedly hanged himself could not have supported his weight;
- the custody record stated that he was alive one hour after he actually died;
- attempts had been made to erase a later entry claiming he was still alive;
- his solicitor said he had seen Marlon in a different cell but the police denied moving him, and the custody record did not record a move; and
- the cell in which he had been found dead had been cleaned before the death was investigated.

A Home Office study looked at the reasons for deaths in custody. According to the official sources on which it was based, only 6 per cent were attributable to police actions.[88] That means Marlon Downes' death would be attributed by this study to his own actions. So the research almost certainly understates the role of the police. Even so, based on the more than 600 deaths occurring over the 13 year period 1990–2003, the 6 per cent estimate amounts to over 30 deaths attributed to police actions—yet we have seen that only 11 of these led to unlawful killing verdicts and/or prosecutions. I am not suggesting that in many—or perhaps even any—of these cases the deaths were deliberately caused by the police. But many were the result of accident, negligence, excessive force, and so on. In many cases this would be manslaughter. And in many the detainees were drunk, drugged, mentally ill or otherwise clearly unstable. Too little was done to save them from themselves.

The point here is that vulnerable suspects are brought into a virtually unregulated place—the police station—where no one is present most of the time to speak up for, and to protect, the suspect. To take a simple example, the researchers in one study were interviewing suspects in their cells. When they finished they pressed the call button but this had been immobilised by the custody officer. They shouted and beat on the door for 30 minutes before being 'rescued'.[89] That is more than enough time for a suicidal suspect to kill himself.

The lack of regulation, though, goes further, and goes back to the question of (virtually unregulated) arrest and detention. The Home Office research found that there were warning signs or explicit warnings (for example, suicide markers on the Police National Computer) in over 30 per cent of all deaths by deliberate self-harm. The same research found most of the dead detainees had been arrested for drink- or drug-related offences (49 per cent) or minor thefts (11 per cent). Why are we detaining people who would probably not be jailed if they were prosecuted and convicted? Why, especially, when we know that some of them will die? The PCA study mentioned earlier concluded that 'drunken detainees should

---

[88] A Leigh, G Johnson and A Ingram, *Deaths in Police Custody: Learning the Lessons* (Home Office Police Research Series paper 26) (London, Home Office, 1998).
[89] T Newburn and S Hayman, *Policing, Surveillance and Social Control* (Cullompton, Willan, 2001) 123.

not be taken to police stations in other than the most extreme circumstances'.[90] This is ignored, because it is the police who take drunks to, and who authorise the detention of drunks in, police stations.

The police argue that they inappropriately detain suicidal, drunk and mentally ill people because hospitals and facilities for mentally ill people frequently refuse to take them. They acknowledge that these people are vulnerable in custody, but say they do the best they can in near-impossible circumstances. These are not problems that they seek.[91] In many instances, the police are rescuing people from dangerous situations, and—dangerous though the police station clearly is—it may be that for most of these people this is the least bad alternative. We can legitimately shift the blame for many—probably most—deaths in custody from individual officers, but this does not absolve the combination of the PACE regime and government complacency from responsibility. The PACE regime fails to require expert assessment of potentially vulnerable people, even when a Police National Computer search reveals explicit suicide markers and even though the police rarely fail to take into account a criminal record when deciding on bail. The PACE regime also allows the police to exercise poor observation and care, does not allow relatives, friends and carers all-hours access, encourages interrogation and isolation techniques that push vulnerable people to (and sometimes over) the edge of what they can bear, and enables officers to abuse detainees and to cover their tracks when they do so.

## VI  Taking stock of the argument so far

This paper has asked three questions:

- to what extent *are* coercive police powers effectively controlled or regulated?
- *can* coercive police powers be effectively controlled or regulated? and
- insofar as either are possible, *should they be* controlled or regulated?

The answer to the first is that they are not as effective as one would expect when looking at the formal rules. It is true that much, perhaps most, of what happens to suspects when detained by the police, is lawful. But that is because the law allows the police to engage in tactics aimed at breaking resistance—aimed, in other words, at getting suspects to do that which they do not want to do (as good a definition of coercion as one might wish for). These tactics include low-level coercive practices such as isolation, deception, destabilising, disorientation, the creation of fear and psychological undermining. When lawful tactics, even such

---

[90]  D Best and A Kefas, *The Role of Alcohol in Police-Related Deaths* (London, PCA, 2004).
[91]  These views were vociferously expressed at the conference and colloquium on Policing and Defending in a Post-PACE World at the University of the West England and the University of Bristol, 29–30 March 2007. See further ch 4 in this collection.

as these, do not work, the police sometimes resort to unlawful tactics. To put this in the terms of section II above, we have seen that the legalistic approach is inadequate—it simply does not describe reality. A combination of cultural and structural approaches is needed. Thus to effectively control and regulate the police we need to understand why they break or stretch some of the rules some of the time (and are frequently aided and abetted in this by government and the courts).

The answer to the second question (*can* coercive police powers be effectively controlled or regulated?) is in two parts. First, as we have seen, control is largely illusory. Secondly, the PACE regime is largely one of self-regulation. For example, custody is regulated by the police themselves, and their actions are recorded by their own custody records. The death in custody of Marlon Downes—just one of the more shocking examples of a shockingly frequent phenomenon—illustrates the illusion of this regulation, when the custody record stated that he was alive an hour after he died, and there is even doubt over the cell he was in. But even if control is not possible, regulation could be—just not in the way PACE ostensibly establishes.

Regarding the third question (*should* coercive police powers be controlled or regulated?), the 'post-regulatory state' debate might lead us to believe that the State has more or less given up attempting to control, and that regulation—particularly self-regulation—is the norm across the board. Arguing that the regulation of the ways the police exercise their powers should be part of this pattern follows naturally. In fact, as Hillyard and Tomlinson point out, the idea that the State is retreating from attempts to control all arenas of social life through directly coercive powers is empirically untrue. Stop and search has been increasing for years, ever more draconian terrorism legislation is being promulgated and increasingly used on ever wider groups of people, and the prisons are full to bursting. The increase in the use of regulation is not inconsistent with the increased use of coercive powers.[92] It nonetheless remains true that regulation is exceptionally permissive in some other contexts: business and finance for example.

So any argument on the lines of 'the era of state control is and should be over' is quite simply wrong. Where the state wants to control it attempts to do so (whether effectively or not is another matter). Where it does not wish to do so, it uses 'law as last resort'.[93] So whether or not coercive police powers should be effectively controlled or regulated is not a question that can be answered by looking at general trends in control and regulation. For general trends are hard to discern. Moreover, we saw earlier that the government does regard it as appropriate to control the use of powers by some investigative agencies—we saw that

---

[92]  P Hillyard and M Tomlinson, 'Patterns of policing and policing Patten' (2000) 27 *Journal of Law and Society* 394.

[93]  The apt title of a recent study of the HSE: K Hawkins, *Law as Last Resort* (Oxford, Oxford University Press, 2003).

non-police agencies have to seek warrants to search and so forth in a very considerably higher proportion of cases than do the police. If these agencies can be controlled, at least to this extent, so can the police. The questions are whether this is desirable, and what criteria we should use to judge this. If it is desirable we need to go onto ask: 1. Are these powers abused in the absence of effective control/regulation?; 2. If so, what would be (are) the most effective ways of regulating/controlling their use?

If we return to section III above, regulation should contain clear goals (rules and standards), and monitoring and re-alignment mechanisms. Most PACE and PACE-type rules and standards are reasonably clear, but most monitoring is done by the police themselves, usually on the basis of information from the officers seeking the power. And re-alignment mechanisms are also largely in the hands of the police. Where other bodies are involved, such as government tribunals, the results are no better. Re-alignment mechanisms where deaths occur—where one would expect the most rigorous mechanisms—are virtually non-existent.

# VII　Towards effective regulation: the need for anchored pluralism

We saw that the answers to the questions in section VI were that there is no attempt to control most coercive police powers, and that attempts to regulate them are largely ineffective; that they can be effectively regulated through a combination of methods; and that control or 'hard' regulation is not necessarily inappropriate per se in the post-regulatory state. I suggest the reverse: coercive police powers entail doing what, in any other context, would be criminal acts; and sometimes, as with many deaths in police custody, they are criminal acts even in this context. Take driving at excessive speeds. We do not want to stop people driving just as we do not want to stop the police exercising their powers appropriately, we simply want to stop excessive forms of both behaviours. We do not rely on drivers, or their representative organisations like the AA and RAC, to self-regulate; so nor should we rely on the police to self-regulate.

We have seen that, as things stand at present, coercive police powers are often used wrongly. This does not necessarily mean that they are usually abused. However, just as the Philips Commission failed to ascertain how much abuse of police power there was in the 1970s, we have little more knowledge three decades later. But just as criminal laws against violence and sexual assault are intended to influence and control only a relatively small number of people rather than the majority of citizens (for the majority of citizens would not engage in this behaviour even if there were no such laws), so we need effective ways to regulate and control police power for a relatively small number of officers (or policing situations) rather than the majority of officers or policing situations. Just because something is unusual it does not mean that we should not guard against it. Similarly, just because police behaviour is better in the UK than in comparable institutions, and has improved over the years, it does not mean that we should not seek to improve it further. The fact that we can usually walk the streets at night without being attacked by passers-by does not lessen the need to control and regulate those who do occasionally attack innocent victims. The same applies to police officers. Most may never abuse their powers, but we know for a fact that some do. Putting in place measures aimed at the effective control of abusive officers need not be seen as an attack on the integrity of all officers, just as laws against rape need not be regarded as impugning the morality of all men. There is as yet no clear answer to whether we can effectively control the use of these powers. But we do know that at present, control and regulation is not effective enough, and further moves towards the self-regulation end of the spectrum are likely to lead to even less effective regulation than exists now.

At the very least, the idea of 'anchored pluralism' needs to be taken seriously in the control of police behaviour. This would entail the empowerment of lay visitors and social services, and even of family members and friends, to be present in the station whenever they wished (subject to some kind of challengeable limits). It would also entail greater empowerment of legal advisors. At present the PACE regime gives suspects an illusion of freedom: suspects can choose whether or not to seek visitors, telephone calls and legal advice. Only vulnerable suspects are forced to accept help (from an appropriate adult) and that is because they are deemed to have limited capacity to make their own decisions. But the idea that we should respect the (perhaps) articulated wish of suspects to not seek help when in involuntary custody when we completely fail to respect their wishes not to be in custody in the first place is Alice in Wonderland logic. If we are prepared to subject them to the coercion documented here, we should also be prepared to subject them to unsolicited help. When suspects say they do not want help, this is usually not an absolute statement—it is made in the context of involuntary detention. For example, since involuntary detention, and the fear of violence and humiliation that goes with it, is what most suspects hate most, anything that extends it is undesirable. Legal advice is often (correctly) perceived as extending it—after all, if legal advice has to be requested, delays are inevitable. But if legal advisors were actually waiting in police stations for clients, the situation would be very different.

This sounds impractical as it would be so expensive. It would be nearly as expensive as having police lawyers (that is, the CPS) in police stations. So one might think that neither could happen. Except that, as a result of 'statutory charging', introduced by the Criminal Justice Act 2003, we do now have prosecutors in police stations. If the money can be found for the prosecution, presumably it could be found for the defence.

Moreover, measures such as these would mean that Paul Croker, Christopher Alder and Marlon Downes—and probably many other suspects who die in police custody—would perhaps be alive today. Rather than the police deciding if a drunk or high suspect should see a doctor, an objective person would decide. A risk assessment could be made—balancing the seriousness of the alleged offence for which the suspect was arrested against the risk of being kept in custody while possibly ill, intoxicated or suicidal. Many deaths in custody would be avoided if this were done.

At present much help, such as provided by legal advisors, is compromised by the control the PACE regime gives the police.[94] Legal advisors need police cooperation to discover the police case against their suspects, for example, and this becomes a matter of bargaining: the more adversarial solicitors are, the less ammunition the police will give them to be effectively adversarial. But why should ammunition be in the gift of the police if suspects are innocent until proven guilty?

My argument, in short, is that the PACE model gives the police huge power, and it gives outside bodies (including suspects and their representatives) little power. That police power is largely self-regulated, and largely ineffectively regulated. Indeed, the police station is, like the street, a largely unregulated place in reality. Dixon, like most other policing scholars, disagrees.[95] I have reached this contrary conclusion by utilising the lens provided by regulatory scholars, rather than continuing to use the somewhat out-dated concepts that are central to the policing literature. Applying the insights of the regulation literature shows that the best way of making regulation more effective would be to disperse it among those who have an interest in making it effective—that is, community and suspect representatives. This would entail giving legal advisors, for example, real power by giving them the right to information held by the police and the right to observe, support and advise throughout the period of a suspect's detention.

The only arguments against allowing suspects this kind of monitoring and support are that they would obstruct police attempts to break resistance. These are also arguments in favour. It all depends on whether we truly wish to regulate coercive police practices or not. Just as vested political interests watered down Patten's proposals for Northern Ireland, so that the dispersal of power over policing is more apparent than real,[96] we can expect similar vested interests to resist this type of proposal in relation to 'normal' policing. Indeed, as a result of the Macpherson Inquiry, there are now Independent Advisory Groups that operate locally to work with the police on local strategies. These do work to some extent, and in some areas more effectively than others. But they are police-led and often neither police nor local communities have a clear sense of their purpose.[97] As with Patten, there is in reality little dispersal of power. But setbacks such as

---

[94]  See further chs 8 and 9 by Ed Cape and Tony Edwards in this collection.

[95]  See, eg M Maguire, 'Regulating the police station: the case of the PACE Act' in M McConville and G Wilson (eds), *Handbook of the Criminal Justice Process* (Oxford, Oxford University Press 2002).

[96]  P Hillyard and M Tomlinson, 'Patterns of policing and policing Patten' (2000) 27 *Journal of Law and Society* 394.

[97]  J Foster, T Newburn and A Souhami, *Assessing the Impact of the Stephen Lawrence Inquiry* (Home Office Research Study 294) (London, Home Office, 2005).

these should not stop us from uncovering the minimal regulation provided under the 'PACE model' and arguing for real regulation. We can agree with Dixon that PACE, in many respects at least, led to improvements by comparison with what went on before.[98] But if we value human dignity, we should not be satisfied with this. There is scope for more improvement, but only if we explore the potential of anchored pluralism.

---

[98] See Ch 2 in this collection.

# 4

# PACE: A View from the Custody Suite

JOHN COPPEN

## I  Introduction

This essay is a practitioner's view of police detention since the introduction of the Police and Criminal Evidence Act 1984 (PACE). Comment will be made on other legislation and outside influences that in the author's view have undermined the original Act.

There are few references to academic research and most of the text is based on the author's observations and experiences.

The author is currently a member of the Joint Central Committee of the Police Federation of England and Wales (PFEW). This means that I do not now take part in what is sometimes called 'front line policing' but as the lead spokesperson in matters relating to police custody issues for the PFEW, I regularly visit police stations and speak with custody officers. I have also had the experience of being a custody officer both pre and post PACE.

The PFEW supports a National Custody Officers Forum which meets quarterly in various locations around the country. The meeting is made up of current custody practitioners and discussions cover a wide range of topics relating to police detention. The aim of the Forum is to achieve practical solutions to problems identified by custody practitioners and, where possible, to influence future policies and legislation relating to the detention process. The Forum has achieved a number of successes for members of the PFEW and this has resulted in a further extension of membership to other UK police forces, including Scotland and Northern Ireland. It is hoped by way of this introduction to have given the impression that I and the PFEW are very much involved with, and supportive of, the practitioners when it comes to the applications of PACE.

So what do the ordinary practitioners think about PACE? Where do they see it evolving, and what could be improved from the users' point of view? Is it just a straightforward case of reviewing the legislation or are there other influences now undermining PACE that were not evident when the Act was originally brought in? Before I try to answer these questions it is useful to look at what was happening before PACE was implemented in 1986.

# II Policing prior to PACE

The police service of England and Wales is very good at taking national strategies and directives and turning them into 43 different versions of that one thing. Anything that is not codified strictly in law can be subject to local misinterpretation and subsequent misuse.[1] This is important to grasp if you are to understand how police detention operated prior to PACE. There was no one way of dealing with people who had been arrested. Each police force had its own Force Orders which dictated how and where a suspect would be detained, but these Orders were largely concerned with the physical practicalities of the task rather than strict compliance with legal obligation.

Anyone who was involved in the criminal justice process prior to 1986 will remember the relative ease with which a person under arrest went from the streets to the cells, with only the minimum of scrutiny in between. The laws of the time stipulated quite clearly what was and was not an 'arrestable offence' but made little or no mention of how the power to arrest was to be applied. Suspects were given the choice of cooperation and responding to being 'invited' to the police station, or being arrested and taken to the police station. The only difference was that a charge sheet would be completed at some stage for the suspect under arrest, and an entry in the 'Persons brought to the station' ledger completed for the invitee.

Both would at some stage be interviewed, sometimes at length, with little or none of the conversation recorded. It was only deemed necessary to record significant statements made, or the suspect's confession to the alleged wrongdoing. The location and duration of any interview was the subject of police discretion.

Nothing I have said so far should be viewed as shocking or in any way derogatory of the police officers of that time. That was the system and rules under which society was content for the police to operate.

Many of the systems that were employed to record information at that time were manual and there was, by and large, far less paperwork and bureaucracy. Things that were recorded were those likely to be of use to the police in the future or necessary to comply with local orders or the criminal law.

It was more important to spend time with witnesses and victims and get accurate information than it was to put statistical information on a computer

---

[1] More recent examples might include the competency related threshold payment scheme, or the work based assessment promotion scheme, both of which were negotiated nationally and then implemented differently at force level.

database. Knowing that your division (now a Basic Command Unit or BCU) had moved above another similar division at the other end of the country in a league table for detecting burglary was less important than arresting and prosecuting local offenders for committing the burglaries in the first instance.

The late 1970s and early 1980s saw the beginning of the age of pro-forma policing. Simple 'tick the box' type forms were being introduced to cover everything from road traffic accidents to neighbour disputes, but of course, in 43 different varieties. Forces were encouraged to gather data on these issues and submit it to the Home Office. Based on the statistical information supplied, the Home Office began to direct previously autonomous chief constables in how and why resources should be deployed and the road to target-led policing was embarked upon. This was also the era that saw the introduction of 'fixed penalty notice' policing, and with it (although at the time we did not know it), the beginning of the end of an individual officer's ability to use discretion.

In the early 1980s, working as an acting sergeant in a busy rural market town, it was not uncommon for the author to act as custody officer for a detainee (by entering the prisoner's details onto a voluminous charge sheet), and then go out and take statements from witnesses regarding the same incident. The next day, depending on the nature of the offence, the author might well be asked to prosecute the matter at the local magistrates' court.

Evidence obtained to support the prosecution was obtained under 'Judges Rules'. Judges Rules were specific about how a suspect should be informed of his or her status on arrest, and how evidence might be obtained from that suspect in any subsequent interview. What they were not specific about was how long that process might take, and what treatment the suspect might hope to enjoy whilst detained by the police.

It was common practice that whoever was doing desk relief at the police station was responsible for any prisoner detained in cells, and how much attention the prisoner received depended on how busy the desk officer was. Many of the basic safeguards for detainees that we now take for granted were not only absent, but often not even considered. There was no automatic right to free legal advice, nor were the police obliged to inform anyone that you were under arrest and being detained.

It seems incredible now to think that such a system operated for so long, but it must be remembered that far fewer people were actually arrested then, and the diversity and complexity of modern offending behaviour was only just beginning to emerge.[2]

---

[2] As well as large scale disorders, the early 1980s saw the rise of the animal rights movement, organised international terrorism, and computer crime to name but a few.

# III Introducing PACE

Britain in the early 1980s was in a state of social change. There was high unemployment, and an upsurge of all the social problems associated with it. Certainly the words most police officers who policed that era associate with it are unemployment, strikes, bombings, and above all, riots.[3]

This is not the appropriate place to comment on the conduct of any of the policing operations relating to the many incidents of those times, (the author took part in policing riots in Bristol and Liverpool, and spent many weeks both at Greenham Common and various coal mines in the north of England). However, it is true to say that many people thought that the police had allowed themselves to be used as enforcers of a political doctrine rather than acting in a free and unbiased manner. As a result, in many parts of the country, the police are still living with the aftermath of events that took place in the 1980s. Whatever the rights and wrongs, the reputation of the British police service did not come out of those years untarnished.

Lord Scarman, tasked to look at the underlying causes of the Brixton riots concluded that there was blame on both sides, and went on to recommend changes to policing methods; the recruitment of more black and ethnically diverse police officers, and the establishment of a public police complaints authority (the PCA). The Scarman report was not the main driver of PACE, but it could be viewed as illustrative of the background climate of that time.

As noted above, the Police and Criminal Evidence Act 1984 was implemented in 1986. PACE was not universally well received when first introduced. As Chapter two by David Dixon in this collection documents, there were those on the civil liberties side who saw it as giving the police too much power (particularly in respect of searching without a warrant), whilst some within the police service disliked the many onerous duties placed upon them by PACE, and thought the system would grind to a halt with every last detainee wanting to see a doctor and a lawyer. I myself well recall the doom-mongers among long-serving officers foretelling the end of civilisation. To the constable on patrol, however, little changed immediately, as few forces made any serious attempt at training their officers prior to implementation. The newly appointed custody sergeants were at least given a copy of the Codes of Practice and told to go away and study it. PACE was not the only thing new in 1986. The Crown Prosecution Service (CPS) also came into being. The CPS mandate was to bring oversight and clarity to the charging process by relegating the police to the role of evidence gatherer, rather than evidence evaluator and presenter.

Twenty years on, the police view PACE as a fundamental guide to conducting an investigation. It is not perfect, but by abiding by the Codes of Practice the

---

[3] 1981 saw riots in Brixton, Toxteth, Wolverhampton, Brighton, Reading, Luton, Chester, Hull, Preston and Bristol.

police can ensure that any future prosecution has at least been founded on a legally sound basis. Libertarians too acknowledge that PACE has brought about a system that is much more transparent and open to challenge.

One area in which change is very evident is interviewing. Most interviews in the pre-PACE era were confrontational. The object was primarily to gain an admission from the suspect. Today interviews are far more balanced. Most start with a very open question that encourages the detainee to give an account of their actions rather than to answer specific questions. There is hardly any repetition of questions and few raised voices.[4]

Another area in which clear change has taken place is the role of the defence solicitor. Prior to the advent of PACE most suspects rarely spoke to a solicitor prior to being charged with an offence. Solicitors were a rarity within a police station, and usually only became involved prior to charge in serious cases such as murder and rape. The experience or worth of any particular solicitor was not a factor in their selection; it was a question of who the suspect requested and who the police could get to attend.

Certainly there was none of the rapport that exists now between defending solicitors and custody staff. Some may question the value of any such rapport either to the suspect or the police, but, from the latter perspective, experience suggests that much more can be achieved by interacting with the suspect's solicitor than by ignoring them. It is all a matter of trust and trust is built up over a period of time. Custody officers quickly identify the solicitors with whom they can have 'honest' conversations in respect of their client's detention. This may include doubts over their suitability to be interviewed at that time, concerns around their long-term medical status, and other background issues that have come to the notice of the custody staff, and, although not strictly relevant to the case, would be relevant to the detainee's overall well-being. These conversations go both ways and help to facilitate a more open environment in which to operate. PACE has been the catalyst for this. It creates an environment where the custody sergeant has a vested interest only in the welfare and proper treatment of the detainee, and therefore is free to make decisions that do not necessarily favour either the interviewer or the detainee, but are fair and unbiased.

## IV   The accountability of custody officers

There are, in my view, two main reasons why PACE has endured into the twenty-first century. First, the Act has been regularly reviewed and updated, and

---

[4]  A police officer 20 years ago would have known the points that had to be proved before any specific charge could be levelled, but that is not necessarily the case today. Some police officers do not now conduct interviews at all, as some police forces employ non-police officers as interviewers. Some of these interviewers have no police background (as is the case in Wiltshire, my own force area).

therefore has remained relevant despite the myriad of new legislation that has impacted upon it.[5] Anyone who doubts the robustness of the subsequent reviews need only examine the growth of the Codes of Practice since the enactment of the original legislation.

The second reason is that the Act is clear and concise in specifying to the police precisely who has responsibility for any given action in respect of a detained person.

The basic clarity given to the role of custody sergeant has been the main and principal strength of the Act. That there is more or less uniformity in the way custody units (or latterly custody 'suites') are run throughout England and Wales, is a direct result of PACE conferring responsibility on a single individual, the custody sergeant. This is also true of other sections of PACE relating to identification, searching, and the taking of samples from suspects.

I refer back to my earlier remarks in respect of chief officers taking policies and interpreting them in 43 different ways, and ask the question, 'Would PACE have become so embedded in modern policing had it been left to individual forces to decide at what level the decisions necessary for PACE to work were to be made?' Experience tells me the answer is 'No'. But if you accept that well run custody suites revolve around the custody sergeant having control, the flip side must be liability when something goes wrong.

As custody sergeant, being complained against is part of the job. In my own experience, I have been accused of everything from unlawful imprisonment to failing to supply a detainee with a cigarette. Some sergeants treat complaints glibly whilst others take matters to heart. Their response to complaints often reflects their current levels of stress.

Obviously the more serious the complaint, the more stress and anxiety is induced. The ultimate concern is always will a 'death in custody' happen on my watch? Such deaths inevitably attract complaints from the public and the attention of official bodies set up to oversee the police. The system for handling such complaints was recently overhauled by the Police Reform Act 2002, which created the Independent Police Complaints Commission (IPCC). The IPCC became operational in April 2004, and, as well having a legal duty to oversee the whole police complaints system, they specifically investigate or cause to be investigated, any incidents where a fatality occurs to a member of the public who has been involved with the police.

Deaths in actual police custody are rare. That is worth stressing. The IPCC produces an annual report into the number of deaths it believes occurred in the previous 12 months following or during police contact. The deaths are categorised into four main areas: fatal road traffic incidents, fatal shooting incidents, deaths in or following police custody, and deaths during or following other types of police contact. According to their statistics, from April 2005 to 31 March 2006,

---

[5]  In particular the Police Reform Act 2002.

3 people actually died in a police cell. A further 19 died in hospital having been taken there from police cells. Many of the deceased detainees had taken non-prescription drugs, consumed alcohol and been involved in violent behaviour prior to police involvement with them. They were, in short, typical of many of the 1.1 million detainees who went through police detention in that period.[6]

Whilst any death is a tragedy for the families of those concerned and is to be regretted, I believe the figures illustrate just how seriously custody sergeants take the responsibilities placed upon them by PACE. I recently attended a five star hotel in the centre of London to take part in a seminar examining deaths in police custody. Being early for the seminar, I spoke with the duty manager who appeared distressed. His anxiety had been induced by the death of a fifth person within a year in one of the hotel's bedrooms. I mention this to illustrate that whether in contact with the police or otherwise, deaths occur.

Any custody sergeant unfortunate enough to be on duty when a death occurs is subject to intense and often unfair scrutiny. Every word of every line of the relevant custody record and all other custody records open at the time of the death, are minutely examined with a view to finding fault. In this context, PACE is not helpful to the custody sergeant as it is very prescriptive as to how and when actions must be taken in dealing with certain types of detainees. A detainee who is drunk for instance must be roused and spoken to at least every half an hour. These stipulations pay no regard to the number or type of other detainees held at any one time[7] nor does it specify how many staff should be deployed in safeguarding their well-being.

There are set time limits for investigating custody staff in a death in custody investigation, but procrastination and delays in decision making mean that they are seldom met. If the CPS decides that there should be no criminal charges levelled at the custody sergeant (as happens in the vast majority of cases), the matter is then returned to the IPCC for them to decide whether internal discipline proceedings should be brought. If the sergeant is charged with a disciplinary offence, it invariably relates to a failure to discharge a duty under PACE.

This process of responding to a death in custody can and does take years. The whole procedure is adversarial, costly, and in my experience, prolongs both the agony of the bereaved family members who want closure, and causes stress and disenchantment to the sergeant under investigation. There are no winners, only losers. A simple amendment to PACE similar to the discretion allowed to a police officer when giving a criminal caution could assist here. Legally it is not the exact

---

[6] Figure taken from the R Teers and S Menin, *Deaths during or following Police Contact: Statistics for England and Wales 2005/06* (London, IPCC, 2006). It is necessary to read the 'descriptions' section to obtain the actual figure. The figure for annual number of detainees is taken from the Home Office website.

[7] Custody staff acknowledge that there is no reliable index on which to base desirable staff to detainee ratios, as every individual detainee will introduce a different risk factor.

wording that is important but the meaning that is conveyed and understood. In terms of PACE this would mean that the spirit of compliance was the important element, not whether something was done in a particular way or strictly in accordance with a time deadline. It is not uncommon for custody staff under investigation to be charged with misconduct for failing to visit a detainee within PACE guidelines even if the error was recognised and the detainee visited five minutes later than prescribed. Such rigorous application of PACE where it has had no bearing on the outcome of any incident being investigated serves only to encourage custody staff to adopt an attitude of non-cooperation with those investigating matters.

Latterly, the IPCC has stated their intention to try to move away from a blame culture, and to foster a more constructive approach, whereby the object of any enquiry will focus on learning the lessons (if there are any), rather than persecuting custody officers for minor breaches of PACE. It remains to be seen if their future actions reflect this desire. Regardless of the efforts of custody staff, and despite any amount of legislation, there will always be those that die in police custody; the challenge is to keep the number to the bare minimum.

Complaints, serious or otherwise are one of the main reasons why some sergeants fight shy of performing the role of custody officer. The other main reason is stress, mostly caused by inappropriate staffing levels, and poor facilities.

# V   Training

Training for the role of custody officer is a postcode lottery. There are some forces that provide excellent in-house training to sergeants prior to their taking up the role, and others which do not. My own experience was not a happy one. I was issued a copy of the Codes of Practice on a Thursday, and told I would be acting as custody officer (Swindon on this occasion) on the following Monday. In recognition of the fact that I would have to read the Codes on my weekend off, I was told I would be starting on a day shift to break me in gently. That was in 1990. I performed my last duty as a custody officer in 2002 and never received any formal training in respect of the role during that 12 year period.

This may be a good juncture to comment on the selection of custody sergeants. In the past, custody sergeants were selected under two criteria. The first was 'career development', (a euphemism for 'make a fuss and you won't have a future career'). Operational need dictated that someone had to do the job and it was, in the eyes of your manager, your turn. The second was because the individual had caused offence to the senior officer with control over the posting to custody, and the posting was the subsequent punishment for that offence. Neither criterion could be described as scientific or fair. In practice, heavy reliance was placed on the knowledge and experience of the individual sergeant to make a success of the situation. Far more care is usually applied to the selection process now, though the two criteria above have not been totally eliminated.

In 1998, the Police Complaints Authority (the fore-runners to the IPCC), carried out a survey of chief officers and asked them to provide statistics in respect of what training custody sergeants receive and when they could expect to receive it. Four forces were found to have no specific training for their custody officers. Of the remaining 39, only seven insisted on any training being given prior to the sergeant going into the suite, whilst a further 20 generally sent sergeants to be trained first, but not always. Whilst some forces gave 15 days training on PACE and other related matters around detention, others gave just one day. The average across the 39 forces was six days. This chaotic approach to training was occurring despite the introduction in 1997 of a nationally agreed training course for custody sergeants.[8]

The situation today has changed for the better. All 43 forces now give some form of training, and chief officers believe that none of their staff are deployed in custody suites without being trained. Sadly this is not the case. Whilst permanent staff are trained, untrained officers are often used to fill in when abstractions and vacancies occur. Moreover, the content, length and timing of the training still vary widely.[9] The only constant is legal instruction on the responsibilities imposed by the Codes of Practice in PACE. The more enlightened forces employ a form of certification to ensure the skill sets required for the modern custody suite are kept up to date, but they are a minority.

Too few forces give any thought to updating or refreshing the knowledge of their custody staff.[10] This fits with the general police attitude to training, which is that it represents an expensive abstraction from policing duties. The volume and variety of new criminal laws that have been created in the last decade have swamped the police service and only the most critical are given any serious training consideration. To illustrate this point one need only refer to the recent sweeping amendments to the law of arrest (discussed in chapter eight by Ed Cape in this collection). In response to the changes brought in by the Serious Organised Crime and Police Act 2005, which came into effect from midnight on 31 December 2005, several forces circulated an e-mail on the afternoon of that day outlining the necessity test criteria for making arrests and the impact necessity was to have on the assessment for grounds for detention.

In 2006, the National Centre for Policing Excellence (NCPE) on behalf of the Association of Chief Police Officers and the Home Office published 'Guidance on the safer detention and handling of persons in police custody'. This publication is based upon the Codes of Practice within PACE but goes further in that it deals with pre-arrest issues, transportation of arrested persons, custody suite staffing

---

[8]  Police Complaints Authority, *Custody Officer Training: Investing in Safety* (London, PCA, 1998).

[9]  The author recently surveyed 21 forces at random, including the three biggest in the UK. Courses varied between four weeks and five days.

[10]  Three Forces of the 21 surveyed carried out refresher training, three days every three years.

issues, training, and the standard of buildings used for detaining those in police custody. It is considered by many to be the 'gold standard' of how police detention should be carried out,[11] but few forces are anywhere near being able to comply fully with the recommendations made within it owing to budgetary restraints. Currently there is no incentive to comply, as compliance does not yet form part of any Home Office target.

The few custody practitioners who have seen 'Guidance on Safer Detentions' welcome what they regard as an attempt to further professionalise the working practices within a custody suite. They suspect however that the real intention is to pave the way to civilianising custody suites altogether. An amendment to PACE prohibiting those who have not received training under a nationally accredited scheme from working within a custody suite would go a long way to ensuring a safer and more professional process.

# VI  Information technology

When I first stood behind a custody desk, the computerised system that I used was a stand-alone system, devised by a local ex-custody sergeant and our force IT department. A simple windows based application, it was relatively easy to operate and captured all the information that was required at that time. Given a compliant sober detainee, it was possible, (though not always desirable), to process the individual within 10 minutes. The drawback of the system was that it could not share information with other systems or custody units within the force.

By the late 1990s this system had progressed further, and was linked to the other two custody suites within the force area. The data capture had extended to include questions around the wellbeing of the detainee, the circumstances surrounding the arrest, and whether any physical force or restraint had been used on the detainee prior to or during the arrest. The process then took around 20 minutes for that same compliant detainee. My force custody computer system worked well, but again, it could not be linked to external systems, nor could it be viewed from outside of the force IT system. Most forces had by this time, installed some form of computerised system. Video and audio coverage of the custody desk and cell passage was also now a well established feature of a modern custody suite.

In June 2004 the Bichard Inquiry report was published following the conviction of Ian Huntley for the murder of Holly Wells and Jessica Chapman. Central to its recommendations was the creation of a national criminal intelligence system, together with a code of practice for the creation, editing and sharing of criminal intelligence by all police forces across England and Wales. Part of the

---

[11]  The author was involved in the consultation for the document, and all the recommendations made by the PFEW custody practitioner forum were ignored!

intelligence gathering process would include details of persons arrested and detained in police custody, together with a host of personal information about that individual and their offending behaviour. This had long been an aspiration of the police service, but in practice each of the 43 forces had purchased the system their financial resources allowed. Work on a national system was taking place prior to the Bichard report, but the recommendations gave added impetus to the project.[12] Here then was an opportunity to create a new system from scratch, which would be standard across the whole of England and Wales, would capture the relevant information in a 'one time', easy to use process, and once captured, could produce court paperwork cutting down the bureaucracy and time spent by front line police officers in preparing files.

Well that was the theory. At least seven years and millions of pounds later, no such system exists. Some forces do have systems that link custody with file preparation in some fashion or other; others have information systems which supply information about a detainee as soon as nominal details are entered into a custody record. Chief officers are still deciding which technology they will buy, based on what their force budgets allow. There are few shared priorities, with some forces placing the emphasis on custody and file preparation systems, while others focus on intelligence.

What has this to do with PACE? Where these new systems are employed, booking that compliant detainee into the custody unit now takes between 40 and 50 minutes. This means less time for the custody staff to exercise all the other requirements of PACE in respect of those already in custody. The systems are not user friendly and require far more information than is required by PACE or the custody suite staff. Custody staffs are spending their time servicing the needs of complex computer systems and concentrating less on the welfare of detained persons. Frustration at the time required to populate the systems is leading to custody sergeants suffering even more stress. Despite their best intentions, the police service are introducing systems that not only fail to assist the already overworked custody staff but in fact add to their burdens. They are prolonging the custody process and adding little of value to the outcome. Adding to the custody officer's woes, the new system of CPS charging is operating to similar effect.

# VII CPS charging

Introduced in May 2004, 'Guidance to Police Officers and Crown Prosecutors' was issued by the Director of Public Prosecutions under section 37A of PACE. It effectively eliminated large areas of the decision making powers of custody

---

[12] The author recalls visiting in 2000 a Chippenham based company which at that time was working on a custody and case preparation system for the police service.

sergeants in respect of the charging of detainees. Apparently, custody sergeants were making too many wrong decisions, leading to too many discontinued cases.

The initial interpretation of the guidance in at least some areas was to the effect that in all but the simplest public order, theft and road traffic matters, any decision to charge a detainee had to be referred to a crown prosecutor.[13] On the face of it, asking a lawyer with specific knowledge of the criminal law to decide if all the elements of any given offence are present prior to charging does not seem unreasonable. One might think that this innovation would be welcomed by the overworked custody sergeant. Potentially all they need to do now is direct the investigating officer to consult with the duty crown prosecutor and act upon any advice received. Again, the reality is far from the simple process envisaged.

Crown prosecutors, unlike police officers, do not like the dark. At least that is the conclusion that most custody sergeants have come to, as the one person you will not find at night in a custody suite is a crown prosecutor. They are rather scarce at weekends too, and should you stray into a custody suite away from one of the larger metropolitan areas, it is unlikely that you will find a crown prosecutor in the custody suite, as they only appear between certain hours on certain days. This is not the fault of the prosecutors. There are simply too few of them to service the number of cases and custody suites that exist.

Most investigating officers make contact with a prosecutor by telephone, and then, at the latter's request, spend considerable time faxing documents, statements etc, to the prosecutor so that a decision around charging can be made. This is now a major cause of police officers being abstracted from front line policing.

Of even greater concern is the effect it is having on the processing of suspects. Delays to the PACE custody process of many hours are not uncommon. Custody staff are concerned by these delays and believe that the power conferred by PACE to detain a person to decide whether to charge, is being, in effect, abused. They are fearful that they may face criticism or disciplinary action should the practice be challenged. The official guidance covers situations where a prosecutor cannot be contacted, and recommends the detainee be bailed pending a decision being made later. What it does not cover is how long custody staff should continue to detain a person pending a decision from a prosecutor. In any case, bailing suspects to return to police stations further adds to the congestion in custody suites. This is because returning suspects require all the initial rights and entitlements conferred by PACE and the re-opening of the original custody record. Risk assessments also have to be reconsidered. All of this is necessitated because an appropriate charge could not be preferred by the custody sergeant during their original visit.

There is also room for concern about the substantive decisions that prosecutors are likely to make in the realm of charging. All police forces in England and

---

[13]   This interpretation of the guidance appears to have been unduly restrictive, perhaps as a result of over-zealous instructions from chief constables to custody officers and criminal justice units. For a legal analysis of the guidance see ch 10 by John Jackson in this collection.

Wales are obliged to set and meet targets in respect of 'sanctioned' detections. A 'sanctioned' detection is the disposal of an alleged crime in a manner which correlates to criteria set down by the Home Office. In short, if it does not conform to the criteria, it does not count as a 'detection'. Detections can be persons charged, cautioned, or latterly, issued with a fixed penalty notice. CPS targets, by contrast, focus on conviction rates for those placed before a court. Very little mental acuity is required to realise that these targets are not mutually compatible. Anecdotally, police officers state that the CPS are reluctant to put before a court anything other than cast iron cases so as better to meet their performance targets. Thus cases that could realistically be charged as serious offences are either not charged at all or downgraded to something that is easier to prove.

Custody sergeants and many investigators question whether any real benefit has been derived from the CPS charging system as it was initially implemented. If crown prosecutors were available in every custody suite 24 hours a day, every day, there would at least be some logic to the decision to exclude custody sergeants from the decision making process. The more cynical among the custody suite staff see CPS charging as yet another way of undermining the status of custody sergeant in order to make it easier to civilianise the role. Latterly discussions have taken place to restore (de facto) some of the custody sergeant's powers to charge in a greater range of cases (in line with the official guidance) and the CPS now accept that far too much time has been spent in needless file preparation. The re-introduction of the short prosecution file system is to be welcomed, and should help reduce the queues in custody suites across the land.

# VIII  Mental health

Section 136 of the Mental Health Act 1983 places a duty on uniformed police officers to remove to a place of safety any person in a public place that appears to be suffering from a mental disorder. 'A place of safety' is defined within the Act as a hospital, or any other designated medical facility, or a police station. The power to detain a person suspected of suffering from a mental disorder exists to provide suitably qualified medical professionals with the opportunity to examine and diagnose whether the individual is in fact suffering from such a disorder. The Act allows detention for up to 72 hours to carry out this procedure.

There are few medically qualified persons routinely in police stations in England and Wales, and yet in the twenty-first century an estimated 11,000 mentally ill people will be taken to police cells every year. The estimation is based on my own research carried out through the Custody Forum. I asked the representatives of the 8 police regions in England and Wales to provide figures for the number of section 136 arrests brought to custody suites. Further study of the figures provided indicates that the mentally ill spend on average twice as long in a police cell as those arrested for criminal offences (12 hours compared with six hours). Clearly this has an impact on the ability of custody staff to discharge their duties to other detainees. The mentally ill often require one-to-one supervision to prevent them from self harming. The supervision is usually undertaken by an ordinary police officer with no specialist training, called in to the suite from their street policing duties. Apart from the impact on the custody suite, local policing resilience, and the detrimental effect on the individual being locked up for being sick as opposed to being a criminal, I find it hard to justify the situation given that this is the twenty-first and not the eigtheenth century.

I have raised this issue at the highest level, and obtained agreement from every quarter that the situation is unsatisfactory and needs to change, but as yet there are no concrete legal proposals to do so. Hospitals, despite being places of safety, refuse to accept the mentally ill for a variety of reasons. The most common excuse is that they do not have the facilities, or the staff to cope with them. Close behind is that the detainee may have taken non-prescribed drugs or be under the influence of alcohol.

The whole issue of the care and treatment of persons suffering from a medical complaint, drink or drug overdose requires urgent review. It is the contention of the PFEW that the Health Services do not do enough to assist in this area, and should be mandated to do so. It makes no sense at all that a person too drunk to look after themselves or a person suffering the effects of a drugs overdose, should be cared for by untrained custody staff at a police station because they were deemed too unruly to go to hospital. Custody sergeants would like to see a clear statement in any revision of PACE that the police are not healthcare providers and that only those persons suffering from minor ailments or injury should be brought to a custody suite.

The PFEW together with the Mental Health Alliance are campaigning to have police stations removed from the definition of a place of safety in the new Mental Health Bill which is currently making its way through parliament. It is unlikely that they will succeed. The IPCC statistical research shows that almost half of those dying in police custody are, or have been, under treatment for a mental illness.

As a fall back position, an amendment to PACE limiting the time the mentally ill can be detained in police cells to six hours (the first review period) should be introduced. This would have the effect of negating most of the hospitals' concerns around drugs and alcohol, allow even the most under-resourced or incompetent local authority mental health team to assess the detainee, and most importantly, reduce the risk of further deaths in police custody.

# IX  The future

When I asked a number of custody sergeants where they saw PACE going in the future, there was little enthusiasm for any changes. This was because most of those I spoke to did not believe that they or future police sergeants would be in the custody suites to benefit from any change. They view as ironic the publication by the Home Office of a consultation paper on reviewing PACE,[14] whilst at the same time a number of chief constables are drawing up business cases to remove police officers from custody altogether.[15]

Opinion is divided as to whether the PFEW should continue to campaign to retain police sergeants as custody officers, with a minority taking the view that the chief constable should be allowed to civilianise it. Given the stress and pressures custody sergeants are under, the view is understandable though mis-guided. The whole point of PACE is that the detention process is administered by a competent independent individual, who is directly answerable at law for their actions. That requires that the custody officer be an office holder not an employee of a chief constable.

But let us say that common sense prevails, and custody sergeants remain at their posts. What practical alterations to the existing Codes of Practice would benefit custody staff as a whole?

There are many sections within the Codes of Practice which place duties on custody staff to perform tasks within set time frames, but none that place time restraints on any other individuals or agencies involved in the custody process. This often means police officers are waiting around for other professionals to attend the custody suite. Patrol time is lost, the detainee spends longer in custody and, in more complex enquiries, valuable time is lost from the investigation PACE clock. It would be desirable therefore to place time limits on the attendance of some of these other professionals, or if that cannot be achieved, the PACE clock should be stopped until such time as they can attend. Interpreters, appropriate adults, doctors and other medical professionals should all be able to attend the custody suite within a set time frame.

Timely attendance is even more crucial when the detainee has been arrested under section 136 of the Mental Health Act 1983. Anyone who has even spent time in a police custody suite will know that it is not a place of safety for the sick and if police stations cannot be removed from the Mental Health Act, PACE should limit the amount of time such detainees can be kept in police cells to a maximum of six hours.

---

[14]  Home Office, *Modernising Police Powers: Review of the Police and Criminal Evidence Act (PACE) 1984* (London, Home Office, March 2007).

[15]  Thames Valley are leading the way by advertising for 15 civilian custody officers. The plan is to recruit retiring custody sergeants.

# X  Conclusion

There is much in PACE that is as sensible and relevant today as it was in 1986. Publications such as *Guidance on the safer detention & handling of persons in police custody* (2006)[16] have taken PACE as a foundation and will no doubt expand upon the diverse strands that the Codes of Practice incorporate. Many of the things that the PFEW has pushed for in respect of better custody facilities, better training for custody staff, and better medical provision within custody suites, are all now on their way to fruition, but the ironic result is that most custody sergeants see no future for themselves within custody units.

Custody sergeants are not against change, and would welcome the help that could be afforded by trained civilian custody assistants. Custody assistants could carry out many of the functions of the custody sergeant, but stop short of having the full powers of a custody sergeant in respect of authorising detention and negotiating the charge and bail process. This would maintain the current clear lines of communication and supervision, vital to keeping the custody process safe. A trained, experienced police sergeant has the power and authority to safeguard the independence and integrity of the process, and does not have the obligations owed by an employee to an employer.

The challenge then, as custody sergeants see it, is to professionalise the profile of custody officer without compromising its integrity by opening it up to non-police officers to fulfil the role. They want better training, a fairer interpretation of the Codes of Practice when things go wrong, and a re-balancing of the Codes to impose some restrictions on other professions which impact on the functions of PACE. They would like to see the return of the power of charging to the custody sergeant, whilst utilising the scant CPS resources for consultation and guidance in more complex cases.

Facilities must also improve in line with the recommendations in *Guidance on the safer detention & handling of persons in police custody* (2006).[17] This is not to say that custody officers are in favour of the recent trend to build 'super bridewells' which house in excess of 50 detainees at a time, because they in turn bring a new set of problems around transportation, evacuation, and general supervision. Finally, they would like to be consulted locally about the changes that are happening to the custody process in their custody suites, as they have an enormous depth of experience which they could share if only they were asked.

---

[16] Available at http://police.homeoffice.gov.uk/publications/operational-policing/Safer_Detention _and_Handlin1.pdf?view=Binary (accessed 12 June 2008).

[17] *Ibid.*

# 5

## Keeping PACE? Some Front Line Policing Perspectives

JOHN LONG*

## I  Introduction

Two decades after its implementation, the Police and Criminal Evidence Act 1984 (PACE) remains the central legal framework within which front line police officers pursue their work. For most currently serving officers it has been the only legislation they have known relating to policing activities such as stop and search, the arrest and questioning of suspects, and the securing of evidence. Of course, the Act has been revised and updated many times but, as far as the practitioners are concerned, PACE has become a way of working life and arguably has actually had an impact on the underlying practices and culture of policing.[1]

That working life has changed significantly in other ways, however. Because of this, whether PACE still represents a framework that achieves the balance in the criminal process that provided the fundamental reason for its inception is a legitimate question. Police reforms, organisational restructuring, resource levels and technological advances raise very functional considerations. Globalisation, organised crime networks and international terrorism all present different natures of threat to those being tackled by the police when PACE was conceived. Societal change and shifting public expectations provide others. This latter context is crucial, as it is arguably the dynamic that exists between front line policing practitioners and the wider public that will determine the success of policing. Having acknowledged this, discussion here will focus on some front line policing perspectives, which may provide indicators of whether PACE still offers

* I would like to thank Martin Jauch (former Chief Superintendent, Metropolitan Police) for his recollections and astute insights on some of the historical context and policing procedures c1984. Also, many thanks to Richard Young for his thoughts and encouragement on my early drafts.
[1] For a discussion on this point see R Reiner, *The Politics of the Police* 3rd edn (Oxford, Oxford University Press, 2000) 182–3 (hereafter Reiner).

the legal framework within which its original objectives may be achieved, or whether it is now struggling to keep pace with over 20 years of change.

## II   Front line policing circa 1984

If aspects of change are to be considered, it is worth reviewing the context within which front line police officers worked in the early 1980s. There are ample commentaries on the arrival of PACE, related police powers and their implications for the police and policing.[2] For police officers at that time it represented probably the most dramatic change to working practices they had yet seen. Coincidently, the author joined the Metropolitan Police in 1984, the very year the Act received royal assent, prior to its full implementation in 1986. It is the case that whilst PACE has often understandably been seen as increasing police powers, to some extent it actually just replaced and rationalised existing powers provided by a melee of long-standing legislation. Arriving at Hammersmith Police Station in 1985, this writer had been trained at the Metropolitan Police training college at Hendon to execute stop and search, arrest and questioning under the Judges Rules[3] as well as under legislation such as the Vagrancy Act 1824; the numerous Metropolitan Police Acts (from 1829 through to 1899); the Licensing Act 1872; the Theft Act 1968; the Firearms Act 1968; and the Misuse of Drugs Act 1971. Outside London, officers enforced similar powers conferred by local by-laws. Although it was to some extent replaced by the Criminal Attempts Act 1981, still of recent infamy was the 'Sus law', the name given to stop and search powers that permitted a police officer to act purely on suspicion. The power originated from sections 4 and 6 of the Vagrancy Act 1824, which made it 'illegal for a suspected person or reputed thief to frequent or loiter in a public place with intent to commit an arrestable offence'.

Arrested persons were booked in by station sergeants, onto vast handwritten sheets, which, despite not carrying the detailed logs of current day custody records, were filed in large protective binders of Dickensian proportions. These

---

[2]   See K Lidstone and C Palmer, *The Investigation of Crime—a Guide to Police Powers*, 2nd edn (London, Butterworths, 1996); D Brown, *PACE ten years on: a review of the research*, Home Office Research Study 155 (London, Home Office, 1997) (hereafter Brown); D Dixon, *Law in Policing* (Oxford, Clarendon Press, 1997); Reiner, n 1 above; A Sanders and R Young, 'From Suspect to Trial', in M Maguire, R Morgan and R Reiner (eds) *The Oxford Handbook of Criminology*, 3rd edn (Oxford, Oxford University Press, 2002) 1034; A Sanders and R Young, 'Police Powers', in T Newburn (ed) *The Handbook of Policing* (Cullompton, Willan Publishing, 2003) 228 (hereafter Sanders and Young, 2003); A Ashworth and M Redmayne, *The Criminal Process*, 3rd edn (Oxford, Oxford University Press, 2005) (hereafter Ashworth and Redmayne); L Jason-Lloyd, *An Introduction to Policing and Police Powers*, 2nd edn (London, Cavendish, 2005); M Zander, *The Police and Criminal Evidence Act*, 5th edn (London, Sweet & Maxwell, 2005); A Sanders and R Young, *Criminal Justice* 3rd edn (Oxford, Oxford University Press, 2007) (hereafter Sanders and Young, 2007).

[3]   See ch 10 by John Jackson in this collection for an interesting perspective on the Judges Rules and related matters.

were separated into 'Charges' and 'Refused Charges'. It is worth noting that the assumption was strongly in favour of a charge and a refused charge was viewed dimly, with 'steps to allay a sense of grievance' (Metropolitan Police General Order 23/25) then being required. This would attract the personal attention of the chief superintendent. Custody facilities dated back to the previous century in some police stations, and even the more modern had poor cell provision, including massive 'drunk tanks' which were used to house several detainees at once until they 'sobered up'. Computer-based systems were years away. Indeed, calls for assistance to the station were still written on note pads. Once dealt with, they were placed on spike holders until filed. Many of the safeguards of PACE now taken for granted were not systematically provided. For example, the term 'appropriate adult' was not yet in use and it was often a matter of personal judgement by the arresting officer or station sergeant as to how the vulnerability of suspects should affect their treatment. The problems that this could cause had been famously illustrated in 1972, in the Maxwell Confait murder case, which was still in the memory of pre-PACE officers.[4] An 18 year-old suspect with learning difficulties had been interviewed without a guardian being present. In 1975, partly as a result of this, he had his conviction overturned.

Unlike the current situation, before PACE the majority of prosecutions at magistrates' courts were presented by police officers themselves. Only in the early 1980s did this role start to pass to designated police court officers, supported by police solicitors departments and prosecution units. For the front line officer, presenting a case at court was often a daunting prospect. Sergeants, for example, could find themselves presenting quite complex and serious cases, albeit those which were either summary only or where trial by jury had not been elected. Offences relating to fatal traffic collisions are a good example. Subsequently, prosecution became the role of the Crown Prosecution Service (CPS) when it was established in 1986, under the Prosecution of Offences Act 1985.[5] The observation amongst many experienced officers is that there is much less opportunity to even give evidence in court as an arresting officer or witness than was the case in the pre-PACE years. This may have had an impact on levels of competence in court, which in some cases may reduce the credibility of the evidence police officers have secured, even though they may have complied fully with PACE.

---

[4] H Fisher, *Report of an inquiry by the Hon. Sir Henry Fisher into the circumstances leading to the trial of three persons on charges arising out of the death of Maxwell Confait and the fire at 27 Doggett Road, London SE6* (London, HMSO, 1977). See ch 3 by Andrew Sanders in this collection for fuller discussion of this case.

[5] See Ashworth and Redmayne, n 2 above, 175.

For the post-Lord Edmund Davies review[6] police officer, it was the Scarman Report[7] into the Brixton riots, which set the tone for much of the change initiated at that time. This followed similar disorders in St Paul's, Bristol in 1980 and Toxteth, Liverpool in 1981. Involvement in the policing of the miners' dispute was another recent experience for many operational front line officers nationally. It was an event which was arguably to change the nature of the relationship between the police and government during the mid-1980s.[8]

A social policy issue of the period, which is often overlooked in terms of its relevance for policing, was the acceleration by the then conservative government of 'care in the community'. Following on from the Mental Health Act 1983 and longer-term health policy to downsize institutional care, many hospitals and institutions specialising in mental health care were closed. This increased the demands on front line police officers as they found themselves managing significantly more incidents involving former patients who had been discharged into the community and who, for many reasons, were struggling with the transition. The police often became the carers of last resort and it is a situation which has not been entirely resolved even today. The safeguards that were introduced by PACE to protect vulnerable suspects therefore had an even wider relevance than perhaps anticipated.

# III   PACE ten years on

In spite of the quite different approaches required to comply with PACE, commentators were able to observe some positive progress in the years following its introduction in the way the police conducted activities within the criminal process.[9] In *PACE ten years on: a review of the research*, Brown provides some evidence of this, albeit still finding a mixed picture.[10] For example, the requirement within section 1 to record stop and search encounters had led to better recording of grounds. This was a long way from the writer's recollection of the pre-PACE situation, where only 'resented' stops were recorded, based on the subjective assessment of the officer involved. However, after 10 years of PACE,

---

[6] The Edmund Davies Review radically changed the pay and conditions of police officers to address the problems in recruiting faced at that time. See Lord Edmund-Davies, *Report of the Committee of Inquiry on the Police* (London, HMSO, 1978); T Newburn, 'Understanding policing', in T Newburn (ed) *The Handbook of Policing* (Cullompton, Willan Publishing, 2003) 1–10.

[7] Lord Scarman, *The Scarman Report* (Harmondsworth, Penguin Books, 1982).

[8] See B Fine and R Millar (eds), *Policing the Miners' Strike* (London, Lawrence & Wishart, 1985); S McCabe and P Wallington with J Alderson, L Gostin and C Mason, *The Police, Public Order and Civil Liberties: Legacies of the Miners' Strike* (London, Routledge, 1988); R Reiner, *Chief Constables* (Oxford, Oxford University Press, 1991); PAJ Waddington, *The Strong Arm of the Law* (Oxford, Oxford University Press, 1991).

[9] See, eg Brown, n 2 above; Reiner, n 1 above.

[10] Brown, n 2 above.

doubts were still expressed regarding the validity of the reasons for search and the disproportionate use on persons from black and minority ethnic groups.[11] Arrests were being made on a more grounded evidential basis but there still appeared to be issues of disproportionality and a lack of scrutiny by custody officers. Detainees were generally being made aware of their legal rights and the proportion obtaining legal advice in the station doubled under PACE.[12] However, this increase in the accessing of legal advice at police stations did not necessarily guarantee that the legal rights of detainees were being protected or advanced, as required by Code C of PACE. For instance, it seems that it is not always the case that the standard of legal advice given by police station lawyers or their representatives is sufficient to achieve this.[13] It has also been argued that often the police employ questionable methods to deny these legal rights in a less visible way,[14] although Brown challenges this to some extent.

Improvements in the conduct of interviews have also been noted in research, particularly around the use of audio tapes, which led to fewer disputes about the content of interviews. For the front line officer, changes to interviewing procedures represented a radical change to working practices, increasing the training need and requiring a different type of experiential learning to be compliant with PACE and to become competent in obtaining evidence through questioning. This latter point gained more importance over time. The immediate post-PACE preoccupation for the practitioner of learning the practicalities of how to use the equipment, apply seals and maintain continuity of exhibits, did not guarantee compliance with the Act. The conduct of the interview was obviously critical too. The increased transparency of this aspect of the investigation, brought about by the audio-taping of interviews, has probably been a contributory factor to the more developed interview methods in which officers are now trained.

In spite of the progress made, Brown concluded that 'it would be difficult to argue that PACE has produced a system that is in a state of balance'.[15] He identified four preconditions for successful regulation of police powers within the pre-trial criminal process. These were: that new rules should be clearly expressed; implementation should be accompanied by adequate training; rules should be backed up by effective sanctions and supervision; and the public needed to be aware of their rights and police powers.

These preconditions will be revisited later. However, the experience of officers regarding the second of these preconditions, namely training, had already been highly variable across different forces. This writer's own experience of the initial

---

[11]  *Ibid*, 245.

[12]  *Ibid*, 244.

[13]  For discussions of this see E Cape and J Hickman, 'Bad lawyer, good defence' (2002) 152 *New Law Journal* 1194; and E Cape and J Luqmani, *Defending Suspects at Police Stations* (London, Legal Action Group, 2006).

[14]  See M McConville, A Sanders and R Leng *The Case for the Prosecution* (London, Routledge, 1991).

[15]  Brown, n 2 above, 254.

PACE training delivered by the Metropolitan Police, prior to a 'dry-run' introductory period in 1985, was that it was delivered on a single day within the police station. It hardly seems credible, in retrospect, that all the legal aspects of PACE relevant to the front line officer could adequately be covered in just those few hours. The Act's objectives, and why the criminal process was being changed to achieve a certain balance, were hardly touched upon at all and this must inevitably have had an impact on how it was interpreted by practitioners. Much of the knowledge of PACE in its early years was gained by officers being required to study for promotion examinations to sergeant and inspector and this did not represent a systematic approach. Of course, the training demands brought about by legislative change are significant and front line officers and staff need to be taken away from their duties on a regular basis to meet these demands. This, however, represents one of the necessary costs of change, particularly where reasonable, proportionate and balanced implementation of legislation is crucial to its objectives.

Going into the early 1990s, the review of the police service undertaken by Sheehy[16] typified the mood for a shift to a more resource-conscious, contracted-out, managerialist and performance-driven model for policing.[17] Sheehy recommended a flatter management structure for the service and the removal of two ranks. In practice, the rank structure, after some initial revision, retained its original format but there was an acceleration of the existing thinning out of the senior posts responsible for front line policing. The reduction of management overheads was often rationalised in terms of returning more officers to the front line but, as the data on police force sizes in the 1990s shows,[18] this actually failed to materialise in terms of absolute numbers. The relevance here for PACE concerns the key roles which that legislation introduced for officers of superintending rank, for example, in relation to road checks for search purposes (section 4); extensions of detention beyond 24 hours without charge (section 42); and the taking of some samples (sections 62 and 63). The trend to amalgamate police Basic Command Units (BCUs) and reduce oncosts lowered the numbers of senior officers available to carry out these functions. For example, there were 1,668 officers of superintending rank in England and Wales in 1994, but this had fallen to 1,256 by 2003, a reduction of 24.7 per cent.[19] Subsequently, the seniority level required for authorisation of the taking of samples has been lowered with more recent revisions of the Codes.

---

[16] Sir Patrick Sheehy, Chairman of British American Tobacco, was appointed to oversee a review of police pay and conditions. See Home Office, *Inquiry into Police Responsibilities and Reward* (London, Home Office, 1993).

[17] See T Newburn, 'Policing since 1945', in T Newburn (ed), *The Handbook of Policing* (Cullompton, Willan Publishing, 2003) 84, which summarises progress in this direction.

[18] M Clegg and S Kirwan, *Police service strength: England and Wales, 31 March 2006*, Home Office Statistical Bulletin 13/06 (London, Home Office, 2006).

[19] *Ibid.*

Another development towards the end of the first decade of PACE, which had a major impact on front line staff, was the introduction of nationally standardised forms for building case files. These were labelled 'MG Forms', alluding to the 'National Manual of Guidance' for file preparation, and they started to appear across England and Wales in 1993. Still in use today (with many additions), they were seen by many practitioners as another significant increase to the bureaucratic burden of police work, introducing numerous specific standard forms for all steps of the arrest, detention and pre-trial process. Completing this paperwork is time consuming, certainly more so than when PACE was first implemented. The introduction of the Criminal Procedure and Investigations Act 1996 (CPIA), covering disclosure, further increased this impact.[20] However, many would see these forms as representing an enhanced professional standard and some forces have reduced the bureaucratic burden through the effective use of technology. As will be discussed later, however, the wide variation in relative resourcing levels between different forces, which affects many areas of service provision, means that the non-adoption of such enabling IT systems can often be attributed to lack of funds rather than a culpable failure to implement best practice. Consequently, competent investigation and observance of both the regulation and spirit of PACE may well be affected by bureaucracy and resourcing levels.

# IV  PACE: Into the second decade

More recent developments in the criminal process and police powers in particular are well covered elsewhere[21] and these contribute to an ever more complex picture of statutory, regulatory and practical matters that the front line police practitioner must take into account. Similarly, the nature of policing and its context has continued to change.[22] A comprehensive review of these developments will not be attempted here. However, five key issues which have had a particular impact on front line policing and PACE are considered in an attempt

---

[20]  See Ashworth and Redmayne, n 2 above, 239.

[21]  Legislation has constantly been introduced and updated over the past decade. For a good appreciation of the ways that this has affected relevant police powers see Reiner, n 1 above; Ashworth and Redmayne, n 2 above; L Jason-Lloyd, *An Introduction to Policing and Police Powers*, 2nd edn (London, Cavendish, 2005); T Newburn and R Reiner, 'From PC Dixon to Dixon PLC: Policing and Police Powers Since 1954' [2004] *Crim LR* 601; M Zander, *The Police and Criminal Evidence Act*, 5th edn (London, Sweet & Maxwell, 2005); Sanders and Young, 2007, n 2 above.

[22]  For some of the more significant and emerging themes during the period see T Jones and T Newburn, *Private Security and Public Policing* (Oxford, Clarendon Press, 1998); Reiner, n 1 above; D Downes and R Morgan, 'The skeletons in the cupboard: the politics of law and order at the turn of the millennium', in M Maguire, R Morgan and R Reiner (eds), *The Oxford Handbook of Criminology*, 3rd edn (Oxford, Oxford University Press, 2002) 286–321; M Matassa and T Newburn, 'Policing and terrorism', 467, T Newburn, 'Policing since 1945', and T Newburn, 'The future of policing' 707, all in T Newburn (ed), *The Handbook of Policing* (Cullompton, Willan Publishing, 2003).

to gauge whether the Act has kept pace with developments. These are statutory charging, diversity, victim care, terrorism and performance management.

## A Statutory Charging Scheme

When PACE was fully introduced in 1986, the Prosecution of Offences Act 1985 had maintained police powers to bring charges. This changed with the Criminal Justice Act 2003, which introduced the provisions that now allow for the CPS to institute criminal proceedings against individuals. For the front line officer, the main outcome of this change is experienced through the statutory charging scheme. The aims of the statutory charging scheme are to sift out 'hopeless cases' earlier; produce stronger prosecution cases; reduce delays between charge and disposal; and lower the number of cases that later 'crack' at court through the acceptance of pleas to reduce charges.[23] Through this scheme, all but the more minor offences are referred to a CPS lawyer for charging decisions.[24] A threshold test is applied by the custody officer to ensure relevant cases are dealt with in this way.

The scheme represents a major change and it is hard to disagree with Ashworth and Redmayne's comment that 'the police may need to change their outlook and the CPS may need to satisfy them of their competence to reach sound charging decisions'.[25] The statutory charging scheme does, however, have some practical problems that need addressing.

The placement of CPS staff at police stations to work more closely alongside the police was piloted in different forces prior to the scheme being instituted. CPS lawyers are now regularly deployed in police custody suites to facilitate statutory charging. However, the level of service provided can vary from place to place. It seems clear that the CPS on occasion struggles to sustain such a presence on its current resources. Officers have either to make appointments to see lawyers when they are in attendance or deal with matters on the telephone, using the services of CPS Direct. On occasion this can create some tension between operational officers, who have to deal with arrested persons on a seven days a week basis whilst on shift work, and their counterparts in the CPS who are also under time and resource pressures. This can literally take hours, with in some places officers actually queuing for long periods waiting their turn to see a CPS lawyer! Until recently, this was exacerbated by the fact that section 42 of PACE only permitted a person to be detained without charge on an extended basis 'to secure or preserve evidence relating to an offence for which he is under arrest or to obtain such evidence by questioning him'. Technically, a detainee was not to be held longer merely so the CPS could be consulted for pre-charge advice or a charging decision. Therefore, delays had real implications for investigating officers and

---

[23] See I Brownlee, 'The Statutory Charging Scheme in England and Wales: Towards a Unified Prosecution System?' [2004] *Crim LR* 896.

[24] See further ch 10 by John Jackson in this collection.

[25] Ashworth and Redmayne, n 2 above, 178.

relevant time. The use of bail could be considered on occasions but was not always be appropriate, particularly when a suspect was being held for a serious offence. Victims of certain types of offence, for example domestic violence, could be vulnerable should the detainee be released on bail prior to a delayed charging decision.

This position has now been addressed by the Police and Justice Act 2006, which brings about an amendment to section 37(7)(a) of PACE, effective from 15 January 2008. The outcome is an explicit power to detain and therefore extend detention, on the authority of a superintendent and to seek CPS advice after the necessary threshold test has been applied. However, whilst this means that investigations are not compromised in the ways already explained, there will be those who may well argue that, in the event of any logistical CPS delays, a suspect may be in danger of being held longer under investigative conditions than they need be. On this basis, arguably, the original spirit of the Act is potentially in tension with later developments. It is important, therefore, that the CPS is sufficiently resourced to support statutory charging.

## B Diversity

Just as the Scarman Report[26] was part of the context for the introduction of PACE, so the second decade of policing under the Act saw another hugely influential report urging change within the service. The Macpherson Report[27] detailed the findings of the Inquiry into the murder of Stephen Lawrence, which occurred on 22 April 1993. It not only highlighted the shortfalls in the way the murder was investigated but also the gap that still existed between the police and some ethnic minority communities.

The report is lengthy, with its 70 recommendations covering many areas of police activity, such as stop and search, incident response, investigation and victim care. However, the headlines were made by the Inquiry's conclusion that the police were institutionally racist. This indictment had a significant impact on many police officers for whom the accusation struck deep. Police practitioners will recall the immediate aftermath of the report as a period of low morale and high concern. This had various effects. For example, in the aftermath of Macpherson most forces saw a 25 per cent drop in the use of PACE stop and search powers between 1998 and 2002. Recommendation 60 of the Stephen Lawrence Inquiry Report had stated that existing stop and search powers under PACE should remain unchanged. However, many officers were apprehensive as to whether their discretion and judgement in using these powers would unreasonably be called into question. In reality, very few officers have actually been the

---

[26] Lord Scarman *The Scarman Report* (Harmondsworth, Penguin Books, 1982).
[27] W Macpherson, *The Stephen Lawrence Inquiry—Report* (Cm 4262–1) (London, HMSO, 1999).

subject of discipline as a result of a complaint being substantiated arising from an instance of stop and search. The fact is, however, that on the front line stop and search reduced, even as concerted management efforts were being made across forces to enhance the effectiveness of the tactic.[28]

Some observers argue that a reduction in the use of stop and search powers in itself increases its effectiveness. Arrest rates appear to increase as stop and search levels fall, perhaps reflecting 'the fact that the more often you perform a task, the less discriminating you tend to be'.[29] Commentators have observed that, ironically, this fall in stops has a further, more negative effect.[30] The reduction in stops on white people was sharper than the drop witnessed in their use against black people. This actually increased the disproportionate use of stop and search powers. More recently the use of stop and search powers has started to increase again, with a 14 per cent rise nationally during 2004/05.[31]

Recommendations 61, 62 and 63 of the Macpherson Report also merit attention. Recommendations 62 and 63 required Police Authorities to monitor the use of stops and searches and to ensure public awareness of these powers. Recommendation 61 proposed that *all* police stops should be recorded where a person has been asked to account for themselves, whether a search took place or not, with a copy of the record being given to that person. The Home Office reported that this recommendation had been implemented in all forces in England and Wales from 1 April 2005.[32] Initially, some practitioners and senior officers saw this as a further addition to the already significant burden of bureaucracy. This may have added to the reluctance of some to engage in stop and search tactics, but the provisions are now fully in place and it remains to be seen to what extent front line officers apply their powers and adhere to the safeguards. Changes to Code A of the PACE Codes of Practice were effected to outline how encounters were to be conducted and recorded, albeit that stops that do not involve searches are not provided for under statutory powers. This is an area where clarity for practitioners can be elusive. Police do not have a power at law merely to stop and question, so the inclusion of this activity within the Codes must not be interpreted by officers as providing that power. The existing legal ambiguity about how questions may be put when there is a power to search is challenging enough to understand. Recommendation 61 adds another aspect of

---

[28] Attempts to reinvigorate the use of these powers are discussed in N Bland, J Miller and P Quinton, *Managing the Use and Impact of Searches: A review of force interventions*, Police Research Series Paper 132 (London, Home Office, 2000).

[29] Sanders and Young, 2007, n 2 above, 97.

[30] *Ibid*, 83–4; B Bowling and C Phillips, 'Policing Ethnic Communities', in T Newburn (ed), *The Handbook of Policing* (Cullompton, Willan Publishing, 2003) 528.

[31] M Ayres and L Murray, *Arrests for Recorded Crime (Notifiable Offences) and the Operation of Certain Police Powers under PACE: England and Wales, 2004/05*, Home Office Statistical Bulletin 21/05 (London, Home Office, 2005).

[32] Home Office *Lawrence Steering Group 6th Annual Report 2005* (London, HMSO, 2005).

complexity for the practitioner, let alone for the lay person who, under Recommendation 63, police authorities must make aware of stop and search powers!

Since the Macpherson report, officers have received enhanced training in how to manage racist incidents, first aid (the standard of which at the scene of Stephen Lawrence's murder was criticised by Macpherson) victim care, investigative techniques, and stop and search. The police have also sought to establish more effective means of understanding the perspectives of diverse communities, notably through the establishment of Independent Advisory Groups (IAGs). Having initially been formed by the Metropolitan Police Service in 1998 as a response to the ongoing Macpherson Inquiry, IAGs have emerged in many forces nationally. They receive particular attention in the Morris Inquiry report,[33] which recognised their importance and urged that IAGs be properly resourced, transparent and accountable. Advising police on the sensitive application of their PACE powers in different communities is a common activity for IAGs.

This improvement in professional standards is obviously important as a direct response to the tragedy of Stephen Lawrence's death. More generally, analysis of the Inquiry report arguably raises two key points that have particular importance for front line police officers. These are that communities and individuals want to know that their problems are taken seriously by the police; and, secondly, that these problems are then dealt with competently. These are issues that certainly carry over into the policing activities governed by PACE. Some recent research based on the British Crime Survey (BCS) 2004/05 suggests that there may have been progress in the way the police apply their powers and deal with people's problems.[34] As well as the core sample of 45,000 adults surveyed for the BCS, a booster sample of 3,703 respondents from black and minority ethnic groups (BME groups) was surveyed to enable a more detailed analysis by ethnicity. Based on the reported experiences of the respondents, the research found that people from mixed, Asian and black ethnic groups were more likely to be stopped by police when in a vehicle, compared with people from white, Chinese and other ethnic groups.[35] However, there were no differences between the groups in the likelihood of being stopped when on foot.[36] The research also found that: 'The reasons for, and emotional reactions to, and the outcomes of being stopped were mostly similar between groups'.[37] A factor that was associated with a positive rating of the police was 'having some level of confidence that the Criminal Justice System is effective in bringing people who commit crimes to justice'.[38]

---

[33] W Morris, *The Report of the Morris Inquiry. The Case for Change: People in the Metropolitan Police Service* (London, Morris Inquiry, 2004).

[34] K Jansson, *Black and minority ethnic groups' experiences and perceptions of crime, racially motivated crime and the police: findings from the 2004/05 British Crime Survey*, Home Office Online Report 25/06 (London, Home Office, 2006).

[35] *Ibid*, 26–7 and 32.

[36] *Ibid*, 26.

[37] *Ibid*, 32.

[38] *Ibid*, 24.

For front line policing, issues of diversity are clearly important and any revision or replacement of PACE must continue to take account of this.

## C Victim Care

It is probably fair to say that it is the police practitioner who, amongst criminal justice system professionals, is likely to observe most closely the impact of a crime on the victim. As the second decade of PACE has progressed, the importance of advancing victims' interests has been re-emphasised in the formulation of criminal justice policy.[39]

Zedner notes how initial contact with police is often a satisfactory experience but that this worsens as cases progress and the victim moves through the pre-trial stage and court proceedings.[40] Here, their main part is as a provider of evidence and they have only peremptory contact with other agencies such as the CPS and Courts Service. The Victims Charter of 1996 attempted to improve victim care but it is unclear to what extent it really succeeded in doing so. Certainly, the perception through the media and some research is that victims and witnesses tend to have negative experiences of the criminal justice system.[41]

The most recent legislative attempt to improve this situation came in the form of the Domestic Violence, Crime and Victims Act 2004. Section 32 of the Act provides for the issuing of *The Code of Practice for Victims of Crime*. This came into full force in April 2006 and requires the police and 10 other agencies, including the CPS and Courts Service, to provide services for victims. Where victims are dissatisfied with the service given by any of the agencies, their complaint can be investigated by the Parliamentary Ombudsman, under the Parliamentary Commissioner Act 1967, as amended by schedule 7 to the Domestic Violence, Crime and Victims Act 2004. Police officers and staff have received training on relevant parts of the Code, which deal with providing information, family liaison, vulnerable and intimidated victims, and contact at key moments of an investigation, such as arrest, charge and bail of a suspect. Section 32 provides for codification of steps that many police officers would have felt were intrinsic parts of 'the job'. However, much of the research over an extended period would suggest these are matters that have not always been satisfactorily pursued.[42] Effective application of the codes, then, should improve matters.

So what relevance has this for PACE? In the same way as other emotive issues are seen on occasion to bring about disproportionate responses (for example, see

---

[39] For a discussion of this see A Crawford and J Goodey (eds), *Integrating a Victim Perspective within Criminal Justice: International Debates* (Aldershot, Ashgate, 2000).

[40] L Zedner, 'Victims', in M Maguire, R Morgan and R Reiner (eds), *The Oxford Handbook of Criminology*, 3rd edn (Oxford, Oxford University Press, 2002) 419–56.

[41] E Whitehead, *Key findings from the Witness Satisfaction Survey 2000*, Home Office Research Findings No 133 (London, Home Office, 2001).

[42] For some examples, see J Shapland, J Willmore and P Duff, *Victims and the Criminal Justice System* (Aldershot, Gower, 1985); T Newburn and S Merry, *Keeping in touch: Police—Victim*

the discussion on terrorism below), the cause of the victim is seen by some as potentially being hijacked by those seeking justification for unwarranted penal measures.[43] The widening of coercive powers under PACE has certainly been seen by many as unwarranted.[44]

At an individual level there is a risk that the operational police officer, in witnessing the impact of an offence on a victim, may feel under a moral pressure to arrest and bring an offender to justice. Reiner touches upon this in describing how officers may see their role as 'protection of the weak against the predatory'.[45] At one extreme, this can manifest itself in what has been termed 'noble cause corruption', the illegitimate breaking of rules to secure arrest, evidence and conviction. More likely is that front line officers may feel that they are an advocate for the victim beyond being just an investigator. Personal contact with victims will often have the potential to strengthen this perception, especially where they feel compassion for their plight.

Amongst the practical implications of this for the police officer are the ways in which they will then engage with other professionals in the criminal process, most notably the defence lawyer or the CPS. In an adversarial system, if an officer feels they are representing a victim rather than just securing evidence, both the suspect and their representative could well feel the brunt of that. Professional advice is given to defence solicitors in police stations to prepare themselves for possible antagonism from arresting or investigating officers when representing their client.[46] However, there are also many police practitioners who could detail examples of antagonistic and unconstructive contributions from members of the legal profession and other agencies. This sort of engagement between stakeholders within the criminal process would need to change in order to move towards something closer to a 'freedom model' of criminal justice as set out by Sanders and Young.[47] They argue strongly that it is essential not only that victims, suspects and offenders respect the criminal justice system[48] but also that 'it is so

---

*Communication in Two Areas*, Home Office Research Study 116 (London, HMSO, 1990); L Sims, and A Myhill, *Policing and the Public: Findings from the 2000 British Crime Survey*, Home Office Research Findings No 136 (London, Home Office, 2001).

[43] For example, D Garland, *The Culture of Control: Crime and Social Order in Contemporary Society* (Oxford, Oxford University Press, 2001); and L Zedner, 'Victims', in M Maguire, R Morgan and R Reiner (eds), *The Oxford Handbook of Criminology* 3rd edn (Oxford, Oxford University Press, 2002) 419, provide critiques.

[44] See the case put by Sanders and Young, 2003, n 2 above, 228; J Spencer, 'Prosecution Powers to Gather Evidence: The Case for Reform', in *Archbold News* Issue 8, September 2005 (London, Sweet & Maxwell, 2005); E Cape, 'Arresting developments: increased police powers of arrest' in *Legal Action*, January 2006, 24.

[45] Reiner, n 1 above, 89.

[46] For example, see E Cape and J Luqmani, *Defending Suspects at Police Stations* (London, Legal Action Group, 2006).

[47] Described in Sanders and Young, 2007, n 2 above, the model they advocate moves the criminal justice system question on from the familiar continuum of crime control to due process. It is mentioned here to illustrate that practitioners may remain working in the adversarial context whilst striving for a system that observes human rights and freedoms.

[48] *Ibid*, 48–9.

important that the police respect the rule of law'.[49] Few, if any, would argue against this latter point and it is true that the freedom of suspects and defendants should ideally be valued by officers alongside the freedom of victims. However, in practice, the legal framework within which stakeholders operate is a strong influence on how all parties engage. For the front line officer, the framework currently provided by PACE is not one which always sits easily alongside the values underpinning the Code of Practice for Victims of Crime. However, expectations around victim care are rightly higher than ever. There may be potential to develop processes to uphold the freedoms and interests of victims without disproportionate impact on the freedoms of suspects. Might this mean that, in the same way that suspects have the option to have legal advice and support, there needs to be an advocacy for victims that is provided independently from the police who are investigating whatever crime is alleged or suspected?

## D Terrorism

Even for the local front line officer, terrorism has been a consistent factor since PACE was implemented. The current intensity of views around 'the war on terror' can cloud the fact that terrorism was already a fact of life for many in the United Kingdom in the mid-1980s. For example, since the late 1960s over 3,000 people have lost their lives as a result of republican and loyalist terrorist activity in Northern Ireland and mainland UK.[50] The Lockerbie bombing, which brought down a Pan Am passenger flight on 21 December 1988, is also a reminder of the international dimensions of terrorism during the period soon after PACE's introduction. Consequently, PACE in its original form had already made particular provision for police officers to apply additional powers with regards to terrorism, specifically around extended periods of detention without charge.

The apparently ever more global and organised nature of international terrorism has heightened the sense of trepidation and intensified government efforts to tackle terrorist activities.[51] Matassa and Newburn list, for example, seven major legislative changes since 1996 that increase the powers to deal with terrorism.[52] The implications of involvement in the Iraq War and the spectre of the suicide bomber have provided an emotive rationale for this in more recent times. Thinking varies on what responses may prove effective across the range of

---

[49] *Ibid*, 49.

[50] A source that brings this into strong focus is D McKittrick, S Kelters, B Feeney and S Thornton, *Lost Lives: The Stories of the Men, Women and Children who Died as a Result of the Northern Ireland Troubles* (London, Mainstream Publishing, 1999).

[51] See Cabinet Office *The United Kingdom and the Campaign against International Terrorism* (London, Cabinet Office, 2002).

[52] See M Matassa and T Newburn 'Policing and terrorism' in T Newburn (ed), *The Handbook of Policing* (Cullompton, Willan Publishing, 2003) at 477–8. See also T Newburn, 'Policing since 1945' in the same collection at 467.

terrorist activity.[53] As far as new legislation is concerned, critics have argued that the outcomes of specific anti-terrorist laws can be counter-productive, especially if there is a disproportionate paring away of democratic values and human rights, as is arguably the case with extended detention without trial.[54] This emphasis on police powers can arise due to the pressure created by the threats posed, their perceived sophistication and the globalised nature of terrorist activities. However, as terrorism is often a political phenomenon, the solution is more likely to lie in the realm of politics than that of policing.[55]

The front line police officer must of course remain alert to the presence or threat of terrorist activity but its main relevance in the context of PACE is probably rather more mundane. Successive revisions of PACE and the additional separate legislation that has further defined police powers have created additional complexity, which is problematic for the practitioner attempting to interpret and apply it. This is also a challenge organisationally, as it will deepen the specialist knowledge required to deal with persons suspected of terrorist offences. Matassa and Newburn pursue the argument that 'the most successful policing strategies in relation to terrorism are precisely those that utilise normal policing methods'.[56] They go on to argue that 'anti-terrorist policing is . . . little different from other areas of policing and . . . with regard to the rules and procedures governing it, should be no different at all'.[57] So, on this basis, the arguments that have been made since the London Underground bombings in 2005, to revise PACE or introduce further laws to extend authorised periods of detention without charge, can be put in a different context. Due to the global nature of terrorism, it has been contended that effective investigation can no longer be achieved within previously accepted timescales. This point, if correct, would probably also equally apply to other forms of organised and trans-national crime. Therefore, the case for extending custodial powers arguably needs to be tested across all scenarios, not just terrorism.

The trend to professional specialisation that complexity in law and procedures can induce also reduces organisational flexibility to move practitioners across the broad range of police activities, as and when needed. Often, this has the effect of requiring greater resources, thus potentially detracting from the government's aim of achieving a cost-effective, efficient and integrated criminal justice system (this 'managerialist' approach is considered further in the following section).

---

[53] Some different perspectives are provided in L Freedman (ed), *Superterrorism: Policy Responses* (Oxford, Blackwell, 2002), including J Gearson, 'The Nature of Modern Terrorism' 7; and M Navias, 'Finance Warfare as a Response to International Terrorism' 57.

[54] For a discussion of this see H Fenwick, 'The Anti-Terrorism, Crime and Security Act 2001: a proportionate response to 11 September?' (2002) 65 *MLR* 724.

[55] A conclusion reached by M Matassa and T Newburn, 'Policing and terrorism' in T Newburn (ed), *The Handbook of Policing* (Cullompton, Willan Publishing, 2003) 467.

[56] *Ibid*, 485–6.

[57] *Ibid*, 495.

In terms of front line policing then, the way that PACE has been affected by responses to the threat of terrorism is an interesting case study in what can happen when legislation is introduced to tackle an issue in isolation from other considerations. For example, the costs of a lack of clarity can be seen from a number of different perspectives, appertaining to human rights, natural justice, effectiveness of the criminal process and resources. From the point of view of the police practitioner, this need for clarity crosses all aspects of police activity touched by PACE and not just the policing of terrorism.

## E Police Performance and 'Managerialism'

Another feature of the latter years of policing in the post-PACE world that marks it out from policing in the 1980s is the move towards what has been termed 'managerialism'. The police have by no means been alone in the public sector in taking on the principles of 'new public management',[58] but a vocabulary that includes 'Best Value',[59] 'Quality of Service Commitment'[60] and 'performance league tables'[61] is now common within the Service.

McLaughlin et al argue that this managerialism is being fostered by government in its attempt to achieve a cost-effective, efficient and integrated criminal justice system.[62] Three aspects that epitomise this new public management are the focus on results; the setting of targets and performance indicators; and the publication of league tables to compare performance. The most obvious manifestation of the application of these aspects for the police comes in the publication of monthly national performance league tables on the system known as 'iQuanta'. Originally introduced by the Home Office Police Standards Unit (PSU), forces and BCUs are each placed in 'most similar families' (MSFs) in order to provide benchmarks for performance. For example, at local level, a BCU will be a member of a MSF of 15 BCUs from across England and Wales (the system does not include Scotland and Northern Ireland), grouped on the basis of having similar characteristics across a range of 17 criteria. These cover factors such as demographics, socio-economics and crime levels. Monthly data is produced showing where a BCU sits in this MSF league table, primarily in terms of crime

---

[58] See E McLaughlin, J Muncie and G Hughes, 'Permanent revolution: New Labour, new public management and the modernization of criminal justice' (2001) 1 Criminal Justice 301.

[59] Home Office, Best Value: Briefing Notes for the Police Service, Audit and Inspection (London, Home Office, 1999).

[60] See, eg, Home Office, The National Policing Plan (London, HMSO, 2003) and Association of Chief Police Officers, Quality of Service Commitment (London, ACPO, 2005).

[61] Again, see Her Majesty's Inspectorate of Constabulary, Report of Her Majesty's Inspectorate of Constabulary (London, HMSO, 2002) and C Banner and A Reid, How is your police force performing? A comprehensive analysis of police performance data (London, Policy Exchange, 2002).

[62] E McLaughlin, J Muncie and G Hughes, 'Permanent revolution: New Labour, new public management and the modernization of criminal justice' (2001) 1 Criminal Justice 301.

levels per 1,000 of the population and the detection rates achieved, expressed as a percentage of the total of each crime type measured. Similarly, forces are also grouped into MSFs in this way.

This systematic approach to driving the performance of the police service was unknown when PACE was first introduced. The currently oft-heard call from senior police managers to instil a 'performance culture' at all levels has had a very real impact on working practices. Police leaders know that they will be held to account for organisational performance through systems such as iQuanta and the Police Performance Assessment Framework (PPAF)[63] and that ultimately organisational performance is driven by the performance of individuals. Constables consequently have their productivity reviewed by their team sergeant; sergeants will report to inspectors and so on. The contemporary BCU commander also knows the experience of being held to account in front of chief officers and peers at performance meetings. The chief constable reports to the Police Authority performance committees and, in the worst case scenario, the force may be subject to performance interventions from Her Majesty's Inspectorate of Constabulary (HMIC) and PSU (now integrated within the National Police Improvement Agency, NPIA). Front line officers therefore have added pressures to those felt by colleagues when PACE was introduced.

It is entirely reasonable that police performance be scrutinised, but this needs to be done with a degree of sophistication to avoid unintended outcomes. The relevance of this for PACE comes where officers are engaged in activities such as stop and search, arrest and the gathering of evidence. They know that they will be judged partly on their levels of productivity. Often this judgement is more likely to be one based on quantitative data than qualitative. How many stops and searches have been carried out? How many intelligence reports submitted? How many detections achieved? However, it is the quality of work done in these areas that will achieve the optimum outcomes. The successful conviction of a dangerous offender or the ruling out from enquiries of an innocent bystander, whilst maintaining proportionality around the rights and freedoms of both, requires a high standard of professional practice. But on the face of it, this is not always what may be measured or rewarded. A detection is easily counted. A quality investigation is not—it takes diligence and time to assess this. The performance manager's maxim that 'What gets measured gets done' has a particular significance here then, and its resultant outcomes may not be those that were originally intended. 'Measure what is important' rather than 'make important what can easily be measured' may convey a truer wisdom.

[63] Home Office, *The National Policing Plan* (London, HMSO, 2003); Association of Police Authorities, Her Majesty's Inspectorate of Constabulary, Association of Chief Police Officers and Home Office Police Standards Unit, *Setting local priorities and assessing performance for PPAF's local policing domain: good practice guidance for police authorities and police forces* (London, Home Office, 2006).

There are other factors in this world of performance that can bring additional complications and tensions when working within PACE at the operational end of policing. For example, the police have the achievement of detections, as determined by Home Office Counting Rules,[64] as a primary indicator of performance. The CPS has a separate set of performance measures, which includes the numbers of cracked trials and unsuccessful prosecutions. This can cause tension between the front line officer and the CPS lawyer making the charging decision. Officers may believe that some offences, where there is sufficient evidence to charge, are not proceeded with due to the CPS being risk averse to a contentious prosecution because a not guilty verdict will affect local CPS performance figures. Conversely, a CPS lawyer may see the officer as merely 'going for the detection'. Neither situation is desirable.

Of course, positive leadership can minimise the risk factors around this. Effective leadership and performance management are currently receiving particular focus within the police service.[65] The front line officer is best directed and supported within an environment that recognises and rewards not only productive but also ethical working practices. It is entirely possible for the police service to achieve this end and bring about a 'virtuous circle'.[66] This is arguably a prerequisite for the legitimacy of policing and an essential precursor no doubt in moving closer to the 'freedom model' of criminal justice mentioned elsewhere.[67]

# V  Keeping PACE? Key issues for front line policing

Whether the Act has actually brought improvement since its implementation, or continues to keep pace with the developments of the last two decades, has been the focus of much commentary and some calls for a rethink about its effectiveness.[68] The argument has been put, too, that merely changing the statute book is not sufficient to ensure progress without cultural and organisational change within the police itself.[69]

The Home Office and Cabinet Office conducted a review of PACE in 2002 within the following Terms of Reference:

---

[64] See Home Office, *Counting Rules* (London, Home Office, 2006).

[65] For a summary see M Long, 'Leadership and Performance Management' in T Newburn (ed), *The Handbook of Policing* (Cullompton, Willan Publishing, 2003) 628.

[66] See P Neyroud and A Beckley, *Policing, Ethics and Human Rights* (Cullompton, Willan, 2001).

[67] Sanders and Young, 2007, n 2 above.

[68] For different perspectives see Brown, n 2 above; Reiner, n 1 above; E Cape, 'The Revised PACE Codes of Practice: A Further Step Towards Inquisitorialism' [2003] *Crim LR* 355; Sanders and Young, 2003, n 2 above, 228; T Newburn and R Reiner, 'From PC Dixon to Dixon PLC: Policing and Police Powers Since 1954' [2004] *Crim LR* 601; J Spencer, 'Prosecution Powers to Gather Evidence: The Case for Reform' *Archbold News* Issue 8, September 2005 (London, Sweet & Maxwell, 2005); E Cape, 'Arresting developments: increased police powers of arrest' *Legal Action,* January 2006, 24.

[69] Reiner, n 1 above; Sanders and Young, 2003, n 2 above.

To undertake a review of the requirements of the Police and Criminal Evidence Act 1984 (PACE), with particular emphasis on, but not limited to, those aspects which govern detention and the custody process.

Without compromising the rights of those that the Act protects, the purpose of the review is to identify possible changes to the rules that could:

Simplify police procedures
Reduce procedural or administrative burdens on the police
Save police resources
Speed up the process of justice

The review will focus on both the PACE Act and the Codes of Practice issued under it.[70]

Taken at face value, this review could have brought good news for the front line police practitioner, weighed down by the complexity and bureaucracy of the system. However, even from a police perspective, one must acknowledge the absence within these terms of reference of so many elements that are key to the workings of PACE and the criminal process generally. Having criticised the report's methodology (including a lack of consultation); superficial appreciation of 'the role and significance of PACE and of the Codes'; the perfunctory consideration of 43 separate issues in a mere 32 pages; and limited reference to research, Zander, a long time commentator on the Act,[71] called the review 'a deplorable report'.[72]

So what direction might a more fundamental and nuanced review of PACE take? Whatever the route, for front line policing there are elements that are prerequisites to the reasonable operation of whatever system might emerge. As noted earlier, Brown touched upon four key points when he noted that 'new rules must be clearly expressed'; 'implementation must be accompanied by training'; that there must be 'effective sanctions and supervision'; and, finally, that there must be 'public awareness'.[73] These points will be discussed here, alongside other issues concerning resourcing.

## A The Need for Clarity

In a critique of the current legal framework, Spencer argues that:

The need for clarity, coherence and accessibility is as necessary in the rules that govern the coercive power of the State to gather evidence as it is in any other area of the

---

[70] Home Office and Cabinet Office, *PACE Review: Report of the Joint Home Office/Cabinet Office Review of the Police and Criminal Evidence Act 1984* (London, Home Office, 2002) 5.
[71] Michael Zander's text, *The Police and Criminal Evidence Act* (London, Sweet & Maxwell, 2005), now in its 5th edition, will need no introduction to many police practitioners.
[72] M Zander, 'The Joint Review of PACE: a deplorable report' (2003) 153 *New Law Journal* 204.
[73] Brown, n 2 above, 252.

criminal law.... The current law on the coercive powers of the police and other agencies to gather evidence is obscure, incoherent and inaccessible.[74]

He goes on to add:

if PACE was a step in the right direction, all subsequent legislative steps have been taken in the wrong one: and in consequence, the resulting law is even messier today than it was before 1984.[75]

This is a view that would probably be supported by many front line police officers and staff. They daily have to contend with the vast array of legislation that underpins their powers to gather evidence. Fairly straightforward investigations can require a very detailed knowledge not only of PACE but also a range of other Acts, together with the ability and professional experience to understand and interpret these in context. This can be illustrated by a hypothetical example.

A typical instance may be where an officer on patrol is approached by a member of the public who alleges a suspect is supplying drugs on a street corner. At the very least, the officer may wish to speak to the alleged suspect and this would require a record to be made, as per Recommendation 61 of the Macpherson Report, which though not covered by statute, is covered by Code A of PACE. Alternatively, a stop and search could be covered by section 1 of PACE, which a lay person might be forgiven for thinking would provide a general power to stop and search. However, it in fact only allows a search to be undertaken for stolen or prohibited articles (for use in burglary, theft, taking a conveyance, committing a deception or criminal damage). In addition, a search for a 'bladed article' as defined by section 139 of the Criminal Justice Act 1988, is permitted under the revised section 1(8) of PACE. These powers were added to by section 60 of the Criminal Justice and Public Order Act 1994 and section 44 of the Terrorism Act 2000, but they do not apply in this case. The officer will need to know that section 23(2) of the Misuse of Drugs Act 1971 also provides a power to search specifically for drugs. It should be pointed out, though, that Code A of PACE still applies to the actual conduct of the search.

In this example the officer may feel that evidence could be lost by making a direct approach to the suspect, so might consider covert surveillance (that is any surveillance done without the knowledge of those under observation), to gather evidence and corroborate the intelligence received. Some police surveillance powers are provided for by part III of the Police Act 1997 (interception of communications), but in this case it will be one of the 82 sections of the Regulation of Investigatory Powers Act (RIPA) 2000 that will provide the power. These sections are very detailed. Spencer quotes *Blackstone's Criminal Practice* when it states the provisions of RIPA 'are so elaborate that only a summary can be

---

[74] J Spencer, 'Prosecution Powers to Gather Evidence: The Case for Reform' *Archbold News*, Issue 8, September 2005, 6.
[75] *Ibid*, 7.

given here'.[76] These surveillance powers are not to be confused with those permitted under the Anti-terrorism, Crime and Security Act 2001. In this street-level scenario, the officer would have to consider the immediacy and continuity of his or her actions in order to establish the nature of authorisation required. The officer will need to know that under sections 28–30 RIPA, authorisation from a superintendent or above may be needed to engage in what is termed 'directed surveillance'. The writer has granted many of these authorisations in the workplace. It is not the work of a moment, and rightly so, but one can sense the weight of legal complexity now weighing down upon the officer on the street corner. If the surveillance is not applied for, granted and then undertaken in the correct way, it may then be the Surveillance Commissioner (appointed under the Police Act 1997), not necessarily the Court, who will be waiting to apply the sanctions.

At this point the front line officer has already had to navigate through 10 pieces of legislation or their related codes and has not yet even spoken to the alleged suspect. They would benefit from having access to a weighty law manual.[77] If a similar summary of the powers and codes that cover the arrest, search and questioning of the suspect were undertaken here, the reader would be occupied for some time. The expectation that the practitioner, whilst still grappling with the professional knowledge required, also applies discretion based on necessity, reason and proportionality at each of these stages starts to have daunting implications for the effectiveness of the process. In the meantime, the outraged member of the public, who saw the drug dealing in their community, will be expecting police action and awaiting the outcome of the investigation.

Due to the 'bolt on' nature of legal measures relating directly or indirectly to PACE, the search for simplicity and clarity at the front line is problematic in other ways too. The change in the right to silence brought about by the Criminal Justice and Public Order Act 1994 meant a change in the wording of the caution delivered by an arresting officer, who must now point out that it may harm a person's defence if they fail to mention something at the time of arrest that they later rely on at court. The warning is a relatively straightforward point of procedure for the officer and the new caution was quickly learned. However, the implications when a detainee questions what this really means, and for how an interview with a suspect is later undertaken, are less clear for most practitioners. Ashworth and Redmayne highlight some of the potential problems.[78]

The Codes of Practice provide the guidance and rules on how PACE will be applied but insofar as PACE is applied in the custody process, the police practitioner now has some further guidance to observe. *Guidance on The Safer*

---

[76] *Ibid*, 9.

[77] This writer resorted to the excellent J English and R Card, *Police Law*, 9th edn (Oxford, Oxford University Press, 2005), but it is unlikely that officers would be able to carry it on the front line, especially in addition to all the PNDs they may also have to carry with them (see below).

[78] See Ashworth and Redmayne, n 2 above, 89–99.

*Detention and Handling of Persons in Police Custody*, known to some practitioners as 'the custody doctrine', contains some 15 sections on the management of arrest and detention, including risk assessment, transportation, detainee care, staffing ratios, deaths in custody, terrorism detainees and CCTV.[79] The aims of the guidance are positive but also illustrate the weight of information, procedures and expectations that front line staff must take on in applying PACE.

Another significant piece of legislation since PACE, for defence, prosecution and police practitioner alike has been the Criminal Procedure and Investigations Act 1996. This did add some clarity to the requirements around disclosure. Inevitably, it also greatly increased the paperwork factor for investigators. Ashworth and Redmayne point out various problems that still can arise around disclosure, however, at different stages of the process.[80] Significant amongst these are the adversarial positions taken by prosecution and defence when applying the disclosure rules. The resolution of these issues was part of the reason for the Criminal Justice Act 2003, but again some of the causes will be cultural and organisational rather than a problem of statute. As far as the police practitioner is concerned, when gathering and presenting the material required for the CPS to disclose to the defence, Ashworth and Redmayne's assertion that 'the prosecution should be seen as the trustee, rather than the owner, of any information gathered during the police investigation',[81] seems sound. However, the complexity of the issue, partly created through the necessity of having to observe two statutes, may hinder awareness or observance of this principle.

The Criminal Justice and Police Act 2001, section 2, provided powers for a constable in uniform to issue a penalty notice for disorder (PND) to a person aged 10 or over, for 18 varying offences.[82] These include drunkenness, false alarm of fire, sale of alcohol to persons under 18, wasting police time, criminal damage and theft. The Penalties for Disorderly Behaviour (Amount of Penalty) Order 2002, as amended, prescribes the penalties. These notices can be issued on the street or at a police station. Police Community Support Officers and 'accredited' persons may also issue notices for the majority of the offences. The powers that a police officer has to grant 'street bail' under sections 30A and 30D of PACE, as amended by section 4 of the Criminal Justice Act 2003, add further discretionary alternatives to the process by which offenders may find themselves being dealt with for certain offences. These powers may be seen as a move away from the 'due process' model of criminal justice towards the 'crime control' end of the spectrum. Ostensibly, of course, they are measures which were designed to speed up the wheels of justice and relieve the front line police officer of some of the

---

[79] Association of Chief Police Officers, Home Office and National Centre for Policing Excellence, *Guidance on The Safer Detention and Handling of Persons in Police Custody* (London, ACPO, Centrex, 2006).

[80] Ashworth and Redmayne, n 2 above, 240–41.

[81] *Ibid*, 241.

[82] See ch 7 by Richard Young in this collection for a more thorough discussion of these powers.

paperwork that successive pieces of legislation have generated since the introduction of PACE. To some extent they achieve this. However, they have introduced yet more legislative complexity and, ironically, new forms of paperwork. On a very practical level, the writer can testify, having witnessed a sergeant colleague lay them all out, that a constable would need to carry *nine* different penalty notice document pads[83] in order to be able to issue the full range of notices available—the weight of criminal justice! Critics might also argue that PNDs may be disproportionately used due to performance pressures.[84]

This is just a selective review of the issues as they affect the practitioner, but perhaps contributes to underlining why there is a collective call for much greater clarity in the framing and operation of the legislative framework governing policing. Having also pointed out the confusion of terminology around 'serious crime', 'serious arrestable offence', 'reasonable grounds', 'reasonable belief' and 'believes', Spencer calls the situation a 'disgrace'.[85] Of course, it may have to be accepted that there will always be a level of complexity—as Einstein is attributed as saying: 'Everything should be made as simple as possible, but not one bit simpler'. But that complexity becomes insurmountable for the front line officer when accompanied by a lack of clarity.

## B Training, Learning and Development

If clarity is achieved within the statutory framework, there is then the matter of ensuring that there is sufficient knowledge and understanding of any legislation in the minds of practitioners. In considering the application of PACE stop and search powers, Dixon *et al* point out that without an adequate model of training, officers may apply the letter of the law without understanding its spirit.[86]

The effectiveness of training delivered to police officers and staff does not appear to have attracted much research interest. However, it is likely that the front line perspective on most BCUs will be that receiving adequate training on the full range of policing activities can be problematic. As mentioned earlier, training is expensive, not only because of the direct training costs but also because officers will normally have to be abstracted from front line duty to receive it. The constant introduction of new legislation, policy and systems means that there are also many competing demands for training. At the time of writing, in the previous 12 months on the writer's own BCU, officers had received training on the National Crime Recording Standard (NCRS), security and counter-terrorism, diversity training, child protection, the use of penalty notices, an incoming

---

[83] More recently this has been reduced to six pads, this down from an original 12! Further national work seeks to reduce this further but is not expected to deliver fully until 2009.

[84] See section IV E above.

[85] *Ibid*, 9.

[86] D Dixon, A Bottomley, C Coleman, M Gill and D Wall, 'Reality and Rules in the Construction and Regulation of Police Suspicion' (1989) 17 *International Journal of the Sociology of Law* 185 at 203.

intelligence IT system, the quality of service commitment, the Victims Code of Practice, self defence techniques, first aid and other disparate issues, all of which were 'a priority'.

If true balance is to be achieved in the criminal process, through PACE or whatever might replace it, training must be accompanied by a deeper learning and development if it is to have a real effect on organisation and culture. As Reiner stresses, 'assimilation of the PACE rules into police culture and working practices has been uneven and incomplete'.[87] This is not a phenomenon unique to the police. For example, a number of commentators remark on the sometimes poor standard of legal advice given to suspects in police stations by defence solicitors.[88] This detracts from the progress made in the uptake of legal advice in police stations since the introduction of PACE.[89] Brown notes that, 'a significant proportion of advice is provided by non-qualified solicitors' representatives'.[90] Interestingly, Cape and Hickman observe that the provision of poor advice by a legal adviser at the police station can even provide a defence in court leading, ironically, to the exclusion of prosecution evidence.[91]

Having identified these factors, and also taking account of the prerequisites probably necessary to move towards a more freedom-based model of criminal justice, one conclusion may be that training should be provided on a multi-agency basis. Developing Ashworth and Redmayne's assertion that the prosecution should be a 'trustee' of evidence within the system,[92] there is a strong argument for making all stakeholders within the criminal justice system, 'trustees' of evidence and individual freedoms and rights. Having identified the aims and objectives of the criminal justice system, and devised the necessary legal framework, the ideal scenario for training must surely be that police, CPS, defence and courts practitioners sit alongside each other and develop a shared understanding of how the criminal process should work. This is not to say that there should be a move away from the adversarial process, merely that it may be supported by the development of greater mutual professional insight amongst all the stakeholders.

## C Supervision

Supervision works on a number of levels. Most obviously officers are subject to supervision on a day-to-day basis from line managers. Certainly, the paperwork that accompanies the activity associated with PACE will be checked by sergeants

---

[87]  Reiner, n 1 above, 180.

[88]  Included amongst these are E Cape and J Hickman, 'Bad lawyer, good defence' in (2002) 152 *New Law Journal* 1194; Ashworth and Redmayne, n 2 above; E Cape and J Luqmani, *Defending Suspects at Police Stations* (London, Legal Action Group, 2006).

[89]  See Brown, n 2 above, and Reiner, n 1 above.

[90]  *Ibid*, xiii.

[91]  Based on an actual case discussed in E Cape and J Hickman, 'Bad lawyer, good defence' (2002) 152 *New Law Journal*, 1194.

[92]  Ashworth and Redmayne, n 2 above, 241.

and inspectors on submission, although this can be inconsistent. Through the statutory charging scheme, evidential tests will be applied by the CPS to ensure there is sufficient evidence to charge. Ultimately, the courts will decide the soundness of the case and pass comment on police practices where appropriate. Police officers and staff will tend to be mindful of these potential sources of scrutiny, criticism and sanction. Although there are variations in local practice, for the most part competency-related shortfalls in case building and police practice are fed back to front line officers as a result of the joint BCU-level performance meetings held between the police and the CPS. Adverse judicial comment may also be addressed through discipline procedures.

Other parties, too, have a part in scrutinising police actions and powers. For example, lay visitors schemes in custody suites have been in operation since 1986.[93] Custody sergeants, detention officers and their front line colleagues will be familiar with facilitating their visits. Research into the working of lay visitors schemes has shown how some early tensions between visitors and police have dissipated and been replaced by more constructive working relationships, although there is still room for improvement.[94] HMIC, the PSU, independent advisory groups and the Independent Police Complaints Commission (IPCC) have also had roles in supervising, passing comment on or sanctioning police actions. The recently created NPIA subsumes the first two of these agencies, along with Centrex (the national centre for policing excellence, formerly the Police Staff College at Bramshill).

In latter years, a significant addition to these arrived in the form of the surveillance commissioners, to oversee the operation of RIPA. As mentioned earlier, the office of the commissioners was created by the Police Act 1997, not only to authorise certain applications but also to have an inspection role, scrutinising police systems and activities under the Act.

Of course, meeting the demands for information from this array of agencies requires a resource commitment from within the police service. Perhaps more fundamental to 'the spirit of PACE' though, is the argument that the establishment of each new regulatory body may move application of the legislation further away from the original intentions of the legislators. Eminent judges though the surveillance commissioners are, is it possible that their interpretation of how RIPA should operate may diverge from the spirit of PACE and mainstream judgements of the courts, thereby eroding clarity for front line practitioners even further?

---

[93] See Home Office Circular No 12/1986 *Lay Visitors to Police Stations*.

[94] M Weatheritt and C Vieira, *Lay visiting to police stations*. Home Office Research Study 188 (London, Home Office, 1998).

Another problem for some critics of the system is that the application of PACE in police procedures is not always easily visible,[95] and so limits the effectiveness of the above stakeholders. There are, though, possibilities for achieving greater visibility in police activities that have historically been a challenge to observe. These include stop and search encounters; contact with detained suspects on their way to the police station; and interaction outside formal interview whilst in custody. If PACE were to be fundamentally revised or replaced, inclusion of provisions or supporting guidance around the use of technology and more integrated working between police, CPS, defence lawyers, courts, probation and treatment agencies, would seem to offer potential ways forward. Certainly, in terms of technology, recording of suspect and some witness interviews has been routine for many years and most custody suites now have CCTV to cover detention areas. Cameras that record street encounters are being trialled by various forces. The digital age will no doubt continue to make the application of these systems more manageable. It is also possible that joint criminal justice system practitioner training and a 'trustee' status for those stakeholders might increase the transparency of the criminal process. In the same way that this would require some cultural change on the part of front line police practitioners, there would similarly have to be a shift in mindset in the legal profession, both on the part of prosecuting and defending lawyers.

## D Public Awareness

Public awareness of rights and police powers has been seen as an important constraint on police actions,[96] but the practicalities of achieving this awareness are challenging. Whilst it is probable that the wider public has a peripheral awareness that the police have powers, it is unlikely that it matches the understanding that is gained in some other nations due to their taught knowledge of their relevant political constitutions. The United States and some Far East nations offer examples. In England and Wales, an understanding of individual rights is part of the citizenship learning in schools within the national curriculum. In the post-PACE years, the front line police officer will often have seen the publication of booklets and leaflets designed to provide information about police powers, issued through front counters, custody suites and community initiatives. Further, many support agencies produce literature for specific groups.

It is not proposed here to assess the effectiveness of these measures but a key point is that, after over 20 years of PACE, some level of knowledge and awareness will have indeed built up. However, what is also likely is that the myriad of additions, revisions and parallel statutes that have been added to PACE since its

---

[95] Expanded upon in D Dixon, A Bottomley, C Coleman, M Gill and D Wall, 'Reality and Rules in the Construction and Regulation of Police Suspicion' (1989) 185 *International Journal of the Sociology of Law* 203; Brown, n 2 above; Reiner, n 1 above; Sanders and Young, 2003, n 2 above, 228.

[96] Brown, n 2 above, 252.

inception will not have helped to sustain that understanding. Any major revisions would need to take account of this in terms of clarification and rebuilding that awareness. This point has been made elsewhere,[97] alongside those who observe that this would 'enhance police accountability, but . . . that the goal of full education is probably unattainable'.[98] Transparency and visibility will mean nothing without the public's awareness about what they are seeing and, for the front line officer, this is crucial in achieving a sense of legitimacy and proportionality when using statutory powers.

## E Resources

In the last decade, the total police officer strength in England and Wales increased by just over 11 per cent, from 126,901 in 1996 to 141,381 in 2006. The majority of this increase was seen in the years since 2003, after a decline in strength in the late 1990s.[99] According to British Crime Survey data, crime levels have fallen possibly by as much as 40 per cent during the same period.[100] Might this allow the police to be more intensively involved and scrutinised, or perhaps allow resources to be realigned so there may be increased emphasis on other forms of justice, such as restorative or diversionary measures? There are a number of factors to consider.

Firstly, demands and expectations of the police have continued to increase. Relevant to PACE have been the increases in the bureaucracy and paperwork caused by issues mentioned elsewhere in this paper, such as MG forms and disclosure. The age of the mobile phone has seen steady rises in calls for service, not necessarily always related to crime reporting. Some of the increase in police strength has been drawn into security and counter-terrorism, especially in the Metropolitan Police Service. The Neighbourhood Policing Model, currently being implemented on the direction of the Home Office, calls for dedicated local teams to close 'the reassurance gap'. This refers to the rise in the public fear of crime, in spite of the reality of reductions in crime levels. Each time a different national standard has been created (for example NCRS) or a form of inspection or regulation emerges (for example RIPA), staff have been required to service the related demands and allied systems and technology have also required significant investment. No surprise then that these factors lead to the front line police officer perspective of being ever busier.[101]

---

[97] D Dixon, A Bottomley, C Coleman, M Gill and D Wall, 'Reality and Rules in the Construction and Regulation of Police Suspicion' (1989) 185 *International Journal of the Sociology of Law* 203.

[98] Sanders and Young, 2007, n 2 above, 91.

[99] M Clegg and S Kirwan, *Police service strength: England and Wales, 31 March 2006*, Home Office Statistical Bulletin 13/06 (London, Home Office, Research Development and Statistics Directorate, 2006).

[100] Home Office *Crime in England and Wales 2005–6: A summary of the main statistics* (London, Home Office, 2006).

[101] This is emphasised in an article entitled 'Sink or Swim?' in *Police*, January 2006, magazine of the Police Federation of England and Wales (Surbiton, Landmark, 2006) 21.

A further factor is the uneven distribution of police resources nationally. It may be quite reasonable to suppose that a more urban force area will have a higher ratio of officers to population compared to a lower crime rural area. This is reflected in the case of the force with the lowest ratio nationally, Lincolnshire at 142 constables per 100,000 of the population, and that with the highest, the Metropolitan Police at 313 constables.[102] However, apparently similar forces can also have quite different police officer levels in terms of the ratio of officers to population. For example, Avon and Somerset Constabulary have 179 constables per 100,000, South Wales 207 and Northumbria 228. The differences are mainly due to historical and local anomalies in government grant and local taxation. These factors were a key reason for the breakdown during 2006 in the plans to amalgamate forces, when it was realised that comparative revenue issues could not be resolved between local authority areas.[103]

When distilled down to a local level the situation can be even more dramatic, due to the 'top slicing' of resources to headquarters and centralised protective services, such as counter-terrorism, firearms, traffic and murder investigation support. A BCU may find itself compared in its MSF with 14 other reportedly 'similar' BCUs, based on the 17 comparative criteria, but with a 40 per cent difference in resource ratio per 100,000 of the population and also crimes per officer. This obviously has a relevance for tackling crime and disorder, compliance with PACE or for the adoption of any new legal framework. For example, differences in resource levels have been observed as critical in achieving the successful detection of crimes, affecting as they do the various investigative stages.[104] Whatever changes may be proposed to improve the criminal process, from the front line policing perspective, no doubt shared by other stakeholders, it is essential that these are accompanied by adequate investment and ongoing funding. If such variances in local resource levels continue to exist nationally, so there will be variances in the capacity to ensure an effective and balanced criminal justice process.

A final reflection on the fall in crime over the past decade is that the links between crime and economic trends are widely acknowledged, even if they are not fully understood.[105] It might be reasonable to suppose that whenever a downturn in the economy occurs there is a threat that crime will again increase. At the time of writing, BCS data suggests that overall crime rates may have

---

[102] M Clegg and S Kirwan, *Police service strength: England and Wales, 31 March 2006,* Home Office Statistical Bulletin 13/06 (London, Home Office, Research Development and Statistics Directorate, 2006).

[103] See 'Police forces merger plan will be scrapped', *The Independent,* 11 July 2006.

[104] J Burrows, M Hopkins, R Hubbard, A Robinson, M Speed and N Tilley, *Understanding the attrition process in volume crime investigations,* Home Office Research Study 295 (London, Home Office, 2005) 125.

[105] See, eg, R Garside, 'Is it the Economy?' (2004) 55 *Criminal Justice Matters* 32.

plateaued[106] and there are reported concerns that poor long-term economic indicators may contribute to a rise in acquisitive crime.[107] If this proves to be the case and the law and order dividend is reduced, the resource issue may be an even more significant background factor to consider in successfully implementing any change.

# VI Conclusion

'Injustice anywhere is a threat to justice everywhere'. The words of Martin Luther King are inspirational when considering the importance of building a fair, compassionate and safe society. In relation to the criminal justice process, PACE remains central to this. But, from the front line policing perspective, has it kept pace with other developments of the past 20 years and does it still represent the best hope of preventing an injustice anywhere?

Arguably, policing is as much about helping communities to thrive as it is about responding to emergencies or upholding the law. The police contribute to this by helping, with others, to enable people to pursue their everyday business, work, education and recreation free from the experience, or, at least, a disproportionate fear, of crime or crisis. But the means of achieving this are crucial if this mission is to be widely accepted and trusted. It is probably fair to say that PACE has helped to move policing on from some of the darker days of community mistrust in the early 1980s. The extent of that mistrust was often articulated in the media of the time—assumptions that prisoners were assaulted; that confessions were fabricated; ID parades rigged; evidence planted during searches and arrested persons 'verballed up'. Since then, PACE has helped to achieve some transparency and a better 'balance' and has further professionalised the police. As Reiner observes: 'The legislation has achieved far more than its civil libertarian critics initially expected, if far less than they would wish'.[108] Whatever the view, after 1984 front line police practitioners certainly had a number of years of greater clarity about their legal powers.

The signs, however, are that PACE may be falling behind the realities of policing in a more globalised, technological, media-sensitive and expectant world. Its original modernist aims of providing balance, order and stability have dimmed as legislation has attempted to deal with more recent developments in human rights, terrorism and technologically facilitated surveillance. PACE appears to have developed critics from all directions. In theoretical terms,

---

[106] Home Office *Crime in England and Wales 2005–6: A summary of the main statistics* (London, Home Office, 2006).

[107] For example, a story entitled 'Secret memo warns Blair of crime wave appeared' in *The Sunday Times*, 24 December 2006, highlighting the threat of future crime increases.

[108] Reiner, n 1 above, 182.

therefore, it may be argued that a more 'affirmative postmodern' approach is now needed that will continue to strive for a better society, developed simultaneously from the perspectives of different stakeholders. In practical terms, this could mean the front line police officer routinely training and working alongside other professionals to achieve a shared vision of a system of justice that is balanced, effective, credible, trusted and which protects the freedoms of all that it serves. These shared objectives would still sit very much within an adversarial system, but a system within which stakeholders have a sense of being privileged trustees and are more alert to the threat of injustice. In its present increasingly complex form, PACE is unlikely to facilitate this.

# 6

# Tipping the Scales of Justice?: A Review of the Impact of PACE on the Police, Due Process and the Search for Truth 1984–2006

BARBARA WILDING*

## I Introduction

Many of the publications and commentaries on the Police and Criminal Evidence Act 1984 (PACE) have been written by distinguished members of the legal profession and academics and focus on the legal perspective or a particular discipline. This chapter takes a wholly different approach in that it is written from a police perspective based on my knowledge and experience gained over 40 years[1] in ranks from constable through to chief constable, together with, I hope, a robust application of common sense.

Like most police officers I joined the service to make a difference and was initially, and somewhat naively, surprised to find that our very complex legal system was not based on establishing the guilt or innocence of an individual. I discovered the 'adversarial system' could often turn a court case into something of a battle between opposing lawyers with the aim of discrediting evidence rather than searching out the truth.

Whilst suspects were well catered for by the voice of the legal profession, victims and witnesses, apart from some police support, had virtually no voice at all. As a female officer, whose role prior to the 1975 Sex Discrimination Act was

* I would like to thank my Staff Officer, Chief Inspector Tony Matthias for his assistance in producing this paper.

[1] I joined the Jersey States Police, (which operated under the 'inquisitorial' system) in 1967 as a police cadet and was attested a constable in 1970. In 1971 I transferred to the Metropolitan Police. I joined Kent Constabulary in 1994 as an assistant chief constable returning to the Metropolitan Police in 1998 as a deputy assistant commissioner. I became Chief Constable of South Wales Police in January 2004.

confined to children and women, I dealt with many sexual offences. In those days, and until fairly recently, prosecution counsel never spoke to victims or witnesses of sexual offences through fear of being accused of coaching. Thus they never saw themselves as acting for those people.

In the early part of my career, I also learnt that within the criminal justice system the police were seen as having 'blue collar' status and accordingly lacked voice and influence. Although issues may have changed, the 'blue collar' thinking is still prevalent today and, in my view, can guide academic and legal professional responses on policing. I thus welcome this opportunity to set out a police perspective for consideration alongside academic and legal professional perspectives on PACE.

Before moving on to develop this perspective in the substantive sections which follow, I would like to begin with a simple outline of certain points that I regard as fundamental. As initially enacted, PACE 1984 and the Prosecution of Offences Act 1985 envisaged the police acting within custody as impartial investigators into the truth. By contrast, the Crown Prosecution Service (CPS) was given the job of trying to prove guilt. However, PACE suffered from the defect of concentrating solely on suspects' rights from interaction with the police during initial enquiry outwith the police station through to charge or other disposal at custody. This bias within the legislation has inevitably led to a series of amendments that seek to give greater weight to the interests of victims, witnesses and the wider community. Unfortunately, in the process the impartial status originally conferred on the police has been eroded. The police now find themselves in an adversarial system once custody is embarked upon. The erosion of our ability to conduct an impartial search for the truth in custody has resulted in a greater, more costly, search for the truth through developing forensics and technology leading to the concerns expressed very recently of the expansion of a surveillance society. It could further be argued that an unintended consequence of PACE has been to raise the bar for the test of 'beyond all reasonable doubt' with no regard to community impact.

All this has taken place in a democratic society under our noses yet few of us have sneezed. Added to this is the increased punitive focus successive governments have forced on society by introducing targets for the police which are measured through 'sanction detections' and 'offenders brought to justice'. To achieve a sanction detection custody has to be embarked upon. There are no targets or measures for establishing the truth, diverting offenders from the criminal justice system or stopping the behaviour. This has led to the increased criminalisation of our young people in particular, who represent our future.

It is my hope that highlighting this fundamental erosion within our civil society of the impartial search for the truth in custody will encourage deeper and wider reflection on the future of PACE. I contend the debate needs to be bigger

than that currently proposed by the Home Office Review[2] of this legislat.
Mere tinkering is inadequate—a wider justice debate is what is required.


# II  The pre-PACE period

In considering the impact of PACE it should not be viewed in isolation because
the years and events leading up to its enactment played a part in creating
perceptions of the police which in turn shaped the Act. One such perception, as
recorded crime rates soared, was that the police were meeting with limited
success in fighting crime. In 1970 there were 1,555,915 recorded crimes for
England and Wales. During the next 13 years there was a steady rise to 3,247,030
such crimes.[3]

Growing unemployment, rising from 2.2 per cent when I joined the police in
1967 to 9 per cent by 1981, resulted in mounting social and economic tensions,
with the police increasingly drawn in to keep the peace. The year-long miners'
strike (1984–85) saw televised scenes of conflict between police and pickets which
did nothing to reduce fear in the minds of some that the police were being used
as an 'organ of the state'.

The latter half of the 1970s and early 1980s saw social unrest and serious
rioting in several cities, notably Notting Hill (1976), Brixton (1981) and Hands-
worth, Birmingham (1984). Lord Scarman's report into the Brixton riots was
critical of some policing methods and called for changes to the police approach
to community and race relations issues.[4]

Public confidence in policing was further tarnished by a number of high-
profile issues which raised questions about police integrity and ethical standards.
For example, the Fisher Report (1977) into a miscarriage of justice following the
quashing by the Court of Appeal of the conviction of three boys who had
confessed to the murder of Maxwell Confait raised serious questions about
treatment by the police of juveniles and mentally disabled suspects.[5]

In his autobiography, Sir Robert Mark (1978) covered the controversial subject
of police corruption in the Metropolitan Police which had received widespread
coverage in the media.[6] He wrote:

---

[2]  *Modernising Police Powers: Review of the Police & Criminal Evidence Act (PACE) 1984: consultation paper* (London, Home Office, 2007).

[3]  Source: http://www.homeoffice.gov.uk/rds/pdfs/100years.xls (accessed 3 October 2007).

[4]  L Scarman, *The Brixton Disorders*, Cmnd 8427 (London, HMSO, 1981). See also ch 2 by David
Dixon in this collection.

[5]  H Fisher, *Report of an Inquiry into the Circumstances leading to the Trial of Three Persons on
Charges arising out of the Death of Maxwell Confait and the Fire at 27 Doggett Road, London SE6* (HCP
90) (London, HMSO, 1977). For fuller discussion see ch 3 by Andrew Sanders.

[6]  R Mark, *In the Office of Constable* (London, William Collins, 1978) 122.

The CID regarded itself as an elite body, higher paid by way of allowances and factually, fictionally and journalistically more glamorous. It also, unlike its provincial counterpart, enjoyed an immunity from external supervision and investigation. This facilitated for many decades three kinds of wrongdoing. The first, institutional corruption, of a comparatively minor kind but affecting a significant minority of detectives such as charging for bail, suppressing additional and sometimes more serious charges and failing to bring previous convictions to notice. Very often, the dubious cover for this kind of malpractice was 'the need to cultivate informers'. The second more spectacular corruption affecting fewer but more specialised or senior officers, such as those concerned with major crimes like bank robbery, illegal drugs and obscene publications. The third, quite different, a widespread general acceptance that in London, at least, the system of justice is weighted so heavily in favour of the criminal and the defence lawyer that it can only be made to work by bending the rules.[7] In fairness to the CID that view is not confined to them.

Whilst Sir Robert's criticism of a minority of officers was certainly valid, it was seldom acknowledged that it was members of the same force who took the action that brought them to justice.

Criticism of the police was not confined to London. The investigation into the Yorkshire Ripper, jailed in 1981, provides a good example. It was a very difficult cross-border investigation conducted without modern technology and resulted in widespread criticism of policing methods. Sir Lawrence Byford reported that, due to the cost of the inquiry and the need to curtail expenditure on overtime, two separate teams had worked day and night shifts and operated quite independently using two separate card index systems.[8] As an operational detective I was brought in to evaluate technology as an aid to major investigations. I found that apart from the telephone, virtually no technology had been used. The work led me, with a scientist, to write the first ever user requirement for an IT based crime recording system with free text functionality for the police.[9]

My personal experiences in the pre-PACE era echoed the lack of professionalism that existed in the police service. The police force I joined was testosterone driven and fuelled with frustration at a criminal justice system perceived as being loaded in favour of the suspect. Many of my colleagues felt the need to get results as a means to prove they were as good as, or better than, anyone else. In those days promotion systems had not been equality proofed and there were no checks and balances in place to limit abuses. Pressures from senior officers to get results as a means of proving fitness for promotion also played a part in the culture of the day.

---

[7] This bending of the rules became known as 'noble cause corruption'.

[8] *The Yorkshire Ripper Case: Review of the Police Investigation of the Case by Lawrence Byford*, December 1981. (The Report was originally presented to the Home Secretary on a confidential basis but has subsequently been made available on the Home Office website under Freedom of Information legislation.)

[9] This, together with another system, was the predecessor to HOLMES (Home Office Large Major Enquiry System).

Pre-PACE there were abuses of process. Judges Rules were commonly flouted and some detainees were kept in custody for much longer than was necessary and without access to the legal advice to which they were entitled. Many supervisors turned a blind eye to this. They often did so because of a deeply held perception that the criminal justice system favoured the accused and, in consequence, rules that favoured a suspect could be broken. Police-led prosecution inevitably gave rise to a contest between police and defence, and a perceived need to win. As a result, there was growing concern within the legal profession, politicians and the public over the way some investigations were carried out.

For example, a feature of cross-examinations of officers at courts in London was that evidence had been planted on the accused. I can recall chasing a female into the Underground who had a knife and in the tussle that followed receiving a black eye. In the resulting court case it was not suggested that the knife had been planted but, at its conclusion, the clerk to the court gave me a 'knowing' wink and, on handing me the knife, said 'you can put this back in the drawer now.' It clearly indicated how we were all stereotyped as blue collar, lacking in both professionalism and integrity.

I knew of some officers who dealt with prostitution and gaming on the basis of whose turn it was to be arrested and then writing up bail applications with varying strengths depending on factors unconnected with integrity. Many served imprisonment as a consequence. In bending and breaching rules, officers were taking a risk that confidence in the police service would be significantly damaged. This was well evidenced soon after the introduction of PACE when a number of high profile miscarriages of justice came to light.[10] The quashing of the convictions of the Birmingham Six by the Court of Appeal in 1991 resulted in the Runciman Royal Commission to which I will return a little later.

Significant concerns raised over the role of the police and policing methods resulted in the 11th Report of the Criminal Law Revision Committee[11] and the Philips Royal Commission.[12] It was the report and recommendations of the Royal Commission, published in 1981, on which PACE was largely built. Chapter 1 set out the main issues which the Commission sought to address:

> For some years anxiety had been manifestly growing about the continuing rise in the level of crime, about robbery, drug peddling, street crime, fraud, the use of firearms and terrorism. On one side it was asserted that the job of the police in fighting crime and of ensuring that offenders, and particularly dangerous professional criminals were brought to justice was being made unwarrantably difficult by the restraints of criminal procedure and on the other side that the use of their powers of investigation by the police was often open to grave question.[13]

---

[10] Most notably the Guildford Four in 1989 and the Birmingham Six in 1991.
[11] Criminal Law Revision Committee, *Evidence in Criminal Proceedings*, 11th Report, Cmnd 4991, (London, HMSO, 1972).
[12] *Report of the Royal Commission on Criminal Procedure*, Cmnd 8092 (London, HMSO, 1981).
[13] *Ibid*, para 1.1.

Having been an operational police officer during the pre-PACE period I can understand why legislators saw a need to put safeguards in place. Had the level of professionalism in the way we investigated offences always been high then this might not have been necessary.

# III  Due process: the introducton, reception and impact of PACE

I take due process to be a fundamental principle of fairness (guarding against prejudicial or unequal treatment) in all legal matters, especially in the courts. From the police perspective, the impact of PACE on due process has proved to be something of a curate's egg.

## A Key Benefits of PACE

On the positive side PACE introduced a regulatory framework that started to bring clarity to the conduct of an investigation and treatment of detainees, together with sanctions for breaches, that had been missing prior to its enactment. It was a catalyst that paved the way for the level of professionalism that now exists in the way investigations are conducted.

Assurance that an investigation will be conducted with objectivity and integrity is crucial to public confidence in the police service. At the time of its introduction PACE was undoubtedly a culture shock for many police officers who saw it as a threat to the way investigative practice had developed. It was indeed such a threat, and in many ways that was a good thing, because police officers now had a very clear regulatory framework in which to operate and guidance on what was and what was not acceptable in terms of investigative practice and evidence gathering.

I do not know any officers who would wish to go back to the pre-PACE era because PACE undoubtedly ushered in new ethical standards for the service and those standards were welcomed. The television series, 'Life on Mars'[14] is all too accurate in its portrayal of the sort of standards that were commonplace compared with now. This of course has to be viewed against the wider culture of society at the time.

One of the key posts in establishing the new standards was that of the custody officer, a new role totally different to that of the traditional station sergeant. Unlike the station sergeant there was now a clear separation of the custody officer from other policing roles and from the investigation. That separation was

---

[14]  The BBC drama 'Life on Mars' was first screened during 2006.

reinforced by the creation of a detention audit trail in the form of a disclosable written custody record, and the requirement for it to be signed by a detainee to indicate that he or she had been informed of their right to legal representation.

As a result, many police officers who had been used to circumventing the Judges Rules found the new custody officers unwilling to do so. It was a rude awakening for some old-school detectives and I personally witnessed many fierce debates between them and custody officers who refused to compromise their role.

PACE introduced safeguards related to the detention of persons which most police officers welcomed. For example, the requirement placed on a custody officer to keep a record of detention protected officers from false allegations. The requirement to obtain medical treatment for detainees suffering even minor ailments again brought an increased level of security to custody officers who no longer had an option of whether to call a doctor or not. Cost was never an issue for the custody officer, but the mandatory provision of medical services was and is a significant spend in police budgets.

## B The Downside of PACE

The preceding point about the impact of the new regulatory framework on police resources brings me to the debit side of the PACE balance sheet. PACE introduced requirements that led to even a simple arrest taking an officer off the street for several hours. The disappearance of police officers from the street into the station through the attendant bureaucracy and procedural delays has in my view increased public fear of crime. 'The police have left the streets' is a cry I constantly heard from the public until very recently and, in my view, has led to increased fear of crime in a great many of our communities.

This aspect of PACE is seldom commented upon, or appreciated, by those who have looked at PACE from a purely legal or academic perspective. But from a policing perspective, suspects, victims, and indeed the public at large, are all police customers. There were of course deficiencies in other parts of the criminal justice system but in many ways PACE was based on a view that, not only could all the ills be solved through placing safeguards on the police, but that this complex legislative framework could be implemented without extra resources. To put this another way, PACE was drawn up from the perspective of a suspect potentially becoming a victim of a miscarriage of justice rather than a more holistic view that would have taken account of the full impact of the legislation on police resources.

Paperwork for a case even where a guilty plea was guaranteed grew and grew and the result has been fewer officers available for patrol or to respond to the increasing demand for police service from a public constantly calling for more and more police officers.

The impact on suspects and police officers was that prisoner handling was linked to the speed of a custody officer and the number of prisoners he or she had in custody. Compliance with PACE requirements also resulted in detainees spending longer in custody.

PACE introduced an initial limit of 24 hours on detention prior to charge other than in very specific circumstances. From an investigator's perspective this could create problems not of their making. This was because PACE takes no account of delays due to a suspect being unfit through drink or drugs, or whilst waiting for the arrival of a solicitor. Recent research undertaken within my own force found that over a seven day period 35 per cent of detainees were unfit for interview, the average length of time for interpreters' attendance was 3 hours 44 minutes (nine hours on one occasion), and the average time for appropriate adult attendance was 4 hours 33 minutes. PACE takes no account of pressures caused by loss of time that the investigator is unable to influence.

Much of the impact of PACE and its attendant codes of practice was captured by independent research undertaken by the Home Office in 2001 entitled, 'Diary of a Police Officer'.[15] The report posed, and answered, a key question:

> But what accounts for the time operational officers spend in the police station? The two main culprits are the time taken to process prisoners and prepare prosecutions, and the other paperwork which the police must produce. Arresting someone—no matter whether they are a petty criminal or a serious offender—keeps officers off the beat for an average of 3.5 hours—often for far longer. Delays are generally the same for a simple shop-lift as for a much more serious matter. Where a solicitor, appropriate adult or interpreter is required, this can trigger a further wait of an average an hour. If CCTV or an identity parade is involved further substantial delays can ensue.[16]

One of the most unwelcome aspects of PACE from a police perspective was the inclusion of a police station within the definition of a 'place of safety' for vulnerable people.[17] The police service has been called the service of first and last resort and we often find ourselves involved with very vulnerable people who are incapable of caring for themselves but who have no one else to care for them. This group includes the mentally ill and those unfit through self-induced drink or drugs. A difficulty a custody officer has when authorising detention of a person for his or her own safety as, hopefully a temporary measure, is then finding a suitable alternative place of safety.[18] In reality the only alternative is a hospital. In practice, hospitals do not want drunks taking up bed space. It is also very time consuming and difficult to transfer people with mental illnesses to an appropriate hospital and many 'places of safety' are unwilling to receive people direct from the street. The consequence is that police officers in custody suites

---

[15] PA Consulting, *Diary of a Police Officer*, Police Research Series Paper 149 (London, Home Office, 2001).

[16] *Ibid*, 6.

[17] Under the Mental Health Act 1983.

[18] See further ch 4 by John Coppen in this collection.

find themselves having to care for these vulnerable people in inadequate facilities because there is no alternative. I would like to see authorities responsible for other places of safety mandated to take vulnerable people considered by a medical practitioner to be at risk of serious harm and also to provide the transport and escort thus releasing highly trained and expensive professionals back to the role of policing.

Disputes at court over the validity of confession evidence had been a feature of many pre-PACE court hearings and often focused on officers' notes recorded soon after the interview or the validity of signed statements of confession dictated by the accused but written by an officer.

The PACE requirement for interviews to be properly recorded during the interview was welcomed by many police officers as protection from accusations that suspects had been 'verballed' or coerced into false confessions. Initially, the requirement was that:

> The record must be made during the course of the interview, unless in the investigating officer's view this would not be practicable or would interfere with the conduct of the interview and must constitute either a verbatim record of what has been said or failing this an account of the interview which adequately and accurately summarises it.[19]

Whilst the immediate effect was to nullify the flow of an interview to the speed of a scribe and resulted in the need for two officers having to be present for even the most minor offence, one to question and one to record, things improved with tape-recording of interviews, which was brought in gradually, area by area, from 1991. In comparison with contemporaneous notes, tape-recording speeded up the flow of the interview and also made available to a court a record of what was said and how it was said. It also meant that if oppression was alleged then the court could listen to the tape.

Although tape recording speeded up the interview, if proceedings resulted a written record was still required. This is a vexed issue in police circles because of the immense amount of time these records take to prepare. In an ideal world with unlimited budgets it would be possible to provide an adequate number of civilian staff to undertake this work. Unfortunately, in the real world this is not the case, and police officers still spend many hours listening to and laboriously transcribing tapes. The irony is that this is seen as a problem for police because the original intention was for transcripts to be the responsibility of the CPS but funding to allow this never followed. It also begs the question, why do we need a transcript? Whilst court and CPS time is saved, it is at the expense of police officer time and it means that police officers spend more time in a station rather than on patrol.[20]

---

[19] Code C, para 11.3 (b)(ii).
[20] The lack of common technology within the criminal justice system is a problem. Within my own force we record CCTV onto modern DVDs but have to convert these to VHS for the CPS.

Increasing disclosure requirements have resulted in more and more investigations being process driven. For the most serious offences, senior investigating officers keep one eye on the undoubted appeal that will follow, knowing that the defence will search for any procedural irregularity within PACE, or disclosure, or anything that could be used to create an element of doubt. Very often it seems that adherence to the processes is on trial rather than the evidence.

During my service I have been a frequent visitor to the Central Criminal Court, the Old Bailey, and count many former Treasury Counsel as friends and acquaintances. Several have pointed out that since the publication of the Association of Chief Police Officers (ACPO) Murder Manual,[21] senior investigators rarely push the boundaries of ethical investigation, and more and more investigations are process-driven. As a result, investigative flair is being lost in favour of an approach focused on ticking boxes to ensure that all avenues that could give rise to doubt are fully explored even when the evidence is corroborated and overwhelming.

Now that PACE has matured I question whether the same safeguards are necessary for the detention of suspects accused of very minor offences. Currently, whether it be a relatively minor theft or a murder, all suspects go down the same time-consuming track. I similarly question the value of custody for minor offences in cases where a suspect does not deny the offence.

Has the time come to differentiate approaches with the more serious crimes subject to the full-blown PACE requirements, whilst minor offences are subject to a more flexible fast-track approach (taking account of likely outcome) while still ensuring adequate protection for the suspect and society? I am in favour of streamlining the process and fast-tracking minor cases through increasing use of measures such as penalty notices, street bail and on-street DNA and fingerprinting.

In the 21 years since PACE was introduced, policing has been modernised and professionalised beyond all recognition. Today, the police service is more accountable in terms of performance and standards than virtually any other public body. Is it therefore really in the public interest to still have a level of checks, balances and bureaucracy that were thought necessary, for all the right reasons, in 1986?

## C Due Process for Witnesses and Victims?

As I have shown above, PACE was designed to include safeguards to prevent the police from abusing powers granted under the legislation, and many of these safeguards stemmed from legitimate concerns. As a consequence PACE was replete with safeguards that provided protection to police officers as well as to the

---

[21] Murder Investigation Manual produced on behalf of the Association of Chief Police Officers by the National Centre for Policing Excellence (first produced in September 1998).

suspect, for example recording of interviews, use of appropriate adults, requirement for medical examinations of people showing signs of physical or mental ill health and so on.

PACE was and still is very strong on safeguards for the suspect. Unfortunately it included little or nothing in the way of safeguards for victims or witnesses. This was a serious omission in terms of due process. There is no doubt that victims and witnesses often feel trepidation about giving evidence at court and that many of those fears are legitimate. For example, a barrister's badgering of a witness to answer 'yes' or 'no' to a loaded question, intended to make a point to the jury rather than elicit a real explanation, is typical of a tactic that would be condemned as oppressive if used in a police interview. It smacks very much of double standards. One of the indirect impacts of PACE has been to exacerbate and highlight the differential standards of due process at play across police stations and courts.

Moreover, it is one thing to make a statement in a police station, but quite another to face a defendant in court with all the associated fear of reprisal or intimidation by either the defendant or his/her family and associates. And yet, when PACE was introduced, and in some areas still today, witnesses and victims are expected to sit in open foyers in close proximity to the people they will be giving evidence against.

The reluctance of some witnesses to give evidence enables the defence to hold back on a plea until the day of court to assess the evidential strength of a case. If a witness attends, a guilty plea can then be made but if the witness fails to appear then an application to dismiss the case will often follow. In 2004 a series of pilots titled 'No Victim No Justice 2004' found that better witness and victim care resulted in more witnesses attending court which in turn contributed to 'cracked trials' increasing due to the late entry of guilty pleas. The imbalance between suspects' rights and victims' rights that was enshrined in PACE is at last being recognised and, in part, redressed.

# IV  Stop and search

Many view the power to stop and search individuals as the most controversial part of PACE. I now want to look in some detail at its impact on the police and policing.

The Royal Commission on Criminal Procedure had found that stop and search powers varied across England and Wales and were inadequate, uncertain and carried a risk of civil action. The Commission was however unable to reach a consensus. The minority view was that a uniform power of stop and search could further worsen the relationship between police and young people, particularly black youths. This view was linked to the social unrest and riots of the 1980s that had involved black youths in areas like Brixton and had attracted criticism from

Lord Scarman[22] and others who found that insensitive use of stop and search powers had contributed to the breakdown of order. In contrast, the majority view, whilst recognising the above concerns, felt that if Parliament had made it an offence to be in possession of a particular article in a public place then the police should be able to stop and search persons if there were reasonable grounds to suspect a person of committing that offence.

The majority view prevailed and PACE included a general power to stop and search persons or vehicles for stolen or prohibited articles on the basis of reasonable suspicion that a crime had or may have been about to be committed. Safeguards included a requirement to keep records and to inform persons stopped of the reason for the police action.

Since the introduction of the PACE stop and search power and its related Code of Practice A, critics have continued to question the usefulness of the power to stop and search and its need. They point to the adverse effect insensitive and disproportionate use can have on community race relations and question its value in terms of performance indicators that are used to measure its usefulness. I will come back to this latter point a little later.

Concerns at disproportionality and insensitive use of the powers are very real and I share them. If we are to have a civil society then it is of fundamental importance that all people are treated with dignity, courtesy and respect. The power to stop and search is one that must be used in a fair and non-discriminatory way and all in the police service have a responsibility to ensure this is the case.

The development of PACE Code of Practice A has been heavily influenced by concerns that police officers use the power in a discriminatory way. These concerns have been influenced and supported by statistical evidence. What is most striking is that despite numerous amendments to Code A and the huge focus the service has placed on the training of officers and monitoring of stop and search records, the statistical evidence that indicates disproportionate use against some black and minority ethnic groups has shown little change. It is legitimate to ask why.

Let us look first at safeguards within the Code and how these have developed. The original Code A made it a requirement for there to be 'reasonable grounds' before an officer could exercise the power. Reasonable grounds for suspicion were defined in Annexe B as:

> The degree or level of suspicion required to establish the reasonable grounds justifying the exercise of powers of stop and search is no less than the degree of level of suspicion required to effect an arrest without warrant for any of the suspected offences to which

[22]  L Scarman, *The Brixton Disorders*, Cmnd 8427 (London, HMSO, 1981).

these powers relate. The powers of stop and search provide an opportunity to establish the commission or otherwise of certain kinds of offences without arrest and may therefore render arrest unnecessary.[23]

The guidance was somewhat confusing. If the level of suspicion was the same as for a power of arrest then officers could quite legitimately arrest and search back at the station.

Successive versions of the Codes have focused on providing a workable definition and in doing so have increased the amount of guidance given. For example, in the 1991 version of Code A 'reasonable grounds for suspicion' were covered in three paragraphs. In the 2005 edition, the guidance had increased to ten paragraphs.

I have great sympathy for the persons charged with drafting this Code because their difficulty stems from the fact that they are trying to produce a definition that, based on available and arguably flawed statistical evidence, suggests that in spite of repeated attempts to clarify how it should be used, the police will use it in a discriminatory way unless the guidance is watertight. As a result they have clearly felt the answer lies in more detailed guidance that will cover all eventualities. I think they have done a good job and that the source of the problem does not lie in a lack of guidance.

As well as changes to guidance, over the years police powers have also changed. For example, the ability of an officer to search a person in the street on a voluntary basis disappeared. The Code effective from 1 April 1991 included the following guidance:

> Nothing in these codes affects the ability of an officer to search a person in the street on a voluntary basis. In these circumstances an officer should always make it clear that he is seeking the co-operation of the person concerned.[24]

The guidance included a safeguard in that:

> If an officer acts in an improper manner this will invalidate a voluntary search. Juveniles, persons suffering from a mental handicap or mental illness and others who appear not to be capable of giving an informed consent should not be subject to a voluntary search.[25]

However, some felt that police officers used voluntary searches to circumvent the 'reasonable suspicion' safeguards. Professor Michael Zander wrote:

> The police sometimes operate on the basis that if a person consents to a search PACE does not apply. This concept is plainly open to abuse and could drive the proverbial 'coach and four' through the provisions on stop and search.[26]

---

[23] Code A, Annex B, para. 4.
[24] Code A, page 14, para. 1D (b).
[25] Code A, page 15 para. 1E.
[26] M Zander, *The Police and Criminal Evidence Act 1984*, 5th edn (London, Sweet & Maxwell, 2005) section 1.11.

As a result of continuing concerns over police use of the power, the 2003 Code stated:

> An officer must not search a person even with his or her consent where no power to search is applicable. Even where a person is prepared to submit to a search voluntarily, the person must not be searched unless the necessary legal power exists and the search must be in accordance with the relevant power and the provisions of this Code.[27]

The above change was influenced by the Macpherson Report published in February 1999. It included a damning indictment of the police use of the stop and search power:

> If there was one area of complaint which was universal it was the issue of 'stop and search'. Nobody in the minority ethnic communities believes that the complex arguments which are sometimes used to explain the figures of stop and search are valid. ... It is pointless for the police service to try to justify the disparity in these figures purely or mainly in terms of the other factors which are identified. ... Attempts to justify the disparities through the identification of other factors, whilst not being seen vigorously to address the discrimination which is evident, simply exacerbates the climate of distrust.[28]

A consequence was that the Code of Practice on stop and search was seen as ineffective and this led to a radical revision published in 2003. It included further guidance on reasonable suspicion and significant changes to recording. Previous Codes had required records to be kept for searches. The 2005 edition of the Code included a new requirement:

> When an officer requests a person in a public place to account for themselves i.e. their actions, behaviour, presence in an area or possession of anything, a record of the encounter must be completed at the time and a copy given to the person who has been questioned.[29]

The record had to be made on the spot unless there were exceptional circumstances. The copy had to be given immediately, was required for each vehicle and person, and recorded on a national search form. The officer also had to ask the person to self-define his/her ethnicity. It was clearly intended to be a better control against arbitrary and discriminatory searches. Additional detail in the written record was intended to better enable supervisors to monitor and scrutinise figures of searches and their results.

What was the impact of all this on the police? It created a hugely bureaucratic process almost designed to deter police from using the stop account/stop and search power at all or from asking questions of persons acting suspiciously. It also created the need for costly back-office support and systems. It meant that an

---

[27] Code A, page 3, para 1.5.

[28] W Macpherson of Cluny, *The Stephen Lawrence Inquiry* (Cm 4262-I) (London, SO, 1999) para 45.10.

[29] Code A, page 14, para. 4.12.

officer faced with a gang of youths acting suspiciously in a high crime area had the choice of completing a separate form for each of them or of turning a blind eye and not carrying out the stop and search at all. In addition he or she had to ask the person to self-define their ethnicity. To ask a question, the answer to which is self-evident, is not helpful to relations in street encounters and often creates puzzlement and anger from the person being asked. Officers in my own force have told me that often a stop and account/stop and search begins quite amicably but that people frequently become resentful and non-compliant when they are asked to state their ethnicity. As a result, in my force this is one part of the form which is frequently left blank, making monitoring more difficult.

Has the overall impact been to deter officers with legitimate reason from using the stop and search power? Home Office compiled statistics on numbers of searches carried out shows the following:[30]

**Table 1: Recorded stops and searches, 1987–2005 (selected years)**

| Year | Number of searches of persons or vehicles |
| --- | --- |
| 1987 | 118,300 |
| 1990 | 256,900 |
| 1995 | 690,300 |
| 1997/8 | 1,050,700 |
| 1998/9 | 1,080,700 |
| 2000/01 | 714,100 |
| 2002/03 | 895,300 |
| 2003/04 | 749,400 |
| 2004/05 | 851,200 |

Following a rise to a peak in 1998/9, numbers have since fluctuated so that it is difficult to detect a long term trend at this stage. The figures do however show that numbers have fallen significantly since the changes to the Codes of Practice.

From the perspective of the general public, faced with a growing culture in some areas of young people carrying offensive weapons, including knives and firearms as reported on almost daily by the media, do current safeguards provide a proportionate balance or do they tip that balance so as to deter use even in legitimate circumstances? Is the power to stop account/stop and search a deterrent? I have no doubt that it is because I was in the Metropolitan Police when the

---

[30]  G Wilkins and C Addicott, Operation of Certain Police Powers Under Pace, Statistical Bulletin 2/99 (London: Home Office, 1999) and M Ayres and L Murray, Arrests for Recorded Crime (Notifiable Offences) and the Operation of Certain Police Powers Under PACE, Statistical Bulletin 21/05 (London, Home Office, 2005).

Macpherson Report was published. Almost overnight stop and search practically ceased, we lost the streets and crime shot up.

I also question whether the amendments to the Code I have described above were necessary. Do statistics that show apparent discriminatory use of the power over more than 20 years indicates a mass conspiracy on the part of the police service to flout the Code or could there be alternative explanations? I would now like to explore this further.

One of my frustrations with some of the data used to measure success or failure of the police is that it is based on what is available and convenient rather than what is fit for purpose. There has also been a growing tendency to accept statistical data without questioning its validity and to then present conclusions without any qualifying statements on the quality of the source data. Stop and search/stop account data provides a good example. There are significant question marks over the data produced, as I will shortly show, but despite this it is produced year on year and even many of those who recognise its inherent unreliability still go on to draw conclusions and present these as fact.

Police officers recognise that the make up of street populations varies enormously depending on the area and the time of day. For example, the street population of a town centre differs greatly at 2 a.m. from its composition at 2 p.m. Despite this, year on year, stop and search/account statistics are based on resident populations from census data and used as categorical evidence that the power is being used disproportionately. Unfortunately, the fact that measurement of street populations is problematic and not easy means that existing measures continue despite their obvious flaws.

Is there any research that supports this view? Following publication of the Macpherson Report, the Home Office undertook detailed research on stop and search and published the findings in a series of reports.[31] One of these, 'Profiling Populations Available for Stops and Searches', was in response to concerns that comparisons between the ethnic breakdown of stops and searches and the ethnic breakdown of local resident populations are a misleading indicator of ethnic bias in stop and search activity. The research showed that resident population measures are very different from populations actually available to be stopped and searched:

> Specifically, the research suggests that available populations tend to include larger proportions of people from minority ethnic backgrounds than resident populations. Furthermore, when statistics on stops and searches are compared with available populations, they do not show any general pattern of bias against those from minority ethnic backgrounds.[32]

---

[31]  Police Research Series Papers 127–32 (London, Home Office, 2000).
[32]  MVA and J Miller, *Profiling Populations Available for Stops and Searches*, Police Research Series Paper 131 (London, Home Office, 2000) 84.

Further research has produced similar findings.[33]

There is therefore an urgent need for statistical data which accurately reflects the make up of the population available to be searched. It is neither fair nor acceptable to collect and utilise data which does not reflect reality. Until then conclusions will continue to be drawn from data which is inherently unreliable for the purpose it is being used.

The Home Office research also examined the geographical targeting of stops and searches in relation to crime at two sites and found that, 'the patterns of stops and searches appeared, to a large extent, to be justified by the patterns of crime'.[34] The research also found that disproportionality is, 'to some extent, a product of structural factors beyond the control of the police'.[35]

It is evident that the preventative effect of stop and search/account has yet to be properly researched. Again, a convenient and easily available indicator used as a measure is the number of resulting arrests. Is it an appropriate measurement? It should certainly form part of a suite of indicators but it also needs to be put into the context of an intelligence-led modern police service which seeks to prevent and deter crime.

To see stop and search/account as a success only if an arrest takes place is wrong. Reasonable suspicion is often just that, and it results in an investigation or questioning to follow up on that suspicion. In some cases even where the suspicion is found to be substantiated it may not result in an arrest. Police officers have discretion to deal with offences and offenders in a variety of ways and an arrest does not always follow even where there is the power to do so. For example, an officer may choose to deal with a minor possession of drugs by way of a warning.

In my view, the impact of Code A on policing has been very significant. Quite rightly, scrutiny of the power has increased. That has been in response to legitimate concerns. However, the Code has been used to increase levels of bureaucracy to such an extent that it now discourages police officers from using stop and search/account, or has the effect of tying them up for lengthy periods. The effect was most vividly seen in some of our larger cities when recorded robberies increased to such an extent that the government intervened with increased funding and resources to combat the problem. Stop and search was a key tactic in addressing the situation.[36]

The effect of PACE through the many revisions of Code A has been to discourage the use of stop and search. Whilst my view may not sit easily with

---

[33] P Waddington, K Stenson and D Don, 'In proportion: Race, and Police Stop and Search' (2004) 44 British Journal of Criminology 889.

[34] MVA and J Miller, *Profiling Populations Available for Stops and Searches*, Police Research Series Paper 131 (London, Home Office, 2000) 86.

[35] *Ibid*, 87.

[36] The Street Crime Initiative was launched on 17 March 2002 (robbery had risen 28% in the 12 months to March 2002).

available statistics (which are generally accepted as unreliable by most commentators anyway) police officers tell me that faced with a car full of suspicious people, the prospect of filling forms does deter a stop.

The question for me is whether this is justified on the basis of performance measures which are questionable and have been shown by Home Office research to be in need of revision. The emphasis on discouraging the use of the power has undoubtedly stifled the ability of the police to prevent crime. What is also clear from feedback from the public is that most people do not mind being stopped or searched providing that the police officer treats them politely, with dignity and explains why the power is being used.[37]

It is evident that stop and search can undermine trust and confidence in some sections of the community. I would like to see a study of the effects of respectful but non-bureaucratic stop and search practices on police community relations and crime rates. Encouragingly, a Statutory Instrument came into force on 31 August 2006 which enabled the British Transport Police in two areas to pilot the giving of an electronic receipt in lieu of a written record. The intention is to evaluate the impact on police accountability and police bureaucracy.[38]

# V  The impartial search for the truth

I very firmly believe that the criminal justice system should be based on a search for truth with the aim of establishing as far as possible what actually occurred, with the police as impartial examiners of the evidence.

The Philips Commission, which laid the foundation on which PACE was constructed, reinforced the importance of the 'adversarial system' and the need for the prosecution to prove its case beyond all reasonable doubt: 'to respond to a mere accusation, would reverse the onus of proof at trial and would require the defendant to prove the negative, that he is not guilty'.[39]

The Runciman Commission, whilst supporting the adversarial concept, also recognised its drawbacks, 'a thoroughgoing adversarial system ... seems to turn a search for truth into a contest played between opposing lawyers according to a set of rules which the jury does not necessarily accept or even understand'.[40] The Runciman Commission did, however, recognise the importance of a search for truth in its recommendations concerning the usefulness of DNA as a tool for establishing the guilt or innocence of a suspect. In reinforcing the adversarial

---

[37]  On the importance of fair process, see further ch 2 by David Dixon in this collection.

[38]  The Police and Criminal Evidence Act 1984 (Code of Practice) (Revisions to Code A) Order 2006 (SI No 2165).

[39]  *Report of the Royal Commission on Criminal Procedure*, Cmnd 8092 (London, HMSO, 1981) para 4.35.

[40]  *Report of the Royal Commission on Criminal Justice*, Cm 2263 (London, HMSO, 1993) para 12.

concept so strongly, did the Royal Commission miss an opportunity to encourage the establishment of truth as the basis of any investigation? I think it did.

I firmly believe that the police should be impartial investigators. Advocates of the adversarial system argue that false conclusions are more likely to be avoided if evidence is tested rigorously at every stage of the system before prosecution. I agree with that view providing the aim is to establish the truth.

There was a very early opportunity when PACE was being introduced, to focus the criminal justice system on a search for truth. As I have already outlined, pre-PACE the police were responsible for both the investigation and prosecution of offences. As a young detective constable operating from West End Central I can still vividly recall going to court one morning to prosecute all the overnight cases and applications for remands in custody and then, following court, resuming my investigative role into 33 burglaries. Professional legal support in those days was just that, support.

In terms of impartial investigations and the search for truth this was not a healthy position especially when combined with the training of the day, which was based around the definition of offences and the key 'points to prove'. It did have a tendency to encourage police investigations down the road of looking for evidence to secure a conviction.

I was therefore very pleased with the Philips Commission's recommendation to separate investigation from prosecution. It led to the Prosecution of Offences Act 1985 and the CPS. The creation of an independent CPS as the main prosecuting body for criminal matters could have transformed the ethos of the criminal justice system in the direction of a search for truth. There are a number of reasons why this did not happen, which I now intend to explore.

Initially, most police officers received a fairly superficial level of training in PACE involving a course of a day or two which largely focused on powers of the police and the main changes to legislation. As a result, in terms of actual investigations little in terms of police culture changed. Although the separation of the investigative and prosecution role was clear in statute, the essential training needed to accompany this change to refocus the direction of investigations was largely lacking.

The second element concerned the adversarial system. Whilst a CPS was created, the failure to create a Public Defender Service introduced the market economy into the custody suite, because, notwithstanding the duty to defend a client to the full, it was also the case that legal aid provided an important source of income and that prolific criminals became valued clients. The legal aid system also encouraged cases to be drawn out and officers began to experience more and more applications for court adjournments. A consequence was that court hearings took longer to conclude and that legal aid costs spiralled to the extent that the Legal Services Commission is currently seeking ways to significantly reduce the budget.

Surprisingly, whilst PACE laid down clear guidance for the police, it included no such guidance for the legal profession. As a result, whilst demand for lawyers for suspects held in custody suites increased dramatically, in the absence of national direction, those lawyers had to use their own experience and interpretation of PACE and initially, the actual role of the solicitor in the police station was unclear.[41]

This lack of clarity also had the effect of encouraging an adversarial perspective between investigative officers and solicitors, so that in the early days there was little in the way of disclosure largely because of mutual distrust and misunderstanding over roles. Investigating officers often chose not to disclose any information until the interview, which in turn made a solicitor's position more difficult because they could only rely on what their client told them in making an initial judgement on what advice should be given in the best interests of their client.

In the pre-PACE era, interview technique had largely been acquired through experience and by watching and listening to colleagues. The difference between interview and interrogation often depended on how responsive a suspect was to questioning. In contrast, PACE brought a level of accountability that required officers to be properly trained. It led to the PEACE model which was designed around open-ended questioning aimed at eliciting responses.[42] The aim was to encourage suspects to give an account that could be tested against other evidence with the aim of establishing the truth and in line with the objective set out in Code C: 'The purpose of any interview is to obtain from the person concerned his explanation of the facts and not necessarily to obtain an admission.'[43] It placed emphasis on interview not interrogation.

To counter fears of oppressive styles of interview, PACE specifically introduced legislation to prevent such techniques. Section 78 of the Act gave a court discretion to exclude any evidence if it appeared that having regard to all the circumstances, including the circumstances in which it was obtained, the evidence would have such an unfair effect on the proceedings that the court ought to exclude it. Section 82(3) also preserved the common law rules on the exclusion of evidence and the power to exclude evidence if the prejudicial effect outweighed its probative value.

The irony of these sections to many police officers was often seen at first hand in the court room. Having followed PACE requirements in conducting their own interviews in the police station, officers could then witness a 'no holds barred' cross-examination of a witness in court using oppressive techniques. The unintended consequence was to reaffirm the priority of the suspect within the criminal justice system. Thus, many victims of rape would rather suffer in private than face the prospect of being made to suffer again in a public court room at the hands of a barrister. Treatment of victims outside the environment of the court room has improved to such an extent in recent years as to make the contrast with the court experience even more marked. Surely, if oppression is not a tool for the

---

[41] See further ch 9 by Anthony Edwards in this collection.
[42] PEACE—Preparation and Planning, Engage and Explain, Account, Closure, Evaluate.
[43] Code C, Notes for Guidance 12A.

police, equally judges must be prepared to control over-vigorous cross examination by Counsel which can do a great deal of damage to a witness' ability to recall events properly.

The major factor that has impacted on the search for truth relates to the 'right to silence'. The 1972 Criminal Law Revision Committee had recommended changes to the existing right to silence which had proven extremely controversial and were not acted upon. The Philips Royal Commission also took evidence in respect of the 'right to silence' and in many ways this illustrated the differing perspectives of the criminal justice system. The police saw themselves as both impartial investigators and prosecutor and, in evidence to the Philips Commission, put forward the view that it was in the interests of an innocent man to clear himself and, whilst accepting as a fundamental principle that a person should not be asked to self-incriminate, argued that the right of silence protected only the guilty. This view fell on deaf ears. The right of silence was seen as an essential safeguard for the weak, the immature and the inadequate: its removal could increase the risk of false confessions by those unable to withstand police interrogation. The Commission reaffirmed as the 'golden thread' running through English criminal justice that the prosecution must prove a defendant guilty of an offence, beyond all reasonable doubt (a high standard indeed), and if a case is not proven there is no case to answer and the defence does not need to respond.

This recommendation was initially accepted by the government and as a consequence PACE did not provide that adverse inferences could be drawn from a suspect's refusal to answer questions. This meant, however, that a suspect could, with impunity, answer 'no comment' to every question put to him or her. This often negated the effect of the interview. A person charged with an offence could then seek disclosure of the prosecution evidence and use it to help build a defence for use at court without giving the prosecution time to explore its truth.

As a result, less than one year after the introduction of PACE, Douglas Hurd, the then Home Secretary, giving the annual Police Foundation lecture said:

> Is it really in the interests of justice, for example, that experienced criminals should be able to refuse to answer all police questions secure in the knowledge that a jury will never hear of it? Does the present law really protect the innocent whose interests will generally lie in answering questions frankly? Is it really unthinkable that the jury should be allowed to know about the defendant's silence and, in the light of the other facts brought to light during a trial, be able to draw its own conclusions?[44]

The Criminal Justice and Public Order Act 1994 (CJPOA) recognised through legislation that the balance had swung too far in favour of a suspect. The CJPOA allowed adverse inferences to be drawn from failure to tell the police about facts subsequently relied upon by the accused at trial, and from a failure by the suspect

---

[44] The full text of the lecture can be found on the Police Foundation website: http://www.police-foundation.org.uk (accessed 12 June 2008).

to answer specific police questions about objects, marks or substances on or about their person or at the place of arrest, or the failure to account for their presence at the scene of the crime. For such inferences to be drawn the officer had to have told the suspect what offence was being investigated, what fact the suspect would be asked to account for, and that the officer believed this fact might be due to the suspect being involved in the offence. It required the investigating officer to disclose evidence prior to an interview to enable a defence solicitor to be able to advise their client.

The new legislation resulted in a change to the wording of the caution. Prior to 1995 the PACE Code of Practice read: 'You do not have to say anything unless you wish to do so but what you say may be given in evidence'.[45] The new caution read, 'You do not have to say anything. But it may harm your defence if you do not mention when questioned something which you later rely on in court. Anything you do say may be given in evidence'.[46] As a result, whilst a suspect could still refuse to answer questions, it could no longer be used as a tactic that had no consequence to the suspect because both the prosecution and the judge were now allowed to draw inferences from that silence as possible evidence of guilt.

To most police officers the words usually ascribed to Jeremy Bentham still echo true: 'Innocence claims the right of speaking, as guilt invokes the privilege of silence'.[47] The change was very welcome because it encouraged suspects to give explanations. However, an unintended consequence of the CJPOA was to embed the adversarial system more fully into the custody suite through the concept of active defence.[48] Home Office research published in 2000 found that legal advisers reported that they now had to be very careful about advising their clients not to answer police questions in view of the possible implications of silence if the case went to court. They might still advise silence if there was insufficient police disclosure, the evidence was weak or their client was vulnerable. Otherwise they would advise clients to give an account to the police when interviewed.[49]

For the defence, guidance was produced by the Law Society. For example, advice published by the Law Society in 2006 states that:

> It remains the case, however, that silence cannot, by itself, prove guilt (CJPOA 1994 s 38), and inferences can only be drawn if the court or jury first find that the other evidence establishes a prima facie case or is 'sufficiently compelling to call for an answer from the accused.' However, this does not mean that in order for inferences to be drawn the police must disclose evidence amounting to a prima facie case prior to questioning

---

[45]  Code C, effective 1 April 1991, page 57, para 10.4.
[46]  Code C, effective 10 April 1995, page 54, para 10.4.
[47]  Jeremy Bentham, 1748–1832, Jurist, Philosopher and Social Reformer. See further A Lewis, 'Bentham's views on the Right to Silence' (1990) *Current Legal Problems* 135.
[48]  See R Ede and E Shepherd, *Active Defence*, 2nd edn (London, Law Society Publishing, 2000).
[49]  T Bucke, R Street and D Brown, *The right of silence: the impact of the Criminal Justice and Public Order Act 1994* (Home Office Research Study No 199) (London, Home Office, 2000) 25.

the suspect. Despite the inherent unfairness, the courts have consistently held that the police are not under a general duty to disclose evidence to the suspect at the police station.[50]

The phrase, 'despite the inherent unfairness' begs the question, unfairness to whom? To a police officer trying to establish the truth? To a victim who has suffered hurt or loss? The quotation also illustrates how far the adversarial process is now embedded in the custody suite[51] and I know that accepted doctrine for many defence lawyers is that the trial effectively starts from their entry into the custody suite. Active defence is thus now firmly embedded in the custody suite. At this stage the focus is very much on disclosure and on the strength of the *initial* prosecution hand (because forensic evidence that might corroborate other evidence is not available because of the length of time it takes to process).

In many ways this has made a search for truth harder because disclosure, rather than facilitating a search for truth, can become a tactical pre-interview battle between the police and a defence representative in which the police can be reluctant to disclose information which could forewarn a suspect of a potential line of questioning whilst the lawyer expects to receive full disclosure in order to be able to gauge the strength of evidence in order to be able to properly advise their client. But does this have to be the case? Is there scope within the adversarial process for police officers and defence lawyers to work towards a search for truth? I think there is.

Code C, note 6D states that: 'The solicitor's only role in the police station is to protect and advance the interests of their client'. In many cases, the best interests of a client faced with overwhelming evidence of guilt lies in trying to minimise the sanction. Disclosure of evidence can therefore be mutually advantageous to a search for truth. The same applies to a person who is innocent and who has information that could enable the police to pursue exculpatory lines of investigation. However, in many respects the current adversarial system is not conducive to a search for the truth and does invite negative tactics on the part of defence solicitors.

What then of defence tactics? PACE had defined the purpose of an interview as an opportunity to gain an explanation of the facts. However, many procedural opportunities have been developed to frustrate this purpose. For example, Law Society advice published in January 2006 includes the following:

> If the client's instructions, having regard to the relevant law, indicate that they are guilty of the alleged offence(s) the solicitor should consider the strength of the police evidence. ... If the police evidence is weak, or the solicitor is unclear of the strength of the police case, the solicitor should consider the advantages and disadvantages of

---

[50]  E Cape (on behalf of the Law Society Criminal Law Committee), *Police Station Advice: Advising on Silence* Criminal Practitioner's Newsletter, Special Edition—January 2006, Issue 63 (London, Law Society) 4 (citations omitted).

[51]  See further ch 10 by John Jackson in this collection.

remaining silent at this stage. Remaining silent may mean that there is insufficient evidence to charge or insufficient evidence to secure a conviction.[52]

Quite legitimate tactics, but hardly conducive to a search for truth.

The difficulties associated with interview evidence under the PACE framework has led to the belief that forensics and technology are of greater evidential value to an investigation, particularly in serious cases. The impartial search for the truth in custody has been replaced by a greater, more costly, search for the truth through developing forensics and technology, leading to concerns that we are witnessing the expansion of a surveillance society.

Since PACE was introduced, police performance measures have increased dramatically and some see this as an impediment to the police role as impartial investigator because forces are closely monitored in relation to how they perform against targets. They see the advent of bonus payments for chief constables as a further impediment to impartial investigations arguing that targets drive forces in particular directions. I feel fortunate that I had the choice of whether or not to link my pay to performance and I chose not to. Colleagues no longer have a choice.

I have a real concern that establishing the truth has never been a performance indicator for the police or any part of the criminal justice system. In my view this is a major failing because such a performance indicator could dramatically alter how the criminal justice system operates. I do however accept that some targets can create inaccurate perceptions. Whilst I am not against targets per se, I do believe that too many of them are related to what is easy to measure rather than what should be measured. Personally, I would not want my pay linked to a bonus scheme.

I would now like to turn to developments related to statutory charging and developments linked to the 2005 edition of the PACE Codes of Practice (published 1 January 2006). Having spent the greater part of my career as an operational detective, I am in no doubt that the main strength of our criminal justice system lies in its constituent parts—investigation, prosecution and adjudication—being separated constitutionally.

The police role is distinct and very clear. We have a duty to undertake impartial investigations and to gather evidence to establish the truth. Only when we are satisfied that there is a case to answer should the case move to the next stage, to the prosecution. The CPS, from its independent perspective, considers the evidence and makes the decision as to whether a prosecution should follow. The courts provide impartial consideration of the prosecution and defence cases. The separation of these three elements (police, prosecution and courts) adds great strength to the integrity of our system.

---

[52] E Cape (on behalf of the Law Society Criminal Law Committee), *Police Station Advice: Advising on Silence* Criminal Practitioner's Newsletter, Special Edition—January 2006, Issue 63 (London, Law Society) 10.

I have therefore watched recent developments in relation to locating CPS lawyers in custody suites with concern. Whilst I fully appreciate arguments that have led to the new system, that professional legal expertise in the custody suite should result in fewer charges being amended before a hearing, I do have serious reservations as to whether it is necessary and, more importantly, whether it will lead to CPS lawyers eventually directing investigations. Already, there is evidence that this is happening and, if it continues, there is a danger of returning to the pre-Philips era, when criticism was made that the investigation and prosecution were in the hands of one body, at that time the police. The erosion of the distinction between police and prosecution puts in jeopardy the safeguards that this separation of function brings with it.

A personal concern is that performance targets can and do influence decisions as to charging. The danger is that if targets for guilty pleas and convictions are set too high it will result in the victim being marginalised because cases will be decided by a CPS lawyer, perhaps chasing their individual targets, rather than a court. Whilst the police may have been criticised in the past for charging too many suspects, the fact remains that in many instances the circumstances and evidence warranted a victim the opportunity of being heard at court.

It is also the case that a CPS lawyer has personal key performance indicators that are linked to guilty pleas at court. It brings into the system an element of inconsistency in decision-making and leads to questions being asked as to whether the basis of the current charging standard, based on a realistic prospect of conviction and public interest, incorporates too much subjectivity.

# VI Conclusion

The 2002 Joint Home Office and Cabinet Review of PACE quoted Professor Ed Cape's view that 'despite legitimate criticism that may be made of PACE and the Codes of Practice ... [it] is considered by many to be a model for a fair, rational approach to police accountability and to securing fair trial'.[53] The Review noted how police and solicitors spoke of PACE having standardised and professionalised police work and ventured the view that 'the operational approach of the police can be said to have been fundamentally altered by the Act'.[54] In many ways I would agree with these views. PACE did lead to many benefits which helped to professionalise the police service.

The key question now is whether it is fit for purpose. In considering this question I would like to refer back to the opening chapter of the report of the

---

[53]  Home Office/Cabinet Office, *PACE Review* (London, Home Office, 2002) 9.
[54]  *Ibid.*

Royal Commission. It referred to the need for: 'A balance to be struck here between the interest of the whole community and the rights and liberties of the individual citizen'.

As I hope I have shown, when it was introduced, PACE erred on the side of caution and the safeguards it introduced were at the expense of the whole community because they took police officers away from the streets. The safeguards were the result of legitimate concerns over policing at that time. However, over the course of the 21 years since the introduction of PACE the police service has undergone a radical transformation in its professionalism. In addition, levels of inspection and accountability, both formal through complaints procedures, and informal through intrusive examination of methods of operation by courts, inspecting bodies, the media and individuals, are higher than ever before.

My view is that issues which impacted on the 'fundamental balance' at the time of the Philips Commission have significantly changed and that safeguards thought necessary some 20 years ago now need to be redressed. Some might argue that to water down the PACE safeguards would be a retrograde step that could lead to a return to the lax standards of policing that were a feature of the pre-PACE era. I do not subscribe to that view. PACE led to changes which are now part of policing culture and a modern highly accountable professional service. Society has changed and so has policing, which is now widely recognised as a professional service. I therefore very much welcomed the 2007 review[55] because it is time to move forward so that the unintended consequences of PACE can be properly scrutinised and the role of the modern police in the current criminal justice system identified.

Just as importantly, I have a real concern that the criminal justice system has lost its way and that the object of stopping criminal and anti-social behaviour is being steadily eroded through short-termism typified by the current performance management regime. Indicators used to measure sanction detections and offenders brought to justice provide good examples. They are having the effect of bringing more people, particularly young people, into the criminal justice system because the emphasis is on counting detections regardless of how minor the offence is.[56] Just treatment and fairness is taking a back seat to a target driven regime, and the result has been the criminalisation of our young people.

The complexity of the legislative framework governing policing is a further issue that requires attention. Since PACE was introduced considerable amounts of case law have developed creating difficulties for the police to stay up to date with developments. Part of the reasoning behind PACE was the need to give clarity to the law through drawing together related legislation that had developed independently over the years. In recent years the amount of primary legislation passed has increased exponentially. The law, both statute and case law, is now

---

[55]  *Modernising Police Powers: Review of the Police & Criminal Evidence Act (PACE) 1984: consultation paper* (London, Home Office, 2007).
[56]  See further ch 7 by Richard Young in this collection.

extremely complex, and a review that would simplify and draw together related elements into one overarching Act as occurred when PACE was introduced would be very welcome.

Any review of PACE should look at the whole of the criminal justice system and not just at the police in isolation, as happened in the mid-1980s. It is my hope that the 2007 Review will focus on pragmatic outcomes, re-establish the search for truth, and recognise and restore the role of the custody suite as a site of impartial policing.

# 7

# Street Policing after PACE: The Drift to Summary Justice

## I Introduction

In this chapter I examine the drift towards summary justice within the realm of street policing. By summary justice I mean the imposition of penalties on citizens without a formal, adversarial trial in open court presided over by an impartial adjudicator according to rules of evidence designed to promote reliable and fair outcomes. Contemporary forms of summary justice therefore include cases disposed of by a guilty plea at court, conditional cautions issued by the Crown Prosecution Service (CPS), as well as cautions, reprimands, warnings (including formal warnings for cannabis possession) and fixed penalty notices (including 'penalty notices for disorder' (PND)) issued by the police, community support officers,[1] and 'accredited persons'[2] (such as local authority wardens[3]) whose remit runs to public areas.

---

* I would like to thank Ed Cape, John Long, Bronwen Morgan and Julie Vennard for their help during the process of writing this chapter.

[1] See sch 4 of the Police Reform Act 2002 as extended by s 46 of the Anti-Social Behaviour Act 2003. Under the legislation community support officers *may* be provided by their Chief Constable with powers to issue 'penalty notices for disorder' for some or all of the offences covered by that scheme save for theft and littering (although for the latter they may issue a local authority fixed penalty notice): The Criminal Justice and Police Act 2001 (Amendment) and Police Reform Act 2002 (Modification) Order 2004, Art 4; Home Office, *Criminal Justice and Police Act 2001 (s 1–11) Penalty Notices for Disorder Police Operational Guidance* (March, 2005) (hereafter *Home Office Operational Guidance*, 2005) 7; Home Office, *Criminal Justice and Police Act 2001 (s 1–11), Supplementary Operational Guidance for Community Support Officers* (no date), 1. The Home Office guidance cited in this chapter is available from http://police.homeoffice.gov.uk/operational-policing/crime-disorder/index.html (accessed 12 June 2008).

[2] See sch 5 of the Police Reform Act 2002 as extended by s 46 of the Anti-Social Behaviour Act 2003 and ss 15–16 of the Police and Justice Act 2006.

[3] Provision for local authorities to issue fixed penalty notices (and keep the receipts) for a range of matters was made by the Anti-Social Behaviour Act 2003 (s 43) and the Clean Neighbourhoods and Environment Act 2005. In 2005–06, 33,033 on-the-spot fines were issued for littering according to *The Times*, 17 September 2007.

The contemporary importance of police-imposed summary justice can be seen in Table 1, which concerns notifiable crimes 'cleared up'.[4]

|  | No of detections | % of all detections[5] |
|---|---|---|
| Charge or summons[6] | 725,539 | 47.8 |
| Offences taken into consideration at court | 117,730 | 7.5 |
| Cautions | 311,155 | 20.5 |
| Penalty Notices for Disorder | 105,698 | 7.0 |
| Cannabis warnings | 63,635 | 4.2 |
| Non-sanction detections (NFA) | 192,685 | 12.7 |
| ALL DETECTIONS | 1,516,442 | 100.0 |

We can see from Table 1 that almost a third of the notifiable crime that was cleared up in 2005/06 was dealt with not through a court process but rather through the imposition of a police penalty, caution or warning. If one adds to this figure the 'non-sanction detections', that is cases where the police believe they have identified who committed a specific offence but decide not to take any further action (NFA),[7] the proportion of 'cleared up' notifiable crimes dealt with through police processes alone climbs to 44.4%.

Cautions, penalty notices and cannabis warnings can all be thought of as police-imposed summary justice of a formal kind. But the academic literature on policing has highlighted that summary justice can also be informal, with police actions geared towards 'social disciplining'.[8] By this is meant that the police sometimes use their powers not with the primary purpose of investigating crime or securing the imposition of a formal penalty but rather to impose discipline. Thus, for example, stop and search powers are sometimes deployed to subordinate or deter those individuals and groups perceived to be posing a threat to public order.[9] And the power to arrest under section 5 of the Public Order Act 1986 is sometimes used to uphold police authority and enforce respect 'for the

---

[4]   Source: A Walker, C Kershaw and S Nicholas, *Crime in England and Wales 2005/6*, Home Office Statistical Bulletin 12/06 (London, Home Office, 2006) 139. Notifiable crimes are those that are notified to the Home Office—they exclude most motoring offences and some other summary offences.
Table 1: Police Detections by method of detection, 2005/06

[5]   The figures in this column do not sum to 100 due to rounding.

[6]   Police detections include charges or summons as cleared up crime even though many of these cases will be discontinued or result in a not guilty verdict. The 'offences brought to justice' measurement, by contrast, substitutes 'convictions' for 'charge or summons'.

[7]   To qualify as non-sanction detections, the police must have sufficient evidence to charge, and must tell both offender and victim that they consider the matter 'cleared up'.

[8]   See, in particular, S Choongh, *Policing as Social Discipline* (Oxford, Oxford University Press, 1997).

[9]   Home Office, *Stop & Search Manual* (London, Home Office, 2005) 38.

cloth'.[10] A decision to detain and interrogate someone in a police station may be motivated by similar considerations. In other words, in these cases the process becomes the punishment, and (assuming that the process is seen as *sufficient* punishment) the formally recorded outcome is likely to be 'no further action' (NFA).

The outcome of NFA is particularly likely where the police lacked legal justification for the use of their powers in the first place, as this ensures that there is no independent scrutiny of their actions such as that which a court might engage in. NFA is also a likely outcome where the legal pre-condition for the exercise of a power had little substantive content (as where no individualised or reasonable suspicion is required). This is because in the vast majority of such cases no evidence of crime will be found.

However, another way to avoid independent scrutiny of the use of police powers, or to 'get a result' where sufficient evidence to prosecute is lacking, is to impose a formal penalty which effectively terminates the process prior to the possibility of such scrutiny arising. At the time the Police and Criminal Evidence Act (1984) (PACE) was enacted, the paradigm example of such a penalty was the police caution,[11] and this is so notwithstanding the benign intentions (of avoiding criminalisation) that often underlay its use. Now, the paradigm example is the PND (where, as we shall see, quasi-criminalisation *is* the intention). The important point, for introductory purposes, is to note that informal and formal forms of summary justice can overlap and feed off each other. This overlap makes it difficult to gauge the extent of social disciplining. Where informal penalties and formal penalties overlap, the original motivation for the exercise of police power is usually impossible to detect.

Analysing the drift to summary justice within street policing must therefore involve a consideration of police process powers such as stop and search and arrest, as well as police outcome powers such as the imposition of a caution or PND. As the focus of this book is on PACE and subsequent developments, no attempt is made to cover all police powers that can be used on the street. Arrest for breach of the peace, for example, long pre-dates PACE and will not be examined here. I will also avoid repeating material covered by other contributors to this collection. Thus I will say little about general powers of arrest as post-PACE developments in that sphere are covered in chapter eight by Ed Cape in this collection. I will also not attempt to cover public order powers,[12] or the

---

[10] D Brown and T Ellis, *Policing Low-Level Disorder: Police Use of Section 5 of the Public Order Act 1986*, Home Office Research Study 135 (London, Home Office, 1994) 42–3 (hereafter Brown and Ellis).

[11] Evidence that the police sometimes ignore the procedural safeguards surrounding cautioning is summarised in A Sanders and R Young, *Criminal Justice* 3rd edn (Oxford, Oxford University Press, 2007) 349–50 (hereafter Sanders and Young). See also ch 10 by Jackson in this collection, text accompanying n 42.

[12] Such as the many powers provided under the Public Order Act 1986 and the Criminal Justice and Public Order Act 1994 (to prevent raves, regulate assemblies and processions, and so forth).

myriad of powers aimed at tackling the amorphous concept of anti-social behaviour, such as powers to 'disperse' intimidating 'groups',[13] or remove children from public spaces,[14] or the use of acceptable behaviour contracts,[15] despite their obvious importance to analyses of informal summary justice. This is because PACE itself did not attempt to regulate policing in general but rather concerned itself with police powers to investigate crime. Finally, the emphasis on street policing means that I am not concerned with those penalties issued by regulatory agencies other than the police such as the CPS, the Health and Safety Executive or HM Revenue and Customs. At the heart of my analysis will be a consideration of the penalty notices for disorder scheme. But to put that analysis in its appropriate context, we need to start by looking back to PACE as originally enacted, and the debates that surrounded that landmark piece of legislation.

# II  The Royal Commission on Criminal Procedure

The Police and Criminal Evidence Act 1984 is recognisably based on the recommendations of the Royal Commission on Criminal Procedure (the Philips Commission). The Philips Commission was set up in February 1978 and its report, delivered three years later, remains the natural starting point for any review of particular aspects of the past, present and future of PACE.

## A The Terms of Reference and What they Excluded

The Philips Commission's own starting point was its terms of reference.[16] What is apparent from those terms and, indeed, from a reading of PACE as originally

---

[13]  The Anti Social Behaviour Act 2003 (as amended) allows areas reasonably believed to suffer persistent anti-social acts by 'groups' of two or more persons to be designated as dispersal areas. Designation provides individual police officers who reasonably believe that the presence in the area of particular groups of two or more persons has resulted, *or is likely to result*, in any members of the public being intimidated, harassed, alarmed or distressed with the power to direct those persons to disperse, or to leave the relevant locality (if not a resident within it). More than 800 areas were designated for dispersal between 2004 and 2005: Hansard, 18 January 2007, col 950. See further A Crawford and S Lister, *The Use and Impact of Dispersal Orders: Sticking Plasters and Wake-Up Calls* (Bristol, Policy Press, 2007).

[14]  Section 16 of the Crime and Disorder Act 1998 (as amended) gives the police the power to 'remove' school-age children in certain circumstances from public places. The same Act allows local authorities and chief constables to introduce child curfew schemes and s 15 allows the police to remove a child found in breach of such a curfew to the child's place of residence.

[15]  Supposedly voluntary agreements entered into as a way of avoiding more formal court-ordered measures such as Anti-Social Behaviour Orders. More than 13,000 acceptable behaviour contracts were made between October 2003 and 2005: Hansard, 18 January 2007, col 950. See further P Squires and D Stephen, *Rougher Justice* (Cullompton, Willan, 2005) ch 5.

[16]  Royal Commission on Criminal Procedure (RCCP), *Report*, Cmnd 8092 (London, HMSO, 1981) iv.

enacted, is that the focus was firmly on the investigation of criminal offences, pre-trial procedure (including the preparation of prosecution cases) and related features of criminal procedure and evidence. In other words, the Philips Commission was not asked to review police powers in general, but only those police powers that related to the investigation of crime.[17]

This distinction between investigative powers and other police powers is problematic. In practice, the ability to bring investigatory powers to bear is enhanced through the availability of other kinds of street powers. Thus a power to hold football fans behind a containment line at the exit to a railway station in order to prevent a breach of the peace provides ample opportunities to generate suspicion sufficient to justify the use of investigative powers such as stop and search.

The Royal Commission's terms of reference did not extend to a consideration of the substantive criminal law either: 'We have also accepted the scope of the criminal law as given' (para 1.9). This is important because of the Philips Commission's reliance on the concept of reasonable suspicion of an offence as a vital pre-condition of the police exercise of investigatory powers. If criminal offences are defined very broadly, or in vague terminology, then the pre-condition of reasonable suspicion is unlikely to amount to much of a constraint on the exercise of police power.

It was for this reason that a minority of the Philips Commission opposed the proposal to extend stop and search powers to cover the carrying of 'offensive weapons', a term covering any article so long as intent to cause injury with it can be shown (section 1, Prevention of Crime Act 1953). The majority concluded that: 'If there is imprecision in the definition of the offence, the remedy for the difficulty perceived by our colleagues lies in removing that imprecision rather in refusing the police the power to search' (para 3.21). But, because their terms of reference did not extend to the criminal law, no recommendation was made about this matter and parliament did not take the hint.

As we shall see in subsequent sections, the vagueness and reach of the criminal law has grown substantially in the post-PACE era. Thus, irrespective of other developments, the ambit of police powers, when assessed by reference to the kinds of behaviour which can trigger their use, has expanded correspondingly.

## B The 'Fundamental Balance'

The Royal Commission accepted that identifying the 'fundamental balance' between the interests of the community in bringing offenders to justice and the rights and liberties of persons suspected or accused of crime was the central

---

[17] Thus the RCCP accepted that public order powers lay outside its terms of remit: *ibid*, para 3.23.

challenge it faced.[18] Some critics have pointed out that the apparent dichotomy here is false, and that the failure to recognise this led the Philips Commission into error.[19]

The argument that the dichotomy is false takes the form of two related points. First, that the community has the same interest in the protection of the rights and liberties of suspects as do individual suspects. Second, individual suspects have as much interest in offenders being brought to justice as the community does. These points can be grounded in a number of different ways.

At the most simplistic level, it is inevitable that innocent members of the community will sometimes fall under police suspicion. These people will naturally want their liberties protected while remaining keen to see the real offenders brought to justice. Then there are all those who commit crimes who will be keen on their own liberties being preserved within the criminal process (and who may hope to 'get off on a technicality') whilst nonetheless remaining supportive of the idea that offenders in general should be brought to justice effectively. Who would seriously argue that shoplifters are opposed to the prosecution and punishment of rapists and murderers? Finally there is the point that we all have a stake in a fair criminal justice process (and in seeing offenders brought to justice) regardless of whether or not we are at risk of becoming suspects (or becoming a victim of crime), just as we all have an interest in the National Health Service whether we have 'gone private' or not. We are not atomistic individuals concerned only with our narrow self-interest but rather flourish within, and are defined by, relationships with other people, including our civic relationships in which we show mutual concern for one another as fellow citizens. Thus, we all have an interest in living in a fair society based on a meaningful degree of social solidarity.

Yet another way of expressing doubts about the 'fundamental balance' is to note that those who characteristically make up the bulk of the suspect and defendant population (the 'lower classes', the relatively young, men) also make up the bulk of the victim population).[20] Thus there is a huge overlap between complainants, witnesses, victims, suspects, defendants and offenders. To posit the interests of the community in bringing offenders to justice as if we are talking about a quite different set of people from those whose liberties are at stake within the criminal process is misconceived. That is one reason why the government's

---

[18]   *Ibid*, para 1.11.

[19]   See, eg Sanders and Young, *Criminal Justice* 2nd edn (London, Butterworths, 2000) 127–9.

[20]   See R Morgan and T Newburn, *The Future of Policing* (Oxford, Clarendon, 1997) 26–7. There are offences where this general pattern does not hold true, such as rape and domestic violence.

current rhetoric that it is seeking to rebalance the criminal justice system 'in favour of the law-abiding majority'[21] and 'putting victims at the heart of criminal justice' is open to criticism.

Did the false dichotomy at the heart of the Philips Commission's terms of reference actually lead it into error, however? The Philips Commission itself pointed out that the notion of a 'fundamental balance' raised a number of difficult and perhaps insoluble questions.[22] They noted that a possible way forward would be to accept that 'some of the powers of the police might be increased, if their use was likewise subjected to reciprocal and stricter controls'.[23] But for this to be acceptable, proposals should be 'based on an objectively established body of knowledge about how pre-trial procedures work in practice, and on considered assessment of the likely effects of possible changes'.[24]

In line with this stance, the Commission highlighted the findings of research which established that the police rely heavily on members of the public for reports of, and evidence about, crime. The Commission noted, in particular, the importance of police interviewing of suspects in allaying or strengthening suspicion and in producing confessions and (subsequently) guilty pleas.[25] It concluded:

> There is, then, a critically important relationship between the police and the public in the detection and investigation of crime. This alone makes it essential that the public should have confidence in the way the police go about the process of investigation, so that ordinary citizens will continue to cooperate in that process. The success of the police depends upon public support and this should be reflected in the arrangements for investigation.

In other words, the detection and investigation of crime would suffer if the police lost legitimacy in the eyes of the public. It was therefore crucial that the police exercised their powers in a fair manner. The Commission is not operating here with a false dichotomy between an imaginary 'law-abiding public' and 'suspects'. Rather it accepts that suspects are drawn from the public and that the coopera-tion of the public (including the cooperation of suspects) is vital if the police are to be effective.[26]

To achieve this it argued that the new arrangements should be fair, open and workable. As Ed Cape notes in discussing these concepts in chapter eight in this collection, this leaves open the question of where the balance between coercive police powers to investigate crime and the rights of citizens (for example, to

---

[21] Just how large and how law abiding the 'majority' really is can also be questioned: S Karstedt and S Farrall, *Law-Abiding Majority?: The everyday crimes of the middle classes* (London, Centre for Crime and Justice Studies, 2007), available from http://www.kcl.ac.uk/depsta/rel/ccjs/middle-class-crime-2007.pdf (accessed 3 October 2007).

[22] RCCP *Report*, n 16 above, para 1.12.

[23] *Ibid*, para 1.33.

[24] *Ibid*, para 1.33.

[25] *Ibid*, paras 2.14–2.17.

[26] See also *ibid*, paras 10.3–10.4.

privacy) should lie. The Commission's position on this point was that the minimum threshold for interference with such rights was 'reasonable grounds for suspicion' that a citizen had committed a specific crime. Moreover, use of a police investigative power had to be necessary in all the circumstances and proportionate in the sense that sufficient account is taken of the seriousness of the suspected offence, and of 'the effectiveness of the power in investigating the offence concerned and of the importance that society places upon bringing those suspected of it to trial'.[27]

This approach was reflected in the provisions of PACE and its associated Codes of Practice, albeit with some differences in detail. So PACE can be characterised as based on the same 'joined-up thinking' that underpinned the report of the Royal Commission, in which fairness to suspects is seen as crucial to police legitimacy and policing effectiveness. Unfortunately, such thinking was not always seen in the implementation and subsequent 'development' of the PACE framework, as we shall now see.

# III  PACE (then and now)

## A  PACE street policing powers

PACE did not sweep away all pre-existing street police powers. Notably, the power of any officer to stop vehicles under road traffic legislation remained in place.[28] Turning to PACE itself, the main powers of interest to this chapter are:

- the uniform, national power to stop and search where there is reasonable suspicion that a person or vehicle is carrying stolen or prohibited items (section 1);
- the power of a senior police officer to authorise a road check (the mass stopping of vehicles) where reasonable grounds exist to believe that someone who is unlawfully at large, or who has committed (or intends to commit) a serious arrestable offence (or a witness to such a offence) would be in the locality where the checks are to take place (section 4); and
- the powers of summary arrest (that is, without judicial warrant) provided under sections 24–5 which generally required reasonable suspicion of a specific (arrestable, that is fairly serious) offence.

Since PACE was enacted, the effective ambit of these powers has grown in two main ways. The first is through a widening of the powers themselves. For example, the concept of 'prohibited items' (which triggers the availability of the

---

[27]  *Ibid*, paras 3.4–3.5.
[28]  Now to be found in s 163 of the Road Traffic Act 1988.

section 1 stop and search power) has been extended to cover anything with blades or sharp points, items intended for use in causing criminal damage, and prohibited fireworks.[29] The powers have also been widened by 'rebalancing'. The fulcrum of the balance between police powers and citizens' rights to liberty and privacy has shifted decisively in favour of police powers. Thus summary powers of arrest now apply to all offences rather than just those which are fairly serious, and the ambit of section 4 road-checks have been extended to cover any indictable offence.[30]

The second way in which the ambit of the original PACE powers has grown is through the prodigious growth of the criminal law. It emerged in August 2006 that the 'New Labour' administration had, since 1997, created over 3,000 new criminal offences, including 1,169 through primary legislation. The preceding Conservative administration is reported to have introduced new crimes at half this rate, which is still a remarkably expansionist stance when one considers that for much of the twentieth century it was rare for there to be more than one Criminal Justice Act a decade.[31] While many of these offences might be depicted as the 'modernisation' of existing provisions, or cover esoteric areas such as the importation of Polish potatoes,[32] others have brought about significant extensions to the effective reach of police powers.

The most germane example of such an extension is section 5 of the Public Order Act 1986, which makes it an offence to use threatening, abusive or insulting words or behaviour, or disorderly behaviour, within the hearing or sight of a person likely to be caused harassment, alarm or distress thereby. There are four main problems with this. First, the *actus reus* element includes 'disorderly behaviour', a vague concept left undefined by the Act. Secondly, the elements of the offence do not require that anyone is actually caused alarm, harassment or distress; it is only necessary to show that such a consequence of a person's behaviour was *likely*. Thirdly, no evidence is needed from any member of the public as to their perception of the behaviour which led to criminalisation; police evidence alone is sufficient to ground a conviction. Fourthly, it is enough that a police officer felt alarmed, harassed or distressed by the behaviour; there need be no member of the public present at the relevant time.[33] A caution or a summary conviction (following a guilty plea) is the likely outcome of a section 5 charge, since it is difficult for a citizen to challenge police evidence of something so

---

[29] These additions were effected by the Criminal Justice Act 1988, the Criminal Justice Act 2003 and the Serious Organised Crime and Police Act 2005 respectively. This development is in line with the expectations of the Philips Commission: RCCP *Report*, n 16 above, para 3.20.

[30] Changes effected by the Serious Organised Crime and Police Act 2005.

[31] http://news.independent.co.uk/uk/politics/article1219484.ece (accessed 20 March 2007).

[32] *Ibid.*

[33] *DPP v Orum* [1988] 3 All ER 449.

nebulous as 'disorderly behaviour'. As noted earlier, the reasonable suspicion criterion provides little safeguard if an offence is drawn as broadly as this.[34]

The elements of the section 5 offence can now be seen reflected in other statutory provisions which form part of the current government's vigorous anti-social behaviour strategy. Thus, for example, section 1 of the Crime and Disorder Act 1998 allows the police, local authorities, and others, to apply for an anti-social behaviour order against someone who has acted in a manner that caused or was likely to cause harassment, alarm or distress to one or more persons not of the same household as himself. The vagueness inherent in section 5 now infects a huge swathe of policing and regulatory activity.[35]

## B Post-PACE Street Policing Powers

PACE was not the last word on policing powers. This sub-section will set out briefly some of the most important new additions to the police's legal armoury. Extra powers to stop and search vehicles and pedestrians were introduced by the Criminal Justice and Public Order Act 1994 (CJPO), section 60[36] and were subsequently extended by the Knives Act 1997. Use of these powers can be authorised for a 24 hour period by a senior officer where the police wish to stop and search for guns, knives or other weapons but there is no individualised reasonable suspicion. Authorisation allows the police to stop and search anyone where there is a reasonable belief in relation to a particular locality that 'incidents involving serious violence may take place'[37] or persons are carrying 'dangerous instruments or offensive weapons'.[38]

Further wide-ranging powers were provided by sections 44–47 of the Terrorism Act 2000 and the Anti-terrorism, Crime and Security Act 2001 (building on earlier anti-terrorism provisions). The police may stop any vehicle or person for the sole purpose of searching for articles of a kind which could be used in connection with terrorism 'whether or not the constable has any grounds for suspecting the presence of articles of that kind' (section 45(1)). While the 'sole purpose' restriction may sound impressive, arrests arising out of such stops need not be in connection with terrorism. Thus, if the police search for evidence of terrorism but find evidence of cannabis use or simple theft they can arrest for

---

[34] Similar points could be made about arrest for breach of the peace, drunkenness or possession of an offensive weapon: C Kemp, C Norris and N Fielding, 'Legal Manoeuvres in Police Handling of Disputes' in D Farrington and S Walklate (eds), *Offenders and Victims: Theory and Policy* (London, British Society of Criminology, 1992) 73.

[35] See further H Carr and D Cowan, 'Labelling: constructing definitions of anti-social behaviour' in J Flint (ed) *Housing, Urban Governance and Anti-Social Behaviour* (Bristol, Policy Press, 2006).

[36] The CJPO also contained powers to stop cars and direct them away from raves (s 65) and trespassory assemblies (ss 70–71).

[37] CJPO, s 60 (2). See also Code A, para 1.8.

[38] Knives Act 1997, s 8, amending CJPO s 60. This also allows the 24 hour period to be extended by a further 24 hours.

those offences. Like section 60 CJPO, the power is confined to an area specified in a prior authorisation by a senior officer but, unlike section 60, the 2000 Act makes it clear that this area can extend to an entire police force area. An authorisation could therefore cover, for example, the whole of London,[39] or the whole of Northern Ireland, or even straddle a number of areas, potentially covering the whole country. Authorisation has to be by an officer of at least the rank of assistant chief constable who must judge it 'expedient for the prevention of acts of terrorism' (section 44(3)); and the period may last for 28 days (renewable). Authorisation must be confirmed by the Home Secretary.

These new powers to stop and search run entirely contrary to the Royal Commission's emphasis on individualised reasonable suspicion of a specific offence committed by a specific individual as providing the justification for an invasion of a citizen's right to liberty. They mark what can be seen as a formal shift to 'actuarial justice' or 'risk management' inasmuch as they allow the police to use coercive legal powers to regulate risky areas and groups.[40] In the next section I examine the question of whether the police have exploited the opportunities afforded to them by their new powers. This will involve an assessment of whether the due process safeguards surrounding ever-increasing police power have restrained problematic police behaviour.

## C The Use of PACE and Post-PACE Powers by the Police

The safeguards recommended by the Philips Commission, designed to ensure that the police did not use their powers in a disproportionate or unaccountable way, have not worked well in practice. Whereas some progress has been made in regulating what takes place in the police station through such safeguards as custody officer supervision; custody records; reviews of detention by senior officers; CCTV; access to, and provision of, free legal advice; tape-recording; use of appropriate adults; and independent inspections by lay visitors, it is widely accepted that it has proved much harder to regulate street policing.[41] Here patrol officers usually operate without any meaningful supervision and with no defence lawyer or appropriate adult in sight. Sometimes deviant police behaviour is caught on CCTV or by a tape recorder carried by a suspect, but this remains rare.

---

[39] Such an authorisation was upheld by the House of Lords in *R (on the application of Gillan & Anr) v Commissioner of Police of the Metropolis & Anr* [2006] UKHL 12.

[40] Feeley M and Simon J 'Actuarial Justice: The Emerging New Criminal Law' in Nelken D (ed), *The Futures of Criminology* (London, Sage, 1994).

[41] See, for an overview, M Maguire, 'Regulating the police station: the case of the Police and Criminal Evidence Act 1984' in M McConville and G Wilson (eds) *Handbook of the Criminal Justice Process* (Oxford, Oxford University Press, 2002).

What safeguards there are, such as the giving of reasons for, and the making records of, stop and searches (intended to guarantee that the 'reasonable suspicion' criterion was not watered down in practice) have not proved effective.[42] One sign, and result, of this is the low arrest rate achieved by stop and search (a rate which declines the more the police use the power). This is shown in Table 2:

**Table 2: Recorded stop and searches (where reasonable suspicion is required) and arrest rates**[43]

| Year | Stop and Searches | Arrests | % of stops leading to arrest |
|---|---|---|---|
| 1986 | 109,800 | 18,900 | 17.2 |
| 1987 | 118,300 | 19,600 | 16.6 |
| 1988 | 149,600 | 23,700 | 15.8 |
| 1989 | 202,800 | 32,800 | 16.2 |
| 1990 | 256,900 | 39,200 | 15.3 |
| 1991 | 303,800 | 46,200 | 15.2 |
| 1992 | 351,700 | 48,700 | 13.8 |
| 1993 | 442,800 | 55,900 | 12.6 |
| 1994 | 576,000 | 70,300 | 12.2 |
| 1995 | 690,300 | 81,000 | 11.7 |
| 1996 | 814,500 | 87,700 | 10.8 |
| 1996/97 | 871,500 | 91,106 | 10.5 |
| 1997/98 | 1,050,700 | 108,700 | 10.3 |
| 1998/99 | 1,080,700 | 121,300 | 11.2 |
| 1999/00 | 857,200 | 108,500 | 12.7 |
| 2000/01 | 714,100 | 95,400 | 13.4 |
| 2001/02 | 741,000 | 98,700 | 13.3 |
| 2002/03 | 895,300 | 114,300 | 12.8 |
| 2003/04 | 749,400 | 95,100 | 12.7 |
| 2004/05 | 851,200 | 94,600 | 11.1 |

Another indication that the reasonable suspicion criterion has failed to prove much of a safeguard is the huge racial disproportionality in the stop and search

[42] For details of the research findings on the operation of stop-search safeguards see Sanders and Young, n 11 above, 87–96.

[43] Sources: G Wilkins and C Addicott, *Operation of Certain Police Powers under PACE, England and Wales 1997/8*, Home Office Statistical Bulletin 2/99 (London, Home Office, 1999); M Ayres and L Murray, *Arrests for Recorded Crime (Notifiable Offences) and the Operation of Certain Police Powers under PACE: England and Wales, 2004/05*, Home Office Statistical Bulletin 21/05 (London, Home Office, 2005) (hereafter Ayres and Murray).

figures. It has been the case for many years that black people are around six times more likely (and Asian people twice more likely) than white people to be stop and searched under section 1 of PACE.[44]

The somewhat arcane methodological debate that now surrounds these ratios, with some attempting to explain them away by reference to the concept of the 'population available to be searched',[45] misses the central point that the police are targeting individuals within 'available populations' on the basis of something rather less than reasonable suspicion (that is, unlawfully).[46] That 'something rather less', whether it takes the form of 'hunch', 'generalised suspicion', or 'targeted intelligence-led policing' (notions that are inevitably influenced by stereotyping, including racial stereotyping) amounts to indirect racial discrimination. This is because the differential impact on ethnic minority and ethnic majority populations of police practices in this area cannot be justified by reference to a legitimate factor. It is not legitimate for the police to ignore the rule of law, notwithstanding that they believe (often with good reason) that doing so will enable them to clear more crime up. Thus, even if it were to be shown that the police target young lower-class males (regardless of ethnicity) on the basis that they were the group most involved in street-crime, this would still amount to indirect racial discrimination. Focusing the use of section 1 stop and search powers on young people (amongst whom ethnic minorities are over-represented) is not a legitimate strategy in the absence of individualised reasonable suspicion at the point when the power is used.[47]

Indirect racial discrimination has continued even in the wake of the Stephen Lawrence Inquiry in which the problems caused by stop and search practices became a major focus of concern and attempted remedial action. A 'Macpherson effect' can be detected in the large reduction in the number of recorded stop and searches which occurred at the turn of the century (see Table 2) and research confirmed a decline in confidence in the use of the section 1 PACE power in the wake of the Lawrence Inquiry.[48] But should we welcome the fact that confidence is evidently returning? As can be seen from Table 2, when stop and search numbers fell, arrest rates increased; when they began to recover, arrest rates fell. In other words, it looks as if the tide has once more turned away from stop and searches based on reasonable suspicion. A large-scale Home Office funded study set up to assess the impact of the Lawrence Inquiry found that:

---

[44] Home Office, *Race and the Criminal Justice System: An Overview to the Complete Statistics 2004–05* (London, Home Office 2006), 11.

[45] MVA and J Miller, *Profiling Populations Available for Stops and Searches*, Police Research Series Paper 131, (London, Home Office, 2000) 84; P Waddington, K Stenson and D Don, 'In proportion: Race, and Police Stop and Search' (2004) 44 *British Journal of Criminology* 889 at 899–900. See also ch 6 by Barbara Wilding in this collection.

[46] The complex evidence on this point is reviewed in Sanders and Young, n 11 above, 67–73, and see also the discussion of the 'Macpherson effect' below.

[47] I leave to one side here the point that focusing on street-crime (as opposed to, say domestic violence and white collar crime) is also likely to have racialised implications.

[48] See, eg M Fitzgerald, *Stop and Search: Final Report* (London, Metropolitan Police, 1999).

observed officers reported a climate in the aftermath of the Inquiry in which 'people were too afraid' to stop and search for fear of being accused of racism. This effect seemed to be particularly powerful in [the Met.], where officers said the use of searches dramatically declined . . . It also appears that the Inquiry brought into focus officers' uncertainty and confusion about the legitimate use of their powers. As one officer explained: 'It makes police officers scared. If I saw a black youth on a street corner I would probably not search him, unless he's done something physically tangible that I have seen, I won't do it'[49]

This, of course, is exactly what reasonable suspicion requires—something tangible. As the researchers go on to observe:

> It seems likely that because officers felt under increased scrutiny in the aftermath of the Inquiry, and that they might therefore be held to account for their actions, there were times when they realised they could not always account for their conduct. Officers reported that the perceived increase in scrutiny meant that they could no longer go on 'fishing trips' where they knew they did not have proper grounds for searching. The climate before the Inquiry appeared to have made it either acceptable and/or possible for some officers to break rules in relation to stop and search. Since the Lawrence Inquiry Report this was perceived to be more difficult.[50]

The difficulty does not appear to be insurmountable, however, as indicated by the recent rises in the stop and search figures, which have been particularly marked in the case of ethnic minorities.[51] Thus ethnic disproportionality, despite the concerted efforts that have been put into tackling the issue by government, police authorities and supervisory police officers, is now worse than before the Lawrence Inquiry reported.[52]

Safeguards surrounding the use of stop and search powers that do not require reasonable suspicion have fared no better. As we have seen, the main safeguard is that the powers cannot be applied by street-level police officers until a senior officer authorises their use in a specific place for a specific time. The reality of how this works in the context of the Terrorism Act section 44 power emerged as a result of the case of *Gillan*. Following inquiries made by the pressure group Liberty, it became apparent that the Metropolitan Police and the Home Secretary had, since the coming into force of section 44 on 19 February 2001, adopted the practice of issuing successive authorisations for the whole of London. The Court of Appeal upheld this practice, commenting that: 'It did no more than enable the commander in a particular area to have the powers available when this was operationally required without going back to the Secretary of State for confirmation of a particular use.'[53]

---

[49] J Foster, T Newburn and A Souhami, *Assessing the impact of the Stephen Lawrence Inquiry*, Home Office Research Study 294 (London, Home Office, 2005) 29–30.

[50] *Ibid*, 30.

[51] See Sanders and Young, n 11 above, 83.

[52] Home Office, *Race and the Criminal Justice System: An Overview to the Complete Statistics 2004–05* (London, Home Office 2006) 11, fig 3.2.

[53] *Gillan* [2004] EWCA Civ 1067 at para 51. Confirmed by the House of Lords in *Gillan* [2006] UKHL 12.

In short, the capital's police have, with the connivance of the Home Secretary and the courts, turned an apparently exceptional power into a routine one. This is important because powers that lack the formal requirement of reasonable suspicion are particularly prone to be used on the basis of social stereotypes. Thus, Bowling has found that CJPO section 60 stops are 27 times more likely to be used against blacks, and 18 times more likely to be used against Asians, than they are against whites: 'Wherever officers have the broadest discretion is where you find the greatest disproportionality and discrimination.'[54]

## D The drift to Summary Justice

That the post-PACE developments have witnessed a drift to summary justice can be demonstrated in a variety of ways.

First, there has been a massive increase in the extent to which the police use their investigatory powers. As Table 2 shows, in 1986 there were 109,800 recorded stop and searches based on reasonable suspicion leading to 18,900 arrests. By 2004/05 the number of recorded stop and searches had increased eight-fold and arrests had soared to 94,600. It is well known that these figures are not wholly reliable as they are affected by police practices. However, successive sweeps of the British Crime Survey have found a rise in stop and searches from 295,000 people in 1987 to 1.1 million in 2000.[55] Rises in (recorded) stop and searches that do not require reasonable suspicion have also been marked, as can be seen from the second column of Table 3, which shows an increase in CJPO stop and searches of around 600 per cent in under a decade.

Table 3 also shows how most arrests which are made under section 60 do not relate to the ostensible reason for the stop and search.[56] Thus in 2004/05 almost four times as many arrests were for unrelated matters as for offensive weapons. It is not surprising that so many arrests are for matters unrelated to the ostensible reason for the original search given the research that shows that the police tend to stop on the basis of generalised suspicions (rather than holding suspicion in relation to a specific offence).[57] One of the factors underpinning the drift to summary justice is the usefulness of stop and search powers (at least in the short term) in detecting crime.

---

[54]  Quoted by Dodd, *The Guardian*, 21 April 2003. See also B Bowling and C Phillips, 'Disproportionate and Discriminatory: Reviewing the Evidence on Police Stop and Search' (2007) 70 *MLR* 936.

[55]  For references and further analysis see Sanders and Young, n 11 above, 99.

[56]  This lack of relationship is probably true of all stop and search powers, but the way the statistics are usually presented does not allow this to be established definitively.

[57]  Summarised in Sanders and Young, n 11 above, ch 2.

**Table 3: stop and searches under s 60 of CJPO Act 1994 (violence and offensive weapons)**[58]

|         | Total searches | Persons found carrying offensive weapons | Arrests for offensive weapons | Unrelated arrests |
|---------|----------------|------------------------------------------|-------------------------------|-------------------|
| 1996    | 7,020          | 187                                      | 132                           | 371               |
| 1997/98 | 7,970          | 377                                      | 103                           | 332               |
| 1998/99 | 5,500          | 213                                      | 91                            | 84                |
| 1999/00 | 6,840          | 59                                       | 36                            | 195               |
| 2000/01 | 11,330         | 357                                      | 309                           | 411               |
| 2001/02 | 18,900         | 1,367                                    | 203                           | 485               |
| 2002/03 | 44,400         | 1,568                                    | 356                           | 2,142             |
| 2003/04 | 40,400         | 557                                      | 299                           | 1,248             |
| 2004/05 | 41,300         | 275                                      | 242                           | 941               |

The use of the arrest power has also soared. A careful analysis by Hillyard and Gordon found that arrests rose over the whole period from 1981 (1.27m) to 1997 (1.96m), 'with a more rapid increase since PACE became law in 1986'.[59] The Home Office indicated in the late 1990s that 'just under 2 million persons suspected of committing an offence are arrested every year'.[60] Arrests for *notifiable* offences rose from 1,277,900 in 1999/00 to 1,353,800 in 2004/05.[61]

One implication of the huge increase in the use of stop and search and arrest since PACE was enacted is that there has been a corresponding increase in the number of times people experience informal summary justice each year. The 'usual suspects' who routinely come under the purview of the police[62] are now subject to far more social disciplining through the use of formal power than was the case when PACE came into force. Thus a recent Home Office report noted that:

---

[58] Stop and searches under s 44 of the Terrorism Act have been subject to wild fluctuations. Between 2002 and 2005 the annual number recorded has been between 32,000 and 36,000: Ayres and Murray, n 43 above, 12.

[59] P Hillyard and D Gordon, 'Arresting statistics: the drift to informal justice in England and Wales' (1999) 26 *Journal of Law and Society* 502 at 508.

[60] Home Office, *Statistics on Race and the Criminal Justice System 1998* (London, Home Office, 1999) 19.

[61] Ayres and Murray, n 43 above, 1.

[62] For citations to the relevant research see Sanders and Young, n 11 above, 70.

In a number of forces stop and search was used as a tool for public reassurance and to prevent people who were seen as creating a public nuisance from gathering in certain places, although there was no reasonable suspicion of a crime. *This is an improper use of the power.*[63]

The arrest power in relation to section 5 of the Public Order Act 1986 is often used in a way which blurs social disciplining with 'bringing offenders to justice'. Thus the research by Brown and Ellis found that:

From many of the section 5 cases and from interviews with arresting officers, the impression comes across very strongly that what is at issue in many of the cases in which the police are the targets of abuse or threats is the enforcement of respect for the police. Arrest is a key resource for achieving this end and section 5 a convenient vehicle because it is very difficult for anyone later to query arresting officers' judgements about whether in the circumstances at the time they were harassed, alarmed or distressed[64]

As this quote signals, another implication of the increased use of police powers to stop and search and arrest is that many more crimes are now detected in a way that virtually guarantees a successful clear up. So, for example, around a third of all arrests resulting from stop and searches where reasonable suspicion is required are for possession of drugs (usually cannabis), where all the evidence needed to clear up the crime is secured through the search itself. The likely outcome is a formal warning for cannabis possession or a caution, with repeat offenders likely to be prosecuted in the magistrates' courts (and likely to plead guilty). Thus the increasing use of stop and search means that an increasing proportion of the outcomes produced by the criminal justice system are likely to take the form of summary justice.

Even more significantly, the post-PACE era has seen a shift from court-based forms of summary justice to police-based forms of summary justice. Thus Hillyard and Gordon have calculated (using conservative assumptions) the outcome of all arrests between 1981 and 1997. In 1981 court disposals accounted for almost 75 per cent of cases, but by 1993 this figure had declined to 49 per cent and by 1997 to 42 per cent.[65] To put this another way, 58 per cent of criminal justice disposals in 1997 were made up of police disposals (NFA and cautions). The picture since then has become more complicated due to the introduction of reprimands and warnings for youths, 'formal warnings for cannabis', conditional cautions by the CPS, and penalty notices for disorder. But we saw in the introduction that, even if attention is confined to 'notifiable offences', most crimes which are 'cleared up' are not prosecuted.

Developments since 1997 have taken place within a particular 'New Labour' discourse in which prime ministerial impatience has been shown with the courts

---

[63]  Home Office, *Stop & Search Manual* (London, Home Office, 2005) 38 (emphasis in original).

[64]  Brown and Ellis, n 10 above, 42–3.

[65]  P Hillyard and D Gordon, 'Arresting statistics: the drift to informal justice in England and Wales' (1999) 26 *Journal of Law and Society* 502 at 517.

(too slow, too bureaucratic, too focused on defendants' rights) and enthusiasm has been expressed for summary justice as a way of bringing 'more offenders to justice' at a cost-effective price.[66] But here the government has encountered a difficulty. PACE cemented the importance of the police station as an evidence-gathering site and the effective start of the adversarial process. In doing this it also cemented in free legal advice for suspects. The more that the police are empowered to collect useful evidence in the police station (for example, through the changes made to the right to silence in 1994),[67] and the more that prosecutors are drawn into that site to advise on, or take, charging decisions, the more compelling the arguments become for acknowledging that many of the safeguards which apply to court proceedings (such as the routine presence of defence lawyers and the full disclosure of prosecution evidence) should also apply to police station proceedings.[68] But this would make cases dealt with in the police station (for example, through police cautions) almost as 'bureaucratic and expensive' as court cases. Couldn't the police just impose 'on-the-spot' fines and march offenders off to the nearest cashpoint for enforcement purposes? When the then Prime Minister first broached this idea in public in June 2000 it drew howls of derision.[69] But, as we shall see in the next section, much of his vision has now come to pass.

# IV 'Penalty notices for disorder'

Promoting the use of summary penalties has become a major policy preoccupation of the current government. This can be seen most starkly by the way in which 'penalty notices for disorder' have, as a result of legislative hyper-activity, ministerial target-setting, and police enthusiasm, become a major feature of the criminal justice landscape.

## A The Legislative Growth of Fixed Penalties

There is nothing particularly new about the police having the power to issue fixed penalty notices. They have long had this power in relation to a wide range of minor

---

[66] Recent policy statements include *Delivering Simple, Speedy, Summary Justice* (London, Department for Constitutional Affairs, July 2006); *Strengthening powers to tackle anti-social behaviour* Consultation Paper (London, Home Office, November 2006) and *Modernising Police Powers: Review of the Police and Criminal Evidence Act (PACE) 1984*, Consultation Paper (London, Home Office, March 2007).

[67] Criminal Justice and Public Order Act 1994, ss 34–7.

[68] See further ch 10 by John Jackson in this collection.

[69] See, eg http://news.bbc.co.uk/1/hi/uk_politics/816949.stm (accessed 12 June 2008) Blair's speech is reproduced in House of Commons Library, Research Paper 01/10, The Criminal Justice and Police Bill (25 January 2001) available at http://www.parliament.uk/commons/lib/research/rp2001/rp01–010.pdf (accessed 12 June 2008).

motoring offences.[70] But the twenty-first century has witnessed a substantial extension of the police power to issue fixed penalties for non-motoring offences, including some which are generally regarded as fairly serious (including criminal damage and theft). The means by which this has been achieved is the 'penalty notices for disorder' scheme as introduced by the Criminal Justice and Police Act 2001. Section 2 empowers a police officer who has 'reason to believe' that a person aged 18 or over has committed an offence covered by the scheme to issue a fixed penalty notice to that person. A person given a penalty notice has three options.

First, pay the fine within 21 days (option 1). This prevents any proceedings being brought for the offence,[71] does not involve an admission of guilt, and ensures that no conviction will be recorded against the person.

Second, do nothing for 21 days. This may, and usually will, result in the police registering a fine with the local magistrates' court with a 50 per cent uplift to the original face value of the fixed penalty amount (option 2a).[72] If a fine is registered then the courts will enforce it as they would any other fine[73] (which could include the use of arrest or bailiffs), but a conviction is not recorded. The police may, instead of registering the fine, charge the person for the original offence (option 2b) in which case the matter may end in conviction and a sentence chosen from those legally available for the offence in question (and the defendant may have to pay court costs).[74]

Third, the person may, within 21 days of the issue of the penalty notice, request to have the matter tried in court (option 3), in which case the matter proceeds as in option 2b.[75]

Ten specific offences were covered by the fixed penalty scheme as originally enacted, as shown below.

## Offences attracting an £80 penalty (upper tier)

1  knowingly giving a false alarm to the fire brigade
2  wasting police time or giving a false report
3  using a public telecommunications system for sending a message known to be false in order to cause annoyance

## Offences attracting a £40 penalty (lower tier)

1  being drunk in a highway, other public place or licensed premises
2  throwing fireworks in a thoroughfare

---

[70]  See Pt 3 of the Road Traffic Offenders Act 1988.
[71]  Criminal Justice and Police Act 2001, s 5(2).
[72]  Section 4(5).
[73]  See ss 9–10.
[74]  Option 2b is not spelt out clearly in the Act but is implicit in the terms of ss 4–5. The point is made explicit (presumably for deterrent purposes) in the PND form prescribed by regulations made under s 3 of the Act, although Home Office guidance states that option 2b 'is not expected to be a common occurrence': *Home Office Operational Guidance* (2005), n 1 above, 9.
[75]  Section 4(1).

**3**     trespassing on a railway

**4**     throwing stones etc. at trains

**5**     buying or attempting to buy alcohol for consumption in licensed premises by a person under 18

**6**     being drunk and disorderly

**7**     consumption of alcohol in a 'no alcohol' designated public space

The upper tier was constructed quite narrowly and essentially covered 'false alarm' offences, while the wider, lower tier was predominantly concerned with alcohol-related offences and protecting the railway network. Keeping the scheme quite narrowly focused on minor disorder by adults, and keeping it 'bottom heavy' (with most offences attracting the lower level of penalty), no doubt helped secure its parliamentary passage. Originally the 2001 Bill had also listed criminal damage, and the Public Order Act 1986 section 5 offence. These offences 'were removed after opposition in the Commons (which was resisted) and the Lords (accepted at the last minute to allow the Bill to become law), on the grounds that these were inherently more serious offences'.[76] However, it did not take long for government to put these offences back into the scheme. Indeed, it has subsequently been extended in such a way as to make its focus stretch far beyond 'minor disorder' by adults. It has also become 'top heavy', with most offences now classified in the upper tier.

There is space here to do no more than summarise the main changes. Section 87(2) of the Anti-Social Behaviour Act 2003 extended the scheme to those over 16 while section 87(3) provided a power to extend the scheme to those aged between 10 and 15. This power was exercised through secondary legislation in September 2004. For those under 16 the upper tier fine was set at £40 and the lower tier fine at £30. As in other areas of criminal justice, once a power or offence has been established, it seems relatively easy to secure increases in the ambit of that measure.[77]

An eleventh offence, section 5 of the Public Order Act 1986, was added (to the upper tier of offences) by order on 22 July 2002[78] *before* the pilots set up to test the operational aspects of the scheme had begun. We have already seen that the creation of this summary offence in the mid-1980s was marked by considerable public controversy, and that Home Office research published in the mid-1990s demonstrated that some police officers were misusing the power as a way of seeking to impose their authority.[79] To add section 5 to the scheme prior to the pilots even beginning thus smacks of a reckless indifference to the possibility that the power to issue penalty notices might be abused.

---

[76] M Wasik, 'Legislating in the Shadow of the Human Rights Act: The Criminal Justice and Police Act 2001' [2003] *Crim LR* 931.

[77] For an account of how public order powers and offences have been widened over time see R Stone, *Civil Liberties and Human Rights* (Oxford, Oxford University Press, 2004) ch 9.

[78] The Criminal Justice and Police Act 2001 (Amendment) Order 2002, SI 2002, no 1934.

[79] As discussed in the preceding section.

Three firework offences were then added from 11 October 2004. Three weeks later, on 1 November, a major expansion of the scheme took place when seven further offences were added, including four alcohol offences relating to underage drinking, and a litter offence. The whole nature of the scheme was radically altered, however, by the final two offences added at this point. The first was retail theft with a value of less than £200 and the second was criminal damage with a value of less than £500. Neither of these offences fall within conventional understandings of 'disorder'. Purchase of alcohol by an under 18 year-old, and selling alcohol to a drunken person, were added from 4 April 2005.

There have also been reclassifications within the scheme. Thus the offences of throwing fireworks and being drunk and disorderly were moved from the lower to the upper tier from 5 March 2004 and 1 November 2004 respectively. The latter date also saw the raising of the lower tier fine level from £40 to £50. The way in which the scheme has become 'top-heavy' can be seen by referring to the Home Office website which includes a table setting out the full list of offences it now covers.[80] To summarise, within four years of the introduction of the penalty notices scheme in 2001, the number of offences it covered had more than tripled from 10 to 31, the lower tier doubled in coverage from 7 to 14 offences, and the upper tier increased almost six-fold from 3 to 17 offences. In some of these cases (for example, those related to the supply and consumption of alcohol) the apparent increase in coverage is attributable at least in part to the redefinition of existing offences (notably through the Licensing Act 2003), and does not, therefore, indicate a substantial broadening of the ambit of the scheme. But other additions (notably section 5 Public Order Act 1986, theft, and criminal damage) represent a massive expansion of this ambit. Whereas once the upper tier was concerned with the relatively rare offences concerned with 'false alarms', it now reaches firmly into the mainstream of criminal behaviour. The way in which the scheme has become 'top heavy' can only be fully appreciated, however, by examining the way in which it is actually used in practice.

## B The Numerical Growth of Fixed Penalties

Some of the current government's innovations to tackle 'anti-social behaviour' were hardly used at all when they were first introduced.[81] The same cannot be said of fixed penalty notices for disorder; exponential growth has been evident here from the outset. Table 4 presents the available statistics on the use of penalty notices for disorder for 2004 and 2005 for those aged 16 and over.[82] The table

---

[80]  http://police.homeoffice.gov.uk/operational-policing/crime-disorder/index.html (accessed 18 March 2007).

[81]  Notably anti-social behaviour orders: E Burney, *Making People Behave: Anti-social behaviour, politics and policy* (Cullompton, Willan, 2005) 32–3 and 89–91 (hereafter Burney).

[82]  Figures for 2004 can be found in Home Office, *Penalty Notices for Disorder Statistics 2004 England and Wales*, Online Report 35/05 (London, Home Office, 2005) but no subsequent statistics

focuses on the six offences out of the 25 covered by the scheme in 2005 where at least 2,500 fixed penalty notices were issued in that year.

**Table 4: Fixed penalty notices issued in 2004 and 2005**

|  | 2004 | | 2005 | |
|---|---|---|---|---|
| Offence | No of offences | % of all PNDs | No of offences | % of all PNDs |
| Wasting police time | 1,171 | 1.8 | 2,525 | 1.7 |
| 'Causing harassment, alarm or distress' (s 5) | 28,790 | 45.2 | 64,007 | 43.7 |
| Drunk and disorderly | 26,609 | 41.8 | 37,038 | 25.3 |
| Criminal damage (less than £500) | 1,190 | 1.9 | 12,168 | 8.3 |
| Shop-Theft (less than £200) | 2,072 | 3.3 | 21,997 | 15.0 |
| Drunk in highway | 2,497 | 3.9 | 3,138 | 2.1 |
| Total of above offences | 62,329 | 97.9 | 140,873 | 96.2 |
| Other offences[83] | 1,310 | 2.1 | 5,608 | 3.8 |
| Total of all PNDs | 63,639 | 100.0 | 146,481 | 100.0 |

A number of points can be made about the figures shown in Table 4.

First, the figures are dominated by just four offences: 'causing harassment, alarm or distress' (section 5 Public Order Act 1986), 'drunk and disorderly', criminal damage, and shop-theft. Together these made up 92.2 per cent of all PNDs in 2004 and 92.3% of all PNDs in 2005.

Secondly, of the specific offences shown only 'drunk in highway' is currently in the lower tier of offences. In 2005, 4,959 PNDs were issued with a lower tier face-value, representing 3.4 per cent of all the fixed penalty notices issued that year.

Thirdly, most offences covered in theory by the fixed penalty notice scheme are rarely responded to in practice with this disposal. Eleven offences attracted fewer than 100 PNDs in 2005.

Fourthly, the figures presented in Table 4 understate the current use of PNDs as a form of summary justice amongst police officers. A written answer in

were available on the Home Office website at the time of writing. On request, Research Development and Statistics Directorate (RDS) kindly supplied the figures for 2005. Pilots for the under-16s have taken place but the results had yet to be reported at the time of writing.

[83] There were 16 other offences covered by the scheme in 2004 and 19 in 2005.

Hansard from the Secretary of State for the Home Office gives the total provisional figures for PNDs for 2006 as 192,583.[84]

The face value of the fines issued in 2005 comes to £11,569,710. That may strike some as a lot of money to be fining the public on a summary basis under a scheme that has yet to be subjected to any independent evaluation. Are there any more compelling objections to the scheme? To answer that question necessitates an analysis of the arguments of policy and principle surrounding it, and evidence of how it is actually used in practice and with what effects.

## C The Policy Aims

Of obvious interest to government is the question of whether its policy aims are being met in practice. However, it has been a feature of much recent policy on criminal justice that the aims are ambiguous. One reason for this is the haste with which law is formulated and pushed through parliament without adequate scrutiny.[85] In the case of fixed penalties for disorder, the timeline was as follows:

1.  30 June 2000; Prime Minister Blair advocates instant payment of 'on-the-spot' fines.
2.  3 July 2000; Senior police officers tell the Prime Minister at a Downing Street 'summit' that they favour a fixed penalty scheme but not 'cashpoint enforcement'.
3.  2 August 2000, the Home Office publishes an 'action plan' on alcohol-related 'crime, disorder and nuisance' which presages a fixed penalty scheme with a power to detain, 'for example, for those who are too drunk to give their personal details.'[86]
4.  26 September 2000, a consultation paper is issued weighing in at just over four sides of A4 paper. The paper states that the government 'regrets that the period available for consultation is relatively short, given that it may seek to introduce legislation on the subject in the autumn'.[87]
5.  25 October 2000; closing date for the consultation exercise.
6.  18 January 2001; the Criminal Justice and Police Bill is introduced into the House of Commons.
7.  11 May 2001; the Criminal Justice and Police Act receives Royal Assent.

The main policy aims as set out in the original consultation paper on the fixed penalty scheme were to:

---

[84] Hansard, 24 July 2007, col 991 (WA).
[85] See the account of the passage of the Anti-Social Behaviour Act 2003 in Burney, n 81 above, 34–5.
[86] Tackling Alcohol-Related Crime, Disorder and Nuisance (London, Home Office, 2000), 8.
[87] *Reducing Public Disorder: The Role of Fixed Penalty Notices* (London, Home Office, 2000) 5.

(a) enable the police to put an immediate stop to disorderly behaviour in public places;
(b) provide the police with a power that would act as a 'real practical deterrent' that in some cases would act as a greater deterrent than the prospect of a 'court appearance some way in the future';
(c) provide the police with the ability to administer a swift punishment for such behaviour; and
(d) reduce the amount of time the police have to spend on paperwork and the time they have to spend in making court appearances.[88]

These policy aims are unconvincing, muddled and conflicting. Policy aim 1 could, of course, already be achieved by the police issuing a warning (for example, that a person will be arrested if they do not desist) or by actually arresting.[89] Policy aim 2 seems somewhat naïve in the light of the literature on deterrence which indicates that it is primarily the prospect of being caught that deters offending. The marginal deterrence achieved through publicising the prospect of one kind of sanction over another, or through announcing an increase in the level of a particular kind of sanction, is usually negligible.[90] The reference to a 'court appearance some way in the future' ignores another aspect of the drift to summary justice (early first hearings) which have allowed defendants acknowledging guilt to be 'fast-tracked' into court for sentencing within 24 hours of charge.[91]

Policy aim 3 can be decoded as seeking to encourage the police to administer summary punishments and thereby increase the likelihood of anti-social behaviour being met by formal sanction. As the Consultation Paper noted, such behaviour 'might at present be dealt with by means of an informal warning' and it explicitly accepted that the scheme might legitimately lead to 'net widening' (that is, drawing more people into the net of formal social control).[92] But if the main effect of the scheme in practice was to displace informal warnings with fixed penalty notices then policy aim 4 would be subverted. Net-widening would entail the police completing fixed penalty paperwork where previously they would have defused or ignored a situation. Moreover, because some of these fixed penalties would be contested, they would also spend more time making court appearances.

---

[88] I have distilled these policy aims (and taken the quoted words) from the vaguely worded paragraph 3 of *Reducing Public Disorder: The Role of Fixed Penalty Notices*, (London, Home Office, September 2000).

[89] Most of the offences to be covered by the scheme were arrestable; the remainder could have led to arrest if any of the general arrest conditions set out in PACE, s 25 were satisfied (eg, doubts about a person's identity existed). As ch 8 by Ed Cape in this collection documents, all offences are now arrestable.

[90] The literature is summarised in A von Hirsch, A Bottoms E Burney and P-O Wilkstrom, *Criminal Deterrence and Sentence Severity* (Oxford, Hart, 1999).

[91] Crime and Disorder Act 1998, s 53; for discussion see Sanders and Young, n 11 above, 487–8.

[92] *Reducing Public Disorder: The Role of Fixed Penalty Notices* (London, Home Office, September 2000) at paras 1 and 18.

In parliament the purpose of the scheme became elaborated by ministers as 'to provide a simple and immediate response to minor offending which will save court and police time'.[93] It follows from the argument presented in the preceding paragraph that court time (just like police time) would not be saved at all if the main effect of the scheme was to displace informal police warnings with formal penalty notices. Indeed, since it is predictable that some of these penalties will not be paid (thus leading to fine enforcement proceedings) and some will be challenged (thus leading to prosecutions) there is evident potential for the scheme to put more pressure on court time.[94] Ministers also continued to portray the scheme as enabling the police 'to deal quickly and firmly with aspects of minor disorder, freeing officers up from paperwork to get back on the streets fighting crime'.[95] But, as highlighted above, if the police issued fixed penalty notices for minor offences where previously they would have used a more informal response then they would necessarily have less time to spend 'fighting' more serious crime. Running counter to my argument is the 'broken windows' thesis (of which the government is much enamoured)[96] which argues that by 'nipping minor offending behaviour in the bud' one can prevent the flowering of more serious crime. I do not doubt that this can sometimes be the effect of zero tolerance strategies but in terms of a general strategy the best evidence we have is that it is counter-productive in the medium to long term, and is likely to produce sharp increases in complaints of police misconduct and violence.[97]

It thus seems that government wanted to have it all ways. In line with its 'tough on anti-social behaviour' and 'zero tolerance' stances, it sought to encourage the police to act more frequently against minor offences, while simultaneously claiming that this would save police paperwork and time. Talk of saving the police and the courts time was in reality a smokescreen for what lay at the heart of these proposals—a deliberate attempt to widen the formal net of social control to take in minor offences.[98]

The immediate policy aims set for the scheme can only be properly understood against the larger backdrop of the key aims the government has set for the criminal justice system as a whole. Towering above all of these is increasing the number of 'offences brought to justice' (OBTJ). Thus the Public Service Agreement 1 target in place at the time of writing is to bring 1.25 million offences to

---

[93] Hansard, 2 April 2001, col 707, per Lord Bassam.

[94] As was pointed out by the courts at the time: Justices Clerks Society, *Response to the Home Office Consultation Paper: Reducing Public Disorder—the role of fixed penalty notices* (October, 2000).

[95] Hansard, 2 April 2001, col 656, per Lord Bassam.

[96] See Burney, n 81 above, ch 2.

[97] J Greene, 'Zero tolerance: a case study of police policies and practices in New York City' (1999) 45 *Crime and Delinquency* 171.

[98] Thus the Explanatory Notes accompanying the Bill stated that, 'the need to focus police and court resources elsewhere means that much minor offending of this kind escapes sanction or consequence under current arrangements': House of Commons Library, *The Criminal Justice and Police Bill* Research Paper 01/10 (25 January 2001) 19.

justice in 2007/08,[99] and all police services have been set targets aimed at ensuring the national target is met. What easier way could there be for these targets to be met than by dipping into a pool of previously unsanctioned behaviour? Certainly issuing 'on-the-spot' fines for disorderly behaviour that police officers come across in person is a lot easier than investigating the average burglary or car theft.

## D Have the Government's Aims been Met?

Has net-widening actually taken place under the fixed penalty scheme? As the scheme was rolled out nationally in April 2004 and has snowballed in popularity since, it is worth looking closely at the data on police detections for recorded crime (that is, excluding the more minor, summary, offences) from 2004/05 to 2005/06. The figures are presented in Table 5.[100]

**Table 5: Police Detections for Recorded Crime by method of detection, 2004/05–2005/06**

|  | 2004/05 | 2005/06 | % change |
|---|---|---|---|
| Charge or summons | 717,691 | 725,539 | + 1.1 |
| Cautions | 249,390 | 311,155 | + 24.8 |
| Offences taken into consideration[101] | 106,346 | 117,730 | + 10.7 |
| Penalty Notices for Disorder | 43,526 | 105,698 | + 142.8 |
| Cannabis warnings | 40,138 | 63,635 | + 58.5 |
| Non-sanction detections[102] | 284,321 | 192,685 | - 32.2 |
| ALL DETECTIONS | 1,441,412 | 1,516,442 | + 5.2 |

As can be seen from these figures, all forms of police-administered sanction detections increased across these two years at the same time as prosecutions also increased. The biggest changes were in cautions (up by 61,765), cannabis warnings (up by 23,497) and penalty notices for disorder (up by 62,172) At the same time there is a large drop (91,636) in non-sanction detections (that is to say, where no further action—or NFA—is classified as a 'cleared up crime'). It thus

---

[99] For details of the target and progress made since the baseline year of 2001/02 see http://lcjb.cjsonline.gov.uk/ncjb/39.html (accessed 16 March 2007).
[100] A Walker, C Kershaw and S Nicholas, *Crime in England and Wales 2005/6*, Home Office Statistical Bulletin 12/06 (London, Home Office, 2006) 139.
[101] Meaning that a court was told of other admitted offences at the time of sentencing the charged offence.
[102] Non-sanction detections are those where the police believe they have identified who committed a specific offence but decide not to take any further action. To qualify, they must tell both offender and victim that they consider the matter 'cleared up'.

seems clear that there has been a large displacement of NFA (much of which would have been experienced as informal summary justice) by police-administered formal summary justice.

Moreover there has clearly been an increase in the number of times people are brought into the social control net to the point of at least NFA. This can be seen in the increase in all detections (up by 75,030). To what extent this is attributable to the 'usual suspects' experiencing a faster rate of detections than previously (rather than new populations being brought into the net) is not known.

The Home Office research into the pilots that were set up to examine the early operation of the penalty notices for disorder scheme also produced evidence consistent with net-widening. In a rather unlovely turn of phrase it was reported that: 'between a half and three-quarters of PNDs issued for disorderly behaviour while drunk and causing harassment, alarm or distress were new business'.[103]

In terms of savings of police and court time, the following findings of the Home Office research are significant:

- there was an estimated saving of between 1.5 and 2.5 hours of police paperwork for each PND that displaced a caution or a prosecution;
- PNDs for section 5 Public Order Act, and drunk and disorderly, were invariably issued in the police station,[104] and in three of the four pilot sites no PNDs were issued on the street at all;
- 51 per cent of PNDs were paid within the statutory period of 21 days;
- 46 per cent of PNDs were registered at court as fines after the 21 day period had elapsed;
- 39 per cent of registered fines were paid, making an overall payment rate of 70%;
- 2 per cent of PNDs resulted in the recipient requesting a court hearing.

It is clear that 'on-the-spot fine' is even more misleading a term than 'penalty notice for disorder'. As the Home Office researchers explained:

> PNDs cannot be issued on the street for alcohol offences as the suspect may not appreciate fully what is going on. Such suspects must be taken to a police station and (in line with the Police and Criminal Evidence (PACE) Act 1984 and its codes of practice) must be sober enough to understand the proceedings. Most of the other incidents which would be suitable for PNDs might have, or had actually, resulted in violence. During interviews officers referred to the 'obvious risk' to them and others of attempting to issue a fine on the street when surrounded by the offender's 'mates' and other interested and inebriated parties.[105]

---

[103] G Halligan-Davis and K Spicer, *Piloting 'on the spot penalties' for disorder: final results from a one-year pilot*, Findings 257 (London, Home Office, 2004), 3 (hereafter Halligan-Davis and Spicer).

[104] This point is to be found K Spicer and P Kilsby, *Penalty Notices for Disorder: early results from the pilot*, Findings 232 (London, Home Office 2004) 4.

[105] Halligan-Davis and Spicer, n 103 above, 4–5.

This quote provides one of the rare glimpses currently available into the reality of the PND scheme. Far from it being a way of officers putting an instant stop to disorderly behaviour through administering 'on-the-spot' justice, it has simply provided a new form of administrative disposal from the police station. Due to the net-widening that has taken place, the implication is that tens of thousands of people are now being taken to the police station for processing when previously they would have been dealt with informally on the street (for example, by being told to choose between going home quietly or being arrested). Whereas before, officers would have been reluctant to take the formal route, not least because of the opportunity costs involved,[106] now the balance of incentives has shifted in favour of arrest and detention (albeit briefer detention than experienced by those who are actually prosecuted).

Mesh-thinning is also taking place within the PND scheme. This refers to the process whereby those brought within the formal social control net are up-tariffed in the sense that they receive a more intensive intervention than would previously have taken place.[107] Thus a Home Office review published in February 2006 reported that 'there were many occasions when PNDs issued for Section 5 had been issued for drunk and disorderly and urinating in a public place without the evidential requirements having been recorded or where the police officer appeared to be the only witness'.[108] This up-tariffing (evident in all 10 police forces reviewed) was being driven by the 'performance culture' that so affects police decision-making nowadays.[109] Section 5 of the Public Order Act 1986 counted as a recordable and notifiable offence (thus contributing to the 'offences brought to justice' target), whereas drunk and disorderly and the bye-law offence of urinating in public did not. Given that performance targets relating to 'offences brought to justice' are set for forces, Basic Command Units, teams of officers, and even for individual officers,[110] it is no surprise to find the scheme being manipulated in this way.

When one combines the net-widening and mesh-thinning that has taken place with the routine use of the police station for processing those brought into the net, and the registration of almost half the PNDs as fines at court (thus triggering

---

[106] As one officer has graphically put it: 'I would feel dreadful if an urgent assistance came over the radio and I was in custody dealing with a tinpot bit of cannabis whilst one of my shift were getting the shit kicked out of them': quoted in Warburton H, May T and Hough M, 'Looking the Other Way: The Impact of Reclassifying Cannabis on Police Warnings, Arrests and Informal Action in England and Wales' (2005) 45 *British Journal of Criminology* 113 at 122.

[107] The seminal discussion of net-widening and mesh-thinning can be found in S Cohen, *Visions of Social Control* (Cambridge, Polity Press, 1985).

[108] Kraina C and Carroll L, *Penalty Notices for Disorder: Review of Practice Across Police Forces*, (London, Office for Criminal Justice Reform, 2006), 11 (hereafter Kraina and Carroll).

[109] See ch 5 by John Long in this collection.

[110] Kraina and Carroll, n 108 above, 23–34.

the need for enforcement procedures)[111] the argument that the scheme has saved the police and the courts time and money becomes difficult to sustain. It is also hard to accept that the scheme has enabled the police to spend more time on the streets tackling more serious crime. They seem rather to be spending more time in the police station (and on the street) processing minor disorder cases. While it would take more rigorous research than the Home Office has so far undertaken to establish the point definitively, it seems likely that the only formal aim of the scheme that has been attained so far is 'bringing more offenders to justice'. But at what cost?

The problem in addressing that question is that we simply do not know. For while the Home Office research made some attempt to look at paperwork savings for police officers in cases where PNDs displaced cautions or prosecutions, it made no serious attempt to look at the police costs of processing so many more people through the police station.[112] More fundamentally, it failed to consider, let alone discuss, the opportunity costs or social costs involved. The roll-out of the scheme nationally was therefore based on rather flimsy one-dimensional evidence. Moreover, the evidence came from only one source—the police.

## E An Evidence-led or Practitioner-led Policy?

For a time the New Labour government nailed its colours to the mast of evidence-led policy.[113] The extent to which this ever represented a deep-seated commitment to be led by evidence (as opposed to values, electoral considerations, and all the other factors that shape policy in reality) is difficult to assess. Whatever commitment there was appears to have waned over time.[114] The last incumbent of the Home Office during the Blair years stated that: 'We have always taken a practitioner-led approach to tackling anti-social behaviour—they have told us what is needed, what works, helped to draft laws and we continue to listen to their feedback'.[115] The practitioners in the case of penalty notices for disorder are the police. It is unquestionable that the PND policy has been practitioner-led (and practitioner-legitimised) rather than evidence-led. And while evidence has

---

[111]  ACPO states that 'people who fail to pay their [PND] then have a warrant issued for their arrest and are actively sought by police': News Release 79/07, 6 March 2007, available at http://www.acpo.police.uk (accessed 19 March 2007).

[112]  It provided a best estimate of half an hour to complete and issue each PND but this estimate did not include custody officer time, or time spent going to and from the police station. A later Home Office Review presented a similarly inadequate cost–benefit analysis: Kraina and Carroll, n 108 above, 9.

[113]  See, eg A Wilcox, 'Evidence-Based Youth Justice? Some Valuable Lessons from an Evaluation for the Youth Justice Board' (2003) 3(1) *Youth Justice* 21.

[114]  M Maguire, 'The Crime Reduction Programme in England and Wales: Reflections on the Vision and the Reality' (2004) 4 *Criminal Justice* 213.

[115]  Foreword to *Strengthening powers to tackle anti-social behaviour* Consultation Paper (London, Home Office, November 2006) 3.

been collected on the operation of the scheme, the practitioner viewpoint has been totally dominant and drowned out all other considerations.

Thus in its supportive public response to the government's original consultation paper on fixed penalties for disorder the Association of Chief Police Officers (ACPO) stated that it had been actively involved in the preparation of the proposals.[116] ACPO support, and its assessment of how the scheme would benefit the police, was cited many times in parliament by government ministers when fending off criticisms of the draft legislation designed to implement these proposals.[117] The government thus made it appear that to criticise the proposals was to criticise, or second-guess, the police—a strategy that few members of parliament presumably find palatable.

The Home Office research into the pilots was similarly practitioner-centred, with all the evidence collected coming directly from the police. As a result, the report of the research was itself dominated by practitioner concerns and policing issues. Officers said:

- that potential recipients generally accepted the issue of a PND;
- that it was desirable to avoid giving repeated PNDs to the same person;
- that therefore a PND database should be created or PNDs should be recorded on the Police National Computer;
- that the scheme should be extended to juveniles and to other offences; and
- that they should be allowed to gather DNA, fingerprint and photographic evidence as part of the procedure.

The police were reported to be developing the scheme to suit their own needs and interests. Thus to make it easier to issue PNDs on the street (where it is harder to check identification), 'Lancashire police force have already developed a PND kit with a leather wallet which incorporates a small ink pad and a street issue penalty notice which incorporates a space for fingerprints'.[118]

A subsequent 'Review of Practices Across Police Forces' carried out by the Office for Criminal Justice Reform was similarly dominated by the police perspective. The review included analysis of quantitative PND data for the 12 months to June 2005 but was 'based primarily on a series of visits and interviews ... with appropriate police officers and staff in the selected [ten] police forces'. Unsurprisingly, then, the report of the review centres on policing issues (although governmental concerns also loomed large). Issues uncovered and discussed included:

- the huge variation across police forces in their PND policies and procedures (for example, PNDs made up 20.7 per cent of all section 5 'offences brought to justice' in Lancashire compared with just 1 per cent in Northumbria);

---

[116] *The Independent*, 27 September 2000.
[117] See, eg Hansard, Standing Committee F, Criminal Justice and Police Bill, 6 February 2001, at 4.30pm (Charles Clarke) and 5.45pm (David Lock).
[118] Halligan-Davis and Spicer, n 103 above, 5.

- 'the latent opportunities that exist to increase sanction detections and OBTJ through the appropriate and ethical use of PNDs';[119]
- the manipulation of the PND scheme (by defining urinating and drunk and disorder as section 5 Public Order Act offences even when evidence was lacking) and the undesirable impact this was having on the national count of violent crime;[120]
- doubt was expressed about Home Office guidance stating that PNDs for recordable offences committed by 16–17 year-olds should only be issued at the police station, the review concluding that: 'notwithstanding the duty of care requirements in respect of juveniles, it may be proportionate and appropriate to consider an out of custody disposal. This approach supports the reduction in bureaucracy for which the PND scheme was, amongst other matters, designed';[121]
- the 'need' to introduce legislation allowing DNA samples to be taken on the street (so that the police could save themselves a trip to the police station);
- redesign of the national template for the PND form so as to prompt the collection of more information, as some forces were already doing through their own locally designed forms. The new information to include 'mobile and home telephone numbers for intelligence and enforcement purposes';
- the inappropriate issue of PNDs in respect of offences not covered by the scheme;
- the manipulation of the scheme by redefining more serious offences as less serious ones in order to make them eligible for a PND;[122]
- the lack of interest in, or tracking of, PNDs that were contested by the recipient, thus making it impossible to check whether some PNDs were being issued inappropriately;
- few front-line supervisory staff appeared to take an interest in any element of the PND scheme; PNDs were rarely 'quality checked' by a supervisory officer; the completeness and quality of information they contained varied considerably;
- officers wished to see the scheme expanded. Possible candidates for inclusion which were mentioned were: all theft to a given value; common assault;

---

[119] *Ibid*, 6.

[120] Section 5 was counted at that time as 'violent crime' which meant that the unintended consequence of police policies and practices was an apparent increase in violent crime with all the adverse media reaction that provokes. No doubt this is the kind of unethical behaviour that really upsets government! The Review recommended dealing with this through moving the performance goalposts again by 1) making urinating in a public place a discrete notifiable and recordable offence subject to the PND scheme, 2) making drunk and disorderly a notifiable and recordable offence, and 3) removing section 5 from the list of violent offences: Kraina and Carroll, n 108 above, 12.

[121] *Ibid*.

[122] The Radio 4, 'Law in Action' programme broadcast on 6 March 2007 gave the example of a barrister who obtained a refund for goods she had not bought. She was given a PND for theft rather than being prosecuted for obtaining property by deception, thus avoiding a criminal conviction and the need to involve the Bar Standards Board.

section 4 of the Public Order Act 1986 (intentional harassment, alarm or distress); possession of cannabis, and all 'volume crime types' in set circumstances such as low value and first offence.[123]

What is missing from the body of Home Office research is an alternative perspective. Neither the research into the PND pilots nor the Review of Practice published in 2006 involved any attempt to discover the views of members of the public. Thus there is virtually no data on what recipients of PNDs think of this use of police time. It is not difficult to guess what some of them think, however. All one has to do is look back to the observational research from the mid-1990s on how the police made use of section 5 Public Order Act 1986:

> In many section 5 cases in which the police are victims, the sequence of events is wearily familiar. The police receive abuse, either completely gratuitously, or during the course of making stops or arrests. They react by providing one or more warnings, as required by section 5 if an arrest is to be made,[124] which further goads the suspect and leads to his or her arrest. In interviews, the police suggested that arrest was necessary in such situations in order to make a stand against a growing tide of disrespect for the police and to show suspects where the line should be drawn. It is hard to believe that, given the apparent attitudes to the police of those involved and the circumstances of the offences, arrest does in fact serve these ends.[125]

Given that the operation of the PND scheme (in which section 5 and related offences have figured so heavily) has resulted in net-widening and up-tariffing, it seems likely that much police activity in this context is similarly seen as illegitimate. Far from 'enforcing respect' it will in many cases be making people less respectful of the police. The fact that the penalties imposed are not related to the ability to pay (unlike court fines) may also be fuelling a sense of unfairness, especially among the poor. Without research into this important issue, we simply do not know.

Another perspective downplayed in the Home Office Review of Practice is that of the victim. By this point in the PND scheme's development, substantial numbers of notices were being issued for criminal damage and theft. The use of a PND effectively means that the criminal courts have been deprived of the opportunity to make a compensation order in favour of the victim. In parliament, Home Office ministers gave specific assurances (in response to much concern about this issue) that Home Office guidance would make it clear that a

---

[123]  Richard Brunstrom, the Chief Constable for North Wales and spokesperson for ACPO on PNDs, has gone still further by arguing that the scheme should be extended to all summary offences. Radio 4, 'Law in Action', 6 March 2007. The police are not a monolithic bureaucracy speaking with one voice of course, as that programme itself demonstrated. Jan Berry, Chair of the Police Federation, expressed concerns that the police are not tracking those with multiple PNDs effectively, and, in an earlier programme on the same subject in this slot (21 November 2006), warned that government pressure on the police to meet crime targets could lead to 'integrity' problems.

[124]  The then statutory requirement to warn prior to arrest was removed by sch 17 of the Serious Organised Crime and Police Act 2005.

[125]  Brown and Ellis, n 10 above, 42–3.

PND should not be used 'where a person can be identified as a victim' but would be reserved for cases in which the victims are unknown or are corporate bodies unlikely to seek compensation in minor cases'.[126] The Guidance itself states that: 'Penalty notices will not be used where there has been a substantial financial/material loss to the private property of an individual'[127] and that 'Officers should seek and record the views of all victims before making a decision on the most appropriate course of action . . . PND disposal will not be appropriate where the victim is non-compliant.'[128] One would have thought, therefore, that some attempt would have been made to interview a sample of victims as part of the Home Office's Review of Practice. Instead, we are given just a tantalising glimpse of the extent to which victims really are now at the 'heart of the criminal justice system':

> In criminal damage cases the views of the victim were rarely recorded on the PND, the highest being Merseyside where this was evident on 40 per cent of the tickets evaluated. Similarly there was no value or estimated cost of damage evident, the highest in this case was West Yorkshire at 36 per cent . . . there is a risk in these cases that PNDs are issued without reference to the victim or for a value in excess of the £300 threshold.[129]

Would victims have much of interest to say? Corporate victims certainly do. The Head of Loss Prevention at House of Fraser spoke on Radio 4 of his concerns, along with those of other retailers, about the operation of the PND scheme. He asserted that PNDs had been used for 'our own staff who steal from us, and in one case a thief who was violent towards our staff and the police. I think more and more the police are using them inappropriately'.[130] What private victims think is anybody's guess. If research is not undertaken to fill that gap, their voices will remain unheard.

Yet another perspective missing from the Home Office research is that of ethnicity. As was noted above, the over-representation of ethnic minorities within processed suspect and offender populations is greatest where officer discretion is greatest. The Home Office has long known that ethnic minorities are over-represented in stop and searched and arrested populations and has invested a huge amount of energy and time in introducing more rigorous ethnic monitoring and tackling racial discrimination (direct and indirect) within the police. Home Office ministers were pressed in parliament to 'ethnically monitor' the new powers to ensure that they were not used in a discriminatory manner[131] and responded by saying that this issue would be dealt with in Home Office

---

[126] Charles Clarke, Hansard, Standing Committee F, Criminal Justice and Police Bill, 6 February 2001.

[127] *Home Office Operational Guidance*, (2005), n 1 above, para 6.4 (emphasis in original).

[128] *Ibid*, para 6.23.

[129] Kraina and Carroll, n 108 above, 28. The figures are based on scrutiny of an undisclosed number of PNDs. The reference to £300 stems from the Home Office Guidance (para 6.18) which sets this as the normal 'cap' other than in cases involving public property.

[130] Radio 4, 'Law in Action', 6 March 2007.

[131] Hansard, 2 April 2001, col 699 (Lord Dhokalia).

guidance.[132] The prescribed PND notice has a box prompting officers to record visual as well as self-defined ethnicity and the Home Office guidance stresses that this box '*must* be completed in all cases'.[133] The Race Relations (Amendment) Act 2000 (in force 2002) placed a duty on the government and the police not to unlawfully discriminate on the grounds of race and, in carrying out their functions, to have due regard to the need to eliminate unlawful racial discrimination and to promote equality of opportunity and good relations between persons of different ethnic groups.

It is therefore deplorable that no data or discussion relating to ethnicity is to be found in the Home Office research (published in 2004) into the PND pilots or in its subsequent 'Review of Practice' (published in February 2006), or in the available Home Office PND statistics for 2004 and 2005 (which *are* broken down by age, gender and offence). Only in November 2006, in its Partial Equality Impact Assessment of the proposals contained in *Strengthening powers to tackle anti-social behaviour*, did the government finally reveal that:

> There is some evidence that BME groups receive a disproportionate number of PNDs relative to their number in the overall population, but the ethnicity of recipients has not always been recorded. Four per cent of PNDs were for Asians (compared with 1.8 per cent in the general population) and 3 per cent for black people (compared with 1 per cent in the general population). . . . The data may be relevant due to the proposal including a discretionary power. Mitigation in the form of active monitoring, supervision and accreditation are included in the proposal.[134]

The proposal referred to here is to give the police the power to issue a 'Deferred Penalty Notice for Disorder' in cases where the offender is willing to enter into an Acceptable Behaviour Contract lasting from three to six months. Breach of the Contract 'will be punished with the issue of a PND for the original offence'.[135] The 'mitigation' the Partial Equality Impact Assessment offers is not persuasive. How is 'active monitoring' supposed to work when ethnicity is 'not always recorded'? Moreover, only nine months earlier the Home Office's Review of Practice had established that no effective supervision of PNDs was taking place—evidence that the Impact Assessment fails to cite. In a world of multiple competing 'priorities' in which the pressure to bring more offenders to justice tops the bill, and alternative perspectives are airbrushed out of the picture, the prognosis for avoiding indirect racial discrimination (or worse) remains gloomy.[136]

---

[132]  Hansard, 2 April 2001, col 714 (Lord Bassam of Brighton).

[133]  Para 12.8. The guidance (which runs to 39 pages) says nothing else about ethnicity.

[134]  *Strengthening powers to tackle anti-social behaviour* Consultation Paper (London, Home Office, November 2006) 48.

[135]  *Ibid*, 46.

[136]  In the policing context it is arguably only when relatively powerless groups (such as those who make use of the police complaints system, or ethnic minorities) are integrated into all stages of the policy process, including the framing of local policy and the development and monitoring of routine practices such as stop and search or complaint investigation, that any progressive reforms will be

## F The Formalisation of Informal Justice

The development of the PND scheme illustrates the way in which informal measures that supposedly do not result in the creation of a criminal record become increasingly formalised through police innovation and adaptation. This happened in the case of police cautions,[137] and it is clearly happening in the case of PNDs.[138] Thus the Home Office researchers noted that: 'Since the pilot, a marker has been introduced on the PNC [Police National Computer] for those arrested'.[139] It is true that these 'markers' do not constitute convictions or admissions of guilt, but at the same time they have legal consequences in the sense that officers are less likely to use the PND option if it has been used before.[140] Moreover, PNDs 'can be used to establish a pattern of bad behaviour and also used under Bad Character provisions in the Criminal Justice Act 2003'.[141] In addition, PNDs can be disclosed as part of a Criminal Records Bureau check, and might therefore affect someone's prospects of employment.[142] So in what sense, exactly, does a PND recipient not have a criminal record?

The pressure for further formalisation will be difficult to resist given that a significant proportion of PNDs are issued for fairly serious offences (such as theft). Thus some defence solicitors have argued that PNDs should be routinely cited in court so that sentencers (or probation officers) seeking to address someone's offending behaviour can be fully appraised of a person's 'record' of 'offending'.[143]

---

achieved. See further G Smith, 'A Most Enduring Problem: Police Complaints Reform in England and Wales' (2005) 35 *Journal of Social Policy* 121 and J Foster, T Newburn and A Souhami, *Assessing the impact of the Stephen Lawrence Inquiry*, Home Office Research Study 294 (London, Home Office, 2005) chs 5–6.

[137] Cautions were originally informal police warnings. Over time they began to be systematically recorded on local police databases and from December 1995 they were recorded on the Police National Computer. The Criminal Records Bureau will disclose details of cautions following a request for disclosure of a person's criminal record. Statutory provision (Crime and Disorder Act 1998) has been made for youth cautioning such that it will usually be the case that no more than two cautions (now known as reprimands and warnings where youths are concerned) can be given. A caution now has various legal consequences. For example, cautions for some offences can result in the cautioned person being entered on the Violent and Sex Offenders Register.

[138] However benign the motivations of individual police officers may be in seeking to use cautions or PNDs to keep first offenders 'out of the system', the problem is that such 'diversionary measures' morph into part of that very system.

[139] Halligan-Davis and Spicer, n 103 above, 5.

[140] In South Wales, after 'the issue of a second PND for s 5 or other instance of low-level anti-social behaviour, a letter is written to the parent or guardian advising them of the incident and that if there is a re-occurrence, or further reports of similar behaviour, application may be made for an ASBO. Evidence from the PNDs would be used in support of the application': Kraina and Carroll, n 108 above, 35.

[141] *Ibid*, 17. The bad character provisions are set out in Part 11, ch 1 of the Criminal Justice Act 2003.

[142] Police National Legal Database (an information website maintained by ACPO). http://www.askthe.police.uk/content/Q223.htm (accessed 19 March 2007).

[143] Radio 4, 'Law in Action', 6 March 2007.

The PND scheme is also becoming formalised as a method of evidence gathering. From the very inception of the scheme it was recognised that it could be brought into disrepute if the recipient's identity was not established at the time of issue. That is why those operating the Police National Computer permitted the recording of DNA and fingerprints 'where these have been taken' and 'anticipated that Fingerprint and DNA will be taken for ALL Penalty Notices for Disorder'.[144] At the time of the pilots section 61 of PACE (as amended) stipulated that fingerprints and DNA could only be taken prior to charge if they tended to confirm or disprove involvement in the suspected offence, or for the purpose of establishing identity. Now, as a result of amendments by sections 9 and 10 of the Criminal Justice Act 2003 (which came into force on 5 April 2004), PACE allows DNA samples and fingerprints to be taken as a matter of routine once a person is detained following an arrest for a recordable offence. The vast majority of PNDs which are issued are for recordable offences.[145] The incentives for police officers to arrest and convey to the police station (rather than simply issue the PND on the street) have thus grown.[146] And the legal restrictions on them doing so in the case of minor offences have been removed by the Serious Organised Crime and Police Act 2005 (which makes all offences arrestable, however trivial they might be).[147] It is hardly surprising that the PND scheme has grown so spectacularly.

The government revealed its own intentions for the future of summary justice through its 2007 Consultation Paper on PACE. It pursues the theme that police efficiency and effectiveness should be maximised through 'freeing up officers' time for operational activity on the street'.[148] From the policing and government's perspective, the only major problem with the PND scheme is that it is not saving as much time as it possibly could. As we have seen, the need to take potential recipients of a PND to the police station (to sober them up, calm them down, or isolate them from 'their mates', to collect physical evidence (such as DNA), and to confirm identity) works against the policy aim of keeping officers on the street.

What are the solutions proposed? First, to allow the police to take fingerprints, DNA samples and footwear impressions on arrest for all offences, not just those

[144] Letter from Customer Support Team of the Police Information Technology Organisation (to Liaison Officers) dated 1 September 2003 (emphasis in original); reproduced as Appendix J to Kraina and Carroll, n 108 above. Note how the push to record PNDs on the Police National Computer fuels the push to extract physical evidence from PND recipients 'to reduce the possibility of litigation where the data was wrongly recorded against an individual', *ibid*, 17.

[145] Recordable offences are those that are imprisonable and miscellaneous other offences (see National Police Records (Recordable Offences) Regulations 2000 (SI 1139). Theft, criminal damage, s 5 Public Order Act and various drink-related offences are all recordable.

[146] Police officers are under pressure (within the performance culture) to make arrests and this too can militate in a preference for the arrest and detention route rather than the 'on-the-spot' fine: Kraina and Carroll, n 108 above, 23.

[147] See further ch 8 by Ed Cape in this collection.

[148] *Modernising Police Powers: Review of the Police and Criminal Evidence Act (PACE) 1984* (London, Home Office, March 2007) para 15.

that are recordable.[149] If this proposal is acted upon then in future the police will have yet more of an evidence-gathering incentive to arrest those they reasonably suspect of committing an offence, however trivial that offence might be. The outcome will often be an 'on-the-spot' fine issued there and then combined with the extraction of physical evidence for adding to crime control databases. But 'on-the-spot' procedures do not work well for the drunk or for the unruly (surrounded by their 'mates'). This is where the second solution becomes relevant. The Consultation Paper suggests that 'short term holding facilities' (STHF) might be set up in shopping centres or town centres:

> The STHF would be under the supervision of a custody officer and would consist of a number of secure holding areas within the accommodation. These would provide secure accommodation but would not equate to the standard cell design. The function of the STHF would be to confirm the identity of the suspect and process the person by reporting for summons/charging by post, a penalty notice or other disposal. Persons detained would be subject to detention up to a maximum of 4 hours to enable fingerprinting, photographing and DNA sampling.... The aim would be to locate STHFs in busy areas to allow quick access and processing of suspects to enable the officer to resume operational duties as quickly as possible.[150]

The Consultation Paper does not discuss whether these 'holding centres' would be subject to any due process safeguards such as access to legal advice, the presence of appropriate adults, the attendance of medical professionals, or scrutiny by independent lay visitors.[151] All that is mentioned is that the facilities will be 'under the supervision of a custody officer'[152] although this may consist of nothing more than virtual oversight through video-conferencing.[153] This is another indication that reforms to PACE are seen almost entirely through a 'bringing more offenders to justice' lens, with mere lip service being paid to 'protecting the balance between the rights of the individual and the needs of the criminal justice system'.[154]

There are a variety of lenses we might use in thinking about this proposal. To a crime control adherent, STHFs are simply an efficient way of processing 'new business' and 'marking' more offences. To the due process adherent, the proposed

---

[149] *Ibid*, paras 3.31–3.38. For the rules on evidence-gathering and how these have chanced since PACE was enacted see ch 8 by Ed Cape in this collection.

[150] *Ibid*, paras 3.29–3.30. This obviously builds on the innovative practice of some police forces which deploy mobile police stations in support of officers working in city centres, thus enabling them to issue PNDs from a nearby location (which in turn increases use of the PND scheme): Kraina and Carroll, n 108 above, 35.

[151] The likelihood of deaths occurring in STHFs is pondered by E Cape, 'Modernising Police Powers—Again' *Crim LR* (forthcoming).

[152] *Modernising Police Powers: Review of the Police and Criminal Evidence Act (PACE) 1984* (London, Home Office, March 2007), para 3.29.

[153] *Ibid*, paras 3.23–3.25; PACE s 45A.

[154] *Modernising Police Powers: Review of the Police and Criminal Evidence Act (PACE) 1984* (London, Home Office, March 2007) para 1.5.

holding centres sound rather like cattle pens designed for branding the disorderly; concerns with human dignity and rights seem entirely absent. To a risk theorist, the centres look like information collection centres, and sites of risk communication, enabling risk profiles of suspect populations to be widened and deepened. To a social disciplinary theorist their key effect will be to enhance the capacity of the police to administer summary punishment without any meaningful oversight. To a freedom model theorist the centres are likely to prove counter-productive in promoting the police's proper mission, which is to promote freedom within society. I will conclude this analysis by using this last-mentioned lens, since it enables the major themes of this chapter to be brought into sharp focus.

# V   Conclusion

The freedom model, as developed by Andrew Sanders and myself,[155] seeks to re-focus the concerns of the criminal justice system away from crime control and towards enhancing and enlarging human autonomy. It makes a distinction between valued ends (the promotion of freedom) and possible means of achieving this (ranging from situational crime prevention, more employment opportunities for youth, different policing strategies, and so forth).

While the attempt to bring more offenders to justice can result in the promotion of such autonomy it does not necessarily do so. It is particularly unlikely to do so when focused at the absolute margins of criminality where the scope for individual police officer discretion is at its maximum yet where the involvement of defence lawyers, prosecutors and judicial officers (who might check that discretion or redress its worst effects)[156] approaches vanishing point. This is the case with the fixed penalty scheme.[157] As we have seen, it has resulted in massive net-widening for offences which turn on such ambiguous concepts as 'disorderly behaviour'. In such a situation, the lessons of earlier research make it reasonable to expect such problems as:

* the criminal law being used as a resource to uphold police authority;

---

[155] See Sanders and Young, n 11 above, 44–52.

[156] Thus B Mhlanga, *Race and the CPS* (London, SO, 1999) found that the CPS discontinued a disproportionately high number of cases involving ethnic minorities on the grounds of evidential insufficiency.

[157] The CPS have made it clear that the initial issue of a PND falls outside of the DPP's Guidance on Charging and that there is no need to refer such cases to them for advice: Kraina and Carroll, n 108 above, 30. In 2005 only 1% of recipients of PNDs requested a court hearing (and therefore came to the attention of prosecutors): Table 3.6 of *Penalty Notices for Disorder Statistics* (provided to the author by the Home Office RDS).

- the social stereotyping of certain kinds of people and behaviours as problematic and worthy of intervention (while other equally problematic groups or forms of behaviour are ignored); and,
- a resultant over-representation of certain social groups in the PND figures (particularly young males from lower class backgrounds—a group in which ethnic minorities are to be found in disproportionate numbers).

It is also reasonable to expect that many of those who are subject to PNDs and allied procedures such as detention in a police station (or holding centre), extraction of DNA and so forth, will see this response as an over-reaction to their behaviour (even if the police refrain from rough handling or insulting language). In their eyes, the police actions are likely to be seen as illegitimate and this will have the knock-on effect of putting police legitimacy more generally in question.[158]

It will not be just the detainees themselves who lose confidence in the police, but also those who hear their stories (friends, parents, children and partners). The predictable result will be a marked decline in confidence in the police amongst those very populations which suffer crime disproportionately. Witnesses and victims are unlikely to seek the help of an institution regarded as illegitimate.[159] Mistrust of the police is already a huge problem in some areas, sometimes bordering on hatred.[160] Detecting serious crime in these areas is already fraught with difficulty. Zero tolerance by the police is likely to lead to zero cooperation with the police when they need it most.

These arguments find support in the existing body of research into police powers such as dispersal orders,[161] stop and search,[162] arrest,[163] and strip-searches,[164] and they are likely to be similarly supported by rounded research (as opposed to police-led research) into the effects of the PND scheme. The main reason why we are not already in a position to ground an analysis of penalty notices for disorder in such research is the lack of joined-up thinking that lies behind the PND scheme. Instead of blundering on myopically, the government should look back to the Royal Commission on Criminal Procedure Report and mark well its emphasis on the vital importance to the investigation of crime of securing confidence in, and cooperation from, *all* sections of the community.

---

[158] On the importance of legitimacy (and for citations to Tom Tyler's groundbreaking research on the issue) see ch 2 by David Dixon in this collection. See also J Jackson and J Sunshine, 'Public Confidence in Policing' (2007) 47 *British Journal of Criminology* 214.

[159] Although the context is very different, this is one of the lessons to be drawn from Northern Ireland: A Mulcahy, *Policing Northern Ireland* (Cullompton, Willan, 2006) ch 4.

[160] See, eg, M Fitzgerald, M Hough, I Joseph and T Quereshi, *Policing for London* (Cullompton, Willan, 2002).

[161] A Crawford and S Lister, *The Use and Impact of Dispersal Orders: Sticking Plasters and Wake-Up Calls* (Bristol, Policy Press, 2007).

[162] The studies are too numerous to cite here, but see Sanders and Young, n 11 above, ch 2.

[163] See *ibid*, ch 3.

[164] T Newburn, M Shiner and S Hayman, 'Race, crime and injustice? Strip-search and the treatment of suspects in custody' (2004) 44 *British Journal of Criminology* 677.

Acting on the basis of an exaggerated dichotomy between 'the law-abiding majority' and those 'who seek to undermine and destroy our way of life'[165] is a road to ruin.

If any part of our 'way of life' is being undermined, it is the notion that the police should be subjected to the rule of law as articulated through the kind of sophisticated regulatory structure embodied in PACE. The necessity and proportionality of police actions under the PND scheme are deeply questionable yet rarely questioned since due process safeguards are minimal, often ignored and easily evaded. The same point can be made in relation to other forms of summary justice such as stop and search. It is difficult to see how PACE-like safeguards can be made to apply, and made to stick, on the street. If summary justice is not reined in, accusations that we are drifting towards 'a police state' may start to resonate more persuasively in some sections of society. One glimmer of hope that some reining in might take place is to be found in growing parliamentary uneasiness about the use of the PND scheme and a post-Blair recognition within the Home Office that there is a need to 'take stock' of both the use of PNDs and the 'offences brought to justice' target.[166]

When stock-taking it is important to recall the lessons of history. By this I do not mean just those concerning how PACE has worked (and been subverted) but also those relating to the relationship between police and public. When one looks back to the creation of the 'new police' in the mid-nineteenth century, the historical record shows that it took time for the police to win the support of lower class communities.[167] That support was always fragile and contingent, and depended in large part on the skilled use of discretion. As Ignatieff writes:

> To win this cooperation, the police manipulated their powers of discretion. . . . In each neighbourhood, and sometimes street by street, the police negotiated a complex, shifting, largely unspoken 'contract'. They defined the activities they would turn a blind eye to, and those which they would suppress, harass or control. This 'tacit contract' between normal neighbourhood activities and police objectives, was sometimes oiled by corruption, but more often sealed by favours and friendships. This was the microscopic basis of police legitimacy, and it was a fragile basis at best. A violent or unfair eviction by the police, for example, could bring a whole watching street together in a hostility to be visited on policeman afterwards, in the frozen silence which would descend when he stepped into the 'local'.[168]

---

[165] This divisive and misleading language, reminiscent of Margaret Thatcher's description of striking miners as 'the enemy within', is to be found in *Rebalancing the criminal justice system in favour of the law-abiding majority: Cutting crime, reducing reoffending and protecting the public* (London, Home Office, July 2006) 4.

[166] Parliamentary unease crystallised in the Select Commission on Home Affairs, Fourth Report, Session 2006/7 (July 2007). The need for 'stock-taking' was expressed in the evidence given to the Select Commission by Home Office minister Mr McNulty (para 19).

[167] See, eg P Rawlings, *Policing: A Short History* (Cullompton, Willan, 2002) 152–62.

[168] M Ignatieff, 'Police and people: the birth of Mr. Peel's "blue locusts"', *New Society*, 30 August 1979 (vol 49) 443–5, reproduced in T Newburn, *Policing: Key Readings*, (Cullompton, Willan, 2005) 28.

When we fast-forward into the present time we find officers working in urban areas reporting similarly hostile experiences. A female police constable working in a deprived borough of London told Fitzgerald et al that '*here,* you even *dare* to say hello to anyone and you get the death stare'.[169] Trading fixed penalties for fixed death stares does not strike me as a good bargain for anyone.

To regard PNDs as just another useful 'tool' in an officer's 'toolkit', in a context where the police are under huge pressure to 'bring more offenders to justice', is thus to overlook the potential for de-skilling of the police. The police have long been highly skilled at 'negotiating nothing',[170] defusing and dispersing problematic situations through conversation, discussion and a pointing out of the available options to the drunk and the disorderly ('go home or we'll arrest you'). This skilful use of discretion has enabled them to win a large measure of community support (or at least grudging acceptance) which in turn has proved crucial in the investigation of more serious crime. While the creation, build-up and use of a DNA database (fuelled by a zero tolerance approach to minor offences) has undoubtedly led to the detection of some grave crimes, community support remains vastly more important. The drift to summary justice thus puts the freedom and safety of us all at risk.

---

[169] M Fitzgerald, M Hough, I Joseph and T Quereshi, *Policing for London* (Cullompton, Willan, 2002) 97 (emphasis in original).

[170] C Kemp, C Norris and N Fielding, 'Legal Manoeuvres in Police Handling of Disputes' in D Farrington and S Walklate (eds), *Offenders and Victims: Theory and Policy* (London, British Society of Criminology, 1992).

# 8

# PACE Then and Now: Twenty-one Years of 'Re-balancing'

ED CAPE*

## I Introduction

In January 2006 police powers of arrest were considerably extended. Prior to the changes powers of arrest, together with other intrusive police powers that were dependant upon the suspected offence giving rise to the arrest, were broadly reserved for more serious offences. The amendments to the Police and Criminal Evidence Act 1984 (PACE) by the Serious Organised Crime and Police Act 2005[1] gave the police powers to arrest for any offence however minor. This represented the latest, but by no means the last,[2] act of 're-balancing' the criminal justice system, a notion that has become the leitmotif of the criminal justice policies of the Labour government that came to power in 1997. In the government's view, the competing interests of suspects and defendants on the one hand, and victims and the 'law-abiding majority' on the other,[3] represent a zero-sum game in which the rights of the latter can only be achieved at the expense of the former.[4] Re-balancing the system continues to be necessary because, according to Tony Blair, the former prime minister, 'the rules of the game have changed'.[5] The then home secretary took up the theme, arguing that the rights of the accused had

---

* I would like to thank Richard Young for his perceptive comments on earlier drafts of this chapter.
    [1] Sections 110 and 11, and sch 7.
    [2] See, eg, the extension of police powers to impose conditional bail on persons not charged with a criminal offence in the Police and Justice Act 2006 s 10.
    [3] Succinctly put in the title of a Home Office consultation document issued in July 2006, *Rebalancing the criminal justice system in favour of the law-abiding majority: Cutting crime, reducing reoffending and protecting the public* (London, Home Office, July 2006).
    [4] See D Garland, *The Culture of Control* (Oxford, Oxford University Press, 2001) esp 142–5.
    [5] In a speech to launch a Respect and Parenting Order Task Force, Hertfordshire, 2 September 2005, quoted in R Morgan, 'With Respect to Order, the Rules of the Game have Changed: New Labour's Dominance of the 'Law and order' Agenda' in T Newburn and P Rock (eds), *The Politics of Crime Control: Essays in Honour of David Downes* (Oxford, Oxford University Press, 2006) 97.

developed in the nineteenth century to mitigate the 'unfairness and savagery' of the Victorian approach to criminal justice, but 'at times they can now seem to overshadow the rights of the victim and the public at large'.[6] Shifting the balance in favour of victims and the law-abiding majority requires, it is argued, giving greater powers to the police, increasing the efficiency of the courts and other criminal justice agencies, and dealing with low-level offences outside of the courtroom.[7]

In this chapter I will examine the changes to the arrest, detention and investigation provisions of PACE in this context. Whilst PACE was amended in the ten years or so before Labour came to power, it is the changes that have been introduced since 1997 that have been most significant in terms of limiting the liberty of suspects, and challenging the principles espoused by the Royal Commission on Criminal Procedure (RCCP),[8] and traditional conceptions of adversarialism.[9] The analysis will commence with the changes to powers of arrest mentioned above. Whilst the government explained them by reference to the need for 'clarification, simplification and modernisation'[10] others regard them as being of constitutional significance and were astonished that they received so little serious parliamentary or academic scrutiny.[11] The next two sections will

---

[6] John Reid, in the foreword to *Rebalancing the criminal justice system in favour of the law-abiding majority*, n 3 above, 3. For critiques of Labour's criminal justice policies generally, see M Tonry, *Punishment and Politics: Evidence and Emulation in the Making of English Crime Control Policy* (Cullompton, Willan, 2004), Morgan, *ibid*, and R Solomon *et al*, *Ten years of criminal justice under Labour: An independent audit* (London, Centre for Crime and Justice Studies, 2007).

[7] See, in particular, *Delivering Simple, Speedy, Summary Justice* (Department for Constitutional Affairs, July 2006) and *Bringing Offenders to Justice: Criminal Justice Penalties and Sentencing* (a consultation paper issued by the government in January 2007, but not attributed to a specific government department, and available at http://www.cjsonline.gov.uk/downloads/application/pdf/Criminal%20Justice%20Penalties%20and%20Sentencing.pdf accessed 19 November 2007). For an account of the shifting of dispository decisions away from the courts see ch 7 by Richard Young in this collection.

[8] See generally the RCCP, *Report*, Cmnd 8092, (London, HMSO, 1981).

[9] Although the 'silence' provisions of the Criminal Justice and Public Order Act 1994, ss 34–8, whilst not amending the PACE 1984, significantly altered the context of the detention and investigation provisions. These provisions, and the right to legal advice, are dealt with in ch 9 by Anthony Edwards in this collection. For a brief, but wider, analysis of the shift away from adversarialism and the implications for the role of criminal defence lawyer, see E Cape, 'Rebalancing the Criminal Justice Process: Ethical Challenges for Criminal Defence Lawyers' (2006) 9 *Legal Ethics* 56–79. See, more generally, N Jorg, S Field and C Brants, 'Are Inquisitorial and Adversarial Systems Converging?' in P Fennell, C Harding, N Jorg and B Swart (eds) *Criminal Justice in Europe: A Comparative Study* (Oxford, Clarendon Press, 1995), P Duff, 'Changing Conceptions of the Scottish Criminal Trial: The Duty to Agree Uncontroversial Evidence' in A Duff, L Farmer, S Marshall and V Tadros (eds), *The Trial on Trial: Volume One* (Oxford, Hart Publishing, 2004), and J Jackson, 'The Effect of Human Rights on Criminal Evidentiary Processes: Towards Convergence, Divergence or Realignment?' (2005) 68 *MLR* at 737–64. See also the commentary on *R v D (Mark Gordon)* [2007] Crim LR 240 to the effect that obligations placed on the accused by the Criminal Procedure Rules 2005 are 'incompatible with an adversarial system of justice'.

[10] *Policing: Modernising Police Powers to Meet Community Needs* (London, Home Office, 2004) 2.

[11] See, eg, J Spencer, 'Extending the Police State' (2005) *New Law Journal*, 1 April, 477, and E Cape 'Arresting Developments: Increased Police Powers of Arrest' (2006) *Legal Action*, January, 24.

consider the changes to the regulation of detention for investigation and questioning and, in particular, the point at which questioning should cease and a decision regarding charge made. Whereas under the common law (as it had developed by the time that PACE was enacted) questioning had to cease and a charge decision made when there was prima facie evidence of guilt, charge can now be delayed, it would seem, to enable the prosecution case to be strengthened. These changes also need to be understood in the context of an enhanced role for prosecutors both in investigations and in respect of the charge decision, issues addressed by John Jackson in chapter ten in this volume. The fourth section will consider the associated question of how long a suspect can be detained by the police prior to charge. Whilst, other than in the case of persons arrested under the Terrorism Act 2000 section 41, the periods have not lengthened, the threshold in terms of the seriousness of the suspected offence in respect of which the person is detained has been lowered. Next to be considered will be police powers that interfere with bodily integrity and/or which require cooperation of the suspect such as powers to take fingerprints, photographs, searches and samples. Finally, police powers in relation to bail will be considered. The chapter will conclude with an examination of whether these changes represent a fundamental, constitutionally significant, shift in the position of the citizen who comes under suspicion, and of their relationship with the state, and whether the protections afforded to them are adequate. However, before embarking on this analysis it is necessary to re-visit the foundational principles underlying the PACE approach to regulation of the investigation of crime.

# II  The RCCP and the principles of criminal investigation

As was noted earlier, the government has invoked the image of a twenty-first century fight against crime being hindered by a nineteenth century approach to the rights of those accused of crime as a justification for rebalancing the criminal justice system and, in particular, for increasing police powers in respect of and over those suspected of crime. This depiction ignores the fact that the RCCP, in developing its recommendations on which PACE was based, engaged in its own balancing exercise. Seeking to avoid the 'diametrically opposed' utilitarian and libertarian arguments that marked the response to the *Eleventh Report of the Criminal Law Revision Committee*,[12] it pursued what it regarded as an evidence-based approach which would enable it to 'strike the proper balance' between the

---

[12]  The recommendations of which on the 'right to silence' were not, given the fierce opposition, pursued by the government of the day.

rights of suspects and the investigative needs of the police.[13] It assumed that the police 'have a responsibility for the investigation of suspected offences and for the collection of evidence sufficient to charge a specific person'.[14] It also recognised the importance of police questioning, particularly in order to secure confessions and thus secure certainty in prosecution.[15] However, it recognised that coercive police powers involve a deprivation of liberty, or an intrusion on someone's person or their property[16] and, given the role played by the public in detecting crime, the importance of maintaining public confidence in the police so that they continue to cooperate.[17]

Public confidence, in the view of the RCCP, required that investigative powers should be based on three principal standards:

(a) Fairness—If a suspect has a right, they should be made aware of it, be able to decide whether to exercise it and, if it is withheld, should know that it is being withheld and why. The principle of fairness also applies to police officers so that they 'should not be required to try to work within a framework of rules which are unclear, uncertain in their application and liable long after the event to subjective and arbitrary reinterpretation of their application in a particular case'.[18]

(b) Openness—This should apply to the impact of investigative procedures on the suspect and to their operation as a whole. Decisions should be explained to the suspect, written down, and be available for subsequent scrutiny. They should also be open to satisfactory supervision and review.[19]

(c) Workability—Rules regulating investigation must enable the police to discharge their duty and ensure that the rights of suspects are properly protected, and they should also take account of resources.

The first two of these principles concern process rather than substance. In other words, they concern how investigative, and in particular coercive, powers should be regulated and implemented but they say little about what those powers should properly be. The third involves the notion of balance between the needs of the police and the rights of the suspect, but says nothing which is of practical use in determining how that balance should be weighed.

However, the RCCP did consider the substantive principles that should inform what powers are available, starting with the assumption that coercive investigative powers either involve an intrusion on a person's privacy or an interference with their liberty. Given this, the use of coercive powers could not be justified, in the Commission's view, unless:—

---

[13]   *Report*, n 8 above, 10–12.
[14]   *Ibid*, 16.
[15]   *Ibid*, 19.
[16]   *Ibid*, 22.
[17]   *Ibid*, 17and 20.
[18]   *Ibid*, 20.
[19]   *Ibid*.

(a) there is certainty of, or reasonable grounds for, suspicion that a specific crime has been, is being or is about to be committed;
(b) use of a particular power is necessary in all the circumstances (reinforced by safeguards that enable immediate challenge to and subsequent review of its use); and
(c) especially in the case of particularly intrusive powers, they are proportionate in the sense that sufficient account is taken of the seriousness of the suspected offence, and of 'the effectiveness of the power in investigating the offence concerned and of the importance that society places upon bringing those suspected of it to trial'.[20]

These principles, of course, left the government of the day, and parliament, with a fair degree of latitude in translating them into legislation, although the Commission was more specific in terms of their application to particular investigative powers. The principles were imperfectly reflected in PACE powers of arrest. In restricting the main general power of arrest to 'arrestable offences'[21] there was a nod towards the criterion of proportionality, although there was no necessity requirement for arrests for arrestable offences, necessity being required only for arrests for offences that were not arrestable offences.[22] Furthermore, arrest under PACE section 24 could be lawfully effected even if the officer did not have reasonable grounds for suspicion.[23] A necessity requirement, but not a proportionality requirement (in that detention was possible however minor the suspected offence), was incorporated into the power to detain an arrested person for the purpose of further investigation,[24] and proportionality was reflected in the rules governing the maximum length of detention without charge (in that detention without charge beyond 24 hours was only possible where a person was detained in respect of a serious arrestable offence). Powers to take fingerprints and non-intimate samples before charge were restricted to circumstances where this was necessary to confirm or disprove involvement in the suspected offence (reinforced by the requirement that it be authorised by a senior officer), and a proportionality requirement could be found in the fact that such powers could only be exercised where the person was suspected of a 'recordable' offence (which broadly included only those offences that were imprisonable). Both principles were also reflected in the regulation of particularly intrusive police powers, such as the power to take intimate samples, which was initially reserved for serious

---

[20]  *Ibid*, 22 and 23.
[21]  PACE, s 24. For the definition of arrestable offence see the text to n 31 below.
[22]  Under PACE s 25.
[23]  For example, 'anyone who is in the act of committing an arrestable offence' could lawfully be arrested (s 24(4)), as could 'anyone who is guilty of [an arrestable] offence' that has been committed (s 24(5)), although whether an offence was in fact being, or had in fact been, committed is something that could only be authoritatively determined by a court after the event.
[24]  Although, as we shall see, it was largely rendered ineffective by police practice and the attitude of the courts.

arrestable offences.[25] However, whilst reasonable suspicion continues to be a (largely ineffective) pre-condition for the most frequently used powers of stop and search, and of arrest,[26] in the period since PACE was first enacted, necessity and proportionality as prerequisites for the exercise of most investigative powers have either been removed or rendered nugatory.

# III  Powers of arrest

The RCCP concluded in respect of the then existing powers of arrest that there was a 'lack of clarity and an uneasy and confused mixture of common law and statutory powers'.[27] Its proposals were based on a desire to clarify and rationalise those powers and, having regard to the overriding principles that it had established, 'to restrict the circumstances in which the police can exercise the power to deprive a person of his liberty to those in which it is genuinely necessary to enable them to execute their duty to prevent the commission of offences, to investigate crime, and to bring suspected offenders before the courts'.[28]

Whereas the Commission regarded both necessity and proportionality as being essential principles, in enacting PACE parliament, in effect, treated them as alternatives, and even then, only imperfectly so. As noted earlier, the necessity principle was not incorporated into the power to arrest for an arrestable offence under section 24,[29] although a version of it was to be found in the general arrest power under section 25 which permitted arrest for a non-arrestable offence only if it appeared to the police officer that service of a summons was impracticable or inappropriate because any of the general arrest conditions were satisfied.[30] An arrestable offence was defined as being an offence for which the sentence was fixed by law (essentially murder) or one that carried a sentence of at least five years' imprisonment.[31] To this extent, proportionality was built in but only, of

---

[25]  Defined by PACE, s 116 and sch 5 as inherently serious offences such as murder, manslaughter and rape, or any arrestable offence that led to, or was likely or intended to lead to, specified consequences. See further the text to n 82.

[26]  For a discussion of stop and search powers introduced since PACE was enacted that do not require reasonable suspicion see ch 7 by Richard Young in this collection. An arrest may still be lawfully effected without the need for reasonable grounds for suspicion under PACE s 24(1)(a) and (b), and (3).

[27]  *Report*, n 8 above, 41.

[28]  *Ibid*, 44.

[29]  A point confirmed in *Al Fayed and others v Commissioner of Police for the Metropolis and others* [2004] EWCA Civ 1579.

[30]  The general arrest conditions were set out in s 25(3) and included that the name or address of the person was unknown or that there were reasonable grounds for doubting those given, or that the officer had reasonable grounds for believing that arrest was necessary to prevent the person, inter alia, causing physical injury to himself or others, suffering physical injury, committing an offence against public decency or causing an unlawful obstruction of the highway.

[31]  Section 24(1)(a) and (b).

course, to the power under section 24. Provided the conditions were satisfied, a person could be arrested under section 25 for any offence that was not an arrestable offence as defined by section 24. However, the definition of an arrestable offence was extended by section 24(2) beyond those carrying a relatively lengthy period of imprisonment to a (limited) number of offences which could not be regarded as serious by reference to the maximum sentence criterion including, in particular, offences of taking a motor vehicle without consent (contrary to the Theft Act 1968, section 12(1)) and going equipped to steal (contrary to the Theft Act 1968, section 25(1)). Thus arrest powers under PACE continued to be available in circumstances where arrest could not be said to be necessary, and in respect of some offences that were not regarded as serious.[32]

PACE did largely limit the power to arrest to circumstances where the relevant constable had reasonable grounds for suspicion, as proposed by the RCCP,[33] but the objective of clarifying and rationalising arrest powers was only partially achieved. Although section 26 abolished powers of arrest contained in statutes passed prior to PACE, this was subject to exceptions in the case of arrest powers under more than 20 statutes.[34] Furthermore, the common law power of arrest for breach of the peace was left intact.

What happened thereafter meant that the RCCP's aim of rationalising and simplifying arrest powers was overwhelmed by a plethora of new statutory powers of arrest and additions to the list of arrestable offences in section 24(2). For example, in the year that most of the PACE provisions were brought into force, the Public Order Act (POA), 1986, created specific powers of arrest in respect of affray (POA 1986, section 3(6)),[35] and subsequently the Criminal Justice and Public Order Act (CJPOA) 1994 empowered the police to arrest for aggravated trespass (CJPOA 1994, section 68(4)), both of which offences carried a maximum sentence of less than five years' imprisonment. Moreover, such arrest powers were often more limited than the PACE arrest powers, for example, by only permitting arrest where the suspected offence was in the process of being committed and/or by requiring the arresting officer to be in uniform. This pattern of creating specific arrest powers was repeated many times over. In addition, the list of arrestable offences in section 24(2)[36] (that is, offences that

---

[32]   At the time that PACE was enacted, going equipped for theft was a summary offence. While taking a motor vehicle without consent was then an either-way offence, it was reclassified as a summary offence by the Criminal Justice Act 1988, s 37(1).

[33]   But see n 26. For a critique of 'reasonable suspicion' as a due process safeguard, see A Sanders and R Young, *Criminal Justice* (3rd edn) (Oxford, Oxford University Press, 2007) 135 (hereafter Sanders and Young).

[34]   PACE, sch 2. This was further complicated by the fact that it was subsequently held that powers to arrest under the Criminal Justice Act 1967, s 91(1) (drunk and disorderly in a public place) and the Vagrancy Act 1824, s 6, were not repealed by s 26 (*DPP v Kitching* [1990] Crim LR 394 and *Gapper v Chief Constable of Avon and Somerset Constabulary* (1998) 2 July (unreported) respectively).

[35]   And other offences such as causing harassment, alarm or distress.

[36]   Subsequently, PACE sch 1A.

were arrestable under section 24 despite having a maximum sentence of less than five years) was regularly added to so that by the time that the new arrest powers came into force in 2006, the list contained arrest powers in respect of offences under more than 26 statutes, several of which did not even carry a sentence of imprisonment.

Thus, from the foundation of relative rationality and simplicity created by PACE, over a 20 year period successive governments created the 'complex and often bewildering array of [arrest] powers and procedures'[37] that provided the rationale for the changes that took effect in 2006. The reform of arrest powers was contained in the Serious Organised Crime and Police Act 2005 (SOCPA),[38] which was rushed through parliament in the run-up to the 2005 general election and which, as a result, meant that it received little scrutiny and almost no attention from the media.[39] Whilst promoted by the government as simply 'modernising' police powers, the legislation significantly extended their powers of arrest so that 'the police will be able to arrest anyone without warrant for anything, whether trivial or serious'.[40] Thus by removing the reference to 'arrestable offence' the amended section 24 of PACE extended the power to arrest to any offence. In broad terms it retained the reasonable suspicion requirement, but that had become a minimal safeguard (if it ever was an adequate safeguard[41]) against arbitrary arrest. Whilst the court in *Castorina v Chief Constable of Surrey*[42] had determined that reasonable suspicion incorporated an objective test, in applying the test to the facts it came to the surprising decision that the arrest was lawful. Further, in *O'Hara v Chief Constable of the RUC*[43] the House of Lords held that in reviewing the decision the court should concentrate on what was in the mind of the officer, and that minimal information from another officer could found the basis for a reasonable suspicion.[44] In fact the decisions did no more than confirm that which had been established by research as the practice of police officers in exercising their arrest powers.[45]

---

[37]   *Policing: Modernising Police Powers to Meet Community Needs*, n 10 above, 4.

[38]   Section 110 and sch 7.

[39]   E Cape, 'Ever increasing police powers', February 2005 *Legal Action* 8.

[40]   J Spencer, 'Extending the police state', 2005 *New Law Journal* 1 April, 477.

[41]   See the concerns expressed to and by the RCCP concerning reasonable suspicion in relation to powers to stop and search: *Report*, n 8 above, 29.

[42]   [1988] NLJR 180.

[43]   [1997] 1 All ER 129.

[44]   It has been held that in forming a suspicion a police officer can take into account information of particular opportunity for a suspect to have committed the offence (*Al Fayed*, n 29 above), and can take a 'broad brush' approach to identifying the suspected offence (*Coudrat v Commissioner of Her Majesty's Revenue and Customs* [2005] EWCA Civ 616). Furthermore, the fact that a small number of people are identified as the only ones capable of having committed the offence may afford reasonable grounds in respect of all of them (*Cummings and others v Chief Constable of Northumbria Police* [2003] EWCA Civ 1844). For a relatively rare example of a decision that the arresting officer did not have reasonable grounds for suspicion see *R v Olden* [2007] EWCA Crim 726.

[45]   For a summary of the research, and consideration of the factors that do influence police decision-making see Sanders and Young, n 33 above, 135–50. See also D Brown, *PACE ten years on: a review of the research*, HORS 155 (London, Home Office, 1997) ch 4, which also refers to some

The other major innovation of the amended section 24 was the requirement that an arrest can only be carried out if the arresting officer has reasonable grounds for believing that arrest is necessary for one or more of a number of specified reasons (section 24(4) and (5)). In principle, the requirement that the officer should have reasonable grounds for *believing* that arrest is *necessary* should amount to a strong test which belatedly gives effect to the RCCP proposal that use of a coercive power be restricted to circumstances where it is really necessary. This is reinforced by Code of Practice G, the *Code of Practice for the Statutory Power of Arrest by Police Officers*, which was introduced at the same time as the amendments took effect,[46] which states that arrest 'represents an obvious and significant interference' with the right to liberty and that officers must 'consider if the necessary objectives can be met by other, less intrusive means. Arrest must never be used simply because it can be used' (Code G, para 1.3).

There is some reason to doubt the efficacy of these apparent due process safeguards. The weaknesses of the 'reasonable grounds for suspicion' formula have already been noted and although section 24(4) employs the term *belief* rather than *suspicion*, research evidence as to the influences on police decision-making and the scope for judicial interpretation to place the primary focus on what was in the officer's mind (which is closer to a subjective rather than an objective test), mean that its protective effect is likely to be minimal. Code G sets the tone by stating that the circumstances that may satisfy the necessity criteria 'remain a matter for the operational discretion of individual officers' (Code G, para 2.7). Section 37(2) of PACE uses the same formula in requiring a custody officer to have *reasonable grounds for believing* that detention is necessary in order to detain a suspect without charge. Research shows that this almost never inhibits custody officers from authorising detention for the purpose of further investigation. For example, Phillips and Brown found in their sample that 60 per cent of arresting officers believed that there was sufficient evidence to charge at the time of arrest, yet in only one case did the custody officer refuse to authorise detention.[47] The courts, whilst indicating that section 37(2) imposes an objective requirement on the custody officer (that is, there must be some objective basis for the decision such as would satisfy a neutral observer),[48] have been unwilling to place on them an obligation to do any more than decide on the basis of information supplied by the arresting officer. Thus it was held in *DPP v L*[49] that a custody officer was under no obligation to enquire into the legality of the arrest before deciding whether to detain them. The custody officer must, under section

---

contrary findings. By contrast, where reasonable suspicion is the threshold for a protective provision, such as the requirement to caution, it is invested with a meaning amounting to a high threshold. See, eg, *R v Shillibier* [2006] EWCA 793.

[46]   See PACE (Codes of Practice) Order 2005 SI 2004/3503.

[47]   C Phillips and D Brown, *Entry into the criminal justice system: a survey of police arrests and their outcomes*, HORS 185 (London, Home Office, 1998) 49.

[48]   See, eg, *Al Fayed*, n 29 above.

[49]   [1999] Crim LR 752.

37(2), have reasonable grounds for believing that detention is *necessary*. If detention is not necessary, the arrested person must be released. As explained later, despite the assurances of the then Home Secretary, 'necessary' has come to mean merely 'convenient' and research evidence demonstrates that this is how it is viewed and implemented by custody officers.

The necessity of an arrest was challenged in *R (on the application of C) v (1) Chief Constable of A (2) A Magistrates' Court*,[50] and although the court declined to decide the point, it indicated that whilst it is arguable that 'the rigour of the test to be applied has been intensified', the test to be applied by the courts will be that based on *Wednesbury* principles.[51] In other words the court will consider the decision-making process, but provided the officer takes into account only relevant considerations, it will not impugn the conclusion that arrest was necessary. Following the decision in *Castorina*, the *Wednesbury* test should only be applied after the court has determined that the belief was objectively reasonable, but it remains to be seen whether the courts will adopt this approach in relation to the new necessity requirement.

The relevant considerations in determining whether an arrest is necessary are set out in section 24(5), and this raises the second reason for concern about the new arrest powers; that the necessity conditions are so extensive that it is difficult to conceive of circumstances where an officer could not reasonably believe that at least one of them is satisfied. In particular, section 24(5)(e) provides that arrest may be necessary in order to allow the prompt and effective investigation of the offence or the conduct of the person in question. It is difficult to see what the investigation of conduct adds to investigation of the offence, but more importantly, if an officer determines that arrest is necessary for investigative purposes, how will it be possible to demonstrate that the officer did not reasonably hold such a belief? In the case of a minor offence, especially one of strict liability, it may be possible to argue that arrest is not necessary for the purposes of investigation. However, if the officer states that he or she arrested the person in order to interview them, and thus give the arrested person the opportunity to explain why they are not guilty, it is unlikely that a court would determine that arrest was not necessary.[52] In any event, if the person does not have proof of identify on them, arrest may be justified under section 24(5)(a) or (b) (the officer does not know or cannot readily ascertain the person's name or address, or has reasonable grounds for doubting the information given). It might be argued that an arrest immediately followed by the grant of unconditional 'street bail' (under

---

[50] [2006] EWHC 2352 (Admin).

[51] *Ibid*, para 26.

[52] In *R v McGuinness* [1999] Crim LR 318 it was held that it was permissible to continue questioning a detained suspect despite the fact that there was 'sufficient evidence to prosecute' them because that phrase 'must involve some consideration of any explanation or lack of it coming from the suspect'. Although not directly concerned with the meaning of 'necessary', it may be argued that an arrest is necessary in order to conduct an interview so as to determine whether the suspect wishes to put forward an innocent explanation.

section 30A) means that arrest was not necessary (especially if justified under section 24(5)(e) given that it is to enable the *prompt* and effective investigation of the offence), but given the courts' approach to reviewing arrest decisions, this is unlikely to be successful.

There may be a greater likelihood of a successful challenge to an arrest justified under section 24(5)(e) where the arrested person indicated to the police that they were willing to cooperate with the investigation. Many police investigative powers, such as search of the person[53] and premises, fingerprints, photographs and non-intimate (but not intimate) samples can be carried out with the consent of the person concerned and thus do not require an arrest. This point was argued unsuccessfully in *Al Fayed*,[54] but this was decided before the introduction of the necessity requirement. In *R (on the application of C)*, concerning an arrest carried out after the amendment of section 24 by SOCPA, it was argued that the proper course of action following execution of a search warrant was for the police to have asked C if he would be willing to attend the police station voluntarily for the purposes of an interview. If he did so indicate, then an arrest could not be justified under section 25(5)(e). In fact, C was arrested 'automatically' without any such enquiry. As noted earlier, the point was not decided and it remains to be seen whether a court would, in effect, require an officer to consider this possibility before arresting a person. The courts may well be reluctant to interfere with the exercise of discretion in this way, particularly because it would mean that in many cases where a suspect voluntarily attends at a police station, an arrest could not be justified by reference to the necessity requirement. However, if that is the case, the government's assurance that the necessity requirement would be an adequate due process protection in the face of extended powers of arrest would be worthless.[55]

In terms of the regulation of arrest, we have seen that the RCCP's principles were partially reflected in the relevant provisions of PACE as originally enacted. Section 24 embodied the notion of proportionality to a certain extent, and section 25 reflected a necessity requirement, although the picture is complicated by the fact that certain relatively minor offences were included within the definition of 'arrestable offence' and within the preserved powers of arrest. The period up to the end of 2005 saw even that distorted reflection removed by the addition of an increasing number of minor offences to the list of arrestable offences in section 24(2) (subsequently schedule 1A), and the creation of a large number of statutory arrest powers that were not subject to the necessity requirements of section 25. Whilst the SOCPA amendments have introduced a necessity

---

[53] Note that Code A para 1.5 provides that consent of the person is not sufficient to justify a stop and search where no power to search is applicable. This was introduced in 2003 because the police had avoided the recording and information requirements of PACE part I where consent was given.

[54] See n 29 above.

[55] In proposing the necessity requirement, the government stated that it 'places the emphasis on the need for arrest' (*Policing: Modernising Police Powers to Meet Community Needs*, n 10 above).

requirement, there is good reason to believe that it will be invested with little significance. The proportionality principle has been removed from PACE altogether. It is now for the individual police officer to determine whether an arrest is proportionate, subject only to a rather weak exhortation in Code G that the power be exercised in a proportionate manner. Not only does this place an unfair burden on police officers but, taken together, the arrest provisions now contained in PACE represent a radical extension of police powers to restrict the liberty of the citizen.

# IV   Detention for investigation

Whilst a necessity test was not built into section 24 as originally enacted in PACE, it was explicitly incorporated into the power to detain a person for investigation once they arrived at a police station. In fact the RCCP felt that a full necessity test was impracticable at the point of arrest, but that it should be implemented in full at the police station.[56] It recommended that at that stage, detention of an arrested person should only be authorised on the basis of one or more of a number of criteria, only one of which was eventually incorporated into section 37(2): that 'the custody officer has reasonable grounds for believing that ... detention without being charged is necessary to secure or preserve evidence relating to an offence for which [the person] is under arrest or to obtain such evidence by questioning [them]'. The RCCP recommended that in taking a detention decision the custody officer should be required to have regard to the nature and seriousness of the suspected offence, the nature, age and circumstances of the suspect, and the nature of the investigation required, a recommendation that did not find its way into PACE.[57] As enacted, section 37 required the custody officer to engage in a two stage process. He or she must first decide whether there is sufficient evidence to charge (section 37(1)). If there is, a charge decision must be made (section 37(7)). If there is not, the arrested person must be released unless the necessity test described above is satisfied. Section 37(1) and (2) have remained unchanged but, as we shall see, section 37(7) has been transformed.

Thus deciding whether there is sufficient evidence to charge is a key decision in determining both initial detention and whether a charge decision should be made. The RCCP did not directly consider the meaning of this critical phrase, and it was not, and has not been, statutorily defined. It is particularly problematic because, to an extent, different considerations may apply at the two stages. I have

---

[56]   *Report*, n 8 above, 45.

[57]   It is, perhaps, salutary to note that in part the recommendation was, in view of the implications for the liberty of the individual, motivated by a desire to 'diminish the use of arrest'. The RCCP recommended the introduction of a 'notice to appear at a police station' procedure which would avoid unnecessary arrest and detention, a recommendation that was not adopted in the legislation.

argued elsewhere that since the expression reflected the pre-existing common law rule, and since parliament did not legislate for a different meaning, it should be interpreted as meaning whether there is enough evidence to establish a prima facie case.[58] As will be seen when the decision to charge is considered, its meaning for that purpose has, arguably, been altered by the *Guidance on Charging* issued by the Director of Public Prosecutions (DPP).

Research evidence quickly established that regulation of the detention decision was ineffective. When asked, custody officers expressed surprise that the detention decision could be anything other than automatic[59] (some even asked for a rubber stamp containing the words of section 37(2)[60]), and researchers failed to find any case where detention was refused.[61] This was exacerbated by the fact that there was no procedure applicable if detention was refused.[62] The courts have also been prepared to invest the decision with little real meaning in terms of acting as a filter to prevent unnecessary detentions. As noted earlier, it was held in *DPP v L*[63] that in determining whether there is sufficient evidence to charge, custody officers are entitled to take the arresting officer's version of events at face value and, in particular, are not under a duty to enquire into the lawfulness of the arrest. In *R v Mehmet*,[64] where a person was arrested on suspicion of possession of unlawful drugs, the court held that the custody officer was entitled to take the view that there was not sufficient evidence to charge until the alleged drugs had been forensically examined. The contrary view was taken in *Martin v Chief Constable of Avon and Somerset Constabulary*,[65] but the custody officer was, nevertheless, entitled to detain because (despite the fact that the suspect had confessed to possession immediately prior to arrest) he was not sure that it would amount to 'good evidence'. Cases on the similar phrase 'sufficient evidence to prosecute', found in a former version of Code C, para 16.1, have interpreted it as involving some consideration of any explanation, or lack of explanation, coming from the suspect.[66] Thus even if there is apparently sufficient evidence to charge,

---

[58] E Cape, 'Detention Without Charge: What Does "Sufficient Evidence to Charge" Mean?' [1999] *Crim LR* 874.

[59] M McConville, A Sanders and R Leng, *The Case for the Prosecution* (London, Routledge, 1991) 44.

[60] I McKenzie, R Morgan and R Reiner, 'Helping the Police with their Enquiries' [1990] *Crim LR* 22 at 24.

[61] D Dixon, A Bottomley, C Coleman, M Gill and D Wall, 'Safeguarding the Rights of Suspects in Police Custody (1990) 1 *Policing and Society* 115, 130. This has been an enduring feature of the detention decision, confirmed by subsequent research. See C Phillips and D Brown, *Entry into the criminal justice system: a survey of police arrests and their outcomes*, n 47 above.

[62] McKenzie, *et al*, n 60 above. There remains confusion as to whether, in these circumstances, a custody record should be opened.

[63] [1999] Crim LR 752.

[64] 13 June 1989, CA (unreported).

[65] 29 October 1997, CA (unreported).

[66] See *R v Elliott* [2002] EWCA Crim 931 for a review of the relevant case law. For further analysis see M Zander, *The Police and Criminal Evidence Act 1984* 5th edn (London, Sweet and Maxwell, 2005) 147–8.

the custody officer is permitted to detain in order to give the suspect an opportunity to provide an explanation or put forward a defence.

If there is not sufficient evidence to charge at the initial stage, the custody officer must determine whether detention is necessary. In explaining the use of the term 'necessary' during the passage of PACE through parliament the then Home Secretary, Douglas Hurd, said that detention must be necessary, 'not desirable, convenient or a good idea but necessary'.[67] That was, at best, wishful thinking, but more likely mere rhetoric which resonates with the government's approach two decades later to the extension of police powers of arrest. As indicated earlier, it was held in *Al Fayed* that while the question of whether the custody officer has reasonable grounds for their belief that detention is necessary is an objective question, the issue of necessity is to be determined by reference to whether the officer acted reasonably in determining that detention was necessary. Despite the fact that research has demonstrated that detention decisions are automatic, there have been no reported cases of a successful challenge to a decision that detention is necessary.

# V  The charge decision

The evidence is thus overwhelming that, in the words of a Home Office research report, the avoidance of 'unnecessary detentions … was not being achieved'.[68] Once a person is arrested, if the officer chooses to take them to the police station for investigation, nothing will prevent their detention irrespective of whether detention, judged objectively, is really necessary. Having been detained, an important question is then at what point must a decision about prosecution be made. As noted earlier, PACE section 37(7) has always employed the expression 'sufficient evidence to charge' as the threshold, and on the meaning of this the RCCP was uncharacteristically silent. Its meaning is important because underlying it are two important questions: to what extent can the police use detention as a means of building a prosecution case; and to what extent can the individual citizen be required to cooperate with that process? During detention a legally innocent person is, of course, deprived of their liberty and is subject to a range of coercive investigative measures—things that the RCCP was at pains to confine to circumstances where this was both necessary and proportionate.

When PACE was first enacted, the charge decision was that of the custody officer. Section 37(7) provided that once the custody officer determined that there was sufficient evidence to charge, the person had either to be charged or released by them. The questioning of a detained suspect had to cease *as soon as* the officer in the case believed that there was sufficient evidence for a successful

---

[67]   Hansard, HC, Standing Committee E, col 1229 (16 February 1984), quoted in Zander, *ibid*, 140.
[68]   Brown, n 45 above, 57.

prosecution and that a prosecution should be brought (Code C, para 11.2).[69] At that point the officer had to take the suspect to the custody officer without delay, who was then responsible for taking the charge decision (Code C, para 17.1). Thus whatever the precise meaning of 'sufficient evidence to charge', once the police had decided that there was such evidence they could not continue to question and/or detain the person in order to strengthen the prosecution evidence still further. They could, of course, continue their investigations (although generally not by questioning the suspect), but could not use continued detention for this purpose.

In the period since then, the position regarding the point at which questioning must cease and at which a charge decision must be made has radically changed. In chapter ten, John Jackson explains how responsibility for making a charge decision has been transferred from the custody officer to a prosecutor. From the perspective of the suspect, and the police, this shift in responsibility has also had consequences for the meaning of 'sufficient evidence to charge' and thus the point at which interviewing must cease and the charge decision made.

With regard to the point at which interviewing must cease, having gone through a series of changes over the previous decade, the 2003 version of Code C settled on the following formula (repeated in subsequent versions):

The interview or further interview … must cease when:

(a) the officer in charge of the investigation is satisfied all the questions they consider relevant to obtaining accurate and reliable information about the offence have been put to the suspect…

(b) the officer in charge of the investigation has taken account of any other available evidence; and

(c) the officer in charge or the investigation, or in the case of a detained suspect, the custody officer… , reasonably believes that there is sufficient evidence to provide a realistic prospect of conviction for that offence' (Code C, para 11.6).

A question arises as to whether a 'realistic prospect of conviction' means the same as 'sufficient evidence to charge'. Arguably, the latter amounts to a lower threshold than the former, but the question awaits definitive resolution. In any event, the current Code C para 11.6 appears to make it clear that interviewing can continue beyond the point where the interviewing officer believes that there is sufficient evidence to give a realistic prospect of conviction if they still consider that they have questions to put and/or have not yet fully taken into account other evidence. This purportedly[70] enables interviewing to continue beyond the point at which, under section 37(7), a charge decision should be made. Assuming the custody officer is aware of the information which would lead to a conclusion that there is sufficient evidence to charge, section 37(7) requires them (subject now to section 37(7)(b) which enables them to bail the person without a view to a charge

---

[69] That is, of the version of Code C published in 1986.

[70] 'Purportedly' because a Code cannot alter the meaning of a statutory provision.

decision being made[71]) to move to the charge stage. However, para 11.6 would seem to encourage interviewing officers to delay taking the suspect to the custody officer, or at least refrain from giving the custody officer the relevant information, until they have put to the suspect all the questions they wish to put to them.

The point is further confused by Code C, para 16.1 which states that the officer in the case must inform the custody officer when they reasonably believe that there is sufficient evidence to give a realistic prospect of conviction, without mentioning the other two conditions in Code C, para 11.6. Leaving that aside, and whether para 11.6 is compatible with section 37(7), the current approach to when interviewing must cease goes well beyond the original formulation in that it permits the officer to continue interviewing beyond the point at which there is sufficient evidence to give a realistic prospect of conviction. A major, although not the only, purpose of this must be to permit police officers to continue interviewing in a coercive setting in order to use the interview to strengthen the prosecution case.

The DPP's *Guidance on Charging*, issued under the authority of PACE section 37A in order to facilitate the new charging arrangements, gives guidance on the meaning of 'sufficient evidence to charge'.[72] It remains the responsibility of the custody officer to determine whether there is sufficient evidence to charge (in accordance with section 37(7)), but normally he or she must then refer the case to a Crown prosecutor for the charge decision to be made.[73] In deciding whether there is sufficient evidence to charge for the purpose of referring the case to the prosecutor under section 37(7)(a) the custody officer must apply the 'threshold test',[74] which is defined as an 'assessment of whether ... there is at least a reasonable suspicion against the person of having committed an offence ... and that at that stage it is in the public interest to proceed'.[75] The prosecutor must then apply the 'full code test', that is, whether there is sufficient evidence to provide a realistic prospect of conviction and whether it is in the public interest to proceed. This is also the test that must be applied by the custody officer in the (exceptional) circumstances in which he or she is permitted to charge.[76]

---

[71]  See text following n 79.

[72]  The *Guidance* is available at http://www.cps.gov.uk/publications/directors_guidance/dpp_guidance.html (accessed 19 November 2007).

[73]  This is subject to certain exceptions where the custody officer retains the power to charge. See the *Guidance*, para 3.

[74]  *Guidance*, para 8.4.

[75]  *Ibid*, para 3.10.

[76]  Although in either case, the *Guidance* states that a charge decision may be made on the basis of the Threshold Test if it would not be appropriate for the person to be released on bail after charge and the necessary information for the Full Code Test is not available (*Guidance* para 9).

The threshold test amounts to no more than the reasonable suspicion require-ment for the purposes of arrest, with the addition of a public interest considera-tion,[77] a point made by the Divisional Court in *G v Chief Constable of West Yorkshire Police and others*.[78] The *Guidance* provides that '[i]n determining whether there is sufficient evidence to charge in accordance with Section 37(7) PACE, Custody Officers *will* apply the Threshold Test'[emphasis added].[79] Given the mandatory language of the *Guidance*, it is arguable that the threshold represented by the phrase 'sufficient evidence to charge' has been lowered. However, this surely cannot have been the intention. It would reduce the threshold to even less than that required for the charge decision prior to PACE and would, in effect, mean that a custody officer would normally be unable to authorise detention under section 37(2) since the threshold for charging in section 37(1) would have been met by the fact of arrest. It is more likely to be interpreted as a test which enables, but does not require, the custody officer to determine that there is sufficient evidence to charge for the purpose of enabling a charge decision to be made by a prosecutor. This is supported by the fact that section 37(7)(b) now permits a custody officer, having determined that there is sufficient evidence to charge, to release the person without charge and on bail for a purpose other than enabling a charge decision to be made. This clearly envisages that despite the fact that there is sufficient evidence to charge, investi-gations can continue, including by further interview when the suspect subse-quently attends the police station to answer to bail.

The complexity and confusion, in particular in the Code provisions and the *Guidance*, hardly satisfy the fairness and workability principles of the RCCP. Since the principles apply to both the suspect and the police, a useful test might be to ask a police officer to explain to a suspect, clearly, so that they may understand at what point a charge decision must be made! Assuming the analysis set out here is correct, and taking into account Code C para 11.6, it would seem tolerably clear that the current approach is that police interviewing can continue beyond the point where there is sufficient evidence to establish a prima facie case and, in particular that it can continue, and the charge decision can be delayed, to enable the police to use continued detention to interview a suspect in a coercive setting in order to strengthen the prosecution case. If so, this represents a fundamental change in the relationship between the citizen and the state which is

---

[77] The *Guidance* states that the public interest for the purpose of the Threshold Test means the same as for the full code test (para 3.10), which is concerned with whether prosecution is in the public interest rather than whether the public interest requires further evidence to be obtained.

[78] [2006] EWHC 3485 (Admin), in which the judge stated 'I do not regard [the Threshold test] as an appropriate test for determining whether there is sufficient evidence to charge'.

[79] *Guidance*, para 8.4. The *Guidance* does not purport to define 'sufficient evidence to charge' for all purposes in s 37, although it is inconceivable that the same phrase should have different meanings within the same section. However, if it does have the same meaning it leads to some odd results. See E Cape, 'Police Bail and the Decision to Charge: Recent Developments and the Human Rights Deficit', (2007) *Archbold News*, August 10, 8.

of constitutional significance, but a change that has been effected by incremental change in the absence of principled debate of the issues involved.


# VI  The length of pre-charge detention

The point at which interviewing must cease and a charge decision made is, of course, subject to the time limits on detention without charge. The RCCP's recommendation as to maximum periods of pre-charge detention[80] were broadly incorporated into PACE, except that the requirement to produce an uncharged suspect before a court was delayed until 36 hours from the commencement of detention as opposed to the 24 hour maximum recommended by the Commission. The RCCP believed that detention without charge beyond 24 hours should only be permissible in the case of persons suspected of a grave crime, its definition of which was broadly translated into 'serious arrestable offence'.[81] Whilst PACE as originally enacted permitted detention without charge beyond 24 hours, and up to 36 hours, on the authority of a superintendent or above rather than a court, it was limited to persons who were detained in respect of a serious arrestable offence. In this way, an element of proportionality was built in to the detention provisions in that detention without charge for lengthy periods of time was limited to circumstances where the detained person was suspected of a serious offence. It is true that the definition of 'serious arrestable offence' was flexible enough to encompass some allegations that were not particularly serious. An offence was serious if it led to, or was intended or was likely to lead to, serious financial loss by any person, and whether loss was serious was to be assessed by reference to the person who suffered the loss (section 116(3), (6) and (7)). Thus, for example, theft of the life savings of a person could amount to a serious arrestable offence even though it amounted to just a few hundred pounds. Nevertheless, in broad terms, detention without charge beyond 24 hours was only possible where a person was suspected of an offence for which, if found guilty, they would be likely to receive a lengthy prison sentence.[82]

This approach remained intact for almost two decades, until the Criminal Justice Act (CJA) 2003[83] amended PACE to permit detention beyond 24 hours and up to 36 hours of persons detained in respect of an arrestable offence rather

---

[80]  *Report*, n 8 above, 55–8.

[81]  Defined by PACE s 116 and sch 5 See n 25.

[82]  Statistics on length of pre-charge detention are not routinely collected or published, although figures on detention beyond 24 hours, and on warrants of further detention, are included in the statistical series mentioned in n 84 below. For a review of the research on detention periods, largely carried out before the mid-1990s, see Brown, n 45 above, 63.

[83]  Section 7, amending PACE s 42(1)(b).

than a serious arrestable offence.[84] The link between length of detention and seriousness was fundamentally altered, although not broken altogether, by SOCPA, which abolished the categories of arrestable and serious arrestable offence, and replaced them for the purposes of extending detention beyond 24 hours with the condition that the person must be under arrest for an indictable offence.[85] The objective behind this change, as expressed in the Home Office consultation paper that preceded the Act,[86] was to simplify the conditions for extending detention (and the other powers affected) whilst preventing their use in less serious offences. In this way, it asserted, a degree of proportionality would be preserved although, rather ominously, it held open the possibility of breaking the link with seriousness altogether in the future.[87] In the case of those powers dependant on a person being under arrest for a serious arrestable offence, such as detention beyond 36 hours, the Home Office clearly understood that it was lowering the threshold so that they would be more widely available and, more specifically, available in respect of persons suspected of crimes that could not be regarded as serious.

Thus, following the changes resulting from SOCPA, the threshold for detaining a person without charge beyond 36 hours has been lowered, and in principle is now available, for example, in respect of a person arrested for theft, criminal damage, assault occasioning actual bodily harm, or affray, however minor.[88] In the case of detention beyond 24 hours and up to 36 hours, as was noted earlier, the threshold had already been lowered by the CJA 2003. The impact of the further change, replacing the threshold of arrestable offence with that of indictable offence, is more complex. Offences that were arrestable offences because they carried a maximum sentence of at least five years are, by definition, indictable offences but since, broadly, any offence that carries at least six months' imprisonment is indictable, detention without charge beyond 24 hours is now much more widely available. However, contrary to the general trend, some (but not all) of the offences that were arrestable offences because they were listed in PACE schedule 1A, such as taking a conveyance without consent, driving whilst disqualified, or

---

[84] Although only amounting to a small proportion of persons arrested and detained, the number of suspects detained without charge beyond 24 hours and subsequently released without charge almost doubled in the year after the threshold was reduced, to 1,132 in 2004/5 from 621 in the previous year, and more than doubled again, to 2,459, in 2005/6 (*Arrests for Recorded Crime (Notifiable Offences) and the Operation of Certain Police Powers under PACE*, Ministry of Justice Statistical Bulletin, October 2007, 16).

[85] Section 111 and sch 7. An indictable offence is one that is triable only on indictment, or either in a magistrates' court or in the Crown Court.

[86] *Policing: Modernising Police Powers to Meet Community Needs*, n 10 above, 5 and 6.

[87] Allowing intrusive powers in respect of any offence 'may be a step too far from where we are currently' (*ibid*, 6).

[88] Statistics for the period after the changes took effect are not yet available. Although the number of applications for warrants of further detention is small, almost all applications are granted. Between 70% and 80% of those in respect of whom a warrant is granted are subsequently charged. See *Arrests for Recorded Crime (Notifiable Offences) and the Operation of Certain Police Powers under PACE*, Home Office Statistical Bulletin 21/05, December 2005, 15.

assaulting a police officer in the execution of their duty, are not indictable so that detention without charge beyond 24 hours is no longer possible in respect of such offences. In fact, only a few offences are affected in this way, but the police are pressing for their powers in respect of such offences, including the power to detain without charge beyond 24 hours, to be re-instated.[89]

Apart from the last category of offences, the effect of the changes since 2003 has been to make extended periods of detention without charge available in respect of a much wider range of less serious offences. Whilst PACE provides that extended detention without charge is dependant upon it being necessary for the purposes of the investigation,[90] there is now only a tenuous link with the principle of proportionality, as gauged by the seriousness of the offence being investigated, and responsibility for determining whether the denial of liberty represented by extended detention without charge is proportionate to the seriousness of the suspected offence, is largely left to the individual officer (in the case of detention beyond 24 hours) or the magistrates' court (in the case of detention beyond 36 hours).[91]

# VII  Powers that interfere with bodily integrity

Reading the careful and reasoned arguments, including the disagreements between Commission members, and recommendations of the RCCP, and the underlying concern to restrict police powers that interfere with bodily integrity, provides an important reminder of how far attitudes, at least of governments and the police, have changed in the last two decades.[92] It is worth reminding ourselves that, according to the Home Office, crime rates now are no greater than at the

---

[89] 'Respondents have requested that these powers are re-instated for those summary offences previously deemed by Parliament as requiring these additional powers to ensure effective investigation and enforcement of those offences.' (*Review of the Police and Criminal Evidence Act (PACE) 1984: Summary of responses to the public consultation exercise (16 March–31 May 2007)*), Home Office, July 2007, available at http://police.homeoffice.gov.uk/news-and-publications/publication/operational-policing/PACEReviewsummary310707.pdf?view=Binary (accessed 19 November 2007). For the consultation paper, see *Modernising Police Powers: Review of the Police and Criminal Evidence Act (PACE) 1984*, Home Office, March 2007.

[90] PACE s 42(1)(a) (superintendent's authority for detention beyond 24 hours) and s 43(4)(a) (warrant of further detention beyond 36 hours), although s 44(1) (extension of warrant of further detention) requires the court to determine that continued detention is 'justified' rather than necessary.

[91] This tenuous link is being placed under even greater pressure by the proposal floated in the consultation paper *Modernising Police Powers* that the 'detention clock' be stopped where prescribed delays, such as those caused by medical treatment or waiting for a defence lawyer to arrive, occur. See E Cape, 'Modernising Police Powers—Again?' [2007] *Crim LR* 934, at 946.

[92] See, in particular, *Report*, n 8 above, 60–69.

time the Commission was considering these issues.[93] In respect of those powers that do not amount to a serious intrusion upon a suspect's bodily or personal integrity, such as fingerprinting and photographing, the RCCP recommended that they should be available where a person had been arrested for any offence if there were reasonable grounds for believing that they would help confirm or disprove the suspect's involvement in a particular crime, or where there were reasonable grounds for doubting their identity. In the absence of consent, they would require the written approval of a sub-divisional commander. Records should be destroyed if the person was not proceeded against or was acquitted. Body samples were regarded as more intrusive, and the Commission recommended that the power to take non-intimate samples without consent should only be available in the case of 'grave crimes' and, again, only on the written authority of a sub-divisional commander. The taking of intimate samples 'seems to us objectionable' and the taking of them without consent should not be permitted.[94] Personal search should be available once a detention decision had been made, but strip searching was regarded as an 'extreme and manifestly disagreeable form of search' which should only be permitted in the case of grave crimes.[95]

In the case of fingerprints, the Commission's recommendations were broadly implemented by PACE. Prior to charge, they could only be taken without consent on the authority of an officer of at least the rank of superintendent who had reasonable grounds for suspecting the involvement of the person in a criminal offence, and for believing that their fingerprints would tend to confirm or disprove involvement.[96] Fingerprints could not be taken simply to establish identity, although the power to take fingerprints (and non-intimate samples) for this purpose was added in 2001.[97] Somewhat oddly, the power to take photographs was not originally provided for in PACE, but only in Code D which stated that before charge they could only be taken without consent if the person was arrested at the same time as others and a photograph was necessary to establish who was arrested. Further, it provided that force could never be used to take a photograph. Following the recommendation of the RCCP, the police were given the power to take non-intimate samples without consent only on the authority of a superintendent or above for the purpose of confirming or disproving involvement, and it was confined to circumstances where the person was suspected of a

---

[93] The risk of becoming a victim of crime 'remains at the lowest level recorded since … 1981'. *Crime in England and Wales 2005/6*, Home Office Research Bulletin 12/06 (London, Home Office, 2006) 13.

[94] *Report*, n 8 above, 68. Intimate samples are currently defined in PACE s 65(1) as including samples of blood and other body fluids, dental impressions and swabs taken from the genitals and body orifices other than the mouth. Non-intimate samples include samples of hair other than pubic hair, samples taken from a nail or under a nail, saliva and skin impressions.

[95] *Ibid*, 62.

[96] PACE, s 61(3) and (4) as originally enacted.

[97] By Anti-terrorism, Crime and Security Act 2001, s 90(2).

serious arrestable offence (section 63(3) and (4)). Taking a sample from a suspect's mouth was not permitted under section 63 because this amounted to an intimate sample (section 65). As now, the taking of intimate samples was only permitted with both the consent of the person and authorisation, but as originally enacted that authorisation had to be given by a superintendent (section 62).[98] Fingerprints and samples taken from a person who was not prosecuted, or who was prosecuted but acquitted, had to be destroyed as soon as practicable, and the person had a right to witness their destruction (section 64). Personal search was permitted on arrest for any offence (section 32(1) and (2)), and also on detention at a police station (section 54), but contrary to the recommendations of the RCCP, strip search (other than one involving a search of body orifices), was permitted irrespective of the seriousness of the alleged offence (Code C, annex A, para 5.). Intimate searches of body orifices were permitted, but only with the consent of a superintendent or above, and only in the same circumstances as currently provided for in PACE, section 55(1).[99]

Whilst PACE in its original form represented some hardening of the Commission's approach to the proper balance between the investigative needs of the police and the rights of suspects, and to the appropriate safeguards, nevertheless it followed the broad contours of the proposed scheme. This approach to the notion of balance and to the appropriate safeguards has, in the past two decades, and step-by-step, been undermined, if not dismantled. It is not possible here to give a detailed account of that process, but the main elements will be traced. In broad terms the level of authorisation required for the exercise of intrusive powers, and the need for justification for exercise of those powers, has been reduced, or removed altogether.

Whilst the Commission's scepticism of the investigative utility of fingerprints has been proved to be ill-founded,[100] the power to take fingerprints has changed from being one that had to be justified by investigative need to one that permits fingerprints to be taken as a routine process. Taking fingerprints from a person in police detention[101] without consent no longer has to be authorised and does not

---

[98] Failure to give consent could, and can now, lead to adverse inferences being drawn (s 62(10)).

[99] That is, if the officer has reasonable grounds for believing that a person in police detention may have concealed anything which could be used to cause physical injury to themselves or other and which they might used whilst in detention or custody, or that they may have a Class A drug concealed on them which they are in possession of for certain purposes such as supply. Authorisation may be given by an inspector.

[100] *Report*, n 8 above, 65. The National Policing Improvement Agency, which now has responsibility for national information systems including those covering fingerprints and DNA, states that it currently processes 100,000 records of arrests per month, and with an average of 6,500 identifications per month, although it does not give figures on the number of detections resulting from fingerprints. See http://www.npia.police.uk/en/5969.htm (accessed 19 November 2007). For a critical report on powers to take and use 'bioinformation' see *The forensic use of bioinformation: ethical issues* (London, Nuffield Council on Bioethics, 2007).

[101] Provided they have been arrested for a recordable offence (s 61(3)(a)). There is currently pressure to permit fingerprints to be taken where a person has been arrested in respect of any offence. See *Modernising Police Powers*, n 89 above, 11.

have to be justified by investigative need nor, indeed, by any consideration other than the fact that they have not already had their fingerprints taken in the course of the investigation of the suspected offence (section 61(3)). Once taken, they can be kept indefinitely even if the person is not charged, or is acquitted (section 64).[102] There is now even a power to take fingerprints from persons who have not been arrested.[103] The power to take and retain non-intimate samples has changed in the same way as for fingerprints and samples from the mouth, originally treated as an intimate part of the body for this purpose, can now be taken under these provisions (section 65(1)).[104] In addition, the police now have the power to take footwear impressions without consent from a person in police detention in broadly the same circumstances that fingerprints can be taken (section 61(A)).[105]

The grounds for authorising the taking of intimate samples remain the same as originally enacted, but authorisation can now be given by an inspector (section 62(1)). In addition, in the case of a person in police detention a sample can be taken for the purpose of testing for Class A drugs where they have been arrested for or charged with[106] a trigger offence[107] or an inspector or above has reasonable grounds for suspecting that the misuse by that person of a specified Class A drug caused or contributed to the offence (section 63B(1A)). Whilst the person's consent is required, failure to give consent without good cause is an offence.[108] The police now have a statutory power to take photographs without consent of persons in police detention (whether or not the suspected offence is recordable) without any pre-conditions. In addition, they have power to photograph arrested persons who are not in police detention, and in some circumstances where the person has not been arrested (section 64A). One consequence of having a statutory power to take photographs is that the police can use reasonable force if

---

[102]   This was unsuccessfully challenged in *R (on the application of S) v Chief Constable of South Yorkshire; R (on the application of Marper) v Chief Constable of South Yorkshire* [2004] UKHL 39; [2004] 1 WLR 2196. At the time of writing, a decision of the European Court of Human Rights involving these applicants was awaited. ACPO guidance, *Exceptional Case Procedures for Removal of DNA, Fingerprints and PNC Records*, 24 April 2006, states that cases where the police should accede to request to remove records will be rare, limited to situations such as where the original arrest was unlawful, or where it is established beyond doubt that no offence had been committed. The guidance is available at http://www.acpo.police.uk/asp/policies/Data/guidance for removal from database.doc (accessed 19 November 2007).

[103]   When implemented, the SOCPA 2005, s 117 will amend PACE s 61 to permit fingerprints to be taken without consent from a person who has not been arrested if a constable reasonably believes that the person is committing or has committed, or attempted to commit, an offence and their name cannot readily be ascertained or there is reason to doubt the name given.

[104]   The inclusion of a swab taken from the mouth as a non-intimate sample was effected by the CJ POA 1994, s 58(1).

[105]   As a result of the SOCPA, 2005, s 118.

[106]   These powers are not currently in force in all police force areas, and in some areas are available if the arrest condition is met, but in others only if the charge condition has been met. See Home Office Circular 3/2006.

[107]   'Trigger offence' has the same meaning as in the Criminal Justice and Court Services Act 2000 Part III, and a list of trigger offences is conveniently set out in Code C Note for Guidance 17E.

[108]   Punishable with up to 6 months' imprisonment (PACE ss 63B(8) and 63C(1)).

the person does not cooperate.[109] Powers to conduct personal searches have remained more or less the same as those originally enacted, except that an intimate search may be authorised by an inspector (section 55(1)),[110] but in addition, a person in police detention can be searched, on the authority of an inspector or above, for the purpose of establishing their identity or to find any mark that would tend to identify them as being involved in the commission of an offence (section 54A(1)).

Thus the approach of the RCCP to police powers that intrude on personal or bodily integrity, based on the need to protect bodily integrity and privacy unless this was outweighed by investigative need relating to an offence of sufficient gravity to justify the intrusion, has given way to one whereby the police have extensive powers, particularly to take fingerprints, photographs and non-intimate samples, without regard to notions of privacy, proportionality or investigative need, and without the (assumed) safeguard of prior authorisation. We have also witnessed the re-definition of an undoubtedly intimate part of the body, the mouth, so that it is treated as being open (literally) to police probing. In the case of fingerprints and non-intimate samples this shift has been driven, in part, by the desire to establish large national databases, which undoubtedly have benefits in terms of crime investigation. One danger of an unprincipled approach to reforming police powers of this kind is the difficulty, as technologies develop and become available (including not only the means of acquiring and analysing such data, but also methods of storing and retrieving it), of determining what the proper limits of those powers should be. Roger Leng has argued, in relation to the 'inference from silence' provisions of the CJPOA, 1994, that they led to a normative expectation that suspects will disclose their defences to the police.[111] The changes to the intrusive powers described here have led not just to a normative expectation that a suspect will cooperate with them but, in respect of most of them, a legal demand that they do, on pain of force being used or the application of some form of sanction.[112]

# VIII  Police bail

Police bail can arise at two distinct stages, bail before charge and bail after charge, and to an extent they raise different considerations. Prior to charge, bail raises the

---

[109]   By virtue of PACE, s 117.

[110]   And intimate drug searches can be conducted by means of x-ray or ultrasound (s 55A).

[111]   R Leng, 'Silence pre-trial, reasonable expectations and the normative distortion of fact-finding' (2001) 5 *International Journal of Evidence and Proof* 240–256.

[112]   There are similarities here with the increasing requirement, post-charge, that defendants provide disclosure, even to the extent of telling the prosecution of weaknesses in their case. See, eg, E Cape, 'Rebalancing the Criminal Justice Process: Ethical Challenges for Criminal Defence Lawyers' (2006) 9 *Legal Ethics* 56, esp 68–70.

question of the extent to which a person's liberty should be restricted (in the sense of having to comply with conditions or having to surrender as and when required) in circumstances where not only is the person legally innocent, but where there is not sufficient evidence to charge them with a criminal offence. Police bail after charge, whilst concerning a person who has not yet been proved to be guilty of the offence charged, does not arise until there is, at least, sufficient evidence of guilt to give rise to the charge and which is inevitably limited in time because the person will be bailed to appear before a court within a relatively short period of time. Furthermore, whilst bail after charge is an alternative to being kept in custody, the alternative to bail before charge is normally unconditional release. Evidence to the RCCP apparently raised no particular concerns with the then current law or practice, other than the danger that the offer or perceived prospects of bail may induce a confession.[113] With regard to pre-charge bail the Commission recommended only that the police should be able to renew bail when a person, having been granted bail, then surrendered. With regard to post-charge bail, in order to encourage the greater use of bail (rather than detention in custody pending the first court appearance), the Commission recommended that the police should be able to attach conditions.

As originally enacted, PACE maintained this division. Prior to charge, the custody officer could impose[114] bail under a number of provisions (for example, sections 34(5) and 37(2)), but no conditions could be attached other than the requirement to re-attend at the police station (section 47(3)). Following charge, there was a presumption that bail would be granted (or the person be released without bail), but it could be withheld if the defendant's name or address could not be ascertained or was doubted, there were reasonable grounds for believing that detention was necessary for their own protection or to prevent them from causing injury, loss or damage, or there were reasonable grounds for believing that detention was necessary to ensure that they appeared in court or did not interfere with the administration of justice (section 38(1)).[115] Contrary to the Commission's recommendation, there was no power to attach conditions to bail granted after charge, although this power was added in 1994.[116] Despite the importance of bail, not only because release is an important consideration for many suspects[117] but also because the police bail decision has a significant impact

---

[113]   *Report*, n 8 above, 58.
[114]   Whilst it is usual to refer to bail being 'granted' to a person following charge, in view of the fact that the alternative to bail is normally unconditional release, it would be more logical to refer to bail being 'imposed' on a person before charge.
[115]   As originally enacted, fear of offences being committed if released was not a specific ground for withholding bail.
[116]   By the CJPOA 1994, s 27.
[117]   A Sanders, L Bridges, A Mulvaney and G Crozier, *Advice and Assistance at Police Stations and the 24 Hour Duty Solicitor Scheme* (London, Lord Chancellor's Department, 1989) 72–3. Bail is also an important bargaining chip for the police. See, eg, S Choongh, *Policing as Social Discipline* (Oxford, Oxford University Press, 1997) 100, and J Raine and M Willson, 'Police Bail with Conditions' (1997) 37(4) *British Journal of Criminology* 593.

on the decision of the court whether to grant bail,[118] neither PACE nor Code C imposed any requirement on the custody officer to listen to representations from the suspect or their lawyer, let alone any requirement that they should have regard to them in taking the decision. Although, in practice, it appears that custody officers do normally listen to such representations, they are still under no duty to do so even though they could be relevant to the decision to grant bail, and could be useful in determining (where this is possible) what conditions may be appropriate.

As with intrusive investigative powers, there have been many changes to the powers of police in respect of bail since PACE was first enacted, but the focus here is on the provisions as they were in 2007 so that a comparison can be made with the position two decades earlier. To be considered first is the major innovation of 'street bail'. When PACE was first enacted, and for many years after, where a police officer arrested a person away from a police station they were required, if the arrested person was not quickly de-arrested, to take them to a police station as soon as practicable (section 30). This was designed to ensure that interviews were not conducted away from police stations, that a custody officer took over responsibility, and that the protective provisions, such as the right to legal advice, became effective as soon as possible.[119] The CJA 2003, section 4 amended PACE so that instead of taking the arrested person to a police station, the arresting officer can impose bail requiring them to attend at a police station at a future date. Criteria for the imposition of 'street bail' were not set out in the legislation, but in a Home Office circular.[120] The principal rationale for the introduction of this power was the efficient use of police resources. It was estimated that it could save 390,000 hours of officers' time annually.[121] Notably, in contrast to the general scheme of police bail, 'street bail' can be determined by police officers of any rank, and normally will be made by those of the rank of constable. No time limit was imposed on the period for which bail could be imposed, and when the

---

[118] Hucklesby found that in the vast majority of cases where the prosecution recommended unconditional or conditional bail, the court followed their recommendation, and that in 86% of cases where the prosecution argued for a remand in custody, this was granted by the court. As a result, Hucklesby argues that since the prosecutor's attitude to bail is informed by police, it is the police who are the real decision-makers: A Hucklesby, 'Remand Decision Makers' [1997] *Crim LR* 269. See also A Hucklesby, 'Court Culture: An Explanation of Variations in the Use of Bail by Magistrates' Courts (1997) 36 *Howard Journal of Criminal Justice* 129, and R Morgan and S Jones, 'Bail or Jail?' in E Stockdale and S Casale (eds) *Criminal Justice Under Stress* (London, Blackstone, 1992).

[119] The requirement to take the person to the police station was, and is, qualified by the requirement that it be 'as soon as practicable after the arrest', and by the fact that delay in doing so is permitted if 'presence of that person elsewhere is necessary in order to carry out such investigations as it is reasonable to carry out immediately' (s 30(1)). Sanders and Young argue that s 30 is a 'messy compromise [that] enables the police to insist on immediate police station interrogation except when they determine that some other course of action is preferable' (Sanders and Young, n 33 above, 237).

[120] Home Office Circular 61/2003, *Criminal Justice Act 2003: Bail Elsewhere than at a Police Station*.

[121] Policing Bureaucracy Taskforce, *Street Bail: an Alternative to Immediate Detention* (London, Home Office, 2004). For an analysis, see A Hucklesby, 'Not Necessarily a Trip to the Police Station: The Introduction of Street Bail' [2004] *Crim LR* 803.

powers were introduced Hucklesby raised the concern that they may be used in a discriminatory fashion and may lead to net-widening.[122] The decision is, of course, made contemporaneously with the arrest by the officer effecting it and, as such, it is not open to scrutiny in the same way as bail granted by a custody officer at a police station, where a defence lawyer may be present, which may be captured by CCTV in the custody office,[123] and which must be recorded in the custody record.

These concerns are exacerbated by the power to impose conditions when imposing 'street bail', which was introduced in 2007.[124] Any condition can be imposed other than residence at a bail hostel,[125] provided that it is for the purpose of securing surrender to custody, preventing the commission of offences, or the interference with witnesses of the administration of justice, or for the person's own protection (PACE, section 30A). The arresting officer could, therefore, immediately impose a condition that the arrested person reside at a specific address, comply with a curfew and report daily to a police station.[126]

Thus any person arrested by the police faces the prospect of being made subject to onerous bail conditions for relatively lengthy periods of time without having been fully informed of the allegation against them, without having the opportunity to give their version of events, and without the right to make any representations as to bail or to the conditions. Given the low threshold for arrest discussed earlier, the net-widening implications of, and the restrictions on liberty represented by, the power to impose conditional 'street bail' are obvious.

Powers to grant bail to persons detained at a police station and not (yet) charged have been extended in a number of ways,[127] mostly relatively recently and ostensibly in order to facilitate the transfer of charging responsibility from custody officers to Crown prosecutors.[128] Amendments to PACE, section 37(7) by the CJA 2003 mean that where a custody officer has determined that there is sufficient evidence to charge a person they may be bailed either to enable a charge decision to be made by a prosecutor (section 37(7)(a)) or 'not for that purpose'

---

[122]   That the police use powers of arrest differentially as between people of different ethnic origin is well established. See *Statistics on Race and the Criminal Justice System 2005* (London, Home Office, 2006). For further sources see Sanders and Young, n 33 above, 81 and 153.

[123]   For CCTV surveillance in custody suites generally, see T Newburn and S Hayman, *Policing, Surveillance and Social Control* (Cullompton, Willan, 2002).

[124]   By the Police and Justice Act 2006, s 10 and sch 6, amending PACE, s 30A.

[125]   Or conditions relevant only to bail granted by a court, or a surety or security.

[126]   As noted in the text to n 133, whilst a person may apply to a magistrates' court to vary the conditions imposed they cannot, other than in exceptional circumstances, challenge the decision to impose bail itself. The decision referred to concerned the imposition of unconditional police bail, but there is no reason to suppose the decision would have differed had it concerned conditional bail.

[127]   As noted earlier, the power to impose conditions when granting bail following charge was introduced in 1994, although the effect is relatively limited in that bail to court is normally only for a relatively short period since by PACE s 47(3A) the first court appearance must normally be no later than the first sitting of the relevant magistrates' court following charge.

[128]   For detailed consideration of this transfer, see ch 10 by John Jackson in this collection.

(section 37(7)(b)).[129] Again, there is no limit to the period for which bail can be granted, and no limit to the number of times that the person may be re-bailed. Since April 2007, the police have been able to impose conditions where they grant bail pre-charge,[130] and whilst the conditions must be justified by reference to the same purposes as for street bail, in addition to the conditions that can be attached to street bail, a surety or security can also be required.[131] Conditions can, therefore, now be attached to bail not only where the police are satisfied that there is sufficient evidence to charge (under section 37(7)(b)), but also when they are not so satisfied(for example, where bail is imposed under section 37(2)).

The power to impose conditional bail on arrest, and at the police station (whether or not there is sufficient evidence to charge), gives the police extensive powers to place controls on people in respect of whom there may, as a result of the low threshold represented by 'reasonable grounds for suspicion' and the 'threshold test', be very little incriminatory evidence. Furthermore, the police have powers of arrest for breach of the conditions imposed (sections 30D(2A) and 47A(1A)).[132] The power to impose lengthy periods of bail was challenged in *R (on the application of C) v Chief Constable of A and A Magistrates' Court*[133] where the applicant, having been arrested in connection with offences concerning child pornography, was then bailed without charge for a period exceeding six months. The applicant argued, amongst other things, that this amounted to a severe restriction of his business activities which frequently took him abroad and regularly required him to make 'fit and proper person' declarations. The court, whilst stating that it was not the case that it would never intervene in a criminal investigation, said that intervention would only be appropriate in the most exceptional circumstances, and this case did not satisfy that requirement. Thus whilst a person may be able to ask a court to vary the conditions imposed,[134] they cannot challenge the decision to impose bail in itself.

The RCCP did not envisage the police having powers to impose conditions on bail granted before charge, and whilst the power to impose conditions on bail after charge may, as the Commission argued, lead to fewer people being kept in custody, this justification is not relevant to pre-charge bail. It is unlikely to reduce

---

[129]  See the text to n 79.

[130]  As a result of amendments to PACE by the Police and Justice Act 2006, s 10 and sch 6 the police may impose conditions where they grant bail under s 37 (2) and s 37(7)(b), but not where it is granted under other sections, eg, s 34(5).

[131]  Note that conditions could already be imposed in relation to bail granted under s 37(7)(a), ie. bail for the purpose of enabling a Crown prosecutor to make a charge decision, although this was introduced as recently as 2004 (by CJA 2003, sch 2, para 5).

[132]  Breach of conditions does not amount to a criminal offence, so the conditions may be unenforceable unless the police or CPS are in a position to charge. Submissions to the 2007 review of PACE include the proposal that breach of bail conditions should be made an offence. See *Review of the Police and Criminal Evidence Act (PACE) 1984: Summary of responses*, n 89 above, 10.

[133]  [2006] EWHC 2352 (Admin).

[134]  Under PACE s 30CB (street bail) and s 47(1C) (bail from police station). The police also have power to vary the conditions.

periods spent in police custody since time spent on pre-charge bail does not count towards the maximum detention time limit. To the contrary, it extends the period for which a person can be subjected to police control. It remains to be seen whether police bail, particularly now that the police have wide powers to impose conditions, can be successfully challenged on human rights grounds. As noted earlier, unlike in court bail proceedings, suspects have no statutory right to make representations regarding police bail, and the police are under no statutory duty to receive them.[135] If bail conditions were so onerous that they amounted to a deprivation of liberty they may fall foul of the European Convention on Human Rights article 5. However, conditions may be very restrictive without amounting to a deprivation of liberty, and the prospects for successful challenge would seem to be limited.[136] The result is that people who the police choose to arrest may be subjected to lengthy periods where they are, in effect, under police supervision and control without any effective mechanism for challenging that limitation on their liberty.

# IX   Conclusions

The government has recently sought to justify the need for changes to criminal justice powers and processes by characterising them as nineteenth century solutions that impede the twenty-first century war against crime.[137] In relation to the investigative stage of the criminal process, this discourse ignores the fact that regulation of this stage of the process was fundamentally reorganised just twenty-one years ago. Ever since PACE was enacted, but particularly in the last decade, that regulatory structure, which in broad terms was designed to reflect the principles espoused by the RCCP, has been continually 're-balanced'. Reasonable grounds as a pre-condition for the exercise of coercive powers has been allowed to wither as a due process safeguard. Necessity has suffered a similar fate.[138] Proportionality, in terms of reserving intrusive powers for the investigation of serious offences, has all but been eradicated from the legislative powers and left to the individual police officer to determine on a case-by-case basis.

---

[135]   This may be contrasted with the right to make representations on review of detention under PACE s 40(12)).

[136]   In a series of decisions concerning control orders the House of Lords has indicated that whilst stringent conditions which include a curfew of 18 hours per day with limitations on movement outside the hours of the curfew may amount to a deprivation of liberty under ECHR art 5, less onerous conditions, such as a 14 hour curfew and a requirement to wear an electronic tag, although restricting liberty, do not amount to a deprivation of liberty. See *Secretary of State for the Home Department v MB and AF* [2007] UKHL 46 and *Secretary of State for the Home Department v JJ and others* [2007] UKHL 45.

[137]   See n 5 above.

[138]   Furthermore, what is regarded as necessary depends in part on how the social, if not legal, responsibilities of persons who comes under suspicion are conceptualised. Without adequate debate,

Although highly controversial at the time,[139] reading the report of the RCCP now, it is clear that its recommendations were based on a careful review of available evidence and principles that are as relevant now as they were then, reflecting those developed in respect of the European Convention on Human Rights. This is in marked contrast to the approach to changing police investigative powers and amending PACE in the period since then, which has largely been unprincipled and lacking in credible evidence.[140] Furthermore, whilst in the first five years or so following the introduction of PACE the government, and in particular the Home Office, appeared to be interested in conducting and sponsoring research to assess the impact of PACE that interest has all but disappeared, despite the political emphasis placed on 'evidence based policy'[141] by the post-1997 New Labour government.[142]

It could be argued that lack of evidence is not inimical to good policy and law-making since it may avoid the consequentialist approach that Andrew Ashworth has warned against.[143] It could also be argued that the changes described in this chapter are Human Rights Act compliant and are therefore unproblematic in terms of respect for liberty, privacy and the right to fair trial.[144] However, the fact that in the past decade or so there have been continual increases in police powers and limitations on suspects' rights demonstrates that whilst entrenching human rights is a necessary requirement, it is not sufficient. What is required if the drift towards greater and greater police control of citizens is to be halted is a commitment to both the principles espoused by the RCCP and to basing and evaluating change on thorough and objective evidence.

---

criminal justice processes have increasingly been based on managerialist and/or communitarian notions that conflict with adversarial principles that have traditionally informed criminal procedure in England and Wales. For a brief account see Sanders and Young, n 33 above, esp 12–19. See, generally, A Duff *et al*, *The trial on trial: Volume One* (Oxford, Hart, 2004) and *Volume Two* (Oxford, Hart, 2006).

[139]  See Zander, n 66 above, xi–xiii for a brief account of the controversy.

[140]  For criticism of the approach of the Royal Commission on Criminal Justice see M McConville and L Bridges (eds) *Criminal Justice in Crisis* (Aldershot, Edward Elgar, 1994). For a critical response to the joint Cabinet Office and Home Office *PACE Review*, see M Zander, 'The Joint Review of PACE: a deplorable report' (2003) *New Law Journal* 14 February, 204. For responses to the extension of powers of arrest introduced by SOCPA 2005 see Spencer (n 40 above) and E Cape (2005) 'Legislation and the democratic deficit', August *Legal Action* 9–10.

[141]  See, eg, *Getting the evidence: Using research in policy making*, Report by the Comptroller and Auditor General, HC 586–1 (London, TSO, 2003).

[142]  It is highly unlikely that there would now be enough research to report on to repeat the Home Office review of research *PACE ten years on* (see n 45 above), which was published in 1997.

[143]  A Ashworth 'Crime, Community and Creeping Consequentialism' [1996] *Crim LR* 220.

[144]  Other than in relation to the restrictions on bail introduced by the CJPOA 1984, s 25, there have been no successful challenges under the ECHR or the Human Rights Act 1998. For the successful challenge in respect of s 25 see *Caballero v UK* (2000) 30 EHRR 643.

# 9

## The Role of Defence Lawyers in a 'Re-balanced' System

ANTHONY EDWARDS[*]

## I Introduction

This chapter seeks to identify the role of the defence lawyer prior to the preferment of a criminal charge and to examine the necessity for that role. It suggests that the role, to advance and protect the rights of the suspect, has a sound justification but that it results in different advice as the underlying law is changed. It argues that, with further changes in the law planned, the role needs to remain clearly recognised in law and firmly established in rules of professional conduct, and needs to be fully understood by all involved in the investigative process.

The only clear definition, at present, of the specific role of the defence lawyer advising at the police station is set out in the Police and Criminal Evidence Act 1984 (PACE) Code of Practice C, Note for Guidance 6D:

> A detainee has a right to free legal advice and to be represented by a solicitor. The solicitor's only role in the police station is to protect and advance the legal rights of their client. On occasions this may require the solicitor to give advice which has the effect of the client avoiding giving evidence which strengthens a prosecution case. The solicitor may intervene in order to seek clarification, challenge an improper question to their client or the manner in which it is put, advise their client not to reply to particular questions, or if they wish to give their client further legal advice.

This provision was introduced by an amendment to Code C in 1995 because so much uncertainty existed. The concern was as much about solicitors who failed to understand their role as it was about the police. The word 'only' was added at the specific request of the Law Society.

That definition required clarification and the creation of an accreditation process to ensure that it was properly understood, but its meaning is now clear

---

[*] The author wishes to thank Ed Cape for his comments and assistance in writing this chapter.

and it should enable solicitors and their representatives to deal confidently with the constant 're-balancing' of the criminal justice process that significantly affects the advice that they are required to give.

# II  Developing the role

The protection of the rights of suspects in order to ensure a fair trial and reliable conviction has a long history. The Judges Rules are thought to have originated in a letter dated 26 October 1906 from the then Lord Chief Justice Lord Alverstone to the Chief Constable of Birmingham. The rules were originally formulated in 1912, and again in 1918. They were much criticised for lack of clarity and efficacy in protecting persons who were questioned by police officers, but also for unduly hampering the detection and punishment of crime. A new set of rules was issued by the judges of the Queen's Bench Division in 1964. They commenced:

These rules do not affect the principles

(a)  That citizens have a duty to help a police officer to discover and apprehend offenders;

(b)  That police officers, otherwise than by arrest, cannot compel any person against his will to come to or remain in any police station;

(c)  That every person at any stage of an investigation should be able to communicate and to consult privately with a solicitor. This is so even if he is in custody provided that in such a case no unreasonable delay or hindrance is caused to the processes of investigation or the administration of justice by his doing so;

(d)  That when a police officer who is making enquiries of any person about an offence has enough evidence to prefer a charge against that person for the offence, he should without delay cause that person to be charged or informed that he may be prosecuted for the offence;

(e)  That it is a fundamental condition of the admissibility in evidence against any person, equally of any oral answer given by that person to a question put by a police officer and of any statement made by that person, that it shall have been voluntary, in the sense that it has not been obtained from him by fear of prejudice or hope of advantage, exercised or held out by a person in authority, or by oppression.

The principle set out in paragraph (e) above is overriding and applicable in all cases. Within that principle the following Rules are put forward as a guide to police officers conducting investigations. Non-conformity with these Rules may render answers and statements liable to be excluded from evidence in subsequent criminal proceedings.

However, a series of miscarriages of justice, including convictions based on unreliable confessions, led to the appointment of the Royal Commission on

Criminal Procedure (the Philips Commission)[1] in 1978, which reported in 1981. The report was entitled 'The Balance of Criminal Justice' and its conclusion was prescient. Identifying areas of difference between the Commissioners it stated that:

> Taken overall, however, all of the Commission's main recommendations are unanimous or have the support of a large majority of the Commission. Upon this basis the Commission concludes that it is for Parliament to strike the balance between the rights of the individual and the security of society and to keep it under regular review.

The Philips Commission researched the right of the police to question people who might turn out to be a suspect but, in referring to the availability of legal advice, it gave no consideration to the nature of such advice. The Commission noted two points in particular:[2] there was no right for a solicitor to be present when a person in custody was questioned; and the right to have someone notified of the suspect's arrest,[3] which right included notification to a solicitor, was subject to the proviso that its exercise was a matter of police discretion.

The research published by the Philips Commission showed that relatively few suspects sought a consultation with a solicitor.[4] About 10 per cent of suspects requested legal advice, one third of which were refused by the police. The request rate increased to 20 per cent when suspects were told of their right to consult a solicitor. Chapter 4 of the Philips Commission report dealt with police question-ing and the rights of suspects, and it concluded that there could be no adequate substitute for police questioning in the investigation and prosecution of crime. The Commission was much exercised by the need for reliable and accurate recording of statements made to the police, and by the cost of tape-recording.

The Philips Commission found that both the notion of voluntariness in the Judges Rules, and the application of the Rules, caused much difficulty to the police and to the courts.[5]

> 5.15. We rule out proposals for an independent third party (whether a magistrate, solicitor or other person) to be present to monitor the conduct of interviews and approve the record of the product of questioning (4.62, 4.99–100). We wish, however, to make the right of access to legal advice, stated as a principle in the present Judges' Rules, an effective right (4.87). It should be made effective by the development of duty solicitor schemes and the provision of adequate remuneration to solicitors (4.97–98)

> 5.18. All the foregoing provisions should be included in the statute regulating the treatment of suspects in custody (4.115). This should additionally incorporate a code of practice for the regulation of interviews, designed to protect the suspect from oppres-sive questioning and to ensure, to the extent possible, the reliability of any statements

---

[1] Royal Commission on Criminal Procedure, *Report*, Cmnd 8093 (London, HMSO, 1981) Appendix 1.
[2] *Ibid*, para 86.
[3] Governed by the Criminal Law Act 1977 s 62.
[4] *Report*, n 1 above, para 87.
[5] *Ibid*, para 4.70.

made (4.109–114). All but one of us recommend that in general breaches of the code should not render any subsequent statement inadmissible as evidence but should be relevant to the assessment by the court of its reliability (4.131). To mark the seriousness of breaches of the rules prohibiting violence, threats of violence, torture or inhuman or degrading treatment, these should result in automatic exclusion of subsequent statements (4.132) … We consider that the present uncertainty of status and effect of the rules on the treatment of suspects in custody should be removed. The remedies for the breach of these rules and of the provisions relating to the exercise of all the investigative powers of the police should be made more effective. To this end police supervisory arrangements should be improved. The placing of the rules in statutory form will bring their enforcement within the ambit of the police disciplinary code. The fuller record keeping that we recommend should facilitate subsequent review and remedy for the purposes of disciplinary action, the complaints procedure and civil actions (4.118–122).

The Commission attempted to cost the introduction of the arrangements that it recommended. It estimated an outlay of £30 million a year[6] at August 1980 prices if every suspect sought advice. If 20 per cent requested advice the cost would be £6 million a year. The Commission attached 'great importance to securing that the right to legal advice is effective and consider[ed] that it warrant[ed] making the appropriate financial provision a high priority' to ensure that legal advice was actually available.[7] It stated that:

> We consider that schemes for the provision of solicitors for these purposes cannot be left to grow sporadically and piecemeal across the country and that central and systematic action to develop schemes which guarantee availability of solicitors round the clock will be necessary.[8]

It recognised that systems of remuneration would be critical and that the only available form of legal aid then available, the 'green form' scheme, would not be acceptable.[9]

Notably absent from the Commission's conclusions was any specific definition of the role of the defence lawyer, save that it clearly disapproved of the solicitor acting as a independent monitor of the interview.[10] It contrasted this with 'look[ing] after the interests of his client; the suspect'. The solicitor could not be regarded as independent when it was not only police conduct that may be relevant, but also the suspect's behaviour.

The recommendations of the Philips Commission were given practical effect by sections 58 and 59 of PACE. The latter enabled the Law Society, which then administered the legal aid scheme, to extend the magistrates' court duty solicitor

---

6    *Ibid*, para 4.94.
7    *Ibid*, para 4.95.
8    *Ibid*, para 4.97.
9    *Ibid*, para 4.98.
10   *Ibid*, para 4.99.

scheme so that solicitors with suitable experience would be available at police stations nationwide for those suspects who did not already know of a solicitor.[11] Section 58 provided that:

(1)  A person arrested and held in custody in a police station or other premises shall be entitled, if he so requests, to consult a solicitor privately at any time …

(4)  If a person makes such a request, he must be permitted to consult a solicitor as soon as is practicable except to the extent that delay is permitted by this section.

(5)  In any case he must be permitted to consult a solicitor within 36 hours from the relevant time, as defined in section 41(2) above.

Essential detail was added to these provisions by the PACE Codes of Practice, but the original version of the Codes contained no positive definition of the solicitor's role; only negative statements were included.[12] Thus Code C para 6.9 provided that '[t]he solicitor may only be required to leave the interview if their conduct is such that the interviewer is unable properly to put questions to the suspect. See Notes 6D and 6E.' Note 6D stated that '[p]aragraph 6.9 only applies if the solicitor's approach or conduct prevents or unreasonably obstructs proper questions being put to the suspect or the suspect's response being recorded. Examples of unacceptable conduct include answering questions on a suspect's behalf or providing written replies for the suspect to quote'.

The Law Society's professional practice rules proved inadequate to deal with the new responsibilities created by PACE, describing the role of the solicitor in only general terms. The Solicitors' Practice Rules 1990, rule 1, defined the solicitor's role in the following terms:

A solicitor shall not do anything in the course of practising as a solicitor, or permit another person to do anything on his or her behalf, which compromises or impairs or is likely to compromise or impair any of the following:

(a)  the solicitor's independence or integrity;

(b)  a person's freedom to instruct a solicitor of his or her choice;

(c)  the solicitor's duty to act in the best interests of the client;

(d)  the good repute of the solicitor or of the solicitor's profession;

(e)  the solicitor's proper standard of work;

(f)  the solicitor's duty to the court.[13]

Rule 1(c) is the only rule specifically applicable to defence work in the police station, thus avoiding the problem of reconciling two or more conflicting principles 'in the public interest',[14] an issue which now raises increasing difficulty

---

[11]  The legal aid provisions are now contained in the Access to Justice Act 1999 s 13.

[12]  As noted at the beginning of the chapter, a positive account of the solicitor's role was not added until 1995.

[13]  Note that solicitors are now governed by the Solicitors' Code of Conduct 2007.

[14]  See The Law Society, *The Guide to the Professional Conduct of Solicitors*, (London, The Law Society, 1999) para 1.02.6.

in criminal proceedings. The standard authority on solicitors' conduct, *Cordery on Solicitors*,[15] continues to provide no assistance in this area.

In the early years following the enactment of PACE difficulties arose because the profession had little experience of acting in the police station context. The first attempt to articulate the role of a defence solicitor at the investigative stage in more detail was made by David Roberts, a Bristol solicitor and member of the Law Society's Criminal Law Committee. This led in 1985 to the first edition of the booklet *Advising a Suspect in the Police Station: guidelines for solicitors*.[16] In its preface to the first edition the booklet provided the following account of the solicitor's role at the investigative stage.

> The quality of the advice and assistance given to a suspect in custody can have a material effect on whether proceedings are brought and, if they are, their outcome. Such advice and assistance should be provided by a solicitor experienced in criminal work. Necessity may sometimes dictate that people with lesser qualification or experience perform the task.
>
> It is hoped that all practitioners whatever their experience will find these guidelines of value in the changed circumstances following the implementation of the Police and Criminal Evidence Act 1984. Practitioners should be aware of the provisions of the Act and the Codes of Practice issued under it which are only selectively summarised.
>
> In these guidelines, the use of imperatives is for emphasis only and should not be taken to imply the existence of a duty. The guidelines are meant to describe preferred practice and are not intended to widen a solicitor's duty. They are not a substitute for the exercise by a solicitor of his or her professional judgement …
>
> SERVING THE PUBLIC INTEREST
>
> The purpose of a solicitor's attendance at a police station is to advise the suspect of his rights, and this may include advising him to exercise his right of silence at the investigation stage or assisting the suspect to give an account of his activities which are under suspicion. His presence is designed to relieve the suspect of pressures which can induce false confessions and cause a miscarriage of justice. What advice you give must depend on the particular circumstances facing the suspect.
>
> A solicitor will advise on the weight and admissibility of the prosecution evidence and in appropriate cases of the substantial mitigation advantages of admitting guilt at the earliest opportunity, of assisting the recovery of stolen property, and of clearing up outstanding enquiries.
>
> The presence of a solicitor in the police station means that justice is better secured for the individual; it also leads to savings in police, court and judicial time so that quicker and more economical justice is secured for the community at large. The principles which you should consider are set out in depth in this booklet.

---

[15] London, Butterworths, 1995.

[16] Further editions were published by the Law Society in 1988 and 1991 and, under my authorship, by Sweet & Maxwell in 1998, 2003 and 2006.

ETHICS

A solicitor is subject to the ethics and discipline of his profession and so are those who act on his behalf.

Ethics are dealt with separately in A Guide to the Professional Conduct of Solicitors issued by the Council of the Law Society.

Like other Law Society publications, that preface showed that care had been taken to have regard to political concerns, and in research for the Royal Commission on Criminal Justice (the Runciman Commission) it was criticised for its timidity and lack of assertiveness.[17] The reference to the Guide to the Professional Conduct of Solicitors was certainly of little assistance. Critical research published in 1994 showed that the lack of an adversarial approach pervaded much of criminal defence work.[18]

Meanwhile, the Legal Aid Board (the forerunner of the Legal Services Commission) was increasingly concerned that it should receive good value for its increasing expenditure on police station advice. Demand for legal advice was rising, and by 1997 the take-up of legal advice had increased, with 40 per cent of suspects requesting legal advice, and 34 per cent actually receiving it.[19] The Law Society also had to be ready to withstand the criticism that would come with the report of the Runciman Commission. This all led to the first positive statement, in Note 6D to Code C, of the defence lawyer's role and the introduction of an accreditation scheme for those seeking payment from public funds to give police station advice. This in turn required the Law Society to develop detailed standards of competence.

The need for a clear, proactive role having been identified, it resulted in a series of publications giving a consistent adversarial message—

1991   Advising a Suspect in the Police Station, Law Society (2nd edn)
1993   Defending Suspects at Police Stations, E Cape, Legal Action Group
1994   Police Station Skills for Legal Advisers, E Shepherd, Law Society
1997   Active Defence, R Ede and E Shepherd, Law Society
2000   Criminal Defence Good Practice in the Criminal Courts, R Ede and A Edwards, Law Society

---

[17]   See M McConville and J Hodgson, *Custodial legal advice and the Right to Silence*, RCCJ Study 16 (London, HMSO, 1993), and J Baldwin, *The Conduct of Police Investigations: records of interview, the Defence Lawyer's Role and Standards of Supervision*, RCCJ Studies 2, 3 and 4 (London, HMSO, 1992), and the debate at [1993] *Crim LR* 368, at 371.

[18]   M McConville, J Hodgson, L Bridges and A Pavlovic, *Standing Accused: The Organisation and Practice of Criminal Defence Lawyers in Britain* (Oxford, Clarendon, 1994).

[19]   T Bucke and D Brown, *In police custody: police powers and suspects' rights under the revised PACE Codes of Practice*, HORS 174 (London, Home Office, 1997).

Furthermore, in the 1996 case of *Murray v UK*[20] the European Court of Human Rights held that the right to a fair trial under Article 6 of the Convention extended to the investigative stage, entailing the right to legal advice and assistance at the police station.

*Police Station Skills for Legal Advisers* was the fundamental work underlying the accreditation process developed by the Law Society ahead of its evidence to the Runciman Commission. The accreditation process required a three stage qualification before payment could be made from public funds for criminal defence work at the investigative stage: the written test, requiring a basic understanding of criminal law and procedure; a portfolio of casework, critically requiring that each case be discussed with a supervisor to identify good and bad practice and points for further learning (this was designed to address the inevitably 'lonely' nature of advice-giving in the police station); and a critical incident test, to ensure appropriate levels of assertiveness. The Legal Aid Board adopted the 'defender model', developed in these works, in transaction criteria as part of its quality assurance project (subsequently substantially overtaken by its peer review initiative).[21]

However, the effects of the 'silence' provisions of the Criminal Justice and Public Order Act (CJPOA) 1994 were to be critical. The possibility of inferences from silence following the implementation of CJPOA 1994 sections 34–38 put to the test the understanding of the defence profession of its role during police investigations, and meant that those who did approach the work in an adversarial way could no longer merely advise 'no comment' when unsure what advice to give.

# III  Identifying the role

The Law Society (which administered the legal aid fund prior to the creation of the Legal Aid Board) gave effect to the Philips Commission's recommendations by extending the 'advice and assistance' scheme to cover police station work whatever the means of the suspect. These regulations played a significant part in the process of developing the role of the defence lawyer. In training both lawyers and police officers, the concepts of 'advice' and 'assistance' have been central.

The concept of giving advice was not new to solicitors, although critical advice now had to be given immediately, in circumstances that were often wholly unsatisfactory. A solicitor has to give advice on the basis that much information is withheld by both the police and the client, often at unsocial hours, and in relation

---

[20]  (1996) 22 EHRR 29.

[21]  The Legal Services Commission (LSC) has introduced peer review as a mechanism for assuring the quality of the work of legally-aided criminal defence lawyers. See http://www.legalservices.gov.uk/criminal/contracting/mq_peerreview.asp (accessed 23 November 2007).

to a client who may be in no fit state clearly to understand and act upon it, either as a result of voluntary intoxication or because of their vulnerability. It was critical, in this context, that solicitors realised that the events in the police station are 'the first day of trial' and will fundamentally affect the outcome of an investigation. Therein lies the need for determined and experienced advisers.

The giving of such advice and assistance therefore amounted to a new demand upon solicitors. Its need was explained by the series of miscarriages of justice, based on false confessions, that preceded the Philips Commission—establishing the need for the suspect to have someone in the police station whom they perceived to be 'on their side'. Writing in the 2006 edition of *Advising a suspect at the police station* I dealt with these matters in the following way.

The solicitor will aim to:

(a)  investigate the prosecution case;
(b)  obtain information to assist in the conduct of the defence;
(c)  avoid the client giving evidence which strengthens the prosecution case;
(d)  influence the police not to charge the client; or
(e)  create the most favourable position for the client if he or she is charged.

Many skills are required successfully to undertake this role. There must be a sound knowledge of criminal law and evidence; good communication and negotiation skills with both the police and client; and above all great courage and determination to protect and advance the client's legal rights, however serious or unpopular their alleged crime.

Advice and Assistance

The solicitor's role involves advice and assistance to the suspect. The purpose of advice and assistance in the police station is to maintain the balance between the powers of the police when investigating whether and by whom the relevant criminal offence has been committed and the protection of the rights of the suspect. Only by vigorous protection of those rights will reliable evidence be obtained by the police.

The quality of the advice and assistance given to a suspect in custody can have a material effect on whether proceedings are brought, and, if they are, their outcome.

In his definitive work on police station advice and assistance, Eric Shepherd analyses the role and identifies seven separate aims for the lawyer.[22]

1. To investigate the police case, the prosecution evidence, the police investigation and all police contact with, and conduct towards your client.

2. To assess the extent of your client's vulnerability and ability to comprehend, to cope and to communicate to best effect in any police interview.

---

[22]  *Police Station Skills for Legal Advisers* (London, Law Society, 1996).

3. To identify the safest defence for your client: to remain silent, to provide a written statement or to answer police questions [to which one might add 'and to advise accordingly in private'].

4. To influence the police to accept your client is not guilty.

5. To influence the police not to charge your client. The police should not charge if:

(a)   their evidence is not strong enough;
(b)   they lack admission evidence from your client.

To charge in the context of inadequate evidence constitutes expediency, counter to ethical conduct and to the spirit and letter of the law.

6. To influence the police to make the most favourable case disposal decision for your client. The police should implement the most constructive alternative to charging relative to the circumstances of the case and your client: no further action, release on bail, or the administration of a caution, reprimand or final warning.

7. To create the most favourable position for your client if he or she is charged. The conduct of your client in the light of your advice and the police response to this should constitute the basis for:

(a)   your client to be found not guilty; or
(b)   your client to have mitigation if he or she pleads guilty.

The courts, because of the piecemeal way in which issues arise, have not always appeared to recognise the importance of both advice and assistance. However, the wider view has been accepted in significant decisions.[23]

# IV   Clarification of the legal issues

This substantial attention to the detail of the defence solicitor's role, however, still left unaddressed some legal issues arising from it. These have now received attention either in decisions of the courts or in further professional guidance.

## A Privilege and Confidentiality

The first of these to receive detailed attention was the inter-related but separate issues of legal privilege and client confidentiality. The law on legal privilege was bound to receive early attention once clients began to rely on their lawyer's advice to justify a 'no comment' interview. The identification of the material covered by legal privilege has been the subject of detailed consideration by the courts and is subject to legislative definition. Section 10 of PACE provides:

---

[23]   Contrast *R v Alladice* (1988) 87 Cr App R 380 with *R v Dunn* (1990) 91 Cr App R 237 and *R v Paris Abdullahi and Miller* (1993) 97 Cr App R 99.

10(1) Subject to subsection (2) below, in this Act 'items subject to legal privilege' means—

(a)  communications between a professional legal adviser and his client or any person representing his client made in connection with the giving of legal advice to the client;

(b)  communications between a professional legal adviser and his client or any person representing his client or between such an adviser or client or any such representative and any other person in connection with or in contemplation of legal proceedings and purposes of such proceedings; and

(c)  items enclosed with or referred to in such communications and made
     (i)   in connection with the giving of legal advice; or
     (ii)  in connection with or in contemplation of legal proceedings and for the purposes of such proceedings, when they are in the possession of a person who is entitled to possession of them.

(2)  Items held with the intention of furthering a criminal purpose are not items subject to legal privilege.

A similar definition is used in the Proceeds of Crime Act 2002.[24] The courts have always attached great significance to the ability of a client in a criminal case to receive privileged advice and will not order its disclosure.[25] The primary statutory provisions which, because of their terms or by providing a defence of reasonable excuse, protect privileged material are the Terrorism Act 2000 sections 19, 21A and 38B, and the Proceeds of Crime Act 2002 sections 330(6) and 333(3). The issue has received detailed consideration in the police station context in *R v Condron*,[26] and in more detail in *R v Bowden*.[27]

A solicitor who attends at the police station is a competent and compellable witness for all parties as to what occurs there. However, a solicitor may not disclose privileged material without the client waiving that privilege. This will often be done expressly, so that the solicitor gives evidence at trial at the request of the defendant, but the defendant may also impliedly waive privilege. The court decisions have led to five basic principles:

1.  A client who makes no comment 'on legal advice' does not waive privilege in his instructions or the advice.
2.  The giving of a more specific reason for making no comment (which is more likely to be persuasive, but which can then be tested) does waive privilege.
3.  However, if the disclosure of the instructions to the lawyer is made purely to rebut an allegation at trial of recent fabrication, privilege is not waived.
4.  Observations of fact made by the lawyer which do not disclose privileged material do not raise issues of privilege.

---

[24]  See, eg, s 330(10), (11) and s 342(4), (5).
[25]  *R v Derby Magistrates' Court ex p B* [1995] 4 All ER 526.
[26]  [1997] 1 WLR 827.
[27]  [1999] 1 WLR 823.

5.   Advice given on a non-privileged occasion such as in the presence of police officers during interview, does not of itself waive privilege although care must be taken not to refer back to privileged material.

Knowledge of the law on the waiver of privilege is an important aspect of the critical advice (considered below) as to whether a client should respond to an investigator's questions. Whilst no suspect is bound to waive privilege, the disclosure of their reasons for making no response (which would thus waive privilege) means that their explanation is more likely to be believed.[28]

The law on client confidentiality (as that on disclosure to clients) is essentially contractual and covered by professional conduct rules. Confidentiality, unlike privilege, can be overridden, both under the professional conduct rules and because of statutory provisions to that effect. The conduct rules allow disclosure of confidential, but not privileged, material—

1.   When the lawyer is being used by the client to facilitate the commission of a crime.
2.   When disclosure is necessary to prevent the commission by the client or another of a crime which the solicitor believes is likely to result in serious bodily harm.
3.   In exceptional circumstances involving physical or sexual abuse of children.
4.   Where a court orders confidential information to be disclosed, or issues a warrant which authorises the seizure of confidential information.[29]

The nature of material, and whether it is confidential or privileged, often calls for careful consideration. Thus if, in order to obtain advice from their solicitor a suspect admits to them past involvement in an act of terrorism, no disclosure may be made to the police by the solicitor without the client's authority. However, if in giving instructions, the suspect disclosed that a further terrorist act was about to take place the solicitor should inform the police because (i) this is not privileged material as it does not relate to a matter on which the suspect seeks legal advice, and (ii) any confidentiality is overridden by the conduct rules. If the suspect merely asks what they should say about future acts without giving details, the solicitor must advise on the statutory duty of disclosure but the decision whether to disclose is that of the client alone.

## B Conflict of Interests

The avoidance of conflicts of interest between different clients has always formed part of the solicitors' professional practice rules, albeit directed at non-contentious rather than contentious work, and in civil rather than criminal litigation. Driven either by a wish to assist progress on an enquiry or by the wish

---

[28]   See *R v Condron*, n 26 above.
[29]   See the *Guide to the Professional Conduct of Solicitors*, n 14 above, ch 16.

to increase the number of their clients, defence solicitors have been poor at recognising potential, and in some cases actual, conflict. The issue was properly left to them by PACE Code C Note 6G, which provides:

> Subject to the constraints of Annex B, a solicitor may advise more than one client in an investigation if they wish. Any question of a conflict of interest is for the solicitor under their professional code of conduct. If, however, waiting for a solicitor to give advice to one client may lead to unreasonable delay to the interview with another, the provisions of paragraph 6.6(b) may apply.

But the response of solicitors has often lacked professionalism—including an unwillingness to recognise the risks. As a result the Law Society has adopted and published guidance which has clarified the position and provides a checklist for use at the police station.[30]

## C Perverting the Course of Justice

However, an extraordinary ignorance prevailed on the application of some basic criminal law principles to the police station situation. As a result of conflicting messages being given on the training courses of major providers, in my capacity as professional head of the Public Defender Service (PDS) I issued guidance to public defenders in 2005.[31] Without it there was a significant possibility that lawyers would risk being arrested for attempting to pervert the course of justice. Two particular matters gave rise to difficulty:

(a) the extent to which a lawyer can continue to act at the police station for a client who is, to their knowledge, using a false name (as this may mislead an investigator and prejudice an enquiry); and

(b) the extent to which a lawyer may pass information from one person in detention to another (as this may enable them to put together a consistent but untrue explanation for crime).

The offence is committed when a person acts in such a way or embarks upon a course of conduct which has a tendency to and is intended to pervert the course of public justice.[32] The course of justice begins as soon as an incident is made known to the police and certainly by the time an investigation begins. This will therefore cover all stages of police station work.[33] However, a positive act to pervert the course of justice is required; inaction in itself is insufficient.[34]

If a client is, to the lawyer's knowledge, using a false name, I advised that a lawyer should continue to advise the client. Such advice does not have a tendency

---

[30] Available at http://www.lawsociety.org.uk (accessed 12 June 2008).
[31] Available at http://www.legalservices.gov.uk (accessed 12 June 2008).
[32] *R v Vreones* (1891) 1 QB 360.
[33] *R v Rowell* (1977) 65 Cr App R 174; *R v Cotter* [2002] Crim LR 824.
[34] *R v Andrews* (1973) QB 422; *R v Clark* [2003] Crim LR 558.

to pervert. It involves no third party. It will often include advice that the client may, by acting in this way, commit the offence of perverting the course of justice. However, the decision whether to desist or continue is for the client to make. However, having advised generally, if the client continues in the deception, the lawyer is bound to withdraw from the case as they otherwise become a party to the crime.

In my judgment the lawyer is limited in these circumstances in the making of representations to any police officer and should not attend upon the client in a police interview. It has been argued that it is proper to remain in the interview if no positive step is taken on the client's behalf and there is to be no intervention. However, this means that the best advice may not be given in interview and, in any event, attendance is itself a positive act: it does, and is intended to, give support to the client against the pressures that such an interview inevitably creates. When withdrawing, the lawyer must not give any explanation to the police as to his or her reason as this would amount to a breach of the duty of confidence to the client.[35]

If a lawyer is asked to see two or more suspects in the same case great care has to be exercised. To pass information from one to the other in a way that knowingly assists that other to present a consistent but untrue defence would amount to the offence of perverting the course of justice. If there is any concern, the lawyer should act only for one suspect. The need to avoid the improper transfer of information should be kept constantly in mind by lawyers working in the police station.

It is because a solicitor must not be party to a crime that, whilst advising on the points to prove and defences to all relevant crimes, they cannot 'invent' a defence. The solicitor cannot advise a client to commit a criminal offence, but having advised on the options it is for the client to decide. A solicitor must similarly be careful not to pass inappropriate messages that may enable evidence to be destroyed. Further, they cannot remain in a police interview whilst facts are put forward which, to their knowledge, are false.

# V  Applying the role

Having established the role of the criminal defence solicitor, its application in the constantly 're-balancing' criminal justice system can be examined. I will start by setting out the list of issues contained in Advising a Suspect in the Police Station (n 16 above) before proceeding to analyse the key issues in turn.

---

[35]  See the *Guide to the Professional Conduct of Solicitors*, n 14 above, ch 16.

## Advice

Ensuring that the suspect understands what facts are being alleged; what criminal offences are under investigation; the legal elements necessary to prove them; the defences available; and the burdens of proof involved.

Explaining the powers and duties of the police as they affect the suspect, especially the limitations on the power to detain.

If the police intend to conduct an interview, advising the suspect in private to decide whether to refuse to answer questions; or whether to place on record his/her reactions to the allegations against him/her, either by way of denial, explanation or admission; whether to do so by prepared statement or in interview or whether to make a statement at charge, explaining carefully the advantages and disadvantages of each course of conduct.

Advising on police powers when the police wish to carry out statutory procedures to obtain samples (fingerprints, DNA, photographs and footwear impressions), obtain or preserve evidence, eg undertaking a search, or holding an identification procedure and advising where appropriate on the issue of consent and the consequences of refusing.

If charges are preferred, advising on the formalities where appropriate of bail and drug testing.

## Assistance

Providing support for the suspect. The presence of the solicitor in the police station is designed to relieve the suspect of pressures which can induce false confessions and cause a miscarriage of justice.

Protecting throughout the wellbeing of the suspect. The solicitor should ensure that a suspect, whilst in police detention, is aware of his/her rights and is treated fairly and in accordance with the Codes.

Attending at any interview to ensure that it is conducted fairly and to maintain an independent record of what takes place.

Making representations about and attending identification procedures to protect the suspect and maintain an independent record.

Making representations at reviews of detention and to the magistrates' court on any application for a warrant of further or extended detention.

Making representations as to searches, and the taking of samples, fingerprints, or footwear impressions.

Making representations as to bail.

Securing evidence relevant to the defence (e.g. a relevant video or to support an alibi).

Discussing with the suspect whether legal representation at court is advisable, and if so by what means: representation order; by the court duty solicitor; or privately. Communicating with sureties and witnesses.

Throughout maintaining full, timed and accurate records of everything material
said and done whether by the police, the suspect, or the solicitor, so that this
may be available if required at trial.

## A Advice

Although the advice role, as now understood, does not change, the significant
amendments that have been made to criminal law, evidence and procedure have
greatly changed the content of the resultant advice.

### (i) Ancillary Issues

The client's first concerns are always about ancillary matters, primarily about the
period for which they will be detained and letting others know where they are.
For major enquiries it is essential that clients appreciate the period for which an
investigation will disrupt their lives. It is essential that solicitors give realistic
answers on timing as the client will then concentrate on the advice about
interview, which is the real matter to be addressed.

Solicitors are aware that requests to pass messages must be handled with skill
to avoid assisting in the destruction of evidence, whilst maintaining the client's
confidence in their independence. Advice on police powers (particularly in
relation to the growing list of powers to take samples),[36] because these are taken
on detention, is now required at a far earlier stage and great skill is needed to
persuade the client that the solicitor is 'on their side'. Police officers routinely use
solicitors to persuade a 'difficult' client to cooperate with the process and the law
is such that solicitors have to advise clients to cooperate in order to avoid
additional allegations of assault on or obstruction of a police officer in the
execution of their duty. Later in the process similar issues arise around drug tests
and, with greater consideration of the other available evidence, x-rays and
ultrasounds.

At one time the giving of intimate samples, which require the suspect's
consent, called for anxious consideration by the solicitor, but in the majority of
cases the ability to analyse even the smallest samples of DNA derived from
non-intimate samples reduces the concerns.

### (ii) Investigation

The key issue remains the advice as to whether or not the suspect should answer
police questions. The possibility of inferences from silence significantly affects
that advice. Many police officers expected that as a result of the inference
provisions of CJPOA 1994 a 'no comment' interview would become a rarity. It is

---

[36] DNA samples, fingerprints, photographs and footwear impressions. See the detailed analysis by
Ed Cape in ch 8 of this volume.

a great credit to the defence profession that each case is still considered on its own merits, with the starting point remaining that solicitors should advise no comment until persuaded by the facts and issues placed before them that a different approach should be taken. Clear guidance is of assistance and in *Advising a Suspect in the Police Station* I suggest the following approach:

> Is the prosecution likely at trial to be able to establish a case to answer by admissible evidence that will then be available (ss 36 and 37 of the CJPOA may themselves raise such a case)? If the prosecution is unable to do so consider advising your client to remain silent. If you have been able to consult with your client in private for an adequate time and you have received sufficient disclosure on the basis of which you are satisfied about the strength of the prosecution case, consider advising your client to provide answers (by prepared statement or preferably in interview), unless to do so may do more harm than good but note;

- the final decision is that of the client;
- if in doubt hold back;
- the facts of individual cases may make it appropriate to move from the normal starting point.

This indicates that the solicitor must be aware of the nature of the prosecution's evidence, and the level of disclosure is critical. This issue was well addressed by Rose LJ in *R v Roble*:[37]

> Good reason for silence may well arise if, for example, the interviewing officer has disclosed to the solicitor little or nothing of the nature of the case against the defendant, so that the solicitor cannot usefully advise his client, or, where the nature of the offence, or the material in the hands of the police is so complex, or relates to matters so long ago, that no sensible immediate response is feasible.

Solicitors are aware that full disclosure need not be given[38] but that they must be proactive in their requests for information, particularly in relation to the information provided by modern technology.[39] Evidence may be excluded under PACE section 78 if the police are misleading in their response to any request.[40] Solicitors make critical judgments about their advice depending on the way investigators handle disclosure.[41] Few police officers sufficiently analyse the way in which to handle the issue. If CJPOA 1994 sections 36 or 37 are relevant, and special warnings have been given,[42] there will almost certainly be a prima facie case and, if there is an explanation, a suspect will normally be advised to give it because a charge is likely if no comment is made. In relation to CJPOA 1994 section 34 the position is different. A case to answer cannot be created only or

---

[37] [1997] Crim LR 449.
[38] See, eg, *R v Argent* [1997] Crim LR 346.
[39] As to video evidence see *R v Imran and Hussain* [1997] Crim LR 754.
[40] *R v Imran and Hussain* (*ibid*); *R v Mason* [1988] Crim LR 139; *R v Kirk* [1994] All ER 698.
[41] Problems continue even in obtaining a full custody record (inclusive of property list and medical findings) as a result of changes to Code C para 2.4.
[42] See Code C paras 10.5A and 10.5B.

mainly by an inference from silence.[43] Thus police officers must make disclosure sufficient to show that a charge is likely if a solicitor is to advise that answers be provided.

Changes in the law, and the increasing use of defence burdens of proof to avoid liability, have had a significant impact on the advice given. The complexity of the law demonstrates the need for experienced advisers. An important area of change is in relation to sexual crime. Advising silence was easier when honest but mistaken belief in consent could amount to a defence, for instance, to rape. But now that the belief must also be reasonable the need for early explanation is significant. The use of the statutory presumptions in the Sexual Offences Act 2003 sections 75 and 76 raise a complex series of issues for careful analysis before good advice can be given. The introduction of the offence of statutory rape of a girl under 13 years leads to equally difficult considerations. Without an admission, many cases could not be proved. Yet if DNA evidence becomes available, the opportunities for diversion from prosecution of a boy who is little older and often of lesser sexual experience than the complainant may, in the absence of an admission, be lost.[44]

Equally significant changes have been made, in relation to the deaths of children and vulnerable adults, by the Domestic Violence, Crime and Victims Act 2004 section 5. Where advice to make no comment was once commonplace when either of two people may, alone, have caused a death, such an approach would today almost inevitably lead to a conviction. The number of provisions containing reverse burden of proof grows annually.[45] Once the police can show that the basic facts can be made out it is usually wise, in such cases, for the suspect to put forward facts relevant to the statutory defence at the earliest opportunity.

Solicitors are aware that in advising that no comment be made, it is not sufficient that their client genuinely relies on their advice. There must be a reasonable basis for it. Thus their advice must be rational, showing awareness of the decisions of the courts as to when a fact later relied upon at trial can reasonably have been expected to be mentioned. The law, from a series of cases that, despite the claims of the judges involved, are not always consistent, may be stated as follows:[46]

(a) Legal advice is relevant in deciding whether it is appropriate to draw inferences from silence.[47]

---

[43] CJPOA 1994 s38(3); *R v Condron* [1997] Crim LR 215; *Condron v UK* [2000] Crim LR 679.

[44] See *R v G* [2006] Crim LR 930.

[45] See I Dennis, 'Reverse Onus and the Presumption of Innocence: In Search of Principles' [2005] Crim LR 90, and most recently, Inspections and Education Act 2006 s 109 amending Education Act 1996 s 444.

[46] For a review of the effects and interpretation of CJPOA 1994 s 34 see I Dennis, 'Silence in the Police Station' [2002] Crim LR 25.

[47] *R v Argent* (1997) 2 Crim App R 27.

(b)    Inferences should not be drawn if a suspect may genuinely have relied on legal advice.[48]

(c)    In judging whether the reliance may have been genuine, the solicitor's reasoning is relevant: soundly based objective reasons are required.[49]

In *R v Howell*[50] the court held that it was not reasonable to advise no comment when:

(a)    there was as yet no written statement by a witness *provided* there had been good oral disclosure of the complaint; or

(b)    it was believed that the complainant might not be willing to give live evidence; or

(c)    a decision had already been made to charge the suspect.

The last proposition seems very questionable, although it would have been acceptable if there was merely a decision that there was sufficient evidence to charge.[51]

Against the background of these changes the issue of disclosure remains the most critical in giving advice about whether to answer questions. Negotiating skills and techniques of the highest order are required, and they are properly tested by the police station accreditation process. However, many other matters require consideration. In *R v Argent*[52] the Lord Chief Justice identified as relevant the following factors in deciding whether it was reasonable for facts to be mentioned, introducing a remarkably subjective element into an otherwise objective test. The factors include:

(a)    time of day;
(b)    defendant's age;
(c)    experience;
(d)    mental capacity[53];
(e)    state of heath;
(f)    sobriety;
(g)    tiredness;
(h)    personality; and
(i)    legal advice.

*R v Howell*[54] added to that list:

(a)    confusion;
(b)    shock; and

---

[48]   *R v Betts and Hall* (2001) Crim App R 257.

[49]   *R v Howell* [2003] Crim LR 405. See also *R v Beckles* [2005] 1 WLR 2829 and *R v Bresa* [2005] EWCA Crim 1414.

[50]   See *ibid.*

[51]   PACE s 37(7) provides that if there is sufficient evidence to charge the suspect shall be charged or released with or without bail, although amendments have been made to Code C para 11.6 to allow for continuing interrogations before that stage is reached.

[52]   See n 47. The judgment emphasised that the law was not to be construed restrictively.

[53]   The addition of Annex G to Code C was particularly important in this context.

[54]   See n 51 above.

(c)   an inability generally to recollect events without reference to documents that are
      not to hand or to other persons.

By implication, that case also held that insufficient oral disclosure was a good
reason for silence. Other cases have identified as sufficient reason the need for the
defence to 'keep the powder dry',[55] and uncertainty as to whether the Crown
could prove its basic case;[56] but as insufficient, the fact that the suspect was
already subject to other charges (about which intervention could prevent inappropriate questions), and the time needed for the solicitor to consider relevant
documents where the client would have been able to provide sufficient information on their meaning.[57]

The issue of the availability of any evidence at trial has also undergone
significant changes in the law, police practice and evidence. In cases of domestic
violence suspects were historically routinely advised to make no comment. This
became more difficult once police investigators began to collect corroborative
evidence and once the Crown Prosecution Service (CPS) began to let it be known
that a witness summons would be issued against a complainant who withdrew
evidence of serious violence (a policy still in need of sensible refinement). The
provisions of the Criminal Justice Act (CJA) 2003 on the admissibility of hearsay
evidence have also had an impact. Whilst it is unlikely that any statement of a
co-suspect under interrogation will be admitted,[58] the evidence of other witnesses can now be more easily used. Sections 119 and 120, dealing with prior
inconsistent and prior consistent statement, also mean that statements made by
both witnesses and suspects may now be admitted as to their truth as well as on
the issue of consistency.

### (iii) Admission of guilt

Difficulties for lawyers may arise when a client admits their guilt to them. The
lawyer must still be satisfied that the Crown can prove its case, but if this is likely
both the possibility of diversion and, if not available, the issue of discount for
guilty plea have to be considered, each requiring an admission to be made. A
solicitor also has to be careful that an admission will not remove mitigation that
might otherwise, in the absence of other prosecution evidence, have been
available. Notwithstanding the wording of the CJA 2003 section 144 and its
reference to 'proceedings', the Sentencing Guidelines Council, advising that the
highest discount shall be available for those who admit their guilt at the first
reasonable opportunity, considers that this includes the interview in the police
station. However this, for advisers, is not the major issue as there will only be
limited difference between the discount available for an admission of guilt in the

---

[55]   *R v Milford* [2001] Crim LR 330.
[56]   *R v Daly* [2002] Crim LR 237.
[57]   *R v Beard* [2002] Crim LR 684.
[58]   Because of the provisions of s 114(2).

police interview and that where it is not made until the first court hearing. The greater factor is that of remorse. The Guidelines make clear that this is a separate issue to the time at which the admission is made, and the police station is the best opportunity for a suspect, in their own words if possible, to express their regret.

For those who admit guilt, current policies on taking offences into consideration (TICs) raise further matters requiring advice. As is made clear in *R v Miles*,[59] the admission of further offences can increase the seriousness of the total offending behaviour and so lead to a higher sentence. On the other hand, if evidence subsequently becomes available to prove guilt, the policy to prosecute such 'non-admitted cases' leads to a substantial risk of 'gate' arrest.[60]

In all these situations the risks, as summarised by Eric Shepherd, have to be balanced and advice given. No longer is it acceptable for solicitors merely to describe the issues and leave the decision-making to the client. The client is entitled to receive clear advice on whether to answer questions and that advice often needs to be in strong terms. For clients who wish to speak, either with or against the solicitor's advice, casework experience shows that it is essential that they are warned of the dangers of being caught out in a lie—the prosecution case is strengthened, and a case where there might have been a successful submission of no case to answer will often go to a jury where a lie by the defendant can be proved.

### (iv) Ways to answer questions

For those who decide to answer questions there are now two clear options for them to follow, and there is a wide range of opinion within the profession about which choice should be made.

There are strong advantages in letting a client give, in their own words, their explanation for events and there is no doubt that if this is done well it has a powerful impact on magistrates and jurors. However, for some clients this represents too risky a route, either because of their own limitations, the nature of the investigator's evidence, or the complexity of the law. In this situation a prepared statement is to be preferred. Surprisingly helpful judgments have been given on this issue, initially in *R v McGarry*[61] and *R v Ali*[62] and then, importantly, in *R v Knight*.[63] A fact is 'mentioned when questioned' if mentioned in a prepared statement even when no comment is made in interview. Thus, as long as the main 'bones' of the defence are identified, no 'flesh' need be placed on them. Real

---

[59] [2006] EWCA Crim 256.
[60] That is, arrest as the suspect leaves prison.
[61] [1998] 3 All ER 804.
[62] [2001] EWCA Crim 863.
[63] [2004] 1 WLR 340.

dangers in this approach exist and were emphasised in *R v Turner*,[64] especially if an important fact, later mentioned at trial, is omitted, or a client wishes to change their explanation.

There is still an unsatisfactory level of understanding within the police service of the use of prepared statements. From their point of view, they need to have a clear plan as to the identification of relevant facts, not mentioned in the statement, that may be material (including as to alibi: see *R v Lewis*[65]). However, the nature of a prepared statement is often not understood and some of the resulting behaviour is reminiscent of the worst days of police conduct in interview. There can be no objection to a solicitor drafting a statement for a suspect as long as the suspect adopts the statement as their own. Furthermore, if the client chooses to read the statement it is the oral rendition, and not the statement itself, that amounts to the evidence. In such a case the police officer has no right to the document. On the other hand, solicitors unnecessarily object to their client signing a statement if a written document is to be used. If the solicitor is worried about the content it should not be used in any event.

Where a solicitor has advised that answers should be given, but in the form of a statement, they must also consider the best time at which the statement might be made known to the investigator. This may be dependent on the amount of disclosure made at any stage, and the mere making, timing and counter-signature of a statement can negate any suggestion of recent fabrication, even if it is withheld until proceedings are underway. It is only in the case of an alibi defence, a situation that makes the greatest demands on a solicitor in terms of their advice, that such withholding can be disadvantageous because it prevents the investigator checking the facts before the suspect and potential alibi witness can communicate with each other.[66]

## B Assistance

The assistance role is also becoming more demanding as the law continues to develop. It covers a number of heads.

### (i) Record-keeping

The need to create contemporaneous notes as evidence of everything that occurs in a police station, for possible use at court (the police station as the 'first day of trial' approach) remains critical, and modern technology may considerably assist in achieving professional outcomes. The video-recording of most custody areas enables a record to be maintained of disclosure and also, particularly, of representations made by solicitors. These facilities provide a powerful re-enforcement

---

[64] [2004] 1 All ER 1025.
[65] [2003] EWCA Crim 223.
[66] See *R v Taylor* [1999] Crim LR 77.

of the 'defender model' as clients will not be impressed by videos showing their solicitor expressing negative views about them or barely trying to make representations, for instance, as to bail on their behalf. Whilst building a good rapport with investigators does facilitate the provision of greater disclosure, that must now be approached in an entirely professional way.

## (ii) Welfare and support

There is no change in the need for support and protection of the welfare of the suspect. All clients, in the atmosphere of a police station, are vulnerable and many are frightened and unsure. Any weakening of the PACE Code obligations on police staff would be particularly dangerous in this context. Rather, there needs to be better management of police time and efficient use of modern technology. At times, there appears to be no management or prioritisation of police investigations, certainly at the divisional level. Fresh consideration should be given to whether a detention in custody is actually required, is proportionate to the object of the investigation, and as to how long interviews should last. Permitting suspects to voluntarily attend the police station without arresting them and the greater use of street or early bail, would facilitate the co-ordinated arrival of defence lawyers, appropriate adults, interpreters and investigating officers.

Criminal Defence Service (CDS) Direct[67] statistics raise considerable concern about unnecessary expenditure of scarce criminal defence resources.[68] Technological developments have the potential to save significant amounts of time in respect of the documentation and record-keeping required by PACE. However, the inefficient use of modern technology in custody suites is already raising issues of real concern. Where custody records are computerised it is no longer possible for a solicitor's telephone call and details immediately to be logged on the custody record if custody staff are engaged in making other entries. Similarly, where staff whose typing skills are inadequate are making those entries, and so are unable to answer the telephones, enormous delays can build up, making it difficult for solicitors to meet their own performance standards. Records kept by CDS Direct show that in the year to 31 October 2006 27 per cent of outgoing calls to police stations were either unanswered or engaged. Where an answer was obtained, in 23 per cent of cases the police were not ready to deal with the case on the telephone. There is an identified need for further training in areas where computerisation is new and for appropriate delegation in the making of computer entries to those with the necessary skills.

---

[67] CDS Direct has been established by the Legal Services Commission to provide advice in cases where attendance by a lawyer is not normally required. It is staffed by solicitors and accredited representatives.

[68] In the year to 31 October 2006, in 14% of cases where CDS Direct determined that attendance by a solicitor was not required because there was to be no police interview, an interview was in fact held, thus requiring an attendance.

The centralisation of the advice function by CDS Direct has enabled important and objective information to be obtained about the quality of police service across the country and, whilst containing dangers, the government's reform programme may also provide some opportunities to improve communication between defence solicitors and custody suites. There is no reason why email communication should not be introduced as a matter of urgency, enabling messages rapidly and conveniently to be passed and, most significantly, recorded.

Great care will be needed if the number of suppliers (that is criminal defence firms providing advice and assistance under a legal aid contract) is reduced, as anticipated by the Department for Constitutional Affairs in *Legal Aid Reform: the way ahead*,[69] following the report *Legal Aid: A market-based approach to reform.*[70] There is a danger that too close a working relationship between individual lawyers and police officers can dull sensibilities and weaken the adversarial approach. Such an approach has never required hostility, but appropriate levels of assertiveness will need to be maintained. Whatever else comes of the PDS pilot, the code of conduct developed for the PDS has important messages that must be maintained:

> 2.1. The primary duty of a professional employee is to protect the interests of the client so far as is consistent with any duties owed to the court and any other rules of professional conduct. Subject to this, a professional employee shall do his or her utmost to promote and work for the best interests of the client and to ensure that the client receives a fair hearing. A professional employee shall provide the client with fearless, vigorous and effective defence and may use all proper and lawful means to secure the best outcome for the client.[71]

If the number of suppliers is reduced, this duty will be put to the test particularly in urban areas where individual lawyers may spend their working day solely at a particular police station.

## (iii) Intervention in interviews

Intervention in interviews was insufficient in the early days following the introduction of PACE,[72] but solicitors now need to intervene in police interviews less often. The process of investigative interviewing has been the subject of detailed advice to both police officers and solicitors. For investigators this was initially in the form of the PEACE model of interviewing, and that has been followed by regular interview and advanced interview training (in which defence solicitors increasingly participate). For defence lawyers, their better training has led to more work by them to prepare their clients for interview and to anticipate

---

[69]   Cm 6993.

[70]   'The Carter Report', July 2006, available at http://www.legalaidprocurementreview.gov.uk (accessed 12 June 2008).

[71]   *Code of Conduct for Employees of the Legal Services Commission who provide services as part of the Criminal Defence Service* (London, The Stationery Office, 2001).

[72]   See text to notes 17–18 above.

the issues that are likely to arise and how to handle them. This is to be welcomed as, adopting 'the first day of trial' approach, juries are often unhappy with unnecessary intervention by solicitors. However, interventions must be made when required.

In 2006 I summarised the reasons for intervention under the following heads, taken from the work of Eric Shepherd in *Police Station Skills for Legal Advisers*:

(a)   psychological ploys;
(b)   harassment/oppression;
(c)   quality of questions; and
(d)   inappropriate questions.

Whilst there is always a need for vigilance, major issues around psychological ploys and harassment have substantially disappeared, although 'building rapport' with interviewees is an essential part of police training, and many more interviewing officers need to listen to what a suspect is actually saying.

However, the asking of good quality and appropriate questions is hugely demanding and it is not surprising that many problems persist. The requirement in PACE Code C para 11.2A that the interviewing office put to the suspect any significant statement or silence 'at the beginning of an interview' is unfortunate and unnecessary. It inhibits orderly questioning, usually chronologically, as to the relevant events. There is no reason why such a statement should not be raised at some later, more appropriate, point in the first formal interview. Hypothetical questions continue to be asked and are as dangerous now as they have always been,[73] and officers remain unable to distinguish opinion from fact.

Changes in the law on the admission of character evidence, introduced by the CJA 2003, have raised new issues for solicitors to consider both whilst advising a suspect in preparation for interview and often also by way of intervention once an interview is underway. A defendant's character may be admitted under any one of seven gateways. These can be divided into three groups at the investigative stage.

*Group 1: Unlikely to be relevant*   Gateways (a) (all parties to the proceedings agree to the evidence being admissible), and (e) (it has substantial probative value in relation to an important matter in issue between the defendant and a co-defendant)

Few solicitors will advise a client to comment at this stage on the statement of co-suspect and agreement (that is gateway (a)) is for the trial stage.

*Group 2: Issues for the defence to avoid raising in police interview or where intervention will be required as the effect is that defendants may put in their own character*   Gateways (b) (the evidence is adduced by the defendant him or herself or is given in answer to a question asked by them in cross-examination

---

[73]   See *R v Paris, Abdullahi and Miller* [1994] Crim LR 361.

and intended to elicit it, (f) (evidence to correct a false impression given by the defendant), and (g) (the defendant has made an attack on another person's character)

These gateways show the extent to which the trial process has been moved into the police station. Prior to the implementation of the bad character provisions a client who was minded to call a witness a liar was advised carefully, in conference with their advocate, how to address that issue so as not unnecessarily to put in their character under the Criminal Evidence Act 1898. That same process must now take place in the police station, increasing pressure on time and on the skills of the solicitor involved.

*Group 3: Issues going to behaviour or propensity*    Gateways (c) (it is important explanatory evidence) and (d) (it is relevant to an important matter in issue between the defendant and the prosecution)

These are matters that the investigator should raise if they have obtained the relevant information from intelligence and criminal records. In cases of domestic violence, for instance, such behaviour may have a particular bearing and careful consideration will have to be given by the solicitor in formulating their advice. More often than not the admissibility of bad character evidence raises difficult issues of law that will require rulings from the relevant court and are best avoided at the investigative stage.[74]

Furthermore it is seldom the fact of conviction that is relevant to the admissibility of character evidence, but rather the facts behind that conviction (or, occasionally, an acquittal or stay of proceedings). It is not part of the role of the defence lawyer to help the Crown to establish the facts behind such matters and, in the absence of admissions, the Crown will not be able to rely on criminal records but rather will have to call witnesses or find a way of admitting their evidence as hearsay under the CJA 2003 sections 116 or 117.[75] Absent exceptional circumstances there is a need for a clear adversarial approach in an area not previously necessary at the investigation stage. A solicitor must be prepared to intervene in an interview in order to indicate that the client is advised to make no comment on matters going to character.

## (iv) Identification procedures

Technology has brought about significant change in identification procedures and in the responsibilities of defence solicitors. Peer review will need to be particularly robust to ensure that solicitors, faced with a fixed fee for an entire investigation,[76] make all appropriate attendances at critical identification stages.

---

[74]   See *R v Hanson Gilmore and Pickstone* [2005] Crim LR 787.

[75]   *R v Ainscough* [2006] Crim LR 635, confirming *R v Humphries* [2006] EWCA Crim 2030.

[76]   As proposed by the Carter report (see n 70 above) and the government's response (see n 69 above) a fixed fee will replace, in the substantial majority of cases, a fee dependent on the time spent on an individual case.

The decision in *R v Turnbull*[77] emphasised the dangers of erroneous identification. The responsibility of solicitors to require formal identification procedures following street identifications is particularly important so that, following *R v Forbes*[78] and the amended PACE Code D para 3.12, the police are aware that 'the suspect disputes being the person the witness claims to have seen', thus triggering the requirement to conduct an identification procedure. The right under Code D para 3.1 to the 'suspect's description as first given by a potential witness' is one of the few rights to disclosure accorded to defence solicitors.

It is in the area of identification that representations made by the defence solicitor may have the greatest likelihood, if wrongly ignored by the police, of leading to the exclusion of evidence at trial under section 78 of PACE. More significantly, acceptance by a defence representative of an identification procedure has been used by the Court of Appeal as the basis for upholding convictions that depend on evidence of which the court might otherwise have been critical.[79] Advice about participation in identification procedures (particularly where other evidence is weak) has been affected by the latest amendments to Code D[80] that now allow the use of any video film of the suspect. Video footage is now normally available of the suspect's attendance in the custody office.

With the substantial reliance on video identification and the creation of specialist video suites, much of the delay and difficulty of older procedures has now been removed, and to diminish the risks resulting from fixed fees, there is a case for a 'permanent' defence representative at police stations, probably answerable professionally to the professional head of the PDS. Professional standards will need to be assured because the suspect is excluded when identification witnesses view the 'tape'.[81]

## (v) Representations

The making of representations outside the area of identification has less frequently led to the exclusion of evidence at trial, although the risk of losing evidence in this way should always cause the custody officer to draw representations to the notice of investigating officers and cause those officers to have regard to them, and to any made directly to them. This is particularly true of representations concerning vulnerability of the suspect. The addition of Annex G to Code C was a particularly important development and there is a need for solicitors, being careful as to client confidentially, to address the issues in Annex G para 3.[82]

---

[77] [1977] QB 224.
[78] [2001] 1 All ER 686.
[79] See, eg, *R v Martin* [2002] EWCA Crim 251.
[80] Code D para 3.21.
[81] Code D Annex A para 9.
[82] Which provides that in assessing whether the detainee should be interviewed, the following factors must be considered: (a) how the detainee's physical or mental state might affect their ability to understand the nature and purpose of the interview, to comprehend what is being asked and to appreciate the significance of any answers given and make rational decisions about whether they want

### (vi) CCTV evidence

The increasing availability of video footage of most public, and many private, places has been of growing significance and has enhanced the quality of investigations, including those where it is linked to the developing science of facial recognition. Its existence has, with DNA evidence, meant that investigators need place much less reliance on custodial interviews. There is a need for defence solicitors to be particularly proactive in relation to CCTV evidence. Following a substantial number of applications to stay proceedings for abuse of process because of the 'wiping' of recorded material that might have assisted the defence, the court in *R v Feltham Magistrates' Court (ex p Ebrahim); Mouat v DPP*[83] made clear that such applications will fail unless the defence draws the attention of the investigator to the possible existence of such material which would otherwise have been unknown to them. There remains an extraordinary unwillingness on the part of many investigators to seek out such material. The planned introduction of a graduated fee for all legally-aided trial preparation work, places substantial responsibility on the defence lawyer for which they may be effectively unremunerated if the proposed scheme continues as at present designed.

### (vii) Samples/arrest/detention

Representations about samples are now less likely to be made because of the growth of police powers considered below. However, two changes in the law have raised the significance of other representations. The amendment of section 24 of PACE by the Serious Organised Crime and Police Act 2005 (SOCPA) section 110 is only now beginning to be understood fully. It was initially understood to widen the scope for arrest where arrest was necessary for one of the statutory reasons set out in section 24(5) of PACE. However, the position of volunteers and those who could properly be volunteers has been insufficiently considered in cases where samples or searches are not required. Harking back to the original report of the Philips Commission it is likely only to be the award of damages for wrongful arrest that will concentrate minds. If a person is willing to attend a police station voluntarily for interview it is difficult to see how their arrest once they attend the station can be necessary. Section 29 of PACE does not prevent a later arrest if a volunteer decides to leave the station. The fact that a volunteer declines to answer questions is not a relevant consideration as the same inferences (under the CJPOA 1994) are available as if they were under arrest.

The other area which increasingly requires defence representation relates to the expansion of police powers to extend the length of detention without charge

---

to say anything; (b) the extent to which the detainee's replies may be affected by their physical or mental condition rather than representing a rational and accurate explanation of their involvement in the offence; and (c) how the nature of the interview, which could include particularly probing questions, might affect the detainee.

[83]   [2001] 1 WLR 1293.

beyond 24 hours to all indictable offences. Such extensions require that the detention is necessary to secure or preserve evidence relating to an offence or to obtain such evidence by questioning the suspect and that the investigation is being conducted diligently and expeditiously.[84] Despite the expansion of the power to detain, in practice it only arises in a small minority of cases. Indeed, if the power of the police to bail on arrest is sensibly developed the increased use of pre-arranged interviews has the potential to remove some of the staggering inefficiencies of the current investigative and custody office process. However, any change in procedure of this sort creates real difficulties for the government's current proposals for fixed fees for police station advice. It is essential that, from the outset, good comparative data is maintained since changes in police powers and practice of this kind can increase or decrease the amount of time defence lawyers must spend on individual cases.

## (viii) Diversion from prosecution

The fastest developing area for defence representations relates to diversion from prosecution. There is now available a significant range of diversionary procedures that avoid the need for prosecution. In relation to these, the role of the solicitor is to consider the best interests of their client, rather than any wider social purpose.[85] Home Office Circulars 66/1990 and 12/1995 continue to set out the policies in relation to mentally vulnerable suspects, and these are substantially reflected in the Code for Crown Prosecutors. Fixed penalty notices and penalty notices for disorder are available for a number of common offences, including low value thefts.[86] For suspects, they have the significant advantage that they do not count as convictions for the purposes of criminal records, although they are recorded and, as a result of not counting as convictions, they cannot become 'spent' under the provisions of the Rehabilitation of Offenders Act 1974. This causes unnecessary difficulties, as it does in relation to police cautions, and it requires political courage to bring them within the rehabilitation provisions.

The law on adult cautions was updated by Home Office Circular 30/2005, although they remain non-statutory, but there is a statutory scheme for reprimands and warnings for young offenders under the Crime and Disorder Act 1998. The conditional caution, introduced by the CJA 2003 Part 3 is currently being piloted and its use, following the implementation of amendments by the Police and Justice Act 2006, is likely to grow significantly. The amendments will allow conditional cautions to be imposed for the purpose of punishment (by

---

[84] PACE s 42.

[85] In guidance to the Public Defender Service published in January 2005, I made clear that, in approaching advice on diversionary schemes that may lead to a reduction in future re-offending, the solicitor must put first the individual interests of the particular suspect and, in particular, whether the Crown could prove its case.

[86] In relation to penalty notices for disorder see Criminal Justice and Police Act 2001 P 1, ch 1. In 2004 63,639 such notices were issued. See further ch 7 by Richard Young in this volume.

imposition of up to 20 hours of unpaid work or of financial penalties up to £250 or one quarter of the statutory maximum, whichever is lower), as well as for the purposes of rehabilitation of the suspect and/or the making of reparation to the victim.

Following the decision of the House of Lords in *Jones v Whalley*[87] solicitors will need to ensure that all cautions are recorded as being accepted in place of prosecution to avoid the matter later being reopened.

However, an issue of more importance to defence solicitors requires legislative change. All forms of caution require an admission from the suspect.[88] If the evidence disclosed by investigating officers is weak or unknown, solicitors must be cautious about advising a client that such admissions should be made. Yet if the case can be proved, diversion is the better result for the client. The importance of this issue was fully understood by the Court in *DPP v Ara*[89] which held that it was an abuse of process to proceed to prosecute a suspect who had been offered a caution where critical evidence had been withheld from his advisers, so denying him 'informed advice'. In the past an approach would be made by the solicitor to the relevant inspector, ahead of the police interview to see what view was taken about the possibility of a caution, but following the decision in *R (on the application of R) v Durham Constabulary and Another,*[90] normally no such approach should now be made. Furthermore, so as to avoid any suggestion of inducement, the Conditional Cautioning Code of Practice states that there must be evidence that the offender has committed the crime, which must include an admission made by the suspect before there is any mention of a conditional caution.[91] Yet this is wholly unrealistic. If a defence solicitor is at the police station they are bound to discuss such an outcome with a client when advising how to proceed. The code should specifically provide that no inducement is deemed to be offered to a suspect solely because discussions take place between the Crown Prosecutor (or in the case of simple cautions, reprimands or warnings, the police officer) who makes the decision and the defence lawyer.

Very similar problems arise if there is to be an effective use of the powers brought in by SOCPA Part 2 Chapter 2.[92] The Association of Chief Police Officers presently requires that admissions be made before use of the powers can be considered. This will emasculate the provisions. Defence solicitors will need to approach prosecutors in a way that does not create admissible evidence.

These problems are aggravated by an unwillingness on the part of Crown prosecutors to engage with defence lawyers. As the conditions imposed as part of

---

[87]   [2007] Crim LR 74.
[88]   See *R (Wyman) v Chief Constable of Hampshire* [2006] EWHC 1904 (Admin).
[89]   [2002] 1 WLR 815.
[90]   [2005] 1 WLR 1484.
[91]   Conditional Cautioning Code of Practice para 4.
[92]   Which allows for immunity from prosecution and sentence discount where an offender provides assistance to the police or prosecution.

a conditional caution must be proportionate, achievable and appropriate,[93] problems are likely to arise when the defence lawyer, who best understands such issues in relation to a particular client, is excluded from the decision-making process. The CPS needs to be braver and see the benefit in discussions with the defence. It does not commit them to any particular view but may significantly improve their decision-making.

## (ix) Bail

Representations as to bail are amongst the most soul destroying for the defence lawyer since, in reality, any decision to refuse bail is effectively made by the time representations are invited and even the best negotiating skills cannot change that. However, the power to grant bail on conditions re-introduced some reality to the decision-making process, and that will be all the more so now that the Police and Justice Act 2006 section 10 has been brought into force.[94] The power to add conditions when granting bail on arrest or early in an investigation is a power with only limited mechanisms for enforcement. Whilst breach of conditions can lead to arrest, and charge in respect of the substantive offence if the Crown could then apply the 'threshold test',[95] that will seldom be possible at such an early stage in an investigation.

There is a real benefit to the defence and prosecution being able to 'negotiate' sensible conditions, since, although they are effectively unenforceable, a suspect will not want, if later charged, to have to explain a series of breaches. There is also an urgent need for a protocol as to 'bails to return' to the police station. Few solicitors will be able, automatically, to attend at the station when their client surrenders to bail once fixed fees are introduced. There should be a clear responsibility on the police to identify whether a return date is to be effective and its purpose.

## (xi) Following charge

From its earliest edition *Advising a Suspect in the Police Station* has suggested that assistance should be given in making appropriate arrangements following charge. Certainly there needs to be better connection between the investigative and proceedings stage. This has always been true in relation to matters such as finding sureties, securities and suitable residential addresses. The removal of any funding for advice and assistance once a charge is preferred was an error by the

---

[93] Conditional Cautioning Code of Practice para 5.1.

[94] The provision allows the imposition of conditions whenever bail is granted prior to charge, including 'street bail'.

[95] The *DPP's Guidance on Charging* permits a charge decision to be made in certain circumstances where the 'threshold test' is satisfied. The test requires only that there are reasonable grounds for suspecting that the person is guilty, and in *G v Chief Constable of West Yorkshire Police* [2006] EWHC 3485 (Admin) the Divisional Court questioned whether it provided an adequate test for a charge decision to be made.

government which it has now compounded by the plethora of unsatisfactory payment schemes following the introduction of the Criminal Defence Service Act 2006 and means-testing of magistrates' court legal aid. They should all be replaced by a single non-means tested scheme providing payment for two hours of work. This would provide important help to disadvantaged clients and address the continuing delays in the effective first hearing of magistrates' court cases, which will otherwise continue given the need to obtain signatures and supporting documents from the charged suspect who requires legal aid.

# VI  The future role

The role of the defence lawyer at the investigative stage is now more demanding than it has ever been. Decisions which used to be taken at court after significant time for preparation, are now made in the police station. The range of issues extends from the danger of putting a suspect's character into evidence, mentioning facts which if omitted may affect the outcome of the trial, and advising on a widening range of diversion from formal prosecution, many of which (including the use of the sex offenders register) are penal in their effect. Advice on such matters is best given, or actively supervised, by those with extensive experience of the outcome of every form of advice. Yet the government's plans are for a criminal defence service requiring the employment of far less experienced staff. As cases are moved out of the criminal courts to be dealt with on a summary basis, there is an urgent need for the redistribution of the savings in the CDS budget that result so that advice and assistance at the investigative stage is adequately financed.

Adversarial justice only works if there is an effective defence, and there is no better way to discover facts and, in particular, the state of a defendant's mind. A clear definition of the defence lawyer's role is therefore critical. It is not satisfactory that it relies more on a code of practice, albeit authorised by parliament, than upon professional rules. The issue requires attention by the new regulatory authorities for the legal profession. The role should not be dependent on the whim of government or a vague 'interests of justice' test. It requires a formal exposition of the issues of advice and assistance considered in this chapter, incorporating a clear recognition of all the rights established at common law and by the relevant articles of the European Convention on Human Rights. The role must be firmly based upon a clear adversarial model since nothing less will test the quality of an investigation. At the investigative stage the client's interest cannot be compromised by any need for a more efficient criminal justice system. Thus it must not reflect the weakened adversarial model that is the inevitable outcome of the Criminal Procedure Rules introduced in April 2005. These have been rightly criticised by James Richardson in the following terms:

The unpalatable truth is that the overriding object in the Criminal Procedure Rules 2005 (SI. 2005 No. 384) (convict the guilty and acquit the innocent) taken together with the obligation imposed upon each participant in the conduct of a case to "prepare and conduct the case in accordance with the overriding objective" (rule 1.2.(1.2)(a)) is incompatible with an adversarial system of justice.[96]

However, by the time the CPS have authorised proceedings there is the likelihood of at least a case to answer. During the investigation the case is still being identified. A series of miscarriages of justice and two Royal Commissions have shown that the 'search for truth' approach does not work reliably at the investigative stage. Modern investigation methods, including DNA, CCTV and mobile telephone identification and positioning, should enable the interview to be used for its true purpose, not to create a case but to see if there is any explanation that the suspect feels it necessary to give. Police officers who come to understand this reality, and the true role of defence solicitors, will conduct better investigations. But in an adversarial system both parties must be professional and trained to achieve their objectives. If the control of quality of those defence lawyer who attend the police station is to pass back from the Legal Services Commission to the professional bodies then the regulatory body must ensure that there is no weakening of the standards required and the Commission must, in its contractual specification, require standards that are no less than those that presently exist, whatever the financial pressures may be.

[96] *Criminal Law Week* 6 April 2006.

# 10

## Police and Prosecutors after PACE: The Road from Case Construction to Case Disposal

JOHN JACKSON*

## I Introduction

The criminal process has tended to be divided into distinct phases with a contrast made between the investigatory phase where inquiries are made into criminal offences; the accusatory phase where an accused emerges to face charges against him; and what may be called the dispository phase which is concerned with how the convicted accused should be dealt with. Although it may not always be easy to determine in point of time when one particular phase of the process ends and another begins,[1] conventionally the investigatory phase is often described as the pre-trial or pre-court inquiry while the accusatory and dispository phases which constitute criminal proceedings against the accused, take place at court. In recent times the police have dominated the investigatory phase but when they have decided to charge a defendant, they have not normally been able to ask any further questions, and the process shifts to the court which is where the accusatory phase begins.[2]

* This chapter has benefited from observations made of the new statutory charging and cautioning procedures at Thames Valley police stations. I am grateful to Superintendent David Lewis for facilitating a visit there in October 2006 and to Ian Brownlee for facilitating a visit to the CPS in Liverpool in November 2006. Thanks are also due to Ed Cape for his comments on an earlier version of this paper and to participants at the North—South Criminology and Criminal Justice Conference, University of Limerick 20–21 September 2006 and at the conference and colloquium on Policing and Defending in a Post-PACE World at the University of the West England and the University of Bristol, 29–30 March 2007.
   [1] See C Safferling, *Towards an International Criminal Procedure* (Oxford, Oxford University Press, 2001) 54.
   [2] See *Police and Criminal Evidence Act 1984 Code C: Code of Practice for the detention, treatment and questioning of persons by police officers* para 16.5.

It is widely assumed that the introduction of the Police and Criminal Evidence Act 1984 (PACE) marked a watershed in English criminal procedure by transforming the investigatory phase of criminal procedure from a closed unregulated inquiry into a much more transparent investigatory regime. In this chapter, however, it will be argued that much more radical developments have been taking place since PACE which have served to transform the PACE regime itself from a purely investigatory phase into one which includes accusatory and dispository features as well. This transformation is requiring role changes in the way in which professionals conduct their work. Changes made to the right of silence in the 1990s, for example, have changed the police role from one of pure investigation towards also holding suspects to account at police interviews for what they are alleged to have done. It has been argued that these changes are also causing tensions in the role of the defence representative at the interview between acting in their client's best interest and advising what is best in the interests of justice.[3] This chapter will focus particularly, however, on the effect of the transformation that has been taking place in the role of the Crown Prosecution Service (CPS) prosecutor from the passive 'case reviewer' of the police file after investigation,[4] towards a more active 'case builder' working with the police in the police station and also becoming responsible through the expanding system of conditional cautions for disposing of cases altogether before they reach court. This transformation has caused one former Law Lord to argue that we are witnessing an infringement of a constitutional principle held sacred since the Bill of Rights of 1689 that sentencing has always been a matter for the courts and not prosecutors.[5]

This chapter will argue that as we go down the road of prosecutorial disposition within the PACE regime, we may need to introduce safeguards which are just as radical and fundamental as those introduced by the original PACE regime. In order to see how significant these recent developments are, we first compare the changes that were made by the original PACE regime with those that have been more gradually introduced in recent years. The chapter begins by discussing how PACE was first developed as a regulated investigative custody regime. It then traces the development of the PACE interview from a purely investigatory tool into an accusatory venue for testing and examining accusations as part of the criminal proceedings against an accused. The chapter proceeds to examine how prosecutors have been brought into this regime with the result that it is changing again to become an important venue for determining the disposition of cases. The chapter finally examines the traditional safeguards available to suspects

---

[3] E Cape, 'Rebalancing the Criminal Justice Process: Ethical Challenges for Criminal Defence Lawyers' (2006) 9 *Legal Ethics* 56, and ch 9 by Edwards in this collection.

[4] See A Sanders, 'Prosecution Systems' in M McConville and G Wilson (eds), *The Handbook of the Criminal Justice Process* (Oxford, Oxford University Press, 2002) 149.

[5] See HL Debs, col 123, 10 October 2006 (Lord Lloyd of Berwick). The Bill of Rights provides that 'all grants and promises of fines and forfeitures of particular persons before conviction are illegal and void'.

under PACE and what further safeguards may be required to make the new regime compliant with the European Convention on Human Rights (ECHR).

# II The Introduction of PACE—A More Regulated Investigatory Regime

Throughout the course of the twentieth century the police increasingly began to rely on arrest for the purpose of interrogation as a means of obtaining confessions and convictions. In 1984 the House of Lords officially endorsed the practice that, provided the police reasonably suspect an individual of having committed an arrestable offence, they may arrest that person with a view to questioning him or her in a police station.[6] There were certain rules that judges developed to regulate the way in which this procedure should be conducted. There was an old common law rule that any confession made by an accused must be voluntary in the sense that it must not be induced by any promise of favour or by any menace.[7] Also during the course of the twentieth century the judges developed the Judges Rules according to which a caution was administered before any questioning that the suspect was not obliged to say anything unless he wished to do so but whatever he said would be taken down in writing and might be given in evidence.[8] But in practice these rules gave plenty of leeway for police officers to question suspects. Although the caution reminded the suspect of his right of silence, it did nothing to urge him to take advantage of his right. On the contrary, the freedom given to the police to question suspects made it very difficult to exercise it.

It was hardly surprising then that the statements made by suspects often played what Lord Devlin described in 1960 as a great and decisive part of the prosecution case.[9] In their study of Crown Court cases in Birmingham some years later in 1975 and 1976 Baldwin and McConville found that in almost all cases statements had been taken from defendants and confessions were recorded against 88 per cent of those who pleaded guilty and 25 per cent of those who pleaded not guilty.[10] Whatever the precise role played by confessions, statements made by the accused played a crucial role in conviction in many cases. As McBarnet put it in her study of conviction in 1981, the police operated a 'three-stage model' of investigation involving custody, interrogation and charge

---

[6] *Holgate-Mohammed v Duke* [1984] 1 All ER 1054.

[7] See *R v Warickshall* (1783) 1 Leach 263.

[8] The Rules were first formulated in 1912. For an account of the history of the Judges Rules, see Royal Commission on Criminal Procedure, *The Investigation and Prosecution of Criminal Offences in England and Wales: The Law and Procedure* (London, HMSO, 1981) Cmnd 8092–1, Appendix 13. Revisions appeared in 1914, 1930, 1947 and 1948.

[9] P Devlin, *The Criminal Prosecution in England* (London, Stevens, 1960) 48–9.

[10] J Baldwin and M McConville, *Courts, Prosecution and Conviction* (Oxford, Clarendon, 1981).

and the tasks of investigation and incrimination became reversed to become first incrimination and then investigation.[11] The investigation that followed custody was far from a neutral procedure whereby the police gathered information from the suspect in order to determine whether he had committed the offence. Instead it became a one-sided attempt to assemble and 'construct' a case for prosecution.[12]

The potential for miscarriages of justice in this regime was immense but it was not easy for them to be uncovered. Given the significance attached to defendants' statements as a part of the prosecution case, contested criminal trials in the pre-PACE era inevitably centred on what was said and done in interviews and 'voir dires'—trials within trials—were frequently held in which the admissibility of the statements were challenged. This was a particular feature of the Diplock trials in Northern Ireland which dealt with defendants who were subject to an emergency framework outside the PACE regime even when PACE was introduced there in 1989.[13] The difficulty was that without a clear record of what exactly took place in the police station, cases often came down to believing one word—the police's—against the accused, and judges were slow to find against the police on a disputed issue of fact.[14]

In time, of course, some of the abuses that took place were uncovered. Cases such as the Birmingham Six, the Guildford Four, the Maguire Seven and the Bridgewater Four revealed that police officers were prepared to inflict physical and verbal abuse and to engage in wholesale verballing and the manufacture of signed confessions.[15] But it was a case that exposed less extreme but no less harmful practices from the point of view of causing a miscarriage of justice that led to the changes that augured in the PACE regime. In the *Confait* case three boys, aged 14, 15 and 18, falsely confessed to the killing of Maxwell Confait in south east London. The inquiry into the case in 1977 revealed that the officer in charge was quite willing to commit breaches of the Judges Rules and put

---

[11]   D McBarnet, *Conviction* (London, Macmillan, 1981).

[12]   M McConville, A Sanders and R Leng, *The Case for the Prosecution* (London, Routledge, 1991).

[13]   Diplock trials are named after Lord Diplock who recommended that trial by a single judge should be substituted for trial by jury in cases connected with the Northern Ireland conflict. See *Report of the Commission to consider legal procedures to deal with terrorist activities in Northern Ireland* (London, HMSO, 1972) Cmnd 5185. See J Jackson and S Doran, *Judge without Jury: Diplock Trials in the Adversary System* (Oxford, Clarendon, 1995). Diplock trials continue to operate in Northern Ireland under the arrangements provided for in the Justice and Security (Northern Ireland) Act 2007.

[14]   The *locus classicus* for judicial acceptance of police versions of events is to be found in Lord Denning's famous dictum in the civil proceedings for assault taken by the Birmingham Six against the police that if the men won, it would mean that 'the police were guilty of perjury, that they were guilty of violence and threats, that the confessions were involuntary and were improperly admitted in evidence and the convictions were erroneous … This is such an appalling vista that every sensible person in the land would say: "It cannot be right that these actions should go any further."' See *McIlkenny v Chief Constable of the West Midlands* [1980] 2 All ER 227, 239–40. Irish judges gave the Irish police similar leeway. See P Carney, 'Court Attitude to Garda Evidence has Altered' *Irish Times* 18 July 2006.

[15]   For details of these cases, see B Woffinden, *Miscarriages of Justice* (London, Fontana, 1989).

considerable pressure on the boys in his questioning of them without their parents being present.[16] The recommendations made by the inquiry chair, Sir Henry Fisher, involved an overhaul of the Judges Rules with clearer safeguards for suspects including a right to have a solicitor present throughout interviews, the right of young and vulnerable persons to have an appropriate adult in attendance with them in the police station and the appointment of custody officers who would not be involved in the investigation of the case. These provided the foundation for the PACE regime that was brought into effect in England in 1984 and in Northern Ireland in 1989.

The introduction of PACE opened up the prospect of a much more transparent custody regime with custody officers having to maintain a custody record for each suspect, access given to appropriate adults, third parties and legal advisers and a clear record being available of what was said by suspects in interviews. The Royal Commission on Criminal Procedure which recommended the specific changes that were made took as its objectives: fairness, openness and accountability.[17] The result was a system of rules which gave a coherent shape and structure to many of the aspects of the relationship between the police and the suspect, especially in the police station.[18] The procedure for the reception of suspects, their processing, telling them their rights, the monitoring and length of detention, access to lawyers, family or friends, doctors, interpreters and appropriate adults, and the regime in the police station were all brought under a new form of control. Where previously the position on many of these matters was fuzzy and unclear, now it became the subject of detailed and precise rules. Furthermore, the judges indicated early on that in contrast to their attitude towards the Judges Rules, they were prepared to exclude evidence obtained where there had been significant breaches of the new rules.[19]

Fundamentally, however, what PACE did was to give greater legitimacy to the investigative custody regime that had been developed throughout the course of the twentieth century. As one commentator put it, its main effect was to enable more suspects to be taken into police custody and kept there for the purposes of questioning.[20] Given this, it is not perhaps surprising that after initially complaining about the extended rights for suspects and the fear of being engulfed by paperwork, the police came fairly quickly to accept the changes made in the Codes of Practice. They found that they were able to mould the new rules to take account of their own organisational goals which remained the need to obtain statements from suspects and assemble a case against the suspect.

---

[16] *Report of the Inquiry into the Circumstances leading to the trial of three persons arising out of the death of Maxwell Confait and the fire at 27 Doggett Road, London SE 6* (London, HMSO, 1977) HC 90.

[17] *Report* (London, HMSO, 1981) Cmnd 8092, para 2.18.

[18] M Zander, 'PACE Four Years On: An Overview' (1989) 40 *Northern Ireland Legal Quarterly* 319, 321.

[19] D Birch, 'The Evidence Provisions' (1989) 40 *Northern Ireland Legal Quarterly* 411.

[20] T Gibbons, 'Questioning and Treatment of Persons by the Police' (1989) 40 *Northern Ireland Legal Quarterly* 386.

The change that potentially provided the greatest obstacle towards the realisa-
tion of these goals was the requirement that suspects be told of their right to legal
advice and their right to have a legal adviser present at police interviews. Given
the right of silence, the police fear was that legal advisers would stymie their
attempts to obtain statements from suspects by advising their clients to be silent
during police interviews.[21] In practice a number of factors prevented this fear
being realised. Research on the reception of suspects in custody in a number of
police stations found that the police used 'ploys' to dissuade suspects from
seeking advice in over 40 per cent of cases.[22] Although figures did in time show
an increase in the numbers requesting legal advice, further research found that
legal advisers, many of who were very junior or unqualified, did very little when
they attended interrogations and frequently saw their task as facilitating the
police investigation rather than protecting the rights of their clients.[23] All this,
however, did little to diminish the calls that the police began to make after the
introduction of PACE for the right of silence to be curtailed. Although these calls
were motivated by a desire to make it easier to assemble a case against the
accused, the changes that were made paved the way towards the PACE interview
becoming much more than an investigatory tool for the police. In effect the
interview was to become part of the actual criminal proceedings that were taken
against the suspect.

# III Bringing PACE within the scope of criminal proceedings

It was Northern Ireland rather than England and Wales that proved the most
fertile ground for those seeking to change the law on the right of silence.
Although in practice the right was rarely exercised by suspects in England and
Wales, in Northern Ireland the police were facing terrorist suspects who in many
cases did adopt a wall of silence towards police questions.[24] The Criminal
Evidence (NI) Order was enacted in 1988 shortly before the introduction of

---

[21] See the comments of the Metropolitan Police Commissioner, Peter Imbert, on 15 September
1987 cited in J Wood and A Crawford, *The Right of Silence* (London, Civil Liberties Trust, 1989) 22.
[22] A Sanders, L Bridges, A Mulvaney and G Crozier, *Advice and Assistance at Police Stations and the
24 Duty Solicitor Scheme* (London, Lord Chancellor's Department, 1989).
[23] See D Brown, T Ellis and K Larcombe, *Changing the Code: Police Detention under the Revised
PACE Codes of Practice* (London, Home Office, 1992) Home Office Research Study 129, M McConville
and J Hodgson, *Custodial Legal Advice and the Right to Silence* (London, HMSO, 1993) RCCJ Research
Series 16, A Sanders and L Bridges, 'The Right to Legal Advice' in C Walker and K Starmer (eds),
*Justice in Error* (Oxford, Blackstone, 1993), D Dixon, 'Common Sense, Legal Advice and the Right of
Silence' (1991) *PL* 233, M McConville, J Hodgson, L Bridges and A Pavlovic, *Standing Accused*
(Oxford, Clarendon, 1994).
[24] J Jackson, 'Recent Developments in Criminal Evidence' (1989) 40 *Northern Ireland Legal
Quarterly* 105.

PACE in Northern Ireland, permitting the courts to draw inferences against defendants when they failed to account to the police for certain matters or failed to mention facts to the police that were later relied upon. Similar legislation was introduced in England and Wales six years later in 1994 against the advice of the Royal Commission on Criminal Justice and after heated debate.

There was considerable argument at the time about the effect of this legislation, with predictions on the part of the police that it would considerably smooth their path in securing convictions, and civil libertarians, on the other side, arguing that it was a fundamental blow to the rights of the suspect.[25] In practice neither of these claims has proven to be completely justified. The right of silence is a poor protection for suspects when they are subjected to police questions. Not perhaps surprisingly then, research has shown that the curtailment of the right has brought few tangible benefits for the police and prosecutors.[26] Aided by the judgment of the European Court of Human Rights in *Murray v UK*,[27] the legislation has indeed served to reinforce the need for suspects to have access to legal advice in order that they can be advised on the complexity of the new caution that suspects may harm their defence by refusing to answer questions. Whatever the impact of the legislation in terms of assisting the police, however, it brought about a significant legal shift in the nature of the PACE regime, from one that is simply a forum for police investigation towards becoming a formal part of the proceedings against the accused.[28]

PACE was primarily designed, as we have seen, to regulate the investigatory phase, giving the police, inter alia, ample powers to question suspects before they were charged to face accusation. Although this gave the police an opportunity to assemble the case against suspects, suspects could exercise a right of silence by refusing to answer any questions and the legal effect was that they could not be called to account for any allegations made against them. What the silence legislation did, however, was to bring forward the accusatory phase into the PACE regime. A new caution called upon the suspect to account for certain matters and to mention facts which may be later relied on. Prior to the legislation, the suspect was of course put under considerable psychological pressure to respond to questions.[29] But there was no legal duty to do so and no legal consequences could attach to a failure to do so. Following the legislation, however, the interview

[25] For discussion of the debates, see S Greer and R Morgan (eds), *The Right to Silence Debate* (Bristol, University of Bristol, 1990) and D Morgan and G Stephenson (eds), *Suspicion and Silence: The Right to Silence in Criminal Investigations* (Oxford, Blackstone, 1994).

[26] See T Bucke, R Street and D Brown, *The Right of Silence: The Impact of the Criminal Justice and Public Order Act 1994*, Home Office Research Study 199 (London, Home Office, 2000); J Jackson, M Wolfe and K Quinn, *Legislation Against Silence: The Northern Ireland Experience* (Belfast, Northern Ireland Office, 2000), NIO Research & Statistics Series 1.

[27] (1996) 22 EHRR 29.

[28] J Jackson, 'Silence and Proof: extending the boundaries of criminal proceedings in the United Kingdom' (2001) 5 *International Journal of Evidence & Proof* 145.

[29] See G Gudjonsson, I Clare, S Rutter and J Pearse, *Persons at Risk during Interviews in Police Custody* (London, HMSO, 1993) RCCJ Research Series 12.

process in effect became a part of the legal proceedings against the suspect as his responses, including silence, had legal repercussions at his later trial.

This change in the legal status of the interview has been recognised in recent English cases where the Court of Appeal has given both recognition and, as Cape has argued, approval to this state of affairs.[30] A series of judicial dicta have pointed out the constitutional significance of the new silence legislation. In *R v Howell*,[31] for example, Laws LJ said that in contrast to the past when the accused could without criticism withhold any disclosure of his defence until the trial, the police interview and the trial are now seen as part of a continuous process in which the suspect is engaged 'from the beginning'—the beginning presumably being the point at which the new caution is given to him.

It would seem that this change in legal status is also being reflected in changes in the manner in which the PACE interview is being conducted. Rather than simply being an opportunity for the police to assemble a case against the accused, the interview also puts an onus on the suspect to answer the allegations or face inferences being drawn against him. In a number of fairly minor cases observed in research on the questioning of young persons in Northern Ireland police stations,[32] the police did not use the opportunity of the interview for investigating or further assembling the case against the suspect. Instead they proceeded on the basis of an assumption of guilt, telling the suspect that this was his one big opportunity to explain why he was not guilty, although at times it was not clear exactly what the young person was accused of. In other more serious cases the interview was used, first of all to try, without disclosing the case against him, to pin the suspect down to certain movements and actions. In these types of situation, solicitors have a difficult but vital role to perform by getting the police to clarify, first of all, what the evidence is against their client and to work out when it is reasonable for the client to respond to the questions asked. This forces the legal representative to play an active role in the police interview, no longer there simply to protect his or her client by advising silence but to play a role akin to the defence representative in court, objecting to certain questions that are asked and where appropriate ensuring, just as in a contested trial, that explanations for her client's conduct are put on record.[33] The result is that the interview becomes a forum for conflicting versions of events to be recorded, no longer always a purely police dominated procedure.

The silence legislation has thus enabled the investigative custody regime that was legitimised by PACE to be transformed into an accusatory venue for testing and examining accusations as part of the criminal proceedings against an

---

[30] See Cape, n 3 above, 65.

[31] [2003] EWCA Crim 1 para 23.

[32] K Quinn and J Jackson, *The Detention and Questioning of Young Persons by the Police in Northern Ireland* (Belfast, Northern Ireland Office, 2004) NIO Research & Statistics Series 11 (hereafter Quinn and Jackson).

[33] See further, K Quinn and J Jackson, 'Of Rights and Roles: Police Interviews with Young Suspects in Northern Ireland' (2007) 47 *British Journal of Criminology* 234.

accused. Although the PACE regime provided important safeguards for those subjected to police questions, most notably access to legal advice, it did not provide suspects with the safeguards available to accused persons at a trial. In particular, there is no requirement for the police to disclose their case against the suspect before asking the suspect to respond to it.[34] Nor, of course, is there any judicial figure at hand who presides over the proceedings to ensure fairness.[35] Fairness instead has to be negotiated between the police and the legal adviser with the police having the ultimate sanction to exclude legal advisers from the interview room where their conduct is such that the interviewer is unable properly to put questions.[36]

# IV Enter the prosecutors

If the silence legislation augured in an interview process that has become more like a trial process where accusations are tested and examined, it did no more than make the interview a stage, albeit a most significant stage, in the criminal proceedings against the accused. Before proceedings could go further, the police still had to decide whether to charge the suspect and present the case file to the prosecution agency for it to decide whether to prosecute or not. Before PACE the police themselves could determine whether cases should be prosecuted or not but another change that arose from the *Confait* case was that a new prosecution agency, the CPS, was created precisely to determine whether to prosecute the accused. The Public Prosecution Service for Northern Ireland now performs a similar function in Northern Ireland.[37] The idea behind the CPS was to create some distance between investigation and prosecution, with prosecutors providing a much needed check on the institution of proceedings which in the past was a matter for the police.[38] This distinction between investigation and prosecution meant that the PACE regime could do little more than preserve evidence and

---

[34] The courts have, however, acknowledged that the lack of police disclosure may justify legal advice not to answer questions: see *R v Argent* 1997 2 Cr App R 27, *R v Roble* [1997] *Crim LR* 449.

[35] The idea of examining magistrates conducting pre-trial investigations is not one that has ever been seriously canvassed in English criminal procedure. See, however, the comments of the Royal Commission on Criminal Justice, *Report* (London, HMSO, 1993) Cm 2263, 3–4. Lord Devlin once said that an Englishman would not be soothed by the sound of a *juge d'instruction* rustling in with his dossiers. He nevertheless considered there was a vacancy in the English system for the post of judicial intermediary. See P Devlin, *The Judge* (London, Stevens, 1979) 82.

[36] Code of Practice C, para 6.9.

[37] For accounts of the emergence of these two new prosecuting agencies, see B Hancock and J Jackson, *Standards for Prosecutors: An Analysis of the UK National Prosecuting Agencies* (Nijmegen, Wolf, 2006) (hereafter Hancock and Jackson) chs 4 and 5.

[38] *Ibid*, ch 4. For a critique of the principle that the functions of investigation and prosecution should be separated, see R White, 'Investigators and Prosecutors or, Desperately Seeking Scotland: Reformulation of the "Philips Principle"' (2006) 69 *MLR* 143.

present cases to the prosecutor. For the regime to do more and effectively replicate the court system, it would have to be able to deal with cases like a court, with the ability to dispose of cases.

The police have always had an important power of disposal by cautioning (rather than charging) those persons whom they believe have committed crimes. In 1998, moreover, a new statutory scheme was introduced for diverting children and young persons from the court system by allowing the police to issue reprimands or warnings, with those warned being referred to youth offending teams for the purpose of their engagement in suitable rehabilitative pro-grammes.[39] Since these schemes have operated outside the control of CPS prosecutors, this has meant that there can often be direct discussions and negotiations between the police and the defence as to whether the suspect should be charged or merely cautioned.[40] When they arrive at a police station solicitors want to know how seriously the police are taking the case, and whether they have in mind charge and remand in custody or whether the young person is to be bailed and merely reported for caution.[41] The dispositional power of the police extends to less recognised forms of summary justice as well, as Young discusses in chapter seven in this collection. Some police officers in the Northern Ireland research readily admitted that they would use the interview process as a means of delivering an informal caution towards the young person.[42] In one observed case an officer spent the time in interview asking the young person if he knew that he had done wrong. Knowing that the case was likely to go to a caution only, the officer admitted that the interview was used to teach the boy a lesson.

So long as prosecutors were kept out of police stations, however, there was a limit on the degree to which the PACE regime could determine the disposal of cases. Police decisions to charge were referred to the CPS which made an independent evaluation of whether to continue or discontinue the prosecution, albeit one that was heavily dependent on the police file.[43] But this division of function whereby the police were solely responsible for investigation and the CPS for prosecution after charge, led to considerable inefficiencies with a large proportion of cases having to be discontinued or proceeded with reduced charges.[44] Attempts were made to locate CPS lawyers at police stations to advise the police on charging but this still meant that about 23 per cent of all indictments in the Crown Court had to be amended before trial.[45] In 2001 the Auld Review which was established in order to reduce inefficiencies in the Crown

---

[39]  Section 66 of the Crime and Disorder Act 1998.
[40]  See E Cape, *Defending Suspects at Police Stations* 5th edn (London, Legal Action Group, 2006) para 10.47.
[41]  Note 32 above, 80.
[42]  *Ibid*, 115–16.
[43]  For this dependence on the file, see McConville, Sanders and Leng, n 12 above.
[44]  See Auld Review, *Review of the Criminal Courts of England and Wales* (London, HMSO, 2001) ch 10.
[45]  See CPS Inspectorate, *Annual Report for 1999–2000* (London, HMSO, 2000).

Court recommended that in all but minor routine cases the CPS should determine the charge and this recommendation was enacted in an amendment to PACE in 2003.[46]

This has led to major change within CPS practice.[47] Instead of fulfilling the subsidiary role of saying no to a positive decision by the police to charge, they now take on the dominant role of determining what the charge shall be in the first place, with much greater scope for influencing the course of investigations than in the past. There remain certain cases where the police retain the power to charge and the charge is then subject to a review by the Crown Prosecutor.[48] These include minor road traffic cases and cases where it appears to the custody officer that there is likely to be a guilty plea and the sentencing powers of the magistrates will be adequate. In addition, where it is considered that bail should not be granted and there is a need to bring the suspect before a court with a view to seeking a remand in custody but it is not possible to consult a prosecutor before the expiry of the PACE custody limit, custody officers may charge the suspect applying a lower threshold test of reasonable suspicion of commission of an offence. A Crown Prosecutor will then review the case as soon as reasonably practicable when there is enough information to make a decision according to the full test laid down in the Code for Crown Prosecutors, namely whether there is enough evidence to provide a realistic prospect of conviction and that it is in the public interest to proceed.[49] In all other cases where a prosecutor is at the police station or otherwise available, charging decisions are to be made by the CPS.[50]

The new charging scheme gives prosecutors greater control over which cases should and should not be prosecuted and makes the CPS a more effective gatekeeper than before. It remains the case, of course, that the CPS will only make

---

[46]   Section 37 of the PACE has been amended by s 28 Criminal Justice Act 2003.

[47]   See I Brownlee, 'The Statutory Charging Scheme in England and Wales: Towards a Unified Prosecution System' [2004] *Crim LR* 896.

[48]   See *Guidance to Police Officers and Crown Prosecutors Issued by the Director of Public Prosecutions under s 37A of the Police and Criminal Evidence Act* 3rd edn (London, CPS, 2007) paras 3.3–3.4.

[49]   *Ibid*, para 3.9.

[50]   Since the effect of this new change is to give the CPS rather than the custody officer the responsibility of deciding whether defendants should be charged, in all but minor matters, it has been observed that it is unfortunate that parliament has sought to achieve this by amendments to PACE which fall short of a radical overhaul of s 37 which still provides that if the custody officer determines that he has before him sufficient evidence to charge the suspect he must release him or charge him. See *G v Chief Constable of West Yorkshire Police* [2006] EWHC (Admin) 3485, para 8. In this case it was argued that any detention from the point when a custody officer considers that there is sufficient evidence to charge and seeks the advice of a Crown Prosecutor as to the appropriate charge is unlawful. It was held, however, that a sensible construction of the new amendments made the charging decisions of the custody officer contingent on advice from and determination by the CPS. Section 37(7) of PACE has since been amended by s 11 of the Police and Justice Act 2006 which explicitly gives custody officers the power to keep suspects in police detention for the purpose of enabling the CPS to take charging decisions. The change came into force on 25 January 2007 as a result of the Police and Justice Act 2006 (Commencement No 1, Transitional and Savings Provisions) Order SI No 2264.

decisions in respect of those cases that are referred to it and the police are not required to refer cases to the CPS which they do not consider should be charged, the one exception being indictable only offences which the police do not think should be charged but which pass the threshold test of reasonable suspicion of commission of an offence.[51] 'Shadow' and statutory arrangements are now in place at most police custody units across England and Wales and hand in hand with these new charging arrangements has been the presence of prosecutors in key police stations to give prompt face to face advice to police officers including possible lines of inquiry, evidential requirements and pre-charge procedures. In addition to face to face meetings, CPS Direct also provides an out-of-hours telephone service that allows prosecutors to provide advice to the police around the country. The Director of Public Prosecution's Guidance on Charging stresses that Crown Prosecutors must be proactive in identifying and where possible rectifying evidential deficiencies, and identify those cases that can proceed to court for an early guilty plea as an expedited report.[52] When the CPS finally makes a determination on the charge they must do so on the basis of detailed reports which in the case of cases proceeding to the Crown Court or expected to be contested require an evidential report setting out the key evidence upon which the prosecution will rely and any unused material which may undermine the prosecution case or assist the defence including crime reports, initial descriptions and any previous convictions of key prosecution witnesses.[53]

All this is likely to mean that the PACE regime will play a greater role in determining the outcome of the case than before. When the police made the decision to charge, they were often not unduly concerned about the eventual outcome of the case. From their perspective early charging or a caution was a mark of completion.[54] If the case did not result in conviction, they could always blame the CPS or the courts, just as the CPS could blame a faulty police file. The vision of the new statutory charging scheme, however, is to get police and prosecutors to work together to achieve successful prosecutions. As the Attorney General put it when the scheme was launched:[55]

> Charging means that the police and prosecutors will all use their time more productively and more efficiently. It will bring police and prosecutors together as never before, working effectively towards the common goal of convicting the guilty by building robust cases from the start and ensuring that evidentially weak cases are weeded out as quickly as possible.

---

[51] *Guidance to Police Officers and Crown Prosecutors Issued by the Director of Public Prosecutions under s 37A of the Police and Criminal Evidence Act* 3rd edn (London, CPS, 2007), para 8.3.

[52] *Ibid*, para 5.2.

[53] *Ibid*, para 7.2.

[54] See Home Office Circular 30/2005.

[55] See CPS Press Release, *Charging Scheme Already Making a Significant Contribution to Narrowing the Justice Gap*, 28 January 2004. See http://www.cps.gov.uk/news/pressreleases/archive/2004/129_04.html (accessed 12 June 2008).

The right charge from the start means a good deal for the public, as more criminals plead guilty; a good deal for victims and witnesses, as their cases are dealt with speedily; and a good deal for the criminal justice system, as police, prosecutors and courts make the best use of their time.

'Rightness' here is defined as whether the first charge results in a successful, speedy prosecution and in consequence the CPS has striven to reduce discontinuance rates and attrition within the courts. Early indications are that the new arrangements have reduced the discontinuance rate but whether this is leading to more accurate disposals is less easy to say.[56] The danger is that the new management systems being built to forge closer relations between the police and prosecutors will lead to a new 'canteen culture' driven by performance targets to stick to the first charge even when the evidence points to weaknesses down the line when the case gets to court. There are counter-arguments that may be made against this scenario happening. It is always open to the defence to plead not guilty, although with discounts for early pleas defence practitioners need to be careful in advising contests. The danger of a police/prosecutor canteen culture may also be offset if duty prosecutors are made to take the cases they charge through to court. As one prosecutor put it to the author: 'Would you not rather be rebuffed by gung-ho police officers in the privacy of a police station than by a judge giving vent publicly in court to a weak case?' However the new charging scheme develops, it can be said with some confidence that with prosecutors now actively involved with police officers in 'case building', the PACE regime is becoming an ever more important venue for determining the disposition of cases.

## V The power to punish?

When charges are brought, they still of course have to be determined in court. But another development which has come to the fore recently has been an attempt to stem the flow of cases coming to the court by introducing 'simple, speedy, summary justice'.[57] The government has declared that it aims to remove one quarter of the magistrates' court's workload as part of its strategy to 'rebalance' the criminal justice system and deal more effectively with low-level crime.[58] A recent white paper points out that magistrates' courts deal with over 95 per cent of all criminal cases and considers that there are more effective ways

---

[56] For figures on the downward trend in discontinuances, see CPS, *Annual Report 2003–2004* (London, CPS, 2004) and CPS, *Annual Report 2004–2005* (London, CPS, 2005).

[57] Home Office, Department for Constitutional Affairs and Attorney General's Office, *Delivering Simple, Speedy, Summary Justice* (London, Department for Constitutional Affairs, 2006).

[58] See Home Office, *Rebalancing the Criminal Justice System in Favour of the Law Abiding Majority: Cutting crime, reducing reoffending and protecting the public* (London, Home Office, 2006), para 4.24. For a critique of the notion of balancing, see A Ashworth and M Redmayne, *The Criminal Process* 3rd

of dealing with forms of low-level offending than the full court process.[59] The paper proposes to engage with the judiciary, criminal justice practitioners, communities and the public in general about where the balance lies between 'simple and immediate responses to low level misbehaviour and fast, efficient modern court processes'.[60]

We have already seen that the police have for some time had the power to caution offenders instead of taking cases to court. Often, however, this has been a method of disposal for cases that have not merited prosecution in the first place. Indeed under the more recent statutory scheme for warning young persons, a constable may reprimand or warn a young offender only if he is satisfied that it would not be in the public interest for the offender to be prosecuted.[61] The level of offences that reach the courts can only be reduced if cases which would otherwise be prosecuted are disposed of by other means. Sections 22 and 23 of the Criminal Justice Act 2003 introduced a new form of caution, the conditional caution, to deal with these kinds of case. Where prosecutors consider that there is sufficient evidence to charge an offender with an offence, they are given the power to authorise a conditional caution to persons aged over 18 who have admitted their guilt and are prepared to agree to comply with certain conditions as an alternative to prosecution. The Code for Crown Prosecutors makes it clear that a conditional caution may be appropriate where the prosecutor considers that while the public interest justifies a prosecution, 'the interests of the suspect, victim and community may be better served by the suspect complying with suitable conditions aimed at rehabilitation or reparation'.[62] Failure to fulfil any of the conditions makes the offender liable to prosecution for the original offence in which case the earlier decision to caution is rescinded.[63] The conditional cautioning regime began by being implemented in selected police forces and there are now plans to extend its availability to at least part of every police force area by July 2007 with full implementation by April 2008.[64] The government also intends to legislate to create an equivalent scheme for young offenders.[65]

Views differs on whether this new form of disposal represents a radical change from past procedure. As Brownlee points out, on one view the disposal is simply a statutory development of the non-statutory simple caution which has been available for a long time.[66] Like the simple caution, the offender must not contest his guilt. The difference is that for a conditional caution to take effect, the

---

edn (Oxford, Oxford University Press, 2005) 40–43, J Jackson, 'Justice for All—Putting Victims at the Heart of Criminal Justice?' (2003) 30 *Journal of Law and Society* 309.

[59] Note 57 above, para 7.1.
[60] *Ibid*, para 7.7.
[61] Section 65(1) of the Crime and Disorder Act 1998.
[62] *Code for Crown Prosecutors* (London, CPS, 2004) para 8.4.
[63] Section 24 of the Criminal Justice Act 2003.
[64] Note 57 above, para 7.11.
[65] Note 58 above, para 4.25.
[66] I Brownlee, 'Conditional Cautions and Fair Trial Rights in England and Wales: Form versus Substance in the Diversionary Agenda' [2007] *Crim LR* 129.

offender must agree to certain conditions. The Criminal Justice Act 2003 originally limited the kind of conditions that could be attached by providing that these must be intended either to rehabilitate the offender or to ensure that he makes reparation for the offence, or both of these objectives in combination.[67] This emphasis on rehabilitation and reparation may in itself be viewed as a new dimension to prosecutorial decision making.[68] Similar efforts have been made in Northern Ireland with the introduction of a fully statutory scheme allowing for prosecutorial referral of young people who admit all but the most serious offences to youth conferencing schemes under which conference plans are drawn up to be completed by young persons.[69] The emphasis on reparation and restorative justice would seem to fall short of giving prosecutors a power to punish offenders. But on another view, the conditions that can be attached to a conditional caution take on a punitive hue as they give the prosecutor considerable discretion as to what the conditions should be provided they are proportionate to the offence.[70] The prosecutor may be said here to be meting out summary justice in a manner quite unprecedented in previous procedure.

At one level a straightforward answer can be given to the question whether these proceedings are punitive by saying that in deciding not to prosecute, the prosecuting authorities are not proceeding to take any punitive action. The House of Lords has made it clear that a caution, like a warning or reprimand given to a young person, does not have the status of a conviction.[71] Nor, according to the House of Lords in *R (on the application of R) v Durham Constabulary and Another*,[72] does a warning given to a young offender which results in the entry of his name on the sex offenders register involve the determination of a criminal charge for the purposes of Article 6 of the ECHR. Even assuming that there had been a criminal charge against him in the first place, this ceased to exist when a firm decision was made that ruled out the possibility of any trial, or condemnation, or punishment.[73] A process which could only culminate in measures of a preventative, curative, rehabilitative or welfare-promoting kind would not ordinarily be such a determination.[74] The decision has been criticised on the ground that it failed to take sufficient account

---

[67]   Section 22(3) of the Criminal Justice Act 2003.

[68]   See J Jackson, 'The Ethical Implications of the Enhanced Role of the Public Prosecutor' (2006) 9 *Legal Ethics* 35.

[69]   See ss 57 and 58 of the Justice (Northern Ireland) Act 2002. See C Campbell, R Devlin, D O'Mahony, J Doak, J Jackson, T Corrigan and K McEvoy, *Evaluation of the Northern Ireland Youth Conference Service* (Belfast, Northern Ireland Office, 2005), NIO Research and Statistics Series 12.

[70]   See *Conditional Cautioning Code of Practice* (London, CPS, 2004) para 5.1. See also *Director's Guidance on Conditional Cautioning* 4th ed (London, CPS, 2007) para 1.

[71]   *Jones v Whalley* [2006] UKHL 41.

[72]   [2005] UKHL 21.

[73]   Per Lord Bingham, para 12.

[74]   *Ibid*, para 14.

of the substance as opposed to the form of the process.[75] Lady Hale conceded that the domestic characterisation of a measure as preventive rather than punitive cannot always be the end of the story.[76] Reprimands and final warnings carry consequences which may individually be explained away as preventive rather than punitive but which cumulatively amount to a considerable modification of a child's legal status. He faces a higher penalty should he offend again, he must notify the police of his whereabouts for some time and his details are held on a computer to which a large number of people have access. Nor could the perception of an offender and his family that he is punished, as well as being helped, be completely irrelevant to the interpretation of an autonomous convention concept. What ultimately swayed her Ladyship, however, in her decision was that the consequences of the decision not to prosecute did not in this case amount to a penalty.[77]

Whatever the status of the conditions that could originally be attached to conditional cautions, recent amendments to the Criminal Justice Act 2003 have enabled conditions to be attached for explicitly punitive purposes.[78] Section 17 of the Police and Justice Act 2006 provides for conditions which include the performance of up to 20 hours unpaid community work or the payment of a financial penalty as distinct from compensation up to a maximum of £250.[79] The rationale for the original conditional caution was to provide a means of diverting those offenders away from the courts who could be more effectively dealt with by rehabilitative and reparative means. The rationale for the new conditions, by contrast, seems to be more directly focused on the need to keep low level criminal offences out of magistrates' courts. As the Solicitor General said in parliament, the usefulness of the original conditional caution in keeping low level offences out of the magistrates' courts was limited by the requirement that the conditions attached to the caution had to have the objectives of rehabilitating the offender or ensuring that he made reparation. This meant that it was unable to cater for the majority of cases that currently come before magistrates' court that are dealt with by way of a fine.[80] The new conditions are then explicitly punitive and the point has been reinforced by a further amendment to the Criminal Justice Act providing for the arrest of persons who fail to comply with the conditions attached to a conditional caution.[81] It was because of the punitive aims of the new conditional cautions that the House of Lords which had supported the original concept of the conditional caution voted against the amendments in the Police and Justice

---

[75]  See A Ashworth [2006] *Crim LR* 88–9 and G Dingwall and L Koffman, 'Diversion, Punishment and Restricting Human Rights' (2006) 57 *Northern Ireland Legal Quarterly* 478.
[76]  [2005] UKHL 21, para 45.
[77]  Para 47.
[78]  See s 17(2) of the Police and Justice Act 2006.
[79]  See s 17 of the Police and Justice Act 2006.
[80]  Hansard HC, vol 450, cols 1465, 1468, (24 October 2006, Mike O'Brien).
[81]  Section 18(1) of the Police and Justice Act 2006, amending s 24A Criminal Justice Act 2003.

Act.[82] According to Baroness Linklater, the new proposals amounted to a form of administrative justice imposed by the police and prosecutors rather than by the courts.[83] The Attorney General attempted to allay their Lordships' concerns by stressing that there was no question of prosecutors imposing punishment on offenders because offenders will have chosen whether to accept the conditions upon free legal advice and if they do not accept them the case will go to court in the usual way.[84] But in the end this was insufficient to convince enough peers that an important constitutional principle was not being breached. According to the Home Office website, punitive conditional cautions were to be introduced from Autumn 2007, although this timetable appears to have slipped.[85]

# VI Safeguards

It has been shown that the PACE regime has been transformed by recent developments from a purely investigatory regime for investigating offences prior to charge towards an accusatory regime where allegations are put to suspects for response as part of the case against them. On top of this the introduction of the statutory charging and conditional cautioning schemes has given police and prosecutors increasing control over the disposition of cases on the basis of the evidence obtained under PACE. Strong incentives have been created for ensuring that the cases that are brought to court are disposed of on the basis of the charge brought in the police station and there are plans through the new conditional cautions to enable an increasing number of cases to be dealt with without going to court at all. Of course, it was always open to the police to deal with minor offences administratively through a simple warning or caution. What is changing is the scale of the number of cases proposed for diversion from the courts and the punitive steps that may be taken by prosecutors against those offenders who admit their guilt. Whether this new form of administrative justice infringes the long-held constitutional principle that sentencing is for the courts and not for prosecutors depends on one's view of the meaningfulness of the consent which must be given by the offender for the punitive steps that are proposed, a point to which we shall return. The new arrangements undoubtedly change the nature of the PACE regime by enabling admissions obtained therein to be used as a means of punitive disposal and raise questions about the safeguards available for persons subjected to it.

The main safeguard provided by PACE for persons arrested and questioned by the police was access to legal advice. Appropriate adults were also made available

---

[82] An amendment moved by Lord Lloyd of Berwick to exclude the new conditions from the Bill was agreed to by 207 votes to 145. See Hansard HL, vol 685, col 133 (10 October 2006).

[83] *Ibid*, col 128 (Baroness Linklater).

[84] *Ibid*, col 131 (Lord Goldsmith).

[85] See http://www.homeoffice.gov.uk/police/powers/cautioning/ (accessed 12 June 2008).

for young and vulnerable suspects. In their day these were important safeguards for protecting the suspect who was placed into the alien world of police custody, although research has shown that the attendance of an appropriate adult is often a less meaningful safeguard for the vulnerable suspect.[86] But questions must be asked in the light of the new PACE regime as to whether the mere right of access to legal advice is sufficient protection. If, as has been argued, PACE has been transformed from an investigatory into an accusatory and dispository regime, just as at court, then the accused would seem to be entitled to the minimum defence rights guaranteed under Article 6(3) to a fair trial. These go much further than simply enabling accused persons to obtain legal advice. As well as requiring this, everyone charged with a criminal offence is entitled at least to be informed formally of the nature of the accusation against him, to adequate time and facilities for the preparation of the defence, a right to legal assistance which goes beyond advice and to rights of examination and the assistance of an interpreter. This would appear to require a transformation of the role of the defence legal adviser from one of providing advice towards one of active representation and support.

English law has been somewhat ambivalent as to whether a person interviewed under PACE is charged with a criminal offence and is thereby entitled to Article 6 rights. On the one hand, as we have seen the Court of Appeal has acknowledged that the changes in the right of silence have made the police interview and the criminal trial part of a continuous process. On the other hand, there has been a reluctance to see the police interview as the stage at which the defendant is charged and proceedings begin. In *Attorney General's Reference (No 2 of 2001)*[87] the House of Lords held that the point in time at which proceedings should commence should ordinarily be when the accused is formally charged or served with a summons. In *Durham*[88] Lord Bingham doubted whether the Divisional Court was right to accept that Article 6 was engaged when a person has been formally notified that allegations against him were being investigated. In the end his Lordship was prepared to assume with some reluctance that there was a criminal charge against the young person at the beginning of the process by which he appeared to mean at the point of arrest. The European Court has been similarly unclear on this point. The Court has considered that defendants are engaged within the meaning of Article 6 when they have been officially notified of an allegation or 'substantially affected' by the steps taken against them.[89] It has been argued elsewhere that the mere exercise of investigatory powers against a

---

[86] See, eg, J Hodgson, 'Vulnerable Suspects and the Appropriate Adult' [1997] *Crim LR* 785, Quinn and Jackson, n 32 above.

[87] [2001] 1 WLR 1869.

[88] See n 72 above.

[89] *Deweer v Belgium* (1980) 2 EHRR 439 at [46]; *Eckle v Federal Republic of Germany* (1983) 5 EHRR 1.

suspect should not in itself trigger the initiation of proceedings but that proceedings do commence when defendants are held to account for allegations as they are under the new caution.[90] If this is the point at which a defendant is charged, his defence rights under Article 6 would then be triggered and it may be argued that the defendant is not only entitled at this point to legal advice but also to the presence of a legal adviser when being questioned and, something that is not presently provided as of right, disclosure of the case against the defendant as well. Although the solicitor's presence at the interview is important, it is also important that she is able to make representations to the prosecutors who will make the decision on charge or caution. Given that Crown Prosecutors normally refuse to speak to defence lawyers at police stations,[91] this will require a considerable change of culture for prosecutors but one that will have to be taken on if defendants are to be given a meaningful defence at this stage of criminal proceedings.

As well as the right to be provided with certain minimum rights of defence, another essential ingredient of a fair trial is the right for the charge to be determined at a fair and public hearing by an independent and impartial tribunal. The police interview represents only the beginning of criminal proceedings and if the case proceeds to trial the defendant will then clearly have the opportunity of an independent and impartial tribunal to adjudicate upon the charge. If, however, on the basis of any admissions made, the police and prosecutors consider that the case is one better disposed of out of court and by means of punitive conditions, then there is the difficulty that the case will be disposed of without a public hearing and without an independent and impartial tribunal. The CPS prosecutor was introduced as we have seen to instil a degree of independence but this was independence in respect of the police in making the decision to prosecute. Prosecutors are a party to the proceedings and are unlikely to be regarded as an independent and impartial tribunal by the European Court.[92] Furthermore they act under the 'superintendence' of the Attorney General who is a member of the cabinet, the executive branch of government.[93] For these reasons, it has been argued that it is highly questionable whether the English courts would be prepared to accept a regime in which the protection of engaged convention rights, particularly those guaranteed by Article 6, rests solely with the prosecutor.[94]

Of course, it may be denied that the prosecutor is really here 'determining' a criminal charge. In *Durham*, as we have seen, the House of Lords considered that the warning given to the young person in that case did not amount to the

---

[90]  J Jackson, 'The Reasonable Time Requirement: an Independent and Meaningful Right?' [2005] *Crim LR* 3, 19. See *Howarth v UK* (2000) 31 EHRR 861, *Quinn v Ireland* (2001) 33 EHRR 264.

[91]  Cape, n 40 above, para 10.58.

[92]  See *Jasinski v Poland* Appl No 00030865/96 ECHR 883, 20 December 2005.

[93]  Section 3(1) Prosecution of Offences Act 1985. For a critique of this constitutional relationship, see J Jackson, 'Let the Director Direct' (2007) 157 *New Law Journal* 23.

[94]  Brownlee, n 66 above.

determination of a criminal charge. Although we have seen that the conditions of the new conditional caution may now be punitive, it may be argued that they are not, as the Attorney General has said,[95] 'imposed' by the prosecutor, as it is up to the defendant to accept them before the conditional caution can be given and they do not therefore amount to a 'determination' of a criminal charge. But looking to the substance as opposed to the form of the procedure, this can only be the case if there is free and informed consent by the defendant to the conditions and he does not feel railroaded into accepting them. Section 23 of the Criminal Justice Act 2003 and the Conditional Caution Code of Practice issued under section 25 of the Act sets out certain safeguards for offenders. The offender must first have admitted the offence and, to avoid any suggestion that an admission has been obtained by offering an inducement, the prospect of a conditional caution should not be mentioned until the suspect has made a 'clear and reliable admission under a cautioned interview to all the elements of the offence'.[96] At the time the caution is administered, it is also necessary that the offender admits that he committed the offence in addition to having admitted it in interview. The Code provides that in order to give informed consent to both the caution and the conditions, offenders should be advised of their right to legal advice at the point when they are asked to confirm that they have committed the offence.[97] The effect of the caution must be explained to the offender and the offender must be warned that a failure to comply with any of the conditions renders him liable to being prosecuted for the offence. Finally, the offender must sign a document containing details of the offence, an admission that he committed it, his consent to the caution and the conditions attached to it.

These requirements would seem quite strict and it may be questioned whether they should not also apply in cases of simple caution.[98] Nevertheless it is suggested that, particularly in view of the new punitive conditions that have been added to the conditional caution and the proposal to extend the conditional cautioning regime to young persons, they do not go far enough to ensure that consent to the conditions is free and informed and to avoid the effective determination of the case by the prosecutor. Once an admission has been made, there would seem to be clear pressure to accept the conditions as the alternative is that the case will go to court with the prospect of more severe sanctions being meted out at that stage.[99] Yet research has shown that young persons in particular have little idea as to the meaning of the elements of an offence when they are being questioned at a police interview and there is often considerable ambiguity

---

[95] Hansard HL, vol 685, col 131, (10 October 2006, Lord Goldsmith).

[96] *Conditional Cautioning Code of Practice* (London, CPS, 2004) para 4.1.

[97] *Ibid.*

[98] See Hancock and Jackson, n 37 above, 132.

[99] It is unclear what attitude the courts will take towards offenders who could otherwise have been dealt with by conditional caution. Nor is it clear whether those who hold out against admitting their guilt until after charge will be entitled to the full sentence discount.

as to whether they have admitted to an offence or not.[100] Given the significance of an admission, it would seem vital that a legal adviser is present, not just at the end of a phone,[101] to ensure that the offender has a full understanding of what an admission to the full elements of the offence actually means and in order to give advice on whether to make a full admission. This would seem to require that steps are taken to encourage particularly young or vulnerable adults to take up their right to legal advice rather than merely to inform them of the right at the stage of the police interview and at the stage of administering the caution.[102] Secondly, in order that legal representatives can give effective advice, it would seem that full disclosure should be made of all the relevant evidence available to the prosecutor both at the police interview and again at the stage of administering the caution.[103] Thirdly, so far as the conditions are concerned, it may be argued that in addition to being given a full explanation of what they mean and what the consequences of a failure to comply with them are, there should be an opportunity for the offender and his legal representative to make representations on what the conditions should be. At present, the Cautioning Code makes it clear that there should not be any bargaining with the offender over the conditions.[104] If he does not accept them in full, he should be prosecuted. The conditions, as we have seen, must be appropriate and proportionate to the offence but given the repercussions for non-compliance, there would seem no reason why the offender should not be able to propose conditions, query those suggested and suggest alternatives before making a decision as to whether to accept them. This again would take the role of the legal representative out of the realm of purely giving advice and into the realm of making representations and again it would require a change of practice on the part of prosecutors who do not usually speak to defence lawyers at police stations. These kind of negotiations, however, are commonplace at the sentencing stage in court and it would seem hard to deny this to offenders at this stage also. Ultimately, of course, the prosecutor will have the final say on what the conditions should be, and the offender will have to choose whether to accept them or not. But the choice is arguably more voluntary and less constrained if the offender has been given an opportunity to have an input into what the conditions are.

---

[100] Quinn and Jackson, n 32 above, ch 8.

[101] The Conditional Cautioning Code states that advice is available either from a Duty Solicitor or own solicitor free of charge, although in some circumstances this may be limited to telephone advice only: para 4.1, note 6.

[102] Quinn and Jackson, n 32 above, 137.

[103] It has been held that the police should disclose the police interview with a suspect to a lawyer who was absent from the interview to enable advice to be given as to whether to accept a caution: see *DPP v Ara* [2001] 4 All ER 559.

[104] Note 96 above, para 4.1.

# VII Conclusion

In his reflections on the developments of pre-trial processes in England, Lord Devlin claimed that the pre-trial process could be seen as a constant drift always in the same direction from administrative action to regulated judicial proceeding.[105] The introduction of PACE may be seen as an attempt to regulate in a more judicial manner, by rules, the way in which the custody regime should operate when persons are arrested for questioning. The judges played their part in the early years in giving these rules some teeth. But what was not perhaps envisaged was that PACE would be transformed from a process of preparing cases for trial to become a real substitute for trials themselves. Yet this is what we would appear to be witnessing. First, we have in the form of the police interview the opportunity, which in many cases will be the only meaningful opportunity, for the suspect to be forensically examined on the record with defence solicitors playing a role in mitigating where possible their client's inculpation. Then we have a prosecutor acting effectively as 'judge and jury' in deciding whether to charge, caution or take no further action against the accused. Of course, a charge is not a conviction and defendants who are charged still have the opportunity to go to court and plead not guilty. But with incentives on prosecutors not to change the charge and on defendants to plead guilty at an early stage, prosecutors are able to exercise considerable control over the outcome of the case. The new powers to offer conditional cautions as an alternative to prosecution including fines enable prosecutors to bypass the courts altogether. Again suspects may decide not to accept the cautions offered and go to court instead but again there are clear incentives on them to accept the prosecutor's penalty.

With the prospect of large numbers of low-level cases being disposed of out of court and an increasing number of cases that do go to court ending in a plea, the question arises as to what safeguards are necessary for suspects. Are those faced with out of court penalties to be granted the same due process rights presently given to defendants in the courts? This paper has argued that the traditional PACE safeguards—the right of access to legal advice and the right to the attendance of an appropriate adult for vulnerable suspects—are not sufficient in this new post-PACE era of speedy summary justice. In view of the increased significance of the police interview as the forum for calling suspects to account and as the basis for making decisions not only to charge but also for out of court disposals, vulnerable suspects need to be protected against unguarded and ill-informed admissions. To this end, they should be more actively encouraged to seek legal advice before the interview, legal representatives should be given full disclosure of the case against the suspect before the interview and they should be given full access to police and prosecutors to make representations afterwards.

---

[105]  Devlin, n 9 above, 10.

Then to prevent the prosecutor's decision to offer a conditional caution amounting to a 'determination of the charge' which would require the full Article 6 safeguard of an 'independent and impartial tribunal', all possible steps need to be taken to ensure that the suspect gives fully informed consent to the conditions that are being offered including, as in the case of defendants considering a plea in court, a full opportunity through a legal adviser in attendance to make representations to prosecutors on the conditions for accepting a caution. Undoubtedly, this more active defence is something that will require a change of culture on the part of defence lawyers in the police station and on the part of prosecutors who are not used to having to deal with lawyers at the police station.[106] But without such a change enabling suspects to play an active role in the process of agreeing to the conditions offered to them, suspects are unable to give their fully informed consent to them. We are then back to the situation where there would need to be some judicial supervision of the penalties effectively imposed by the CPS. English men and women may not like the idea of a judicial figure rustling in with her dossiers. But if this is what is needed to ensure fairness in the new era of speedy and summary justice, it may be a necessary price to pay.

---

[106] For a detailed review of the more demanding role that is being made of defence lawyers at the police station, see ch 9 by Edwards in this collection.

# Index